D1522779

# TOMBS OF THE ANCIENT POETS

# Tombs of the Ancient Poets

*Between Literary Reception
and Material Culture*

Edited by
NORA GOLDSCHMIDT
AND BARBARA GRAZIOSI

OXFORD
UNIVERSITY PRESS

# OXFORD
### UNIVERSITY PRESS

Great Clarendon Street, Oxford, OX2 6DP,
United Kingdom

Oxford University Press is a department of the University of Oxford.
It furthers the University's objective of excellence in research, scholarship,
and education by publishing worldwide. Oxford is a registered trade mark of
Oxford University Press in the UK and in certain other countries

First Edition published in 2018
Impression: 1

Published in the United States of America by Oxford University Press
198 Madison Avenue, New York, NY 10016, United States of America

British Library Cataloguing in Publication Data
Data available

Library of Congress Control Number: 2018939908

ISBN 978-0-19-882647-7

Printed and bound by
CPI Group (UK) Ltd, Croydon, CR0 4YY

# Acknowledgements

This collection has its origins in a collaborative research project, *Living Poets: A New Approach to Ancient Poetry*, directed by Barbara Graziosi and based at Durham University: we owe a debt of thanks to the European Research Council for funding it. Earlier versions of some of the chapters were presented at a *Living Poets* panel at the Annual Meeting of the American Philological Association in Chicago (4 January 2014); others featured at an international conference hosted by Durham University (12–14 September 2014). We would like to thank all those who took part, whether as speakers or audience members, for their stimulating contributions and scholarly expertise. We are also grateful to all researchers on the *Living Poets* team, especially Erika Taretto, for their help. At Oxford University Press, Charlotte Loveridge and Georgina Leighton took excellent care of this volume, from when we first submitted an exploratory proposal all the way through to publication. The anonymous readers offered perceptive feedback, which substantially improved the book. Our copy-editor, Ben Harris, worked with great precision and speed. We wish to thank Clement Raj and Amanda Gomez for their helpful and precise work of production and proofreading and Kurt Ballstadt for preparation of the index. Finally, a word of thanks to our families, who offered us moral support and practical help, as we worked on this volume amid several competing commitments.

# Contents

## PART III.  COLLECTING TOMBS

## PART IV.  THE TOMB OF VIRGIL

# List of Illustrations

# List of Abbreviations

| | |
|---|---|
| AB | C. Austin and G. Bastianini, eds, *Posidippi Pellaei quae supersunt omnia* (Milan, 2002) |
| *AP* | *Palatine Anthology* |
| *APl* | *Planudean Anthology* |
| Bernabé | A. Bernabé, ed., *Poetae epici Graeci. Testimonia et fragmenta*, part II, 3 vols (Munich, 2004–7) |
| *CEG* | P. A. Hansen, ed., *Carmina Epigraphica Graeca* (New York, 1983–9) |
| *CIL* | *Corpus Inscriptionum Latinarum* (Berlin, 1863–) |
| DK | H. Diels and W. Kranz, eds, *Die Fragmente der Vorsokratiker*, 6th edn, 3 vols (Berlin, 1951–2) |
| *FGE* | D. L. Page, ed., *Further Greek Epigrams* (Cambridge, 1981) |
| *FGrHist* | F. Jacoby, ed., *Die Fragmente der griechischen Historiker* (Berlin, 1923–) |
| G-P | A. S. F. Gow and D. L. Page, eds, *The Greek Anthology: Hellenistic Epigrams*, 2 vols (Cambridge, 1965) |
| G-P, *Garland* | A. S. F. Gow and D. L. Page, eds, *The Greek Anthology: The Garland of Philip and Some Contemporary Epigrams*, 2 vols (Cambridge, 1968) |
| *GV* | W. Peek, ed., *Griechische Vers-Inschiften*, vol. 1: *Grab-Epigramme* (Berlin, 1955) |
| *IG* | *Inscriptiones Graecae*, 12 vols (Berlin, 1873–1981) |
| *IGRR* | R. Cagnat et al., eds, *Inscriptiones Graecae ad res Romanas pertinentes*, vols 1, 3–4 (Paris, 1911–27) |
| *ILLRP* | A. Degrassi, ed., *Inscriptiones Latinae liberae rei publicae*, 2nd edn, 2 vols (Florence, 1963–5) |
| KA | R. Kassel and C. Austin, eds, *Poetae Comici Graeci* (Berlin, 1983–95) |
| *LIMC* | L. Kahil et al., eds, *Lexicon Iconographicum Mythologiae Classicae* (Zurich, 1981–97) |
| LSJ | H. G. Liddell, R. Scott, and H. S. Jones, eds, *Greek–English Lexicon*, 9th edn (Oxford, 1940; with revised supplement by P. G. W. Glare, 1996) |
| Pf. | R. Pfeiffer, ed., *Callimachus*, 2 vols (Oxford, 1962) |
| *PIR*[2] | *Prosopographia Imperii Romani. Saec. I, II, III*, 7 vols, 2nd edn (Berlin, 2006) |
| *PMG* | D. L. Page, ed., *Poetae Melici Graeci* (Oxford, 1962) |

*List of Abbreviations*

| | |
|---|---|
| Powell | J. U. Powell, *Collectanea Alexandrina. Reliquiae minores poetarum graecorum aetatis ptolemaicae, 323–146 A. C.* (Oxford, 1925) |
| P.Oxy. | *The Oxyrhynchus Papyri* (London, 1898–) |
| Reifferscheid | A. Reifferscheid, ed., *C. Suetoni Tranquilli praeter Caesarum libros reliquiae* (Leipzig, 1860) |
| *SEG* | *Supplementum Epigraphicum Graecum* (Amsterdam, 1923–) |
| *SGO* | R. Merkelbach and J. Stauber, eds, *Steinepigramme aus dem griechischen Osten*, 5 vols (Munich, Stuttgart, and Leipzig, 1998–2004) |
| *SH* | H. Lloyd-Jones and P. Parsons, eds, *Supplementum Hellenisticum* (Berlin, 1983) |
| *SupplItal* | G.L. Gregori and M. Mattei, eds, *Supplementa Italica. Imagines. Supplementi fotografici ai volumi italiani del CIL, Roma (CIL, VI)*, I. *Musei Capitolini* (Rome, 1999) |
| *TrGF* | B. Snell, R. Kannicht, and S. Radt, eds, *Tragicorum Graecorum fragmenta*, 4 vols (Göttingen, 1971–85) |
| *VSD* | *Vita Donatiana e Vita Suetoniana desumpta*, in G. Brugnoli and F. Stok, eds, *Vitae Vergilianae antiquae* (Rome, 1997), 9–56 |
| W | M. L. West, ed., *Iambi et elegi Graeci ante Alexandrum cantati*, 2nd edn, 2 vols (Oxford, 1989) |
| Wendel | C. Wendel, ed., *Scholia in Apollonium Rhodium vetera* (Berlin, 1974) |

Abbreviations of ancient authors and texts follow the Oxford Classical Dictionary, 4th edn; titles of journals are abbreviated according to *L'Année philologique*.

# List of Contributors

**Emmanuela Bakola** is Associate Professor in Ancient Greek Language and Literature at the University of Warwick. Previously, she held fellowships at University College and King's College London. She has published a monograph (*Cratinus and the Art of Comedy*, Oxford University Press, 2010) and several articles and chapters which explore the relationship of ancient comedy to other genres. Her current project uses cultural anthropology and theatre space theory to argue, on the basis of dramaturgy, imagery, stage action, and engagement with cult, that Aeschylean theatre is profoundly preoccupied with the human relationship to the earth and its resources.

**Peter Bing** is Professor of Classics at the University of Toronto and Samuel Candler Dobbs Professor of the Classics Emeritus at Emory University. Among his books are *The Well-Read Muse: Present and Past in Callimachus and the Hellenistic Poets* (1988; 2nd edn, Michigan Classics Press, 2008), *The Scroll & The Marble: Studies in Reading and Reception in Hellenistic Poetry* (University of Michigan Press, 2009), and (with Regina Höschele) *The Erotic Letters of Aristaenetus: Introduced, Translated and Annotated* (Society of Biblical Literature, 2014).

**Valentina Garulli** is a Research Fellow in Greek Language and Literature at the University of Bologna, and worked at different stages of her career in Cambridge, Göttingen, Cincinnati, and Oxford. She has published on Greek biography (*Il Περὶ ποιητῶν di Lobone di Argo*, Pàtron Editore, 2004), Greek poetry on stone (*Byblos lainee. Epigrafia, letteratura, epitafio*, Pàtron Editore, 2012), Greek and Latin epigram (particularly Callimachus and Posidippus), and Hellenistic poetry. She also researches the history of classical scholarship, specifically on Wilhelm Otto Crönert, Tadeusz Zielinski, and Laura Orvieto.

**Nora Goldschmidt** is Associate Professor of Classics at Durham University. She is the author of *Shaggy Crowns: Ennius' Annales and Virgil's Aeneid* (Oxford University Press, 2013). *Afterlives of the Roman Poets: Biofiction and the Reception of Latin Poetry*, written under the aegis of the ERC project *Living Poets: A New Approach to Ancient Poetry*, is forthcoming with Cambridge University Press.

**Barbara Graziosi** is Professor of Classics at Princeton University. She held positions at Oxford, Reading, and Durham, where she served as Head of Department and Director, for the Arts and Humanities, of the Institute of Advanced Study. Her most recent monographs are *The Gods of Olympus: A History* (Profile Books, 2013) and *Homer* (Oxford University Press, 2016). She recently directed a major research project, funded by the European Research Council, on visual and narrative portraits of the ancient Greek and Roman poets, entitled *Living Poets: A New Approach to Ancient Poetry*. This volume stems from that project.

**Johanna Hanink** is Associate Professor of Classics at Brown University. She is author of *Lycurgan Athens and the Making of Tragedy* (Cambridge University Press, 2014) and *The Classical Debt: Greek Antiquity in an Era of Austerity* (Harvard University Press, 2017), and co-editor (with Richard Fletcher) of *Creative Lives in Classical Antiquity: Poets, Artists and Biography* (Cambridge University Press, 2016).

**Harald Hendrix** is director of the Royal Netherlands Institute in Rome and Professor of Italian Studies at Utrecht University. He has published widely on the European reception of Italian Renaissance and Baroque culture (*Traiano Boccalini fra erudizione e polemica*, Olschki, 1995), on the early modern aesthetics of the non-beautiful as well as on literary culture and memory. He is currently preparing a book on the cultural history of writers' houses in Italy, from Petrarch to the present day. Recent publications include *Writers' Houses and the Making of Memory* (Routledge, 2008), (with Antonello Corsaro and Paolo Procaccioli) *Autorità, modelli e antimodelli nella cultura artistica e letteraria fra Riforma e Controriforma* (Vecchiarelli, 2007), (with Paolo Procaccioli) *Officine del nuovo* (Vecchiarelli, 2008), (with Philiep Bossier and Paolo Procaccioli) *Dynamic Translations in the European Renaissance* (Vecchiarelli, 2011), (with Lieke Stelling and Todd Richardson) *The Turn of the Soul: Representations of Religious Conversion in Early Modern Art and Literature* (Brill, 2011), (with Geert Buelens and Monica Jansen) *The History of Futurism: The Precursors, Protagonists, and Legacies* (Lexington Books, 2012), and (with Benjamin Arbel and Evelien Chayes) *Cyprus and the Renaissance, 1450–1650* (Brepols, 2013).

**Regina Höschele** is Associate Professor of Classics at the University of Toronto. Her research focuses on post-classical Greek literature, Graeco-Roman epigram, and ancient erotica. She is the author of *Verrückt nach Frauen. Der Epigrammatiker Rufin* (Classica Monacensia, 2006), *Die blütenlesende Muse. Poetik und Textualität antiker Epigrammsammlungen* (Classica Monacensia, 2010), and (with Peter Bing) *The Erotic Letters of Aristaenetus: Introduced, Translated and Annotated* (Society of Biblical Literature, 2014).

**Andrew Laird** is the John Rowe Workman Distinguished Professor of Classics and Humanities at Brown University. His books include *Powers of Expression, Expressions of Power* (Oxford University Press, 1999), *Ancient Literary Criticism* (Oxford University Press, 2006), and *The Epic of America* (Bloomsbury, 2006). He has produced the first comprehensive surveys of Latin writing from colonial Spanish America and Brazil for *Brill's Encyclopedia of the Neo-Latin World* (Brill, 2014) and for the *Oxford Handbook of Neo-Latin* (Oxford University Press, 2015).

**Francesca Martelli** is Assistant Professor of Classics at UCLA. She is the author of *Ovid's Revisions: The Editor as Author* (Cambridge University Press, 2013), and has written articles on a range of Latin authors, from Cicero to Statius.

**Silvia Montiglio** is Basil L. Gildersleeve Professor of Classics at Johns Hopkins University. She has written extensively on many aspects of Greek literature and culture. Her most recent books are *Love and Providence: Recognition in the Ancient Novel* (Oxford University Press, 2013), *The Spell of Hypnos: Sleep and Sleeplessness in Greek Literature* (I. B. Tauris, 2016), and *The Myth of Hero and Leander: The History and Reception of an Enduring Greek Legend* (I. B. Tauris, 2017).

**Irene Peirano Garrison** works on Roman poetry and its relation to rhetoric and literary criticism, both ancient and modern. She is especially interested in authorship, authenticity, and the history of philology and other scholarly practices from antiquity to modernity. She is the author of *The Rhetoric of the Roman Fake: Latin Pseudepigrapha in Context* (Cambridge University Press, 2012). *Eloquentia: Persuasion, Rhetoric and Roman Poetry* is forthcoming with Cambridge University Press.

**Verity Platt** is Associate Professor of Classics and History of Art at Cornell University. She is the author of *Facing the Gods: Epiphany and Representation in Graeco-Roman Art, Literature and Religion* (Cambridge University Press, 2011), and co-editor (with Michael Squire) of *The Art of Art History in Graeco-Roman Antiquity* (Arethusa, 2010) and *The Frame in Classical Art: A Cultural History* (Cambridge University Press, 2017).

**Richard Rawles** is Lecturer in Greek at the University of Edinburgh. He is the author of *Simonides the Poet: Intertextuality and Reception* (Cambridge University Press, 2018) and of several articles on Greek poetry. Together with Peter Agócs and Chris Carey, he edited two volumes on epinician poetry.

**Sam Smiles** is Emeritus Professor at the University of Plymouth and Honorary Professor at the University of Exeter. His research concentrates on British art, focusing especially on the eighteenth and nineteenth centuries, and in particular on the career of J. M. W. Turner. His publications include *British Art: Ancient Landscapes* (Paul Holberton, 2017), *Late Turner: Painting Set Free* (Tate, 2014), *J. M. W. Turner: The Making of a Modern Artist* (Manchester University Press, 2007), *Eye Witness: Artists and Visual Documentation in Britain 1770–1830* (Ashgate, 2000), and *The Image of Antiquity: Ancient Britain and the Romantic Imagination* (Yale University Press, 1994). He is currently completing a book on late style in the visual arts.

# Introduction

*Nora Goldschmidt and Barbara Graziosi*

## THE DEATH OF THE AUTHOR

When he was 51, Virgil decided to retire to Greece and Asia for a three-year period with the single purpose of revising the *Aeneid*, so that he would then be free to devote the rest of his life to philosophy. But when, after embarking on his journey, he met Augustus in Athens, who was returning to Rome from the East, he decided not to stay away but, in fact, to return together with him. Virgil then caught a fever while he was touring the nearby town of Megara in the sweltering heat. He worsened his condition by not breaking up his journey, so that he was in a far more serious state when he put ashore at Brundisium. He died there within a few days, on the eleventh before the Kalends of October, in the consulship of Gnaeus Sentius and Quintus Lucretius. His remains were borne to Naples and laid in a tomb which is on the road to Puteoli, within two miles of the city. On the tomb is a couplet he composed himself:

*Mantua me genuit, Calabri rapuere, tenet nunc*
  *Parthenope. cecini Pascua, Rura, Duces.*

Mantua bore me, Calabria took me away, and now
  Parthenope holds me. I sang of pastures, agriculture, and
  leaders.

(*VSD* 35–6)[1]

---

[1] The Latin text reads:

anno aetatis quinquagesimo secundo impositurus Aeneidi summam manum statuit in Graeciam et in Asiam secedere triennioque continuo nihil amplius

This ancient account of Virgil's death culminates in an epitaph he composed for his own tomb. In a terse two lines, the poet takes on the role of his own biographer and literary historian. He states where he was born (Mantua), where he died (the port of Brundisium in Calabria), and where he now rests (Parthenope, that is to say Naples). It is this last location that most fully exposes the autobiographical conceit of the epitaph: a man is likely to know his place of birth, may realize that he is about to die in a particular place, but has no control over the subsequent whereabouts of his body. He may express a wish, to be sure, but the matter rests in the hands of others. The same is true, of course, of literary reception. After the short biography which opens the epitaph, an even shorter sentence encapsulates Virgil the author, organizing his oeuvre in chronological sequence and ascending order of genre: first the pastoral *Eclogues*; then the agricultural *Georgics*; and finally the martial epic *Aeneid*.

The epitaph extends Virgil's life and oeuvre: it poses as his last work and suggests that the poet still speaks to us from his grave.[2] There is a clear connection between the poem and the genuine works of Virgil: the epitaph echoes several autobiographical passages, or 'seals' (*sphrageis*), contained in his poems.[3] Moreover, the sequence of works—*Eclogues, Georgics, Aeneid*—is already implied within those works themselves. Still, the epitaph makes an important contribution to literary history: the sequence only becomes canonical when set in stone. The life and the oeuvre are sealed by death. We are told that Virgil's original plans were interrupted. He enjoyed no old age, and no graduation from poetry to philosophy. Virgil's *curriculum vitae* thus failed to conform to a standard ancient pattern, according to which epic poetry was propaedeutic

quam emendare ut reliqua vita tantum philosophiae vacaret. sed cum ingressus iter Athenis occurrisset Augusto ab oriente Romam revertenti, destinaretque non absistere atque etiam una redire, dum Megara vicinum oppidum ferventissimo sole cognoscit, languorem nactus est, eumque non intermissa navigatione auxit ita, ut gravior aliquanto Brundisium appelleret, ubi diebus paucis obiit XI Kal. Octobr. Cn. Sentio Q. Lucretio conss. ossa eius Neapolim translata sunt tumuloque condita, qui est via Puteolana intra lapidem secundum, in quo distichon fecit tale.

[2] For the inscription of this epitaph on the so-called 'Tomb of Virgil', and the subsequent epitaphs imagined for it, see Hendrix, Chapter 14 and Smiles, Chapter 15 in this volume, together with Trapp (1984).
[3] See Chapters 12 and 13 in this volume.

to philosophy.[4] Death broke up that sequence, and simultaneously established a new one: the *rota Vergiliana*, 'Virgil's wheel', a poetic career ascending to progressively grander genres of poetry. For centuries, this career remained an important model: poets as different as Petrarch and Wordsworth imitated the *rota* in their own lives and works.[5]

Virgil was by no means the only ancient poet said to have composed his own epitaph. From Homer to Ennius and beyond, Graeco-Roman antiquity engendered a whole series of auto-epitaphs in which poets allegedly set in stone their 'last work'. The poets' self-composed epitaphs followed funerary conventions that also applied more generally: ancient tombs often exhibited inscriptions that stated, in verse and in the first person, 'Here I lie . . .'.[6] In short, even ordinary people became poets after their death.[7] Still, the case of actual poets was different, in at least two respects. Their epitaphs extended and defined their oeuvres—and, in turn, helped to shape their reception. Our opening example illustrates this double function clearly: just as Virgil's epitaph drew from his poetry (and a tradition of poetic epitaphs that extended back to Ennius and Homer), so, too, it shaped the lives and works of later poets for an unusually long period of time, some two millennia to date.[8]

The tomb, then, is the place where life ends and Life begins; where the oeuvre is extended and received; where death is lamented and immortality affirmed.[9] In the case of a poet, immortality means, in

[4] Virgil's contemporary Horace emphatically marks his own transition from poetry to philosophy in *Epistles* 1.1 (esp. 1.1.7–12), where he also presents epic, specifically, as propaedeutic to philosophy. In general, the Augustan poets display an intense interest in the relationship between life and work, and in the way in which autobiographical passages can be used in order to organize their own oeuvre in chronological sequence.

[5] Hardie and Moore (2010), esp. 19; 282–3.; cf. also de Armas (2002) on Cervantes. For the alternative 'anti-career'—that is to say, a deliberate and conscious refusal to imitate Virgil's—see Lipking (1981), 131.

[6] For a discussion of the first-person voice in sepulchral epigrams, see Vestrheim (2010).

[7] This aspect of ancient culture has attracted intense scholarly attention in recent years. *CEG* provides an overview of Greek funerary epigrams on stone; important recent work on inscriptional epigram (not always wholly separable from literary epigram) includes Bing and Bruss (2007), 29–93; Prioux (2007); Baumbach, Petrovic, and Petrovic (2010); and Christian (2015).

[8] See above, n. 5.

[9] See recently Laqueur (2015) for a broader cultural history of mortal remains, which restates the importance of the tomb and of burial as part of 'the enormous amount of cultural work . . . that needs to go into giving a dead body meaning' (p. 46).

the first instance, preservation of the works, so that they may find new readers. In turn, those readers keep the poet alive through their wish to know about his or her life and person. Pliny talks explicitly about this desire for the author. He describes libraries as places where 'immortal spirits speak to us', and comments on the fashion to place portraits of the authors next to their works. He presents it as a form of reception most pleasing to the deceased writer; but he also points out that 'desire gives birth' to the author, even in cases when the author is, in point of fact, unknown:

> non est praetereundum et novicium inventum, siquidem non ex auro argentove, at certe ex aere in bibliothecis dicantur illis, quorum immortales animae in locis iisdem loquuntur, quin immo etiam quae non sunt finguntur, pariuntque desideria non traditos vultus, sicut in Homero evenit. utique maius, ut equidem arbitror, nullum est felicitatis specimen quam semper omnes scire cupere, qualis fuerit aliquis.

> We must not pass over a novelty that has also been invented: portraits made, if not of gold or silver yet at least of bronze, are set up in the libraries in honour of those whose immortal spirits speak to us in the same places. In fact, even imaginary likenesses are made, and desire gives birth to countenances that have not been handed down to us, as occurs in the case of Homer. At any rate, in my view, there is no greater kind of happiness than that all people for all time should want to know what kind of person one was.

> Pliny, *Natural History* 35.9–10

Biography and portraiture are important aspects of a poet's *Nachleben*; they make up for an absence. This can be characteristic of modern as well as ancient responses to literature. In her essays on life writing, *Body Parts*, Hermione Lee speaks of a desire that recalls Pliny's *desideria*: 'what makes biography so curious . . . is that . . . we keep catching sight of a real body, a physical life.'[10] Again, like Pliny, Lee insists that this desire for the body, and for physical contact, happens in the mind of the reader. Her celebrated biography of Virginia Woolf ends with a chapter on her suicide and her suicide note, her death and her last work, as it were. It also describes where she was buried, and what was inscribed in stone (a quotation from *The Waves*). Still, as the final sentence insists, Woolf 'went on living and changing after death'.[11]

In the case of Virgil, the ancient account of his death lives on and changes through many subsequent iterations, most arrestingly perhaps

---

[10]  Lee (2005), 3.     [11]  H. Lee (1996), 767.

in Broch's *The Death of Virgil* (1945). Here, the last hours of the poet's life involve a comparison between the brutalities of Roman society and the beautiful lies of literature, a disgusted rejection of poetry, an eventual agreement to hand over the *Aeneid* to Augustus (in exchange for the freedom of his slaves), and finally a dying vision of a sea voyage. It is not difficult to see in that vision, and the book more generally, the facts of Broch's own life as a Jewish writer who escaped Vienna for Britain and the United States shortly after the Nazi *Anschluss* of Austria. The ancient poet lives on in what others make of him.[12]

The tomb, meanwhile, marks a transition. As Jean-Pierre Vernant points out, it signals an absence, that of the missing person whose bones it holds: 'the being it evokes, like a substitute, appears in the form of the stone as that which has gone far away, which would not deign to be there, that which belongs to an inaccessible "elsewhere".'[13] At the same time, the tomb can also mark a moment of liberation. To adapt the words of Roland Barthes, when it comes to a poet's burial, the death of the author most clearly signals the birth of the reader.[14] Barthes' celebrated essay, 'The Death of the Author', was primarily concerned with the free play of texts once liberated from authorial control—and, written in Paris in 1967, shortly before the student occupation of the Sorbonne, was itself an act of emancipation from the influence of previous generations. What was missing from Barthes' statement, however, and from the vast discussions and publications it subsequently inspired, was an understanding of authors and readers in their full-bodied physicality. There was little acknowledgement that 'poetry emerges from and is attended to by the mortal body', as Platt writes in this volume.[15] This book stems from that realization—from an interest in physical contact and its absence.[16]

---

[12] Broch worked on an earlier version of the novel during three weeks' imprisonment in Bad Aussee in March 1938 and completed it as an exile in the United States. For a poetological reading of *Der Tod des Vergil*, see Heizmann (2016), 179–86. For Broch's biofictional reception of Virgil, see Goldschmidt (forthcoming), ch. 5.

[13] Vernant (1990), 32: 'L'être qu'il évoque, à la manière d'un substitut, se manifeste dans la forme de la pierre comme ce qui s'est enfui au loin, qui ne saurait être là, qui appartient à un inaccessible ailleurs' (trans. Neer (2010), 15).

[14] Barthes (1967).   [15] P. 22.

[16] In this respect, it can be seen as part of a wider movement away from rather impersonal and disembodied models of intertextuality and towards an understanding of literature as grounded in lived experience—specifically, as a form of human contact. In antiquity, the author was seen and created as an embodiment of his or her oeuvre: Graziosi (2002) argued this in relation to Homer; the project *Living Poets: A New*

The point is not just that the tomb physically substitutes for the body of the author, but also that readers may be physically present at the tomb, or imagine themselves to be there. Reading the tomb and reading the work are connected enterprises, because they are embedded in an ancient system of commemoration that involves both literature and material culture. Just as the auto-epitaphs of poets have their roots in wider cultural practices—specifically first-person funerary inscriptions in verse—so all tombs, and not just those of poets, are sites of reading. Jesper Svenbro argued, in an influential monograph, that the boundary between tomb and text is inherently permeable. Meaning 'sign', 'symbol', 'signal', as well as 'tomb', the Greek *sēma* can be read just as much as a text written out on papyrus, calling for acts of interpretation that parallel textual communication strategies.[17] Within this general framework, the tombs of poets are a special case: they mark out an absence and stimulate a desire for the figure 'behind' the texts—something that Barthes, as well as Pliny, acknowledged: 'I *desire* the author, I need his figure.'[18] They are also, and more intensely than other tombs, sites of reading, because the 'reading' of the tomb is in effect intertextual, in dialogue not only with other tombs, but with the oeuvre of the buried author.

This is something contemporary poets understand and know how to exploit. In a recent programme for BBC Radio 4, contemporary British poets Paul Farley and Michael Symmons Roberts describe their pilgrimages to the places where other, earlier poets lived and died: the account works well as an introduction to poetry and has now also been published as a book entitled *Death of the Poets*.[19] In the course of walking in the footsteps of other poets, Farley and Symmons Roberts suggest, to these two readers at least, a few questions about their own eventual deaths, particularly given their emphasis on coincidence of time and place.[20] In *This Is Not a Novel*, David

---

*Approach to Ancient Poetry* explores this aspect of ancient culture from a variety of angles: <https://livingpoets.dur.ac.uk>.

[17] Svenbro (1993). For the multiple meanings of *sēma*, see also Vernant (1990) and (1991); Nagy (1983); Nagy (1990b), ch. 8; Sourvinou-Inwood (1995); Neer (2010), 14–19 and *passim*, and Alcock and Schnapp-Gourbeillon in Henry and Kelp (2016), 1–8 and 205–18.

[18] Barthes (1975), 27. Cf. Burke (1992) for the 'return' of the author in twentieth-century critical theory.

[19] Farley and Symmons Roberts (2017): the book focuses on places of birth and death; tombs are left unexplored.

[20] Ange Mlinko (2017), reviewing the volume for the *London Review of Books*, seems to have had the same idea: 'Farley and Roberts take cover under the impersonal

Markson (writing in his seventies and in poor health) is more explicit: he lists the deaths of some five hundred poets, writers, philosophers, politicians, actors, and athletes, turning towards the end—and in some defiance—to the ancient poets:[21]

> When the city I extol shall have
> perished, when the men to whom I sing
> shall have faded into oblivion, my words
> shall remain.
> Said Pindar.
>
> *Non omnis moriar.* I shall not wholly die.
> Said Horace.
>
> *Per saecula omnia vivam.* I shall live forever.
> Said Ovid.[22]

Markson then adds a diagnosis, which is at once literary and physio-logical: 'Writer's cancer.'[23] *This Is Not a Novel* grows like a tumour, from one death-generating scene to the next, until it suddenly stops—with a valediction, a handing-over: 'Farewell and be kind.'[24]

---

first-person plural as if to say to the gods: "Move on, nothing to look at here".' *Death of the Poets*, however, hardly exploits the possibilities of autobiography and auto-epitaphic poetry, beyond a few urbane suggestions.

[21] Markson (2016), 147.   [22] Markson (2016), 147.
[23] Markson (2016), 148.
[24] Markson (2016), 148. After *This Is Not a Novel*, first published in 2001, Markson went on to write a sort of sequel, *The Last Novel*, published in 2010. Towards the end of that work, too (which turned out to be, in fact, his last), he considered the ancient poets one more time. The passage is quoted here in a posthumous edition (2016), 439–41:

Having died they are not dead.
Wrote Simonides of the Spartans slain at Plataea.

Keats, in a last letter some weeks before the end, telling a friend it is difficult to say goodbye:

I always made an awkward bow.

Tiny drops of water will hollow out a rock.
Lucretius wrote.

. . .

Dispraised, infirm, unfriended age.
Sophocles calls it.

. . .

The old man who will not laugh is a fool.
*Als ick kan.*

In antiquity, the tombs of the poets were presented as extensions of their works not just through the inscriptions they bore, but also through their locations and the behaviour they inspired. Pindar, who celebrated athletic victories, was buried at the racecourse in Thebes.[25] Actors performed the plays of Aeschylus at his grave.[26] The tomb of Stesichorus was an elaborate octagonal monument, which expressed specific theories about musical harmony.[27] A statue of Ennius was placed in the tomb of the Scipiones, in recognition of the poet's role in establishing their name.[28] Horace was buried in the tomb of Maecenas, the great patron of his poetry.[29] Many more examples could be adduced to illustrate the correspondence between tomb and work: in a useful recent monograph, Flore Kimmel-Clauzet offers a vast survey, which we recommend as a companion to this volume.[30] Silvia Barbantani devotes a whole monograph to the traditions concerning just three tombs: those of Ibycus, Stesichorus, and Simonides.[31] In this great abundance of material there is one complication: none of the tombs just mentioned actually survives. All we have are texts that describe real or, in some cases, imagined monuments.

This volume focuses on Greek and Roman poets whose oeuvres are known, and situates their tombs between literary reception and material culture. This aim determines the range of cases considered. Tombs which, on the basis of archaeological and epigraphic evidence alone, can be identified as graves of (otherwise unknown) poets feature here only in as much as they shed light on relevant practices of commemoration.[32] The exception is the tomb of Quintus Sulpicius Maximus, which deserves a whole chapter. Although all we have, in his case, is a funerary monument, the tomb itself preserves the otherwise unknown oeuvre: a substantial hexameter poem, which established Maximus' reputation as a poet when he was only a young boy, is inscribed on two columns, to the left and the right of

---

[25] Paus. 9.23.2.          [26] *Life of Aeschylus* 11, discussed by Bakola in Chapter 6.

[27] See the interpretation offered by Barbantani (2010), 34.

[28] Cic., *Arch.* 9.22, discussed together with other relevant sources by Martelli in chapter 3.

[29] *Life of Horace*, p.4* Klingner.

[30] Kimmel-Clauzet (2013); see also her 'Poets' tombs and conceptions of poetry' at <https://hal.archives-ouvertes.fr/hal-01328536>.

[31] Barbantani (2010).

[32] See, most importantly, the case discussed on pp. 22–3: a cist tomb excavated in Daphne, dating to the fifth century BCE, which clearly contained the remains of a poet.

his portrait. The monument, in this case, makes the oeuvre. At the other end of the spectrum, we discuss tombs of famous poets which exist only as literary constructions. We even include a chapter on the fictional tombs of fictional characters created by poets: they, too, are an aspect of literary reception and, indeed, of material culture. It seems to us that, if the term 'material culture' has any force at all, it must include the imagined materiality of the tomb, as well as the actual materials out of which tombs were made. Between monuments with no literary oeuvres and oeuvres with no monuments, there are many intermediate cases—including that of Virgil, with which this collection ends. Near Naples, an ancient Roman tomb has long served as a site of Virgilian memory, even if there is no reason to assume that the remains of the ancient poet were buried in it. From antiquity onwards, countless visitors paid homage to Virgil at the alleged site of his tomb. To this day, school children from all over Europe leave scribbled messages at the tomb of the ancient poet, asking him for help in love—and good marks in their Latin examinations.

## Topoi

As Liddell and Scott state, the Greek term *topos* can denote not only a physical place, and specifically a place of burial, but a literary commonplace.[33] The tombs of the ancient Greek and Roman poets are both: physical places and/or spaces of the imagination—*lieux de mémoire*, in the words of Pierre Nora.[34] There are direct, tangible ways to interact with tombs as physical objects. Several chapters in this collection explore what people did and do when visiting them: worship, recite, paint, fall asleep, write graffiti, convert from business to literature, and (especially if they are themselves poets) plan the location and design of their own tombs.[35] In the sixteenth century,

---

[33] LSJ s.v. I.5; II.2.    [34] Nora (1984–92); (1989); (1996).

[35] Bakola, Bing, and Hanink discuss, from a variety of perspectives, the relationship between hero cult and the cult of poets: see Chapters 6, 7, and 11 respectively. On reciting poetry at the tombs of poets, see Bakola at p. 126 and Hanink at p. 235; on painting, Smiles Chapter 15; on falling asleep, Graziosi pp. 187–9; on writing graffiti, Hendrix pp. 292–7. The most famous literary conversion is, arguably, that of Boccaccio at the tomb of Virgil: see the account of how he turned from business to literature given by Giovanni Villani (1280–1348) in *Liber de civitatis Florentiae famosis civibus*, ed. Galetti, Florence 1847, p. 17, discussed by Trapp (1984), 10.

the Neapolitan humanist Jacopo Sannazaro built his own posthumous memorial next to that of Virgil. Centuries later, the corpse of the lyric poet, philosopher, and philologist Giacomo Leopardi was buried near there, too. The graves of poets near Naples inspired the collection of another set of tombs: the 'Poets' Corner' in Westminster Abbey. The epigram that Pietro Bembo wrote to commemorate the death of Sannazaro in 1530 insisted on the deceased's proximity to Virgil: when Spenser died a few decades later, in 1599, an epigram celebrated, in similar terms, that poet's burial next to the grave of Chaucer. His tomb in turn led to a steady addition of poets' graves in Westminster Abbey.[36]

There are, then, material ways of engaging with the tombs of poets, including the practice of placing them next to each other, and thus imbuing specific sites with literary significance. At the same time, there are also ways of engaging with tombs that involve no specific, material locations at all. For example, we need not imagine that the epitaphs on the graves of poets collected in the *Palatine Anthology* were ever inscribed on stone. What those poems do, rather than mark specific monuments and places, is create a different kind of 'poets' corner'—an imaginary graveyard through which readers stroll in their mind. In fact, two epigrams allegedly composed to mark the tomb of Euripides insist that 'the whole of Greece' is his grave.[37] As *lieux de mémoire*, the tombs of poets have all and nothing to do with physical location.

Accordingly, chapters in this collection explore the place of both real and imaginary tombs in the reception of literature through key topoi, which are used to structure the collection into four parts. The first governing commonplace is the opposition between literature and material culture, the life of the mind vs the apprehensions of the body. The contrast is not new. Pindar declared with some pride at the beginning of *Nemean* 5: 'I am no sculptor . . .' and went on to point out that his poem would travel 'on every ship and boat' spreading the news that Pytheas won the pancratium competition, whereas a statue of the athlete would have to stay put 'on its pedestal' on the island of Aegina. Horace elaborated on this theme. The last poem in the third book of his *Odes* starts with the now proverbial *exegi monumentum*

---

[36] On the tombs of English poets, see further Matthews (2004) and Höschele's discussion in this volume, pp. 197–201.

[37] *AP* 7.45. 1–3, attributed to Thucydides: see discussion by Montiglio at p. 220; and 7.47, discussed by Platt at p. 31.

*aere perennius*, 'I have erected a monument more permanent than bronze', and goes on to reflect on Horace's own mortality: *non omnis moriar*, 'I shall not wholly die', a phrase that already featured above. Poetry itself is the monument that keeps the memory of the author alive. And yet, the transmission and reception of literature depends on physical survival, since it is stored and circulated on inscribed or encoded objects. All the chapters in the first section of this book break down easy dichotomies between literature and material culture—insisting that just as literature depends upon tangible records, so material tombs need to be interpreted with reference to the literary imagination.

In the Greek world, between the third and the first centuries BCE, the tombs of poets became the focus of sustained attention, both as monuments and as subjects of poetry (as the genre of *epitymbia*, short epigrams that posed as texts inscribed on graves, testifies). Platt explains: 'at a time when literary texts were being feverishly collected, copied, catalogued, canonized and archived, when contemporary poetry was carefully situating itself in relation to an emerging library culture, and when texts were being reframed and circulated in the context of anthologies, the tomb as inscribed marker of the poet's literal *corpus* offered a rich analogy to the physical objects that sustained his or her surviving *corpus* of work.'[38] Poems written on papyrus posed as grave inscriptions on stone. Conversely, inscriptions on monuments that commemorated poets (most famously those carved into the Archilocheion on Paros) were laid out as if they were columns of writing inked on papyrus.[39] What we witness, in this period, is an intertextuality of materials. In Chapter 2, Rawles travels the same route as Platt, but in the opposite direction: rather than insist on the materiality of textual transmission, he points out that inscribed texts were memorized and orally transmitted. This insight provides the key for his reading of Callimachus' 'Tomb of Simonides'—itself a reading of Simonides' own response to the poetics of inscribed epigram (and of his role as the inventor of memory techniques). Rawles argues that 'Callimachus presents Simonides' tomb not as an epitaph, but as a kind of "meta-epitaph"—an elegy which is not itself inscribed, but describes the loss of an inscribed

---

[38] P. 24.    [39] For a later example, see p. 94.

tombstone': liberated from the tomb that once covered his body, the voice of Simonides now speaks through Callimachus' verse.[40]

From early on, funerary practices in Rome developed in dialogue with the Greek traditions set out in the first two chapters of this volume. For example, between the third and first centuries BCE, a grand tomb near the Via Appia served as a funerary monument for the prominent patrician family of the Scipiones. The inscribed *elogia* that commemorated their deaths testify to the influence of Hellenistic literary epigrams on Roman culture—yet this is not the main reason why Chapter 3 focuses on this tomb. As well as generations of Scipiones, the monument was believed to have once contained the statue of a man who did not belong to the family: the poet Quintus Ennius. Martelli considers how Ennius' poetry and his portrait contributed to the circulation of political prestige, and links the story of his statue to a later image of the poet in Varro's *De poetis*. She argues that Varro's collection of author portraits and the practice of erecting busts of authors in libraries (which became fashionable shortly afterwards) are best seen as 'a form of entombment – one that situates the *imago* of the poet alongside those of his literary forebears in a space that recognizes their identity as a group, much like the tomb of the Scipiones, or, indeed, as the atrium in a Roman household collects the *imagines* of a family's ancestors'.[41] Garulli, meanwhile, reminds us that real, biological families are as important as literary genealogies when approaching the tombs of poets. She considers the case of Quintus Sulpicius Maximus, who competed in poetry at the Capitoline Games of 94 CE and died soon afterwards at the age of 11. His parents set up an elaborate funerary monument in his memory, explaining its design: 'lest his parents may seem to have been unduly influenced by their affection for him, his extemporaneous verses have been inscribed here.'[42] The boy's oeuvre is framed by the monument, which provides a rich context for Garulli's reading of it—but as well as the poet's death we need to consider his parents' lives. Their names reveal that they were freed slaves: in terms of social capital, the monument substituted for the career young Maximus never had. Investment in the boy's literary talent and investment in his tomb were both effective means of social advancement. Like Martelli's

---

[40] Pp. 51–2.     [41] P. 78.

[42] For a new edition and translation of all the texts inscribed on the tomb, see pp. 90–2.

chapter, Garulli's excavates the political significance of the tomb—even if in this case the focus is on a family of ex-slaves rather than the grand Scipiones.

Taken together, the chapters in Part I of this volume span a vast period of time, from antiquity to the present. They thus serve as a reminder that the study of classical reception is not the study of what happened after the end of antiquity. It is, in point of fact, inextricable from the study of ancient culture. This is particularly obvious in the piece that concludes this section: Chapter 5 begins with Ovid's own reception of his work, and shows how he writes about the future of his oeuvre with reference to the future entombment of his body. Through a series of case studies, the chapter goes on to illustrate an enduring preoccupation with Ovid's tomb through the centuries: the poet's tomb allegedly contained his lost final work, *De vetula*, and was repeatedly 'discovered' in both Romania and Rome.

Issues of authenticity surface repeatedly in the chapters collected in Part I and become the focus of attention, from a different perspective, in Part II: 'The Poet as Character'—a section that investigates the religious as well as the literary significance of tombs. Poetry and the cult of tombs developed in parallel in early Greece. At the time when Homeric epic began to spread through the Greek-speaking world, local communities devoted themselves to the cult of the great heroes celebrated in epic, typically at the tombs where they were thought to be buried. It can be no coincidence that the characters we find in poetry (for example, Agamemnon, Cassandra, Menelaus, Helen, Odysseus) were also recipients of cult.[43] What is crucial for this volume is a subsequent development: the poets who celebrated the heroes of myth and cult started to be worshipped themselves at their own alleged tombs.

Emmanuela Bakola identifies some key aspects of hero worship in Chapter 6, reassesses the depiction of the poet Aeschylus in Aristophanes' *Frogs*, and connects the play to the cult of Aeschylus' tomb in Sicily. What she offers is a new understanding of hero worship in terms of well-being, prosperity, fertility, and health—which in turn leads to a new interpretation of the relationship between biography, literary reception, and cult. In Chapter 7, Peter Bing focuses on Hellenistic epigrams commemorating the death of minor literary characters: a

---

[43] For further discussion and bibliography, see pp. 151–3 in this volume.

prostitute berated by Sappho, the daughters of Lycambes vilified by Archilochus, and the lovely Baucis, Erinna's friend. His chapter demonstrates how an interest in 'entombed literary figures . . . could manifest itself purely as literature, that is as poetry inspired by poetry, Art by Art, with no real-life component in ritual or cult'.[44] Still, it is no accident that some of the poems he discusses feature also in Chapter 1, where they support Platt's argument about the materiality of literature. And it is also no accident that these poems focus on minor female characters: the materiality of their bodies, once so attractive and now dead, serves as a foil to the enduring fame of the poets who created them in literature.

It seems that the poet's best hope of immortality is to become part of the mythical world s/he created. The final chapter in Part II explores this idea in reverse: it considers the case of a literary character, Orpheus, who was considered the author of real-life mystic texts. Chapter 8 argues that Orpheus the character and Orpheus the author coincide at his tomb. Various ancient sources suggest that the singer carried on performing poetry even after his death: he sang from his tomb and through the landscape. This helps to explain how Orphic authorship worked in antiquity, as well as the reasons why it was so contested. Some ancient critics argued that, far from being age-old works, Orphic poems were in fact recent forgeries. Devotees of Orpheus, meanwhile, could insist that the poet's voice was heard in stones, trees, caves, and birds—that is to say, in nature itself: Orphic authorship, from that perspective, was a matter of attentive reception, rather than fraud. The case of Orpheus is extreme, but the possibility that an oeuvre may continue to grow after the death of its author surfaces repeatedly in this volume: attribution is, after all, a form of posthumous homage.

Part III investigates a third, fundamental commonplace: the literary graveyard. Physical graves can be collected together, as in the assemblages of literary tombs near Naples or Westminster Abbey mentioned above, but the collection of tombs is a crucial topos of literature as well. A nineteenth-century ode may help to introduce what is at stake here: Ugo Foscolo's *Dei Sepolcri* (1807) attempts to create a nation, Italy, by lingering on the resting places of its famous men, particularly those buried in Santa Croce in Florence.

---

[44] P. 153.

Tombs, Foscolo insists, are of no use to the dead ('What compensation for my lost days can a stone be, / a stone that distinguishes my bones from the countless other bones / that death scatters over land and sea?'); what tombs do, rather, is inspire the living.[45] Thus, for example, he suggests that Italy would have deserved a better burial for the poet Parini, and argues that the ancient dead buried at Marathon inspire the modern Greeks, in his day still under Ottoman rule, with a desire for freedom. Tilted as the poem is towards the future, it concludes with ancient hero cult: a blind Homer rummaging through the abandoned tombs of the Troad and recreating, in poetry, the grave of Hector. This may seem like a purely literary enterprise, but *Dei Sepolcri* inspired elaborate acts of material memorialization— including the exhumation of Foscolo's own remains (he died in exile in 1827 and was buried in the cemetery of Chiswick, west London) and their ceremonial entombment in Santa Croce in 1871, in a grand nation-building exercise.

Like Foscolo's *Dei Sepolcri*, ancient literary collections of tombs did not focus exclusively on the graves of poets, and yet granted them special prominence. Through a painstaking reconstruction of ancient epigram collections, Regina Höschele shows how unique 'poets' corners' were created inside poetry books. Silvia Montiglio, for her part, identifies recurrent themes in the descriptions of poets' tombs in the *Palatine Anthology*—many of which feature also in other texts. Thus, for example, poets' tombs are generally characterized by lush vegetation, blooming anew, generation after generation. The vitality of literature is the focus of attention also in Chapter 11, where Johanna Hanink considers how Pausanias treats the tombs of poets in his *Description of Greece*. She presents the buried bones of both ancient poets and heroes featured in poetry as a 'root system . . . that in Pausanias' imagination nourishes the sacred Greek landscape, ensuring that the memories it holds always stay lush with life'.[46] Like Foscolo, Pausanias presents the tombs of poets as underground resources.

The final chapters, collected in Part IV of this volume, focus on a single, grand commonplace—the tomb of Virgil—and make up,

---

[45] Foscolo, *Dei Sepolcri* 12–15: 'qual fia ristoro a' dí perduti un sasso / che distingua le mie dalle infinite / ossa che in terra e in mar semina morte?'
[46] P. 250.

together, an extensive case study.[47] Andrew Laird, in Chapter 12, investigates the epitaphic quality of Virgil's own verse—how it inspired the traditions concerning his burial but also how, in turn, those traditions offer a useful and evocative key for reading his work. Specifically, the landscape of Aeneas' landfall, and of his descent into the underworld, described in *Aeneid* 5-7, is reimagined as a burial site for the poem's author. Irene Peirano Garrison, in Chapter 13, returns to that landscape—and its remarkable system of underground tunnels—in order to explore the earliest traditions associated with Virgil's tomb. She focuses on reports about Silius Italicus and his veneration of the tomb of Virgil, but also considers the ancient topos of the neglected and rediscovered grave. Harald Hendrix, in Chapter 14, focuses precisely on the 'rediscovery' of Virgil's tomb in the Renaissance, exploring its position in the cultures of scholarship and leisure (both of which thrive on the pleasures of reading). Finally, Sam Smiles shows how poetic inspiration can be expressed through the material idiom of painting: the tomb of Virgil inspired English artists on the Grand Tour, and thus contributed to the creation of new material cultures. The reputation of the poet became, for Turner and others, an important means of establishing the social value of artists, despite the materiality of their means of expression.

The purpose of this volume, as a whole, is to make a distinctive contribution to the study of literary reception by focusing on the materiality of the body and the tomb, and by arguing that the 'places', or topoi, outlined here mediate the relationship between classical poetry and its readers. Since Gadamer, Jauss, and Iser, from whom we have inherited the term, 'reception' studies have tended to privilege the aesthetic response of readers in the present over the contexts of authors in the past.[48] It is this approach, centred on the horizons of readers, that Charles Martindale influentially put forward in *Redeeming the Text*.[49] Since then, and in line with broader developments in the Humanities, the study of classical receptions has shifted (to put it crudely) from literary theory to cultural studies, broadly conceived.[50] The present volume can easily be located within that general development: it focuses

[47] All chapters in Part IV take J. B. Trapp's detailed survey of the history of the site as an important point of departure: Trapp (1984), with Trapp (1986).

[48] See especially Gadamer (1975); Iser (1978); Jauss (1982).

[49] Martindale (1993).

[50] See, for example, the essays collected in Machor and Goldstein (2001) and, for a brief and perceptive analysis, Leonard (2009).

on literature, yet insists that readers' horizons include material objects. Our volume also benefits from what art historian Dorothea von Hantelmann recentelly labelled the 'experiential turn', that is to say, a new attention to embodiment, experience, situation, and situatedness.[51] Martindale, in reassessing his own book twenty years after its publication, insisted on the transhistorical, which he defined as 'the seeking out of often fugitive communalities across time'.[52] Our contention here is that the tombs of the Greek and Roman poets, whether real or imagined, are places where such fugitive communalities are established.

---

[51] von Hantelmann (2014).
[52] Martindale (2013), 173. In theorizing the transhistorical, Martindale repeatedly refers to material objects (most prominently and programmatically Pater's response to art)—yet does not draw attention to this fact.

# I

## Material Texts, Textual Materials

# 1

## Silent Bones and Singing Stones

### Materializing the Poetic Corpus in Hellenistic Greece

*Verity Platt*

### IMPLEMENTS FROM THE 'TOMB OF THE POET' (PIRAEUS ARCHEOLOGICAL MUSEUM)

On the journey to the mundane afterlife,
You travel equipped to carry on your trade:
A bronze, small-toothed saw to make repairs,
The stylus and the ink pot and the scraper,
Wax tablets bound into a little book.

Here is the tortoise shell for the cithara,
Bored through with holes for strings, natural sound box.
Here is the harp's wood triangle, all empty—
The sheep-gut having long since decomposed
Into a pure Pythagorean music.

The beeswax, frangible with centuries,
Has puzzled all your lyrics into silence.
I think you were a poet of perfection
Who fled still weighing one word with another,
Since wax forgives and warms beneath revision.

From *Hapax* by A. E. Stallings[1]

[1] Stallings (2006), 19. Reprinted by kind permission of the publisher, Northwestern University Press.

In 1981 a salvage excavation in Daphne, Athens, brought to light a limestone cist grave dating to 430–425 BCE, which belonged to a man in his early twenties.[2] The belongings carefully buried with him (now displayed in the Piraeus Museum) identified the youth as a poet-musician: fragments of a harp, tortoise-shell lyre, and wooden aulos implied proficiency in performance (perhaps even training in the making of instruments, as suggested by a saw and chisel), while a stylus and inkpot, wax tablets and a papyrus roll demonstrated a facility with (and investment in) written texts (Figure 1.1).[3] Gathered as eternal accessories to the poet's profession, this assemblage reminds us that words do not, despite our best imaginings, have wings. Nor are they immortal. Rather, poetry emerges from and is attended to by the mortal body; it makes its way into the world by means of instruments, whether vocal, musical, or notational; and it is stored and circulated on inscribed objects, whether temporary compositions impressed into wax tablets, or more enduring texts inked onto papyrus. Adept in both oral and literary media, the occupant of the Daphne tomb poignantly demonstrates how all poetry depends upon material vehicles for its own survival, whether the singer's jawbone, the decomposed strings of his spindle-harp, or his treasured papyrus (which bears traces of epic verse—tantalizingly lost to posterity, the author(s) unidentified).[4] For A. E. Stallings (a living poet herself), it is the wax lingering on the ancient poet's *polyptychon,* 'frangible with centuries', that proves most haunting, since its malleable capacity for revision by the warm, living body is hardened by time once active composition has been suspended in the coldness of the tomb. The poet's relics thus speak of endless possibilities—of flawless compositions not yet crafted by 'a poet of perfection'— while reminding us that poetry is nevertheless a corporeal, a fallible, and a perishable art.

The Daphne tomb gives us a poet without a name, a craftsman-musician accompanied by the tools of his trade, with no surviving

---

[2] See Pöhlmann (2013) and Lygouri-Tolia (2014).

[3] On the instruments, see Terzēs (2013) on the harp, and Psaroudakēs (2013) on the aulos. On fragments recoverable from the tablets and papyrus (the earliest yet discovered in ancient Greek), see Pöhlmann and West (2012); West (2013) and Alexopoulou and Karamanou (2014), with further bibliography.

[4] See West (2013) and Alexopoulou and Karamanou (2014). For a sensitive exploration of the materiality of writing (and the metaphors to which it gives rise) in antiquity, see Butler (2011).

**Figure 1.1.** Objects recovered from the 'Tomb of the Poet', Piraeus Museum, Athens.

Photograph: Chelsea Gardner.

grave-marker or epitaph. Here we have all the accoutrements of ancient poetry (including the body of an actual bard), but no corresponding works with which to associate them, the poet's instruments 'all empty' of sound. The ancient epigrammatic tradition, conversely, gives us names and epitaphs that float free of their poets' bodies.

Tethered instead to a familiar body of texts, the Hellenistic epitaphs (*epitymbia*) gathered in Book Seven of the *Greek Anthology* draw upon the metapoetic potential of poets' tombs as a means of securing and shaping their occupants' literary legacies.[5] But they do this not in blind celebration of the immortality of the word. Rather, as I argue here, a preoccupation with poets' tombs during the third to first centuries BCE emerges from a keen awareness among living poets of their work's dependence upon its material vehicles—on the fraught relationship between embodied performances and bodies of verse, and the diverse media that make possible poetry's transmission, preservation, and retrieval. Hellenistic *epitymbia* cleave more closely to the Daphne poet's entombed belongings than we might initially assume. For at a time when literary texts were being feverishly collected, copied, catalogued, canonized, and archived, when contemporary poetry was carefully situating itself in relation to an emerging library culture, and when texts were being reframed and circulated in the context of anthologies, the tomb as inscribed marker of the poet's literal *corpus* offered a rich analogy to the physical objects that sustained his or her surviving *corpus* of work.[6]

Tombs signify the presence of the body, but they also mark a site of absence and loss. As Jean-Pierre Vernant observed, the Greek concept of the *sēma*, or tomb, is profoundly ambiguous: while situating the remains of the dead, it simultaneously points beyond itself, to the intangible and dematerialized realm of the departed—to the silenced voices and unread words of Stallings' 'mundane afterlife'.[7] The *sēma* constitutes both a physical marker and a threshold—a monument to be viewed in its own right, and a point of mediation between the living and the dead.[8] It is also an object that both displays and calls for

---

[5] On epigrammatic epitaphs for poets, see especially Gabathuler (1937); Bing (1988a); Bolmarcich (2002); Sens (2003); Klooster (2011), 15–42; and Kimmel-Clauzet (2013), 163–84, with Montiglio, Chapter 10 in this volume. On the programmatic role played by poets' epitaphs within the anthologies of Meleager and Philip, in particular, see Höschele, Chapter 9 in this volume. On the device of the epitaph as applied by poets to their own works, see Peirano (2014). On sepulchral epigram more generally, see Bruss (2005); Tsagalis (2008); Tueller (2008), 65–94 and Christian (2015), 162–228.

[6] On Alexandrian textualization of—and corresponding poetic intertextuality with—the poetry of the past, see especially Bing (1988a); Hunter (1996) on Theocritus; Fantuzzi and Hunter (2004); Acosta-Hughes (2007a) on iambic poetry, and (2010) on Hellenistic reception of Greek lyric, and Klooster (2011).

[7] Vernant (1991).

[8] On the liminal status of the tomb, see Haarløv (1977) and Platt (2012).

acts of writing and reading.[9] At the tomb, the material and aesthetic qualities of the written word are strikingly displayed; at the same time, poetry not only memorializes the dead, but also gives them the power of speech by harnessing the voices of its readers. The *sēma* thus marks the loss of the poet's living voice and the impossibility of witnessing his or her embodied performance, while offering new possibilities for communion, re-enactment, and reanimation. At the poet's tomb, complex relations between text and object, script and voice, are made manifest in the context of enduring tensions between life and death, memory and loss, the material and metaphysical. For literary epigram—an intermedial genre poised between 'scroll and marble' (in Peter Bing's compelling formulation) and exceptionally attentive to poetry's material substrate—the aesthetic potential of fictionalized poets' epitaphs would prove a temptation impossible to resist.[10]

## TOMB AND BOOK

Whether real or imagined, the poet's tomb marks the presence of his or her physical remains. It thus testifies to its occupant's historical, embodied existence and the erstwhile vitality of his or her voice, while pointing incontrovertibly to its silencing in death. In performing remembrance through an inscribed epitaph, the tomb draws attention to the role of the written word in the operations of memory—in both sepulchral inscription and the storage of the poet's words on wax or papyrus. There is a clear relationship between tomb and book, for in highlighting the 'death of the author', the poet's tomb parallels the transition that any literary work undergoes in publication, from the active authorial agency of the composing and performing poet to his or her reception via 'the solemn silence' of the written word.[11]

In marking the poet's physical body and its temporal limits, the tomb thus indicates a crucial transition from living performance to

[9] See the classic analysis of Svenbro (1993).
[10] Bing (2009). On the role of voice in Hellenistic epigram, see in particular the subtle analyses of Männlein-Robert (2007a) and (2007b).
[11] Barthes (1967). On the 'solemn silence' ($\sigma\epsilon\mu\nu\hat{\omega}s\dots\sigma\iota\gamma\hat{q}$) of text, see Pl. *Phaedrus* 275d. On voice and silence in relation to ekphrastic poetry, see Squire (2010).

entextualized script, and to the poet's posthumous survival in the form of an inscribed 'body' of verse.[12] Like the written *sēmata* of the book roll, the sepulchral *sēma* signifies the poet's presence-in-absence through the commemorative power of an inscribed object. Consequently, the *Greek Anthology* includes within its section of poets' epitaphs a poem attributed to Asclepiades that explicitly blurs the categories of epitaph and epigraph, or book tag (7.11):[13]

> ὁ γλυκὺς Ἠρίννης οὗτος πόνος, οὐχὶ πολὺς μέν,
> ὡς ἂν παρθενικᾶς ἐννεακαιδεκέτευς,
> ἀλλ᾽ ἑτέρων πολλῶν δυνατώτερος· εἰ δ᾽ Ἀΐδας μοι
> μὴ ταχὺς ἦλθε, τίς ἂν ταλίκον ἔσχ᾽ ὄνομα;

This is the sweet labour of Erinna, not great in size,
seeing that she was a 19-year-old girl,
but more powerful than that of many others.
Had Hades not come for me
early, who would have had so great a name?

Ostensibly inscribed as the preface to Erinna's Ἠλακάτη (*Distaff*), Asclepiades' text gives voice to the deceased poetess in terms that borrow from funerary epigram, as well as the Doric forms and lamentatory themes of Erinna's own verse.[14] The language of the tomb is combined with a self-consciously literary intertextuality in such a way that the book itself becomes the speaking *sēma* that preserves Erinna's voice in death, its slender dimensions (οὐχὶ πολύς, line 1) a figure for both the aesthetic qualities of her verse and the petiteness of both poetic *corpus* and maiden corpse.[15] Both

---

[12] On 'entextualization' as 'the process by which circulable texts are produced by extracting discourse from its original context' (Sung-Yul Park and Bucholtz (2009), 486), see Bauman and Briggs (1990); Briggs and Bauman (1992); Silverstein and Urban (1996) and Barber (2007).

[13] *Greek Anthology* 7.11 = Asclepiades G-P 28. Text and translation from Sens (2011), 185. For epigrams mourning Erinna, see also 7.12 (anonymous), 7.13 (attributed to Leonidas or Meleager), 7.713 (Antipater), and 9.190 (anonymous), with additional discussion and Montiglio (this volume, pp. 225–6). On these and the series of epitaphs (perhaps falsely) attributed to Erinna mourning her childhood friend Baucis (subject of the *Distaff*) at GA 7.710 and 712, see Höschele (this volume, pp. 207–8, with further bibliography). On Erinna and other female poets as both authors and subjects of literary epigram, see Murray and Rowland (2007).

[14] See Knauer (1935), Neri (1996), Gutzwiller (1997a), Stehle (2001), and Sens (2003) and (2011), 185–93. On lament in Erinna's *Distaff*, see Levaniouk (2008).

[15] Sens (2011), 190 notes that ancient witnesses (e.g. *AP* 9.190.3) set the length of Erinna's *Distaff* at 300 verses.

the book and the tomb it implies stand as *oggetti parlanti* that enable forms of enduring presence through the borrowed voice of the reader, who is encouraged to ventriloquize Erinna both by reading her own verse and by following Asclepiades' shift into the first person with the striking μοι at the end of line 3 (a manoeuvre common to sepulchral epigram, as Rawles discusses in Chapter 2).[16] These practices converge in a later epigram from the same series (attributed to Leonidas or Meleager), in which Erinna's premature death is likened to that of Baucis, the very subject of her *Distaff* (7.13):

> παρθενικὴν νεάοιδον ἐν ὑμνοπόλοισι μέλισσαν
>    Ἤρινναν Μουσέων ἄνθεα δρεπτομένην,
> Ἀΐδας εἰς ὑμέναιον ἀνάρπασεν. ἦ ῥα τόδ᾽ ἔμφρων
>    εἶπ᾽ ἐτύμως ἁ παῖς. "Βάσκανος ἔσσ᾽, Ἀΐδα."

The virgin Erinna, a newly singing bee amongst singers,
    as she was plucking the flowers of the Muses,
Hades snatched for marriage. Yes, the wise girl said
    this truthfully: 'You are envious, Hades.'[17]

Others have commented on the epigrammatic conceit whereby Erinna is here turned into both the subject of her own verse and the prophetess of her own fate; the flowers she gathers in an echo of the Kore-like Baucis are figured as the *anthea* of poetry (and, by virtue of the epigram her maiden death inspires, the 'garland' of Meleager's anthology).[18] In the light of the genre's materializing analogy between book and tomb, we might attend more closely to the use of citation in the epigram's final line ("Βάσκανος ἔσσ᾽, Ἀΐδα."). Like other sepulchral epigrams, both poems take advantage of the reader's voice so that the dead might speak. But Erinna does not address us directly from beyond the grave. Rather, the poet recalls her poetic utterance

---

[16] On the use of the first person in Erinna's verse, and its influence on Hellenistic poetry, see Gutzwiller 1997a. On the notion of 'speaking objects', coined as 'oggetti parlanti' by Burzachechi (1962), see Svenbro (1993) and Steiner (1993); on speaking objects in literary epigram, in particular, see Petrovic (2005); Männlein-Robert (2007b), 157–67; Tueller (2008), 141–65; and Squire (2010), 608–16.

[17] Text and translation from Sens (2003), 82. On the disputed authorship of the poem, see Neri (1996), 213–16.

[18] See Höschele, in this volume, pp. 207–10. On Meleager's *Stephanos* (especially *AP* 4.1) and the use of flowers as a metaphor for verse (and thus, by the second century CE, *anthologiai*), see Cameron (1993), 19–33; Gutzwiller (1997b) and (1998), 78–9; and Höschele (2010), 171–229. On the motif of the maiden's abduction by Hades in epigram, see Cairns (1996).

when ἔμφρων—'in her senses', or, by implication, 'alive'.[19] The words
we encounter in the context of her death are thus mediated by means
of a written text that performs an act of archival retrieval. In this
sense, the epigram-as-epitaph functions not as a means of animation
but as an echo, its ghostly effect serving to underline the tragedy of
Erinna's untimely loss even as it affirms her transformation into the
written *corpus* that enables the poem's conceit.[20] Strikingly, the same
phrase appears in an epigram attributed to Erinna herself, placed later
in Book 7, in which the stele of Baucis encourages the passer-by
to 'Say this to Hades beneath the earth, "You are envious, Hades."'
(τῷ κατὰ γᾶς τοῦτο λέγοις Ἀΐδα, | "Βάσκανος ἔσσ', Ἀΐδα.", lines 2–3).[21]
Given the likelihood that this epigram (the authenticity of which is in
question) also cites the *Distaff*, we are thus presented with a series of
textual echoes in which the dead poetess' words—addressed to Death
himself—are posthumously quoted by poetic successors at her
imagined graveside.[22] Recursively resounding from tomb to tomb,
Erinna, her 'self'-citations and the subjects of her verse are actively
incorporated into the text of Meleager's original *Garland* and its
subsequent iterations.

As made objects that can crystallize the past, create foci for mem-
ories, and transport them into the present, books and tombs both
function as *lieux de mémoire* (in Pierre Nora's phrase).[23] Both are
dynamic objects that 'stop time, to block the work of forgetting, to
establish a state of things, to immortalize death, to materialize the
immaterial'.[24] But they only do so by virtue of the fact that the *milieux
de mémoire*—the active contexts of composition and performance
that generated them—no longer obtain.[25] A preoccupation with
the tombs of late poets such as Erinna by Asclepiades and his

[19] LSJ notes that ἔμφρων gains its meaning of 'in one's mind' or 'sensible' by
explicit contrast with the mad, the dead, and the sleeping, citing Soph. *Ant.* 1237.
[20] I borrow the notion of an epigrammatic echo from Hayden Pelliccia, who
detects Callimachus' use of the device in *Ep.* 28 Pf. (Pelliccia (forthcoming)). On the
pointed use of intertextual allusion (and possible direct quotation) in Asclepiades'
reference to γλυκὺς . . . πόνος at *AP* 7.11.1, see Sens (2003), 79 and (2011), 190.
[21] *AP* 7.712 = 2 G-P.
[22] On the probably spurious attribution of this epigram to Erinna herself, see Neri
(1996), 194–201. On the question of citation in 7.712, see Sens (2003), 83, with further
bibliography.
[23] Nora (1989) and (1996).     [24] Nora (1989), 19.
[25] Nora (1989), 7: 'There are *lieux de mémoire*, sites of memory, because there are
no longer *milieux de mémoire*, real environments of memory.'

epigrammatic successors is a product of the Hellenistic poets' own sense of belatedness: it expresses the complex equivocation between identification and difference prompted by an intense engagement with the poetry of the archaic and classical past accompanied by archival acts of material reorganization. While tombs 'fix' their poets' bodies in spatial and geographical terms, creating a physical site at which to engage with their literary and cultural legacies, books 'fix' their literary output in the form of stable texts, inviting the formation of authoritative editions, literary canons, and displays of knowledge. The once-living voice of Erinna is thus heard in the form of an epigrammatic echo produced by Meleager/Leonidas—a quotation that is only made possible by the *Distaff*'s textual storage and subsequent retrieval by the scholar-poet, the latter in service of anthology-formation, whereby the maiden flower—plucked, epitomized, and transformed into an epigrammatic conceit—is woven into the *stephanos* of literary epigram.

Both book and tomb facilitate what Aleida Assmann defines as 'Storage Remembrance' (*Speichergedächtnis*)—the reification of cultural authority in the form of libraries, museums, and archives, 'institutions of memory maintenance and the mediation of knowledge' in which factual knowledge of the past can be stored, conserved, and retrieved, primarily in the form of externalized material texts.[26] As a repository of the poet's body (as well as his texts and instruments, if the Daphne grave is anything to go by), the tomb is also a 'storehouse', while its epitaph offers a means of recording and preserving information about the deceased.[27] Both book and tomb thus comprise the outsourced media of 'cultural memory' (*kulturelles Gedächtnis*), as opposed to the living, embodied 'communicative memory' that characterizes remembrance of the recent past.[28] In attending to the dormant media of 'Storage Remembrance', however,

---

[26] A. Assmann (1999), 189. The notion of 'storage memory', as opposed to 'functional memory' (discussed below), is outlined in A. Assmann (1999): *Erinnerungsräume. Formen und Wandlungen des kulturellen Gedächtnisses*, 'Commemorative Spaces: Forms and Changes in Cultural Memory', translated as A. Assmann (2011). On the notion of 'cultural memory' as embedded in specific social and cultural frames and aided by means of mnemonic institutions, see also A. Assmann and J. Assmann (1989). For an application of these ideas to a number of premodern cultures (including ancient Greece), see J. Assmann (1992).

[27] On the tomb as a form of *Speichergedächtnis*, see Hendon (2000).

[28] On this distinction, see J. Assmann (2011), 34–41 and A. Assmann (2011).

the sepulchral epigrams of the *Greek Anthology* engage a different commemorative mode, responding to the fact that books and tombs also invite acts of dynamic engagement. This reactivates their content through practices of reading or—in the case of tombs—funerary rituals designed to communicate with the dead.[29] For Assmann, the processes of selection, connection, internalization, and identity-formation generated by such gestures define them as forms of 'Functional Remembrance' (*Funktionsgedächtnis*), which restore the knowledge stored within memory institutions into public space through acts of performance, commemoration, and renewal. 'Storage Memory', in this sense, acts as a reservoir for 'Functional Memory', crossing from one category to the other when it acquires additional dimensions of social meaning.[30]

As a genre that charts, comments upon, and plays with the status of written texts as they move between monuments and books, or ritual performance and literary culture, Hellenistic epigram is concerned with precisely this relationship—between 'functional' modes of remembrance that attest to the continuity of a living poetic culture, and textual means of 'storage' that preserve the words of the dead in accordance with an emerging concept of 'literature'.[31] In this context, fictional epitaphs constitute a dynamic form of reception—a means by which the poetry of the dead might be heard again through modes of functional remembrance that nevertheless acknowledge (and even amplify) the inevitable silence of the past.

## LIFE AND *NACHLEBEN*

In locating and preserving the physical or poetic *corpus*, both tomb and text sustain traces of oral performance, active composition, and authorial presence. Both stand as a fixed point of contact between author and reader that marks a shift from living poet to literary 'afterlife', displacing creative energy from acts of authorial production

---

[29] On allusions to ritual in the context of literary epigram, see below.
[30] A. Assmann (1999) and (2011); see also J. Assmann (1998), with helpful discussion by Erll (2011), 34–7.
[31] On 'literature' and literary criticism as emerging concepts in the Hellenistic period, see Gutzwiller (2010a).

to those of readerly consumption and active reception. If the tomb calls attention to the 'death of the author' by marking the end of the poet's *bios,* it also marks his or her coming-into-being as the protagonist of a posthumous biographical, honorific, and performative tradition—a form of *Funktionsgedächtnis* that is both collective and open to individual elaboration. Epitaphs, like epigraphs, function as a paratextual genre which retrospectively frames the poet's work, shaping and policing the reader's engagement with a literary *corpus*, in the act of marking the poet's literal body.[32]

This process receives self-conscious commentary in a series of epigrams in Book Seven of the *Greek Anthology* concerned with the burial of Euripides (7.43–7). Famously interred in Macedon, rather than his Attic homeland, the playwright also received a cenotaph in Athens.[33] In problematizing the question of where best to commemorate Euripides, this doubling of monuments became a *leitmotif* of his reception history.[34] In the context of epigram, tensions between tomb and cenotaph as loci of commemoration in the Euripidean tradition offered a rich opportunity for exploring parallel tensions between text and voice, as in this anonymous example (7.47):

> ἅπας Ἀχαιὶς μνῆμα σόν, Εὐριπίδη·
> οὔκουν ἄφωνος, ἀλλὰ καὶ λαλητέος.

> All Greece is your tomb, Euripides,
> so you are not voiceless, but even to be talked of.[35]

The use of λαλητέος in the personal sense here (as opposed to the impersonal λαλητέον) is unique: translated by Liddell and Scott as 'to be talked of', but also carrying a sense of necessity (*'must* be talked about'), it elegantly expresses the sense in which voice is relocated in death from the poet to his audience.[36] Euripides speaks because he is spoken *of*, and it is the compelling place his plays have afforded him

[32] On the notion of the paratext, see Genette (1997), with Smith and Wilson (2011) on Renaissance paratexts. See also the papers gathered in Jansen (2014) and Peirano (2014), who addresses the paratextual function of *epitymbia* in particular.
[33] *Vit. Eur. Genos* Ia.10, and Pausanias 1.2.2: see Lefkowitz (2012), 91–2, who observes that possessing two tombs is a sign of heroic status, Burges Watson (2013b) and Kimmel-Clauzet (2013), 154–60 and 171–3.
[34] See Hanink (2010) and (2014), 37, 233–4, with her comments in this volume, pp. 238, 245–6. On the cenotaph theme in literary epigram, and the play it engenders between hidden presence and revealed absence, see Bruss (2005).
[35] *AP* 7.47. My translation.     [36] LSJ s.v. λαλητέος, citing *AP* 7.47.

within literary tradition that ensures all Greece is his 'tomb' and 'memorial', μνῆμα. At the same time, this verbal activity echoes the very 'chattering', λαλία, with which Euripides was associated by his critics (as in Aristophanes' *Frogs*), thereby affording the tragedian the 'last laugh', as his trademark 'chattering' endures beyond the grave.[37] Strikingly, the verb from which the noun is derived, λαλέω, is also employed in epigraphic contexts to denote theatrical performance (such as an epitaph for an actor from Rome which claims χειρσὶν ἅπαντα λαλήσας, 'He said everything with his hands', i.e. in panto-mime).[38] The epigram's use of λαλητέος suggests that Euripides 'must be broadcast', that is, given voice through the continued reperfor-mance of his plays throughout the Greek-speaking world (as we know he was).[39]

This continuing culture of performance testifies to a Panhellenic 'envoicing' of Euripides that is implicitly contrasted with the periph-eral location (and 'voiceless' silence) of his actual tomb, in Macedon.[40] The topos echoes and responds to an epitaph said to have been inscribed on Euripides' Athenian cenotaph, preserved in the *Life of Euripides* as well as the *Greek Anthology*, and attributed to Thucydides or Timotheus (7.45):

> Μνῆμα μὲν Ἑλλὰς ἅπασ' Εὐριπίδου. ὀστέα δ' ἴσχει
> γῆ Μακεδών. ᾗ γὰρ δέξατο τέρμα βίου.
> πατρὶς δ' Ἑλλάδος Ἑλλάς, Ἀθῆναι. πλεῖστα δὲ Μούσαις
> τέρψας, ἐκ πολλῶν καὶ τὸν ἔπαινον ἔχει.

> All Hellas is the monument of Euripides, but the Macedonian
>     land holds his bones, for it sheltered the end of his life.
> His country was Athens, the Hellas of Hellas, and as by his verse he
>     gave exceeding delight, so from many he receives praise.[41]

---

[37] Ar. *Frogs* 954: τουτοισὶ λαλεῖν ἐδίδαξα.

[38] *IG* XIV 2124, an epitaph from Rome for an actor and teacher of acting, cited by LSJ s.v. λαλέω. I am grateful to Hayden Pelliccia for drawing my attention to this example.

[39] On this reception history, see Hanink (2014), 60–91. On epigram and the theatre, see Fantuzzi (2007).

[40] This is, of course, to gloss over the active performance of Greek drama (and associated cultural imperialism) in Macedon itself: see Hanink (2014), 68–74.

[41] Text and translation from Loeb edition. See also Page *FGE* 'Thucydides' or 'Timotheus' 1, pp. 307–8, who dates the epitaph to the early fourth century BCE. The epitaph is quoted in the Euripidean *Vita* (*Genos* Ia10) and Thomas Magister (*Vit. Eur.* 6). For discussion, see Kimmel-Clauzet (2013), 171–3.

Here, the tomb's function as a μνῆμα, a 'memorial' or 'reminder', is explicitly decoupled from its function as a container for the body (Euripides' 'bones') and applied instead to 'All Hellas', and especially to Athens in its role as both Euripides' 'country' and the figurehead of cultured Hellenism. Yet tombs facilitate remembrance by means of their spatial fixity, their material durability, and their capacity to act as points of return, inviting repeated communion with the dead. If these commemorative functions are not aligned with the physical containment of Euripides' 'bones', then how should they be performed? At first reading, we might assume that the tomb's physicality is to be contrasted with the transcendent qualities of reputation (as the preceding epitaph in Book Seven claims, 'This is not your memorial, Euripides, but you are the memorial of it. For this memorial/tomb, μνῆμα, is swathed in your glory').[42] But to accept this interpretation is to suppress the tangible materiality that is both inherent to the μνῆμα as tomb or monument (as opposed to the more abstract μνήμη, 'memory') and fundamental to the epigram's status as an inscribed epitaph (whether real or self-fictionalizing). If Euripides' reputation simply rests on the widespread fame of his works, then why evoke, address, or purport to speak for his tomb or cenotaph at all?

The sequence of Euripidean epitaphs in the *Greek Anthology* is particularly striking for its clear juxtaposition of an epigram apparently transcribed from a known, physical monument (7.45) with more self-consciously 'literary' epigrams that respond to and extend its conceit.[43] As a collective *corpus* of verse, the sequence addresses a fundamental question posed by the original inscription: what is to follow the poet's τέρμα βίου, 'the end of his life'? How is the poet's voice to endure and be heard? And what is the most effective mode of remembrance for a genre that is primarily mediated through embodied performance? The 'empty monument' that Pausanias would later see in Athens offers a powerful object for pondering poetic loss because it signifies a double absence—of both the living poet and his body, relic of and testament to his once-living verse.[44]

---

[42] *AP* 7.46 (also anonymous): Οὐ σὸν μνῆμα τόδ' ἔστ', Εὐριπίδη, ἀλλὰ σὺ τοῦδε. | τῇ σῇ γὰρ δόξῃ μνῆμα τόδ' ἀμπέχεται.

[43] On the incorporation of 'authentic' epigrams into the literary epigrammatic tradition, see Bing (2002), 38–66 and (2009), 116–46; Bettenworth (2007); and Christian (2015).

[44] Paus. 1.2.2: εἰσὶ δὲ τάφοι κατὰ τὴν ὁδὸν γνωριμώτατοι Μενάνδρου τοῦ Διοπείθους καὶ μνῆμα Εὐριπίδου κενόν ('Along the road [from the Piraeus] are very famous

Tellingly, in two further epigrams from the series, both (probably erroneously) attributed to Euripides' contemporary Ion, the location of Euripides' body in Macedon is rationalized by its proximity to the Muses of Pieria, whose 'dark-robed valleys' prove a fitting resting-place for his 'chamber of eternal night' (7.43.1–2).[45] In this way, Euripides' physical remains—traces of the material vessel through which his verse came into being—are situated at the site of inspiration, and associated with the elusive process of poetic becoming, of *poiēsis* itself: in death, the poet, as 'servant of the Pierian Muses', returns to his mistresses (7.44.5–6).[46]

Athens, by contrast, is identified on Euripides' cenotaph as the location where his poetry receives its definitive reception and *Nachleben*—where it generates pleasure (τέρψας) and is garlanded with praise (ἔπαινον).[47] Euripides' physical location in Macedon is both spatially and ontologically dematerialized—assigned to the mythological and cerebral realm of the Muses. The Athenian monument, tied to the urban landscape and ritual contexts in which Euripidean drama was most definitively embedded, stakes its claim as the primary material vehicle of remembrance. As 'Ion' observes, Euripides is the 'ornament of Athens' (κόσμον Ἀθηνῶν, 7.44.3)—the term *kosmos* conveying the notion of a material entity,

---

graves, that of Menander, son of Diopeithes, and a cenotaph of Euripides'). On Pausanias' treatment of poets' tombs, see Hanink, Chapter 11 in this volume.

[45] *AP* 7.43 = *FGE* 'Ion' 1: Χαῖρε μελαμπετάλοις, Εὐριπίδη, ἐν γυάλοισι | Πιερίας τὸν ἀεὶ νυκτὸς ἔχων θάλαμον. | ἴσθι δ᾿ ὑπὸ χθονὸς ὤν, ὅτι σοι κλέος ἄφθιτον ἔσται | ἴσον Ὁμηρείαις ἀενάοις χάρισιν. ('Hail, Euripides, dwelling in the chamber of eternal night in the dark-robed valleys of Pieria! Know, though thou art under the earth, that thy renown shall be everlasting, equal to the perennial charm of Homer.') Text and translation from Paton (1917). Page (*FGE* 157) suggests that *AP* 7.43–4 were erroneously ascribed to Ion of Chios as a well-known contemporary of Euripides, despite the fact that 'Euripides outlived Ion by about a dozen years' (if they were not a deliberate forgery, p. 128). Rather, Page argues, 'the style of the epigrams and their pseudo-epitaphic character suit the Hellenistic much better than any earlier period'.

[46] *AP* 7.44 = *FGE* 'Ion' 2: Εἰ καὶ δακρυόεις, Εὐριπίδη, εἷλέ σε πότμος, | καί σε λυκορραῖσται δεῖπνον ἔθεντο κύνες, | τὸν σκηνῇ μελίγηρυν ἀηδόνα, κόσμον Ἀθηνῶν, | τὸν σοφίῃ Μουσέων μιξάμενον χάριτα, | ἀλλ᾿ ἔμολες Πελλαῖον ὑπ᾿ ἠρίον, ὡς ἂν ὁ λάτρις | Πιερίδων ναίῃς ἀγχόθι Πιερίδων. ('Though a tearful fate befell thee, O Euripides, devoured by wolf-hounds, thou, the honey-voiced nightingale of the stage, the ornament of Athens, who didst mingle the grace of the Muses with wisdom, yet thou wast laid in the tomb at Pella, that the servant of the Pierian Muses should dwell near the home of his mistresses.') Text and translation from Paton (1917).

[47] *AP* 7.45.4 (see above, p. 32).

a made object that gives honour and delight by virtue of its beauty, order, and well-wroughtness.[48]

If 'Euripides'—as distinct from his 'mere bones'—is to be apprehended as a reified ornament, a monument belonging to all of Greece, and especially to Athens, then how is this 'Euripides' to be read? One answer lies in the augmented use of $\mu\nu\hat{\eta}\mu\alpha$ to refer to a 'record' or 'archive'.[49] Although Athens could not lay claim to Euripides' actual body, it could lay claim to a textual archive of Euripides' verse which functioned as the physical body of his work—the definitive entextualization of his plays alongside those of Aeschylus and Sophocles, according to the 330 BCE *nomos* of Lycurgus.[50] As part of the material and cultural fabric of the *polis*, this archival repository effectively established the means of *Speichergedächtnis* that makes the *epitymbia* of the *Greek Anthology* possible—verses that are themselves textually entwined with the epitaph inscribed upon and transcribed from Euripides' Athenian cenotaph. The use of $\lambda\alpha\lambda\eta\tau\acute{e}o\varsigma$ in *AP* 7.47 implies that it is this process of transcription and textual monumentalization that, paradoxically, gives voice to the deceased poet: while the claim that Euripides is still to be 'spoken of' implies a collective mode of remembrance generated by 'estimation' ($\delta\acute{o}\xi\alpha$: 7.46), the implication that the playwright is still to be 'broadcast' or 'envoiced' suggests an active performance culture (a mode of *Funktionsgedächtnis*) that relies explicitly upon the material support offered by archival acts of storage for its acts of ventriloquism. Reinforced by the unusual use of the verb $\lambda\alpha\lambda\acute{e}\omega$ (as opposed to $\lambda\acute{e}\gamma\omega$), this onomatopoeically conveys the sense of 'chattering', and is also applied in Hellenistic poetry to the 'chirping' of locusts or the 'sounding' of musical instruments.[51] Rather than prioritizing the meaning of what is said, $\lambda\alpha\lambda\acute{e}\omega$ emphasizes language's

[48] On the poets (and their tombs) as 'ornaments' of their cities, see also *AP* 7.19.3 (Leonidas on Alcman's *tymbos* as the *charis* of Sparta); 7.52.1 (Demiurgus on Hesiod of Ascra as the *stephanos* of Greece and the *kosmos* of song), and 7.90.2 (Anonymous, on Bias of Priene as the *kosmos* of Ionia). On the significance of *kosmos* as both ornament and symbol of cosmic order, see Bloomer (2000), 15–18; Marconi (2004); Hölscher (2009); and Barham (2015), who provides extensive literary and epigraphic examples.
[49] LSJ s.v. $\mu\nu\acute{\eta}\mu\eta$, A III, citing *Hdn.* 4.8.4 and Cassius Dio 76.14.
[50] The primary source is Ps-Plutarch, *Vit. dec. or.* 841–3. For a discussion of Lycurgus' law in the cultural and political context of fourth-century Athens (and its relations with Macedon), see Hanink (2014), 60–89.
[51] On the use of $\lambda\alpha\lambda\acute{e}\omega$ in Hellenistic epigram, and in relation to animal sounds in particular, see Männlein-Robert (2007a), 214–20, 238–50.

function as a channel of transmission.[52] It gestures to the ambient 'chatter' that comprises Euripides' active and ongoing reception, and the oral 'playback' of reperformance and citation that the mnemonic storage of Euripides' textual *corpus* has made possible. The poetic λαλία for which Euripides was so well known is now itself the object of perpetual λαλία, resounding in an infinite echo chamber of cultural re-mediation—one in which voices are repeatedly layered upon each other as text moves from theatre to stone to scroll, amplified still further by the self-conscious intermedial play of literary epigram itself.

## FROM 'DUST' TO DUST

In their metatextual games with the material vehicles of poetic legacy, *epitymbia* associated with Erinna and Euripides generate a textual *corpus* of their own. As each epigrammatist refers to the works of dead poets and other epitaphs—both real and fictional—within the literary tradition, he also weaves himself into the sepulchral *stephanos* that comprises this particular mode of reception. While the deceased poet's entextualized *corpus* comprises a form of archival storage, the creative acts of intertextuality, emulation, and variation that it generates conduct their own form of *Funktionsgedächtnis*. The poets included in Meleager's *Garland* (and, arguably, its successors right through to the sixth-century Cycle of Agathias) comprise an active 'community of remembrance', generating new vessels for verse (and new textual media) through their dynamic engagement with both the stored and stabilized texts of the past and, crucially, with each other: epigram thereby establishes itself as a living *milieu de mémoire* in which to encounter the dead anew.[53]

As a genre composed for papyrus yet masquerading as text incised into stone, the literary epigram presents itself as verse in motion— poetry that has already departed from its original material support, to

---

[52] Chirping of locusts: Theoc. 5.34, Aristoph. 10.6; musical sounds: Theoc. 20.29. Euripides himself uses the term λάλημα to refer to the 'clever, knavish, deceitful chatterers' (σοφῶν πανούργων ποικίλων λαλημάτων) whose 'Siren words' convince Hermione to act against Andromache at *Andr.* 937.

[53] See above, n. 25, on Pierre Nora.

assert itself in new contexts of reading and reception. If the poet's tomb invites us to consider the stable qualities of definitive textual editions, the literary *epitymbion*—by virtue of its self-fictionalized transition from 'marble to scroll'—also invites consideration of the text's ability to *transcend* the limitations of its physical substrate.[54] In the context of the tomb, the metaphysical properties of text are, inevitably, aligned with a more eschatological notion of the poet's 'afterlife', associated with the immortality of the soul. Consider, for example, an epitaph for Sappho attributed to Pinytus (*AP* 7.16):

> ὀστέα μὲν καὶ κωφὸν ἔχει τάφος οὔνομα Σαπφοῦς·
> αἱ δὲ σοφαὶ κείνης ῥήσιες ἀθάνατοι.

> The tomb holds the bones and the dumb name of
> Sappho, but her skillful sayings are immortal.[55]

Here Sappho's silent bones (ὀστέα) are explicitly contrasted with her clever 'sayings' (ῥήσιες), so that the mortality of her physical body is countered by the immortality (ἀθάνατοι) of her surviving words. Dematerialized and distinguished from her entombed remains, Sappho's 'sayings' are implicitly like the soul in their ability to exist independently of her mortal frame. Her name, by contrast, is bound to the silence of the tomb, its 'muteness' (κωφόν) suggesting the frozen impassivity of the stone surface into which it is (implicitly) incised.

This attention to the written status of 'Sappho', however, alerts the reader to the fact that the posthumous survival of her 'sayings' is itself a figure of speech, since her words are mediated by writing. Gow and Page comment that the epithet κωφός ('dumb') is merely conventional here, yet Pinytus arguably fills the silence of the grave with new life by pointedly evoking the 'sayings' of Sappho herself, alluding to her own envoicing of the death of her poetic voice in Fragment 31: 'For when I look at you . . . no speaking is left in me, my tongue breaks. . . . And I seem to myself to lack little of death.'[56] Sappho's

---

[54] On this notion, see also Klooster (2011), 26–35.

[55] *AP* 7.16 = G-P, *Garland* 'Pinytus' 1 (vol. 2, pp. 464–5). This couplet, dated to the first century BCE/CE, was probably included in the *Garland of Philip*.

[56] Fr.31 Lobel-Page, ll. 7–9, 15–16: ὡς γὰρ εὔιδον βροχέως σε, φώνας | οὐδὲν ἔτ' εἴκει· | ἀλλὰ κὰμ μὲν γλῶσσα ἔαγε . . . | τεθνάκην δ' ὀλίγω 'πιδεύης | φαίνομ' ἔμ' αὔτᾳ. On κοφόν, Gow and Page (1968), vol. 2, 465, citing *AP* 7.48.3 and Peek (1955), nos. 1263 and 1265. On the play of silence and speech in Fragment 31, see O'Higgins (1990); Stehle (1997), 288–94; and Montiglio (2000), 103–4 (who also discusses

comment upon her own mortal silencing—recalled as one of her 'immortal sayings', yet relayed through the textual storage and preservation of her poetic *corpus*—is employed to comment upon the silence of her grave. The play between speech and silence that we might claim as a *leitmotif* of Sappho's own poetic voice is thus applied to parallel tensions between her physical and textual corpora: just as Fragment 31 paradoxically testifies to Sappho's ability to overcome the silencing power of her own desire, so the enduring presence of her sayings in written form overcomes—if only by 'a little'—the silencing power of death. Moreover, this silent envoicing is performed within the context of a literary epitaph that invites its own vocalization by the reader. Crucially, the οὔνομα Σαπφοῦς, as inscribed by Pinytus, is not bound to Sappho's tomb at all, but to the papyrus that supports his fictional *epitymbion*. Here, it resounds in company with other such texts (whether a collection by Pinytus himself or anthologies such as the *Garland of Philip* through which it subsequently circulated), as part of an active community of remembrance sustained by the very textual practices that Pinytus' text self-consciously elides.[57]

This paradox characterizes several literary *epitymbia*, where the textual support that enables poetry's survival is metaphorically dematerialized in service of its transcendent 'immortality', while simultaneously drawing attention to its potential perishability. We might compare an epitaph for Sophocles attributed to Simias, in which the 'tomb and little portion of earth' (τύμβος . . . καὶ γῆς ὀλίγον μέρος) that hold the tragedian are contrasted with the 'extraordinary life that gleams in [his] immortal papyrus columns' (ὁ περισσὸς αἰὼν ἀθανάτοις δέρκεται ἐν σελίσιν), where αἰών refers both to the achievements of his 'lifetime' and the 'eternity' of his literary legacy.[58] Simias' conceit, however, lies in the fact that the insistent materiality of

---

*AP* 7.16–17 briefly on p. 101). On the reception of Sappho in Hellenistic poetry (and epigram in particular), see Acosta-Hughes (2007b) and (2010), 82–92.

[57] Note that Pinytus may also possibly allude here to a play on the tension between voice and silence in a dedicatory epigram 'in the style of Sappho' at *AP* 6.269, in which an object (presumably a statue) dedicated to Artemis claims 'Children, though voiceless I answer if anyone asks . . .' (Παῖδες, ἄφωνος ἐοῖσα ποτεννέπω αἴ τις ἔρηται): see Acosta-Hughes (2010), 83, n. 78, who also wonders if 'the partly conventional opening of this poem . . . is not also meant to recall the broken voice of Sappho fr. 31'.

[58] *AP* 7.21, text and translation from Paton (1917). For discussion, see Edmonds (1931); Gow and Page (1965) ad loc.; and Klooster (2011) 27–8. Simias is better known as the author of Hellenistic *technopaegnia* such as his 'Egg', on which see Méndez Dosuna (2008); Luz (2010); and Kwapisz (2013), 107–37.

Sophocles' tomb (signified by the 'little portion of earth' that holds his body) actually parallels the gleaming columns of his literary archive—that is, the text of the *Antigone*, wherein the 'light cover of dust' (λεπτὴ . . . κόνις) that its protagonist sprinkles on the corpse of her brother proves the catalyst for the unfolding of its tragic plot.[59] The matter of burial, as Sophocles reminds us, is never trivial; indeed it is his complex treatment of this topic that, arguably, generates the authority of his textual monument. Herein lies a further conceit, for the notion of Sophocles' 'immortal columns' introduces an oxymoron that draws explicit attention to the textual vehicles that ensure his work's durability. A σελίς is the column of script that forms the paginated structure of the papyrus roll, yet as Simias' notion of 'gleaming' columns suggests, its primary sense is architectural, referring to a 'cross-beam' used in ceiling construction or a 'block' of seats in the theatre.[60] The papyri that ensure Sophocles' immortality, then, imply a monumental construction that could equally apply to the *tymbos* on which Simias' epigram is (fictionally) inscribed, or the architectural structure of the theatre in which his tragedies are performed. Though Horace would later claim that poetry can transcend the perishability of material monuments (his 'monument more lasting than bronze'), Simias' *epitymbion* demonstrates that while texts may perform their own self-transcendence, they often do so by virtue of materializing metaphors that emerge from the very structural frameworks in which they are heard and read.[61]

The dependence of poetic immortality upon the materiality of its textual support takes us back to Sappho, and a sophisticated engagement with the paradox of textual (im)perishability in a much-discussed *epitymbion* by Posidippus:

Δωρίχα, ὀστέα μὲν σὰ πάλαι κόνις ἦν ὅ τε δέσμος
  χαίτης ἥ τε μύρων ἔκπνοος ἀμπεχόνη,
ἧι ποτε τὸν χαρίεντα περιστέλλουσα Χάραξον
  σύγχρους ὀρθρινῶν ἥψαο κισσυβίων.

---

[59] Soph. *Ant.* 256.
[60] See LSJ s.v. σελίς, A1: 'cross-beam', e.g. *IG* 12.374.58; 42(1).103.163 (a fourth-century BCE inscription from Epidaurus); A3: 'block' of theatre seats, *BMus.Inscr.* 481.157, 440 (first-century CE inscription from Ephesus).
[61] Horace, *Odes* 3.30.1–2: on this text's function as a poetic *sphragis* in relation to epigrammatic *epitymbia*, see Peirano (2014), 231–4. On Horace's *monumentum* as the equivalent to his tomb, see Woodman (1974). On the perishability of poets' tombs, see Rawles, Chapter 2 in this volume.

Σαπφῶιαι δὲ μένουσι φίλης ἔτι καὶ μενέουσιν
    ὠιδῆς αἱ λευκαὶ φθεγγόμεναι σελίδες
οὔνομα σὸν μακαριστόν, ὃ Ναύκρατις ὧδε φυλάξει
    ἔστ᾽ ἂν ἴηι Νείλου ναῦς ἐφ᾽ ἁλὸς πελάγη.

Doricha, your bones were dust long ago, and the band of your
    hair and your perfume-breathing shawl,
wherewith you wrapped the charming Charaxus,
    skin to skin, until you took hold of the morning cups.
But the white columns of Sappho's lovely ode
    are still here and they will go on celebrating
your most fortunate name, which Naucratis will thus treasure
    as long as ships sail from the Nile on the waves of the sea.[62]

Ironically, Posidippus' epitaph for Doricha (the Egyptian courtesan
supposedly resented by Sappho for seducing her brother Charaxus)
has been much on scholarly lips recently for precisely the issues of
physical preservation that the poem itself addresses.[63] This is not the
place to discuss the textual status, literary quality, or poetic signifi-
cance of the 'New Sappho' papyrus, other than to observe that its
reference to Sappho's brothers and their seafaring touches on the very
themes later alluded to by Posidippus. Here, he celebrates the endur-
ing power of the 'white resounding columns' (λευκαὶ φθεγγόμεναι
σελίδες) of Sappho's poetry—ordered, canonized, replicated, and
circulated in its definitive Alexandrian papyrus edition. He does so
in a typically oblique Hellenistic manner, composing an *epitymbion*
not for Sappho herself, but for a famously problematic figure within
her textual *corpus*.[64] The seductive presence attributed to Doricha in
lines 1–4 of the epigram (characterized by sophisticated intertextual

---

[62] Athenaeus 13.696/G-P XVII/122 AB, text and translation: Austin and Bastianini
(2002). See Bing (2005), 131–2, whose interpretation of the epigram is crucial for my
argument here.

[63] For the 'new Sappho papyrus', see Obbink (2014). Sappho's resentment of her
brother's lover is mentioned by Herodotus 2.35, who calls her Rhodopis, and Athe-
naeus 13.596c: see Lidov (2002), who claims the two names must have been connected
to each other in the Hellenistic biographical tradition. On Sappho's relationship with
her brothers, see Ferrari (2014) and Lardinois (2014).

[64] On this phenomenon, see Bing's discussion in Chapter 7, as well as Lidov (2002).
Doricha appears in Sappho frs 7 and 15 LP, though not in relation to her brother
Charaxus. The theme of Sappho's Alexandrian edition also emerges in a series of
epitaphs in the *Greek Anthology* that refer to her as the Tenth Muse, in a play on her
(by then) canonical nine books of poetry, or (as Tullius Laureas expresses it), her
'Nine flowers of song' (*AP* 7.17): see Acosta-Hughes (2010).

play with the Sapphic tradition) may have dissolved into the Egyptian dust (κόνις), yet they have passed into cultural memory, Posidippus suggests, by virtue of the *Speichergedächtnis* applied to Sappho's poetry.[65] It is this monumental literary archiving that ensures a literary reception (and dubious reputation) for Doricha that has been entirely shaped—and even constructed—by Sappho herself.

Posidippus' vicarious epitaph for Sappho (by way of Doricha) is prescient in its nod to the contingency of papyrological survival. As Rosenmeyer and Bing have observed, the poet's claim that Naucratis will treasure Doricha's name 'as long as ships sail from the Nile' may refer to the courtesan's (probably fictional) tomb in Egypt, but also evokes the papyrus trade, and by extension the role of Ptolemaic book culture in preserving and disseminating the literary achievements of the Greek past.[66] Whereas the tomb fixes the body in place, the book roll can travel, converting the 'winged words' of poetic performance into an object that stabilizes text yet simultaneously facilitates its circulation and replication (not to mention its later entombment as the by-product of Egyptian funerary practices). At Athens, the definitive entextualization of Euripides' plays offered a material substitute to his displaced tomb, asserting an enduring 'presence' that tied literary immortality to his *patris*. The definitive Alexandrian edition of Sappho's verse, by contrast, is presented as a means by which her lyrics can transcend the limitations of space and time, even as it provides Posidippus with a device for linking Sappho to Egypt by means of an entombed body other than her own. Furthermore, this textual mobility is precisely what enables Posidippus' epigram to stage its own epigraphic self-fictionalization, whereby the reader is asked to entertain the fantasy that it has been transcribed from tomb to book. In this way, the epigrammatist purports to have it both ways, evoking the solid fixity of tomb and text while celebrating the fluid ontology of his own poetic enterprise.

How fitting, then, that their very retrieval from Egyptian dust has resurrected so many papyrus 'columns' ascribed to both Sappho and Posidippus for an eager twenty-first-century readership (albeit in less 'white' or complete a form than their third-century BCE

---

[65] For the theme of κόνις (dust) in *epitymbia*, see also *AP* 7.34.2 (Antipater on the '*dust* that holds Pindar') and 7.708.1 (Dioscorides on the 'light dust' covering the playwright Machon), both discussed by Montiglio, in this volume, pp. 222 and 227.

[66] See Rosenmeyer (1997), 132 and Bing (2005), 132.

manifestations). As in the case of the Daphne poet's tomb, modern papyrology's dependence upon the physical traces of ancient verse (even as it attempts to liberate word from medium) reminds us that, as far as literary legacies are concerned, texts and tombs—or literary 'dust' and literal dust—are both materially and metaphorically 'entangled'.[67] Indeed, their mutual implication is expressed in quite literal terms on the purported tomb of the poet Archilochus on Paros. Here an extensive third-century BCE inscription by one 'Mnesiepes' commemorating the foundation of the Archilocheion is presented in parallel columns, thereby simulating the appearance of 'a papyrus roll spread out across a marble wall'.[68] It further employs documentary structuring devices such as reverse indentation (*ekthesis*), which is used to indicate citations from other texts, including oracles and Archilochus' poetry.[69] Whereas literary *epitymbia* evoke funerary epigraphy to draw attention to poetry's complex relationship to its material support, the Archilocheion inscription evokes literary strategies of structuring text as a means of asserting its authority as a definitive *bios* of the deceased poet, incorporating a wide range of sources to support a particular reading of more ambivalent aspects of Archilochus' verse (such as scurrilous aspects of his *iambos*).[70] The inscription's efforts to shape the visitor's encounter with Archilochus' actual *corpus* thus parallel its attempts to frame readings of his surviving body of work. This active formation of a 'community of remembrance' around both the literal and literary relics of Archilochus is emphasized by the

---

[67] For some fascinating comments on the relationship between papyrology and archaeology, see Obbink (2011). On the notion of 'entanglement', whereby social groups become invested in the maintenance of complex material worlds, see Hodder (2012).

[68] Clay (2004), 11, citing Kontoleon (1952), 36. Clay's study of the Archilocheion and its cache of inscriptions is still definitive. On the Mnesiepes inscription (*SEG* 15 no. 517; Clay (2004) cat. 2) in particular, see Kontoleon (1952) and (1956); Clay (2004), 10–24, 104–10 (with further bibliography); and Ornaghi (2009). On inscribed Hellenistic poetry organized in imitation of texts on papyrus, see Del Corso (2010) and Garulli (2014). Parallel uses of *selides* can be found on the philosophical inscription of Diogenes of Oinoanada (*SEG* 52.1445), dated *c.*200 BCE, and the so-called 'Pride of Halicarnassus' inscription (*SGO* 01.12.01), dated to the second century BCE: see Isager and Pederson (2004) and Garulli (2014), 146–50.

[69] On *ekthesis* in the Mnesiepes inscription, see Clay (2004), 156 n. 16 and Nagy (2008), 261–2.

[70] See Clay (2004), esp. 10–24; Ornaghi (2009), 176–80; and Rotstein (2010), 293–8.

name of the inscription's author, for Mnesiepes is literally 'He who remembers *epē* ("utterances")'.[71] Mnesiepes thus presents himself as an intermediary between poet and reader: he gathers the fragile traces of Archilochus' legacy into a stable text that claims both the public monumentality and cultic authority of an inscription, and the literary cachet and transmissive potential of a book roll, converting the fluid 'sayings' of oral tradition into a textual 'monument' (μνῆμα) that operates as both archive and tomb. Embodied 'collective' memory is transformed into entextualized 'cultural' memory by means of a monumental storage device which, located at the site of the poet's bodily remains, yokes practices of reading to those of cult in order to ensure a form of enduring *Funktionsgedächtnis* that is both lapidary and literary—both epitaph and epigraph.

## THE LIVING TOMB

For Mnesiepes, the Archilocheion's capacity to serve as a site of active commemoration depends upon ritual performance—both the sacrifices to Apollo that established the tomb's function as shrine and ongoing sacrifices to Archilochus.[72] In communicating between living visitors and the deceased hero-poet, sacrifice plays out on a ritual level what Mnesiepes' inscribed text invites of its readers— repeated reactivation of Archilochus' *corpus* (whether literal or literary) through acts of remembrance. Mnesiepes himself serves as a channel between the material and the metaphysical, mediating between the living and the dead, while his text occupies an interstitial category between oral and textual traditions, on the one hand, and stone and papyrus, on the other. The transcendent qualities of the poetic are thus harnessed to a specific location, monument, and body of texts—indeed, to the very location (the inscription implies) where Archilochus himself

---

[71] As observed by Nagy (1990b), 363–4 and (2008), 263.

[72] See Clay (2004), cat. 2, section $E_1$ II, lines 3–6 (Mnesiepes sacrifices to the Muses, Apollo, and other deities) and line 18 (Mnesiepes sacrifices in the precinct to Archilochus and other deities 'according to the instructions the god gave us in his oracle'). On the Delphic oracles cited by Mnesiepes, see Parke (1958), and on relations between the Archilocheion and Delphi, see Ornaghi (2009), 181–256.

was initiated into his role as poet by the Muses.[73] In contrast to the Euripidean tradition, the Parian Archilocheion unites Archilochus' body and its ritual remembrance with the location of his poetic production and entextualization; it thus yokes the metaphysics of divine inspiration (as in his encounter with the Muses) to the theology of hero cult (inspired by Mnesiepes' communications with the oracular Apollo). Significantly, it is through the physical preservation and commemoration of such encounters—by means of archival storage and its ritual retrieval—that such a transcendent model of poetic production can endure.

By virtue of its mid-third-century BCE date, Mnesiepes' inscription is contemporary with many *epitymbia* in the *Greek Anthology*, and mirrors the literary epitaph in its negotiation of the complex relationship between elusive verse and material monument. In generating virtual encounters with poets' tombs, *epitymbia* likewise address poetry's slippery ontology by drawing on the language and material paraphernalia of cult. In particular, they return repeatedly to the act of libation, as when (in an anonymous epigram) the speaking tomb of the 'divine Homer' requests that the traveller 'pass me not by, but pour a libation (κατασπείσας), just as you would to honour the gods.'[74] Like the ships of the Nile in Posidippus' epitaph for Doricha (where repeated launches from Naukratis suggest the recurrent transmission of Sappho's verse), ritual performance at the tomb suggests continuous communication with and remembrance of the departed. As Jan Assmann observes, 'cultural memory is imbued with an element of the sacred': the tomb's capacity to yoke the transcendent metaphysics of 'immortal' poetry to the commemorative functions of funerary ritual is key to the *epitymbion*'s performance of active remembrance (or *Funktionsgedächtnis*), drawing its readers into a living community of virtual visitors that extends across time, linking poetic past to textual present.[75]

Recurrent observances at the physical site of the poet's *corpus* are thus evoked in *epitymbia* as a parallel to repeated activation of his or her

---

[73] See Clay (2004), cat. 2, section E₁ II, lines 20–40. On Archilochus' epiphanic *Dichterweihe*, see Clay (2004), 14–16; Corrêa (2008); Ornaghi (2009), 133–55; and Rotstein (2010), 293–8.

[74] *AP* 7.2B, lines 2–3 (Anonymous), text and translation from Paton (1917).

[75] J. Assmann (2011), 38. See also A. Assmann (2011), on the mnemonic function of ritual 'scripts' in cultural memory.

textual *corpus*, such as the libations of milk and honey traditionally offered to the dead that Alcaeus of Mytilene (or Messene) claims were poured by goatherds at the tomb of Hesiod: 'For even such was the song the old man breathed who had tasted the pure fountains of the nine Muses' (*AP* 7.55.5–6).[76] As in numerous epigrams that play on the pouring of wine on the tomb of the bibulous Anacreon, the fresh flow of liquid in honour of the dead evokes the ministrations of funerary ritual, while both reifying and reactivating the outpouring of song associated with the poet's living body (and its divine inspiration).[77] Libation ritually figures the process of transmission from one poetic vessel to another, as streams of verse pass from Muse to poet to reader/celebrant, flowing between the metaphysical and the corporeal, the dead and the living.[78] Furthermore, libation materializes the content of the poet's verse in the form of flowing substances that evoke particular genres or aesthetic qualities—whether Anacreon's wine-fuelled sympotic verse or Hesiod's honeyed agricultural didactic.[79] At the same time, the epigram presents itself as an inscribed text that, in inviting us to perform a ritual that reactivates the tomb's function as a memorial, or μνῆμα, collapses the distinction between lapidary and literary modes of reading, inviting us into its virtual space.[80] In this way, the material presence, geographical specificity, and socially embedded modes of remembrance associated with sites such as the Archilocheion are claimed for the textual community of the literary epigram, where the topos of libation generates repeated outpourings of verse as successive poets adopt and extend the conceit, returning time and again to their predecessors' tombs as part of their practice of epigrammatic sociality.

This simultaneous reification and ritualization of poetry in the form of flowing liquid brings us to our final (and most thrillingly

---

[76] *AP* 7.55 (attributed to Alcaeus of Mytilene or Messene): τοίην γὰρ καὶ γῆρυν ἀπέπνεεν ἐννέα Μουσέων | ὁ πρέσβυς καθαρῶν γευσάμενος λιβάδων.

[77] *AP* 7.23.3–4, 7.26.3–4, 7.28.2: for discussion, see Montiglio, Chapter 10 in this volume.

[78] On depictions of libation on Greek pots, and the theological implications of its material fluidity, see Gaifman (2013). On libation in Greek religion more generally, see Graf (1980) and Simon (2005).

[79] Cf. Montiglio's chapter in this volume on the generic significance of plants growing from poets' tombs in Hellenistic *epitymbia*, where the ivy and vine springing forth from the tomb of Anacreon, for example, function in parallel ways to libations of wine.

[80] On the means by which epigrams construct fictional spaces within their anthologies, whether cemetery or gallery, see Höschele (2010), with her discussion of virtual 'Poets' Corners', Chapter 9 in this volume.

complex) example of a textualized poet's tomb—an *epitymbion* for
Sophocles from the *Garland of Philip* attributed to 'Erycias', which
brings together many of the themes explored in this chapter (*AP* 7.36):

αἰεί τοι λιπαρῷ ἐπὶ σήματι, δῖε Σοφόκλεις,
  σκηνίτης μαλακοὺς κισσὸς ἅλοιτο πόδας,
αἰεί τοι βούπαισι περιστάζοιτο μελίσσαις
  τύμβος, Ὑμηττείῳ λειβόμενος μέλιτι,
ὡς ἄν τοι ῥείη μὲν ἀεὶ γάνος Ἀτθίδι δέλτῳ
  κηρός, ὑπὸ στεφάνοις δ' αἰὲν ἔχῃς πλοκάμους.

Ever, O divine Sophocles, may the ivy that adorns the stage
  dance with soft feet over your polished monument.
Ever may the tomb be encompassed by bees that bedew it,
  the children of the ox, and drip with honey of Hymettus,
that there be ever store of wax flowing for you to spread on your Attic
  writing tablet, and that your locks may never want a wreath.[81]

Like many fictional epitaphs, Erycias' poem treats Sophocles' *sēma* as
a physical manifestation of his work, whereby plants adorning it
embody the genre at which he excelled, tragedy.[82] Here the customary
embellishments of the tomb are put to work as signs, *sēmata*, of
literary form, content, and poetics, so that the Bacchic connotations
of ivy recall the Dionysiac setting of the theatre. The plant's 'soft feet'
suggest actors' buskins, while Hymettian honey suggests the 'sweet-
ness' of Sophocles' verse, the Attic qualities of his language, and the
Athenian context for which he wrote.[83]

Erycias takes this conceit further: extending the metaphor of honey
from its role in libations to the dead to the use of beeswax as a surface
for script, he goes on to pray in lines 4–5 'that there be ever store of
wax flowing for you to spread on your Attic writing tablet'. Here the
distinction between tomb and text is fully elided, as the ritual accoutre-
ments of the *sēma* themselves provide the physical surface necessary

---

[81] *AP* 7.36. Translation adapted from Paton (1917). On this epigram, see also
Montiglio's chapter in this volume.

[82] In this sense, the epigram responds to Simias' *epitymbion* for Sophocles, *AP* 7.22
(discussed above), which describes him as crowned with the 'curving ivy of Acharnae'.
Compare the vines, violets, and myrtle that grow upon the tomb of Anacreon—
material embodiments of sympotic verse that, appropriately for this most bibulous of
poets, accompany the drenching of both his ashes and his *sēma* with wine (*AP*
7.23–33), discussed by Montiglio, Chapter 10 in this volume.

[83] On the significance of Attic honey here (celebrated by Aristophanes at *Pax* 252
and *Thesm.* 1192), see Gow and Page (1968), vol. 2, 286.

for textual composition. Not only does the technology of writing preserve Sophocles' works for posterity, Erycias implies, it even offers material conditions appropriate for the production of new work in the context of death. Within the virtual medium of the epigram, the tomb already serves as a (stone) surface for the epitaph's inscription. Yet the image of a *sēma* spread with wax—a veritable beehive of poetic activity—creates a palimpsest of textual surfaces, whereby stone inscription is layered with wax writing tablet and, implicitly, the papyrus roll that supports Erycias' text itself. In this way, the impermanence of the wax tablet—as a surface more appropriate for initial composition than the long-term storage of literary texts—is countered by means of a stone inscription that is nevertheless preserved and circulated in the form of a book roll.

This materialization of remembrance upon the surface of Sophocles' *sēma* parallels the preservation of his tragedies in the material form of the book (recalling, like the *epitymbia* of Euripides, the definitive entextualization of his works in Lycurgan Athens), once more asserting the relationship between tomb and archive as parallel forms of *mnēmata*. At the same time, Erycias' hope that wax might 'always flow' (ῥείη μὲν ἀεί) and that Sophocles will be 'continually crowned with wreaths' (ὑπὸ στεφάνοις δ' αἰὲν ἔχῃς πλοκάμους) expresses a desire for the elusive immediacy of poetic composition and theatrical performance that a book roll (as archival document) can never quite provide.

It was the wax tablets discovered in the Tomb of the Poet at Daphne, we might recall, that so moved the poet A. E. Stallings, who contrasts the crumbling beeswax 'frangible with centuries' now visible in the Piraeus Museum with the pliant substance known to the living poet, 'still weighing one word with another'.[84] As an organic medium created by bees and employed for 'work in progress', the text impressed into wax (rather than inked onto papyrus) maintains the status of an eternal *non finito*, forever suspended in a state of becoming.[85] It is, moreover, the archetypal medium of memory, from Plato's *Theaetetus* (which describes how memories are formed when imprinted into the

---

[84] Stallings (2006), 19 (discussed above).
[85] On the phenomenology of the *non finito*, see Rothstein (1976); Guentner (1993); Carabell (1995) and (2014); Kramer (2008), with Gurd (2007) and Platt (2018) on the aesthetics of the incomplete in Hellenistic epigram. On the ontological complexities of beeswax as a medium for writing and image-making, see Platt (forthcoming).

wax tablet of the mind) to Cicero's model of spatial mnemotechnics derived from Simonides (whereby one stores memories as images within places, 'as a wax writing tablet and the letters written on it').[86] In contrast to the impassive hardness of stone or the brittle surface of papyrus, wax conveys a sense of embodied, active memory that is stored in persons rather than things. As a medium for the storage of thought, it mediates between the material and metaphysical—just as the libations of honey poured on Sophocles' tomb mediate between the living and the dead, and just as the teeming bees that throng it are themselves described as emerging from the dead body of an ox (in an allusion to the *bougonia*, a famous example of 'spontaneous generation' with overtones of resurrection).[87] In marking the textual materialization of Sophocles' *corpus*, then, Erycias reifies his work in media that are traditionally invested with both an organic and a transcendent power.

Pierre Nora observes that 'Memory is a perpetually actual phenomenon, a bond tying us to the eternal present.'[88] In his prayer for perpetually flowing wax, Erycias finds an especially apposite means of materializing the elusive nature of poetry at its very moment of emergence, aligning the enduring ritual present of the honey-steeped tomb with the compositional present of the poet, and uniting the embodied storage of memory (in its Platonic formulation) with both the fluidity of verse and the material inscription of text itself. As the relics of the Daphne tomb remind us, however, wax needs the warmth of living bodies to remain pliable, impressible, and, ultimately, readable. To retain their functionality and avoid obsolescence, textual media must remain active, operating within networks where they can maintain their 'fluidity' through continual reactivation. Ultimately, the poet's tomb both embodies and problematizes an enduring tension between the transcendent qualities attributed to the poetry of the past and the material vehicles that convey this transcendence to

---

[86] Plato, *Theaetetus* 191c–d; Cicero *De oratore* 2.86. On the relationship between wax and memory in antiquity, see Penny Small (1997), and on the role of wax in the phenomenology of memory, Ricoeur (2004), 13–17. On the uncanny organicism of wax as a medium, see Didi-Huberman (1999). On Simonides as the inventor of memory techniques and as the object of memorialization, see Rawles, Chapter 2 in this volume.

[87] The *locus classicus* for the *bougonia* is Virgil, *Georgics* 4.281–314 and 538–58: see Perkell (1989) and Habinek (1990); on bees in the Graeco-Roman poetic tradition, see Engels and Nicolaye (2008) and Carlson (2015).

[88] Nora (1989), 8.

future generations. Whether virtual or inscribed, the *epitymbion* marks out a privileged space for written text as a medium that, in maintaining and even generating poetic memories, holds the potential to circulate them among the living. Yet whether stone, wax, or papyrus, such media exist along a spectrum of impermanence that continually threatens the immortality they attempt to confer. The Muses' gifts may be 'deathless', as Antipater's epitaph for Sappho claims (*AP* 7.14), yet they depend for their survival upon a series of mortal bodies, of which the poet's own is merely the first in a series of perishable vessels for verse.[89]

[89] I am most grateful to Barbara Graziosi and Nora Goldschmidt for inviting me to contribute to this volume, and for the wonderful opportunity to learn from the *Living Poets* project at Durham University. I would also like to thank colleagues who have given me invaluable feedback during the writing of this paper, including Hayden Pelliccia, Pietro Pucci, Alex Purves, Victoria Wohl, Nancy Worman, and the anonymous readers for Oxford University Press. Chelsea Gardner and Carolyn Laferrière provided invaluable help in securing the image of the 'Tomb of the Poet'.

# 2

## Simonides on Tombs, and the 'Tomb of Simonides'

*Richard Rawles*

In this chapter, I discuss the elegy from Callimachus' *Aitia* known as the 'Tomb of Simonides': I argue that the Hellenistic poet commemorates his archaic predecessor by considering Simonides' association with epigram and, more specifically, his take on the epigraphic commemoration of the dead. The language and rhetoric of inscribed poetry (and especially that of epitaphs) can draw attention to its own materiality and relate to its inscribed context, yet can also be experienced apart from its original context. I consider how Simonides responded to this specific feature of the poetic world in which he lived, by focusing in particular on 581 *PMG*, a poem often read as a rejection of the poetics of inscription in favour of non-inscribed poetry and song, but which in my view shows a more subtle and complex relationship with the world of epigram than has usually been perceived. I then return to the voice of Simonides and its relationship to epigram as presented in Callimachus' elegy: I read this poem as receiving and responding to Simonides' own poetics—a poetics, I argue, shaped by the materiality of inscriptions and, simultaneously, by the dynamics of orally diffused poetry.

This chapter is intended as a case study of the poet's tomb (whether real or imagined), seen as a form of literary reception. The epitaph is often a crucial part of this kind of reception, as several chapters in this volume illustrate. The case I discuss here, however, is more complex than most: Callimachus presents Simonides' tomb not as an epitaph, but as a kind of 'meta-epitaph'—an elegy which is not itself inscribed, but describes the loss of an inscribed tombstone. The 'Tomb of

Simonides' does not simply explore the poetics of epigram but, as I argue, Simonides' own poetic response to epigram.

## CALLIMACHUS FR.64 THE 'TOMB OF SIMONIDES'

*ed. & trans. Harder*[1]
*P.Oxy.* 2211 fr.1 verso, 10–28.
⌊*supplements from Suda* σ441 Adler *s.v.* Σιμωνίδης⌋
[*supplements by modern editors*]

οὐδ᾽ ἄ]ν τοι Καμάρινα τόσον κακὸν ὀκκόσον ἀ[ν]δρός
    κινη]θεὶς ὁσίου τύμβος ἐπικρεμάσαι·
καὶ γ]ὰρ ἐμόν κοτε σῆμα, τό μοι πρὸ πόληος ἔχ[ευ]αν
    Ζῆν᾽] Ἀκραγαντῖνοι Ξείνι[ο]ν ἁζόμενοι,
... κ]ατ᾽ οὖν ἤρειψεν ἀνὴρ κακός, εἴ τιν᾽ ἀκούει[ς     5
    Φοίνικ]α πτόλιος σχέτλιον ἡγεμόνα·
πύργῳ] δ᾽ ἐγκατέλεξεν ἐμὴν λίθον οὐδὲ τὸ γράμμα
    ᾐδέσθ᾽]η τὸ λέγον τόν ⌊μ⌋ε Λεωπρέπεος
κεῖσθα⌊ι⌋ Κήϊον ἄνδρα τὸν ἱερόν, ὃς τὰ περισσά
    .....] μνήμην πρῶτος ὃς ἐφρασάμην,     10
οὐδ᾽ ὑμ⌊έας, Πολύδευκες, ὑπέτρεσεν, οἵ με μελά⌊θ⌋ρου
    μέλλο⌊ν⌋τος πίπτειν ἐκτὸς ἔθεσθέ κοτε
δαιτυμ⌊ι⌋όνων ἄπο μοῦνον, ὅτε Κραννώνιος ⌊αἰ⌋αῖ
    ὤ⌋λισ⌊θ⌋ε⌊ι⌋ν μεγ⌊ά⌋λο⌊υ⌋ς οἶκος ἐπὶ ⌊Σ⌋κ⌊ο⌋πάδ⌊α⌋ς.
ὦνακες, ἀλ..ϊ[..]. γὰρ ἔτ᾽ ἦν[     15
    ] ... ωοῦμεδ[    ].βοạιν[
....λμοὐσ[    ].ϊουνδο.[
    .....ηστ.[    ]εν ἀνῆγεν[
...[    ].[.].ετ´κ..[

Not even Camarina would bring so much disaster on you as the tomb
    of a pious man if it is moved from its place.
For my tomb, too, which the people of Acragas built outside the town,
    honouring Zeus the god of strangers,
was once destroyed by an evil man, if you have heard
    of a certain Phoenix, the town's headstrong leader.

---

[1] Harder (2012), i.227–8. The first line of our fragment corresponds to the first line of the elegy; the end of the elegy was probably not much after u.19: Harder (2012), ii.516; Massimilla (2006), 37.

He built my tombstone into the city-wall and had no respect
   for the inscription which said that I, the son of Leoprepes,
was lying here, the holy man from Ceos, who first invented
   the extra letters . . . and the art of mnemotechnics.
He did not shrink back from you, Polydeuces, who once,
   when the house was going to fall down, brought me outside
as the only one among the guests, when—oh dear—the Crannonian
   palace collapsed on the mighty sons of Scopas.
Lords, . . .

(Callimachus fr.64)

In this papyrus fragment from Callimachus' *Aitia*, the voice of the
poem, which turns out to be the voice of the poet Simonides himself,
warns of the danger of moving a tomb: the first line refers to a story
about the people of Camarina, who were warned by an oracle not to
move the lake of the same name. They did so anyway, by draining the
marshes around their city, with the result that Camarina was des-
troyed. Simonides' tomb, at Acragas, also in Sicily, was moved by a
general called Phoenix,[2] who should have been scared, particularly
since Simonides' history with powerful but impious men showed that
he had divine protection. Lines 11–14 refer to a story we know best
from Roman sources (but which was clearly well known in the
Hellenistic period, as this very fragment and other sources named
by Quintilian demonstrate): Simonides composed a song for a noble-
man of Thessaly, which extensively treated the Dioscuri;[3] the uncouth
patron was annoyed by their starring role in the composition and
responded by paying Simonides only half of the agreed fee; later, at a
dinner, Simonides was told that two youths were waiting for him
outside; he left the building; he encountered nobody, but was saved
from sure death, since the building where he was having dinner
collapsed while he was outside. The disaster so mangled the bodies
of the diners inside that their relatives could not identify the bodies—
but Simonides, known as the inventor of memory-systems could, by
recalling the order in which they were seated. This feat enabled them
to be identified *for burial.*

---

[2] Alternatively, Phoenix (the supplement is secured by a mention in the *Suda*
entry, σ441 s.v. Σιμωνίδης) may be an ethnic, referring to the Punic Hannibal who
besieged the city in 406 BCE: Dyer (2000); Livrea (2006); cf. Bruss (2004), 63–4, but also
Harder (2012) ad loc.; Garulli (2007).
[3] Simonides 510 *PMG* (T80 Poltera): Quintilian 11.2.11–16, Cicero, *De oratore*
2.86.351–3.

At this point, the text gives out; ὦνακες ('Lords') must be a direct address to the Dioscuri. The vocative fits into a broader area of interest: the voice of the elegy is hard to pin down, but is strongly marked pragmatically. We have two first persons in 3, an apostrophe with ἀκούεις ('you hear', singular) in 5; a different direct address to the Dioscuri (ὑμέας, plural) and to Polydeuces in 11, in the singular. The address to the Dioscuri is picked up by 'Lords', again in the plural, in 15. The shifts between singular and plural are obscured in Harder's translation but serve to characterize a complex voice, which must be that of Simonides himself. The context evokes the capacity of epitaphs to represent the voice of the deceased—yet this is not an epitaph, but rather describes the destruction of an epitaph. How, then, can the voice of the dead man be coming to life in this poem?

## EPIGRAMS, TOMBS, BODIES

In the light of Simonides' own work, as well as its ancient reception, it makes sense that we find him, here, in the context of an elegy about tombs and inscribed epitaphs.[4] Simonides was known for *threnoi* (dirges), of which fragments survive.[5] Since the publication of the 'new Simonides' in 1992, we can now also appreciate his elegiac treatment of battles in the Persian Wars, which represents in part a commemoration of the dead.[6] His association, in anecdotal tradition, with the burial of the dead is visible in a story known from Cicero and elsewhere, in which Simonides is rewarded for his piety by the ghost of a man whose burial he had ensured. Cicero took this from Stoic sources, and the same story generated two fictitious epigrams.[7] These take us to an area of Simonidean studies between 'works' and 'reception': ancient sources repeatedly attribute epigrams to Simonides, sometimes where there is reason to believe that the attribution is

---

[4] It should be stressed that much of what we see of Simonides' works (and the point can be generalized to other poets) itself reflects a form of reception, through the choices of quoting authors.

[5] Page (1962) classified 520–31 *PMG* as certain or possible fragments from the *Threnoi*; Poltera (2008) gathers his frr. 244–8 under this heading.

[6] The *editio princeps* of *P.Oxy.* 3965 was by Peter Parsons; Simonides frr. 1–18 W².

[7] Cicero *De divinatione* I.56; 'Simonides' *FGE* 84 = *AP* 7.516, 'Simonides' *FGE* 85 = *AP* 7.77. See Davies (2004); *FGE* ad loc. with further references.

false. Many epigrams *might* be genuine, and I am happy to suppose that part of the reason why Simonides was believed to be a poet of epigram is that he was. However, attribution is also a form of reception: later in antiquity it made sense to attribute epigrams, particularly epitaphs, to Simonides, or (as with these two) to generate 'Simonidean' epigrams to accompany a story about Simonides and the burial of the dead.[8]

In Callimachus' elegy, the voice of the poem is the voice of the dead man: the elegy plays on the common capacity of sepulchral epigram to be expressed in the voice of the deceased in this way, and to mark its association with the tomb using various forms of deixis. I argue below that it responds to engagement with the poetics of inscription in Simonides' own work. In order to illustrate and explore this, I now turn to inscribed epigram of the archaic and early classical periods. What follows is not an attempt at a complete account of the poetics and pragmatics of inscribed poetry; I rather draw attention to selected features, with a view to their significance in ancient responses to inscribed poetry, as discussed further below.[9]

The epitaph often marks its association with the tomb using explicit deixis (*mutatis mutandis* this holds for many non-epitaphic inscribed poems, too). We can see this in one epigram securely attributed to Simonides, for the seer Megistias who died at Thermopylae (6 *FGE*, Hdt. 7.228, *AP* 7.677): μνῆμα τόδε, '*this* memorial'. Here the epigram inscribes its own position on the tomb. Similarly, we find τόδε σῆμα, '*this* tomb/sign' and equivalents also in other poems attributed to Simonides.[10] Alternatively, we may find a deictic adverb like ἐνθάδε or τῆδε, 'here'. Thus, in the famous epigram for the Spartans who died at Thermopylae, attributed to Simonides by some sources (22b *FGE*), we read 'we lie *here*.' By such expressions the text marks its association with the monument, and the monument's singular, spatially fixed quality. This can also be true of, for instance, dedicatory epigrams, but with tombs there is a particular fittingness: the singularity and spatial fixity marked by the epigram corresponds to that of the tomb, and thus of the body, and, as stories like the one about Simonides and the

---

[8] On Simonidean epigrams and related questions, see Bravi (2006); Petrovic (2007) (with a full treatment of earlier scholarship); Sider (2007).

[9] For recent work on archaic and classical epigram, see Baumbach, Petrovic, and Petrovic (2010); Day (2010) (on dedicatory epigram).

[10] E.g. σᾶμα τόδε in 'Simonides' 86 *FGE* (*AP* 7.177), apparently a simple one-line inscription which somehow entered the Simonidean tradition.

unburied corpse remind us, the body must be laid to rest in a specific place.

The same impression of singularity and spatial fixity can be intensified and augmented by explicit attention to the monument itself in the words of the epigram. This is much less common than simple deictic marking, but we have epigrams which show a keen interest in the relationship between the inscription, its written 'voice', and the material features of the monument. An example is a tombstone for Mnesitheos of Aegina, buried at Eretria (*CEG* 108, dated to *c*.450):[11]

> χαίρετε τοὶ παριόντες, ἐγὸ δὲ θανὸν κατάκειμαι.
> δεῦρο ἰὸν ἀνάνεμαι, ἀνὲρ τίς τὲδε τέθαππται·
>   ξενὸς ἀπ' Αἰγίνες, Μνεσίθεος δ' ὄνυμα·
> καί μοι μνêμ' ἐπέθεκε· φίλε μέτερ Τιμαρέτε
>   τύμοι ἐπ' ἀκροτάτοι στέλεν ἀκάματον,
> hάτις ἐρεî παριôσι διαμερὲς ἄματα πάντα·
> Τιμαρέτε μ' ἔσστεσε φίλοι ἐπὶ παιδὶ θανόντι.

Greetings, passers-by! I, having died, lie here.
Come here and read out what man is buried here:
a foreigner from Aegina, and Mnesitheos is his name.
And my dear mother Timarete set up this memorial for me,
on the top of the tomb an unwearying stele,
which will say to passers-by continuously for all days:
'Timarete set me up upon her beloved son, dead.'

Here we see an interest in the inscribed, material qualities of the text: an addressee is instructed to read out the answer to the question 'Who is buried here?', and the stele itself, carrying the inscription, will speak to passers-by.[12] The poet is exploring different ways of presenting the relationship between reading, voice, and the monument itself, and the spatial fixity of the text is emphasized by the description of its position and the relationship of its voice to the inscribed stele.

This is more clearly visible in another example, this time a dedication (*CEG* 429, from Halicarnassus, *c*.475):

> αὐδὴ τεχνήεσσα λίθο, λέγε τίς τόδ' ἄ[γαλμα]
> στῆσεν Ἀπόλλωνος βωμὸν ἐπαγλαΐ[σας].

---

[11] For inscriptions cited from *CEG*, I print Hansen's (1983) text, but omit some lectional signs.

[12] Svenbro (1993), 49–50 proposed the reading *HOTIΣ*, and interpreted it as οὖ τις ἐρεῖ 'where some one will tell'; I here assume that Hansen (1983) gives the better text.

Παναμύης υἱὸς Κασβώλλιος, εἴ μ' ἐπ[οτρύνεις
ἐξειπεῖν, δεκάτην τήνδ' ἀνέθηκε θε[ῶι].

3. suppl. Wilamowitz; εἴ με κ[ελεύεις Maiuri

> 'Skilfully wrought voice of stone, say who set up this offering, bringing delight to the altar of Apollo.'
> 'Kasbollios, son of Panamye—if you urge me to speak out—dedicated this tithe to the god.'

The epigram celebrates the voice of the stone, which is to say the inscription itself and its power to name.[13] The reference to the stone emphasizes the 'placedness' of the poem: it seems inseparable from the monument. The voice is of the stone, because the poet is thinking of the inscribed base, rather than the bronze statue on top.

Where inscriptions like these are epitaphs, the human and the body—necessarily fixed in space and time—are commemorated by the monument and its inscription: these retain the spatial fixity of the body, but may claim to endure through time. The voice becomes live each time the inscription is read, and its longevity is thus guaranteed—or limited—by the endurance of the monument. This can be seen as a claim that epigram can perpetuate κλέος (*kleos*), 'fame', or 'resounding renown', as Svenbro put it, emphasizing the importance of sound: the inscription prompts reading aloud and can thus be heard over time.[14] Some epigrams make explicit claims concerning *kleos* which might be interpreted this way.[15] However, this kind of epigrammatic *kleos* can be contrasted with the *kleos* claimed by non-inscribed poetry and song, which lacks such dependence on the material object of the inscription, and as such is not confined in space or time. Epigrammatic *kleos* can look inferior to the commemoration instantiated (for example) by Homeric poetry.[16] Poets of different kinds of encomiastic verse can offer *kleos* free of material fixity to their patrons and sometimes draw attention to this fact.[17]

---

[13] Again Svenbro (1993), 57–61 sought to resist this, interpreting τεχνήεσσα as active, 'skilful', and translating λίθο as 'at the service of the stone', so that the voice is that of a skilful reader of the text on the stone: this seems strained and unlikely.

[14] Svenbro (1993), 4, 14–15.

[15] For epigrammatic κλέος, see e.g. 'Simonides' 20 *FGE* (*CEG* 2.11, ML26); a more explicit claim that the monument and inscription themselves generate κλέος at *CEG* 459 (Rhodes, '*c*.600–575 (?)', probably not an epitaph), *CEG* 344 (cf. Fearn (2013), 244–5).

[16] This is a point made by several scholars, see esp. Ford (2002), ch. 4 (93–112) and, in its application to Simonides, Fearn (2013).

[17] For Homer as κλέος-provider and an analogue for later commemorative poetry, see famously Simonides 11.15–18 W²; the opening of Pindar *Nem.* 5 is the classic instance for contrast between statues, fixed in their places, and mobile song: see e.g.

## EPIGRAMS WITHOUT STONES

The most obvious problem with the dichotomy 'orally transmitted poetry vs inscribed epigram' is that inscriptions *can* break free of their confinement in space.[18] For us, this is common: we have many epigrams which were once inscribed but which we now read without seeing the original stone.[19] In theory, the *kleos* associated with an inscribed monument—for our purposes, an epitaphic monument, but the point can be generalized—could always break free, so to speak, from the stone and join the oral or partly oral tradition characteristic of song and elegy, simply by being repeated and becoming famous. In fact, we have evidence that this often happened.

I have mentioned the Thermopylae inscriptions, functioning (according to Herodotus and others) as epitaphs for those who died and were buried at the site of the battle. Here I give the most famous, accompanied by an apparatus, because the textual variation between sources matters for my argument:[20]

'Simonides' 22b *FGE* (Hdt. 7.228 [no attribution], Lycurgus *in Leocr.* 109 [no attrib.], Diod. Sic. 11.33.2 [no attrib.], Strabo 9.4.16 [no attrib.], *AP* 7.249 [Simonides], *A. Plan.* [no attrib.], *Suda* s.v. Λεωνίδης (λ272 Adler) [no attrib.], trans. Cicero at *Tusc.* 1.101 [Simonides]):

> ὦ ξεῖν᾽, ἀγγέλλειν Λακεδαιμονίοις ὅτι τῇδε
> κείμεθα τοῖς κείνων ῥήμασι πειθόμενοι.

*app. crit. (from Page)*:
1. ἀγγέλλειν Hdt.; ἄγγελλε *Suda*; ὦ ξέν᾽ ἀπάγγειλον Strabo; ἄγγειλον *the rest*.

---

Ford (2002), 98, 119-23; O'Sullivan (2003), 81-5; Fearn (2013), 241-4 (with more references in n. 42) attempts a more nuanced reading (see further below).

[18] Cf., recently, Baumbach, Petrovic, and Petrovic (2010), 17-18 (from the editors' introduction) on 'delapidarisation', using the example of Simonides' epigram for the Spartans at Thermopylae, discussed further below.

[19] For our receptions of ancient texts, a clash between a *claim* about how fame may endure and the fact of how it has or has not endured is likely to be important: one may think not only of inscriptions (Shelley's *Ozymandias*!) but also of other kinds of 'as long as' claims. The survival of Horace's *Odes* was not 'for as long as the priest climbs the Capitol with the silent virgin' (Horace, *Odes* 3.30.8-9), and Virgil's epitaph for Nisus and Euryalus (*Aeneid* 9.446-9) may provoke similar thoughts.

[20] For this epigram and 'delapidarisation', cf. Baumbach, Petrovic, and Petrovic (2010), 17-18.

2. ῥήμασι πειθόμενοι Hdt., *AP*, *A. Plan.*, *Suda*; πειθόμενοι νομίμοις Lycurgus, Diodorus, Strabo, Cicero ('legibus obsequimur').

*trans. Campbell*:
Stranger, report to the Spartans that we lie here, obedient to their words.

The differences between transmitted versions of the first line are perhaps insignificant, but the second half of the pentameter is more striking: our sources diverge between the reading ῥήμασι πειθόμενοι, 'obedient to their words', and πειθόμενοι νομίμοις, 'obedient to their laws'. Regardless of the question which words were actually inscribed at Thermopylae, the divergence is early: it seems to originate, as Page suggested, in early oral dissemination of the text of the epigram.[21] The text does not become well known because lots of people visited Thermopylae, or because it was transcribed by Herodotus (if that is what he did), but because it passed into the mix of tradition associated with the battle as a song might have done. Its circulation—and thus its commemorative power—became independent from the spatially fixed monument. Perhaps this movement is envisaged in the poem itself: the messenger addressed will be able to repeat to the Spartans the poem which he has read.[22]

Another example, this time a dedication, again from Simonides' world, and again attributed to Simonides, comes from Delphi—or, as I argue, does not really come from Delphi:

'Simonides' 17 *FGE* (Thuc. 1.132.2, [Dem.] 59.97, *AP* 6.197 [Simonides]; cf. Paus. 3.8.2 [Simonides]; *other sources*)[23]

Ἑλλάνων ἀρχάγος ἐπεὶ στρατὸν ὤλεσε Μήδων
Παυσανίας Φοίβῳ μνᾶμ᾽ ἀνέθηκε τόδε.

*trans. Campbell*:
When Pausanias, commander of the Greeks, had destroyed the army of the Medes, he set up this memorial to Phoebus.

---

[21] *FGE*, 233–4: in *FGE* Page argued that the reading of Lycurgus, Ephorus (the assumed source of Diodorus) and Cicero must be the 'generally accepted text' in antiquity, and probably right, whereas ῥήμασι πειθόμενοι was told to Herodotus 'at second hand, orally, from his Spartan informants'. Page (1975), 18 had previously printed the Herodotean reading, as does Petrovic (2007), 245.

[22] Baumbach, Petrovic, and Petrovic (2010), 17; Tueller (2010) 57–8, discussing the same Thermopylae epigram, describes 'the *idea* that epigrams would be spread and repeated in other places' (my emphasis) as an impetus for literary transmission and composition of epigrams.

[23] See Petrovic (2007), 267 for a fuller indication of sources.

This text was inscribed on the authority of Pausanias of Sparta, says Thucydides, by the 'serpent column' dedicated at Delphi from the spoils from the defeat of the Persian invasion; but the Spartans 'immediately' (εὐθύς) erased it. A slightly different version of the story is reported by Apollodorus in *Against Neaera*, again quoting the epigram. However, as the quotation in both sources shows, the erasure of the inscription made no difference to its preservation. In the heightened commemorative atmosphere after Xerxes' invasion, the epigram, despite its erasure, passed into a tradition which transmitted it down the generations: a poem composed for inscription and, in fact, inscribed could still perpetuate memory through time independently of the carved stone.

## THE 'MIDAS EPIGRAM'

My next example does double duty. The epitaph of Midas is variously transmitted by various sources, and attributed either to the sage Cleoboulus or to Homer. I outline the main aspects of this variety (some variation of vocabulary and morphology is ignored) below. The multiformity in transmission, probably a consequence of oral dissemination, is what matters for my argument, rather than any particular judgement about the 'correct' text.

Sources: Plato *Phaedrus* 264d3, Diogenes Laertius 1.89-90, *Certamen Homeri et Hesiodi* 15 = 265–70, *Herodotean Life of Homer* 11 = 135–40, *AP* 7.153, *A. Plan.*, [Dio Chrys.] *Or.* 37.38 (Favorinus' *Corinthian Oration*), Philoponus on Aristotle *Analytic Posteriora* 13.3 (ed. Wallies, *Commentaria in Aristotelem Graeca* 13.3 p. 156), anon. on Aristotle *Sophistic Refutations* 171a (ed. Ebbeson, *Commentators and Commentaries on Aristotle's* Sophistici Elenchi [Leiden, 1981], ii.77).

*ed. Marcovich (Teubner) at Diogenes Laertius 1.89–90:*

χαλκῆ παρθένος εἰμί, Μίδου δ' ἐπὶ σήματι κεῖμαι.
ἔστ' ἂν ὕδωρ τε ῥέῃ καὶ δένδρεα μακρὰ τεθήλῃ,
ἠέλιός τ' ἀνιὼν λάμπῃ, λαμπρά τε σελήνη,
καὶ ποταμοί γε ῥέωσιν, ἀνακλύζῃ δὲ θάλασσα,
αὐτοῦ τῇδε μένουσα πολυκλαύτῳ ἐπὶ τύμβῳ,          5
ἀγγελέω παριοῦσι, Μίδας ὅτι τῇδε τέθαπται.

I am a bronze maiden, and I rest here upon the tomb of Midas.
For as long as water flows and great trees flourish,
and the sun shines as it rises, and the splendid moon,
and the rivers flow, and the sea washes on the shore,
remaining here on his much-lamented tomb
I shall announce to passers-by that Midas is buried here.

*How many lines are given?*
Plato, *AP*, *A.Plan.*, Dio Chrys.    1, 2, 5, 6
D.L., *Certamen*                      all six lines
*Hdt. Life of Homer*                  2, 3, 5, 6 *or* all six lines
Philoponus and anon.                  1, 2, 3, 5, 6

*Attributions:*
None: Plato, Dio, Philoponus (but he refers to *Hdt. Life of Homer*)
Homer: *Certamen, Hdt. Life,* anon. in Arist. *Elench. Soph.*
Cleoboulos: Simonides (below), *ut vid.*; D.L. (Homeric attribution
    denied)
Both: *AP*

ἀγγελέω παριοῦσι, 'I shall announce to passers-by', resembles ἐρεῖ
παριοῦσι, 'will say to passers-by', in the epitaph for Mnesitheos (*CEG*
108, above). One may nonetheless doubt whether this was really
inscribed, though there is, I think, no sure reason to rule it out.[24] In
any case, the variety in the form in which this poem is reported by our
different sources is likely to result from oral transmission. Everybody
gives the last two lines, but several sources omit the fourth or the
third and the fourth, and the Herodotean *Life of Homer* omits the
first (some manuscripts include it, but this is probably the result of
contamination).[25]
    Our earliest direct witness is Plato, who gives four lines. This might
be because Socrates claims that the same lines could be given in any
order, and that claim would be hard to make with a longer poem (it
does not quite work even with just the four lines, but would be weaker
with any addition). In any case, the variety of the tradition elsewhere

---

[24]   Peek (1955), 344, i.e. *GV* 1171, wrote 'Phrygien? Aeolis? VII./VI. Jh.'. Herodotus
(1.35) records Adrastos, 'a Phrygian of royal stock', grandson of Midas, which implies
a Midas *fl. c.*600, coherent with a reasonable dating of Cleoboulos. On historical
persons called Midas, see Berndt-Ersöz (2008): the Midas of Hdt. 1.35 is discussed at
1–2, and corresponds to Midas IV in the table on p. 29. Ford (2002) 101–2 treats the
poem as originally a real inscription of the late seventh century.
[25]   Cf. the extensive discussion in Markwald (1986), 34–83.

suggests that this is a 'real' variant rather than Platonic sneakiness.[26]
Simonides' poem (see below), usually read as a response to the epi-
gram, presupposes a longer text than Plato's: Simonides' sun and moon
and ocean whirls correspond to something like lines 3 and 4 of the
epigram as given by Diogenes.[27] The disagreement between our earliest
witnesses, combined with later muddle, suggests a text which is doing
the oral-traditional rounds in archaic and classical Greece and exhibits
the variety we might expect to result from rather messy, uncontrolled
diffusion, while being built into the story-traditions that eventually
result in the *Contest of Homer and Hesiod* and the Herodotean *Life*.

In short, while inscribed epigrams, including epitaphs, often mark
their attachment to a spatially fixed, material monument, they were in
fact *also* encountered in circumstances removed from the deictically
marked context. Rather as we see with markers of occasion in per-
formed, non-inscribed poetry, terms like '*these* men', '*this* grave', or
'lie *here*' would be refocused in these circumstances. Now, instead of
marking the location shared by reader and monument, deictic mark-
ers, like descriptions of the monument itself, evoke the experience of a
reading *in situ* through a kind of re-enactment.[28]

## SIMONIDES AND CLEOBOULUS
## (581 *PMG*, 262 POLTERA)

After the Midas epigram, Diogenes Laertius quotes a poem by
Simonides as evidence in support of attributing the Midas epigram
to Cleoboulus, rather than Homer:

τίς κεν αἰνήσειε νόωι πίσυνος Λίνδου ναέταν Κλεόβουλον,
ἀενάοις ποταμοῖσ᾽ ἄνθεσί τ᾽ εἰαρινοῖς
ἀελίου τε φλογὶ χρυσέας τε σελάνας
καὶ θαλασσαίαισι δίναις ἀντία θέντα μένος στάλας;
ἅπαντα γάρ ἐστι θεῶν ἥσσω· λίθον δὲ                                    5
καὶ βρότεοι παλάμαι θραύοντι· μωροῦ
φωτὸς ἅδε βούλα.

---

[26] Nor should we read the epigram as a Platonic fiction: Ford (2002), 101 n. 29.
[27] This despite the fact that, as transmitted, 4 is problematic: ἀνακλύζῃ is post-
classical, and the rivers are weak, given the water in line 2. It is possible that 4 has been
interpolated to match Simonides: Markwald (1986), 63.
[28] Cf. Morgan (1993) on Pindaric reperformance.

4. ἀντίθεντα codd.; ἀντία θέντα Bergk, ἀντιτιθέντα Schneidewin & Mehlhorn

*trans. Campbell, adapted:*

What man who can trust his wits would commend Cleoboulus, dweller in Lindos, who set against ever-flowing rivers, spring flowers, the flame of the sun or the golden moon, or the eddies of the sea the force of a stele? All things are less than the gods. Even mortal hands break a stone. This was the counsel of a fool.

The sources on which Diogenes Laertius relies assume that Simonides' lines are a response to the Midas epigram and, in my opinion, this view must be accepted. Cleoboulus of Lindos was one of the figures dated early in the sixth century who became known as the Sages, at some time codified as seven in number; Simonides also names and corrects a Sage in a different poem, discussed in Plato's *Protagoras* (542 *PMG*, 260 Poltera). Here, however, the tone is more aggressive: μωροῦ φωτὸς ἅδε βούλα, 'this was the counsel of a fool', is a put-down which puns on Cleoboulus' name (made up of the roots for 'fame' and 'counsel').

Why is Cleoboulus' counsel so bad? For Fränkel, the key phrase is ἅπαντα γάρ ἐστι θεῶν ἥσσω 'all things are less than the gods.' He writes: 'here again the poet is reminding us of the limits prescribed for all that pertains to man.'[29] Fränkel's 'again' caps a discussion of several Simonidean fragments, apparently from *threnoi* (dirges), which indeed emphasize the limitations of human beings, especially in the face of death. In a more recent treatment by Andrew Ford, the significance of this 'theological' aspect is acknowledged,[30] but is subordinated to the idea that Simonides contrasts inscribed poetry and monuments with the power of non-inscribed song: 'in Simonides' vision of song, enduring fame is not achieved by writing on rocks or metal; the only possible fame for mortals comes from ever-flowing oral traditions, as songs are taken up and performed to make the names of the dead sound again in time.'[31]

This kind of reading is hard to reject. Despite the gnomic 'all things are less than the gods', the paradoxical expression μένος στάλας, 'force of a stele', is strongly emphasized in the long first sentence, and the general expression focuses the more specific statement which follows:

---

[29] Fränkel (1975), 307.     [30] Ford (2002), 106.     [31] Ford (2002), 109.

'All things are less than the gods, but as for a *stone*—well, even mortal hands can break that!' It does look like an attack on the claim that a monument can enable *kleos* to be perpetuated through time, particularly an *inscribed* monument: in the Midas epigram, the bronze statue speaks, but Simonides refers to a stele and stone because he has in mind a statue with an inscribed base. This is intended as a correction: it is by virtue of the *inscription* that a statue can preserve the name of the deceased; cf. the stone voice of *CEG* 429, above.[32] The song seems to express hostility to monumental claims to preserve fame, especially with reference to inscribed monuments. We may feel that the point is a validation and celebration of song in a competitive environment—especially in a context which emphasizes the economics of poetry. Song is the better buy.[33]

David Fearn has objected to this kind of reading on various grounds.[34] He feels that it would be strange for the poets of praise to appear to devalue monumental and inscribed commemoration when their patrons were often the same people who commissioned statues and monuments, accompanied by inscriptions.[35] In addition, he finds it troubling for Simonides to polemicize against inscribed poetry when he was himself known as a composer of epigram.[36] The former argument is perhaps less than convincing: it seems that Simonidean praise could sometimes be rather combative and aggressive, even tactless.[37] I am more sympathetic to the biographical argument: the song addressing Cleoboulus, where the narrator confronts an authority from the past, is a passage which contributes to the persona and authority of the poet (not just a narrator), and this seems odd if the point is to devalue epigram. Fearn emphasizes 'poetic one-upmanship' between Simonides and Cleoboulus, and this seems right: Simonides rewrites the plain, list-like language of the epigram using the more heightened language of song.[38] He refers to a stele, and to stone, thereby, I argued, correcting the reference to the speaking

---

[32] Cf. Ford (2002), 107–8. Contra, Bruss (2004), 63 states that 'Simonides' interest in *PMG* 581, of course, is not the written word'.

[33] O'Sullivan (2003), 77–8; cf. the same scholar's reading of Pindaric references to statues, 78–85.

[34] Fearn (2013), building on work by Deborah Steiner and Roy Porter (p. 233; further bibliographical background at 232 n. 2, 233 nn. 8–9).

[35] Fearn (2013), 239–40.    [36] Fearn (2013), 235.

[37] See e.g. Rawles (2013) 194–9 with further references.

[38] Fearn (2013), 234–5.

'maiden' in the Midas epigram. Detailed comparisons are risky because of textual uncertainty, but it appears that Simonides also removes repetition of sense between the water of 2 and the rivers of 4. Still, Fearn's attempt to replace earlier ways of describing what is at stake in Simonides' poem with the idea of poetic one-upmanship can seem reductive.[39] It is with Cleoboulus' βούλα, 'counsel', not merely his poetic skill, that Simonides takes issue.

Attention to the permeable boundaries between inscribed poetry and oral traditions, as described above, may help here. A poem like the Midas epigram focuses attention on the endurance of the monument, which seems intimately connected with the perpetuation of fame. It is easy to respond by pointing out that 'even mortal hands break a stone'. Yet this is not the only way to describe the value of inscribed poetry, and such a response need not constitute rejection either of epigram or of monumental commemoration in general. Rather, the claim of the epigram can be contrasted with a more holistic poetics of commemoration, which might include inscribed and non-inscribed poetry, and which acknowledges the capacity for inscribed poetry to break free of its fixed spatial location and to travel through traditions and memory in the same way that non-inscribed poetry does. This is different from rejection: an epitaph may still carry the deictic markers of its location as it travels through both space and time—they are part of the point—in a way which is analogous to how occasional poetry sometimes carries marks of its original performance context. If an epigram is repeated away from its inscribed location, the fact of the tomb and its location is still part of what is being commemorated, even though the survival and reproduction of the words are independent of the endurance of the monument itself.

This—a disagreement about the poetic claims concerning inscribed poetry, rather than about its value *tout court*—may seem a subtle matter for such aggressively expressed disagreement. To make sense of Simonides' attitude, let us first return to the pun at the end. The designation of Cleoboulus as a φὼς μωρός, 'foolish man', probably plays on an expectation that he might have been named as a sage, a φὼς σοφός, 'wise man'.[40] Cleoboulus' name has two parts: fame-counsel.

---

[39] Up to a point this is what Fearn (2013), 235 seems to do; but I agree that Simonides need not seem to see himself as 'challenged by, or superior to, *all* literary epigraphy or statuary' (my emphasis).

[40] Cf. 542.12 *PMG* (260.12 Poltera), of Pittacus.

We might read it as 'the man famous for his (good) counsel', or as 'the man with (good) counsel about fame'. It helps to focus Simonides' disagreement to think of the second, and thus to think of Cleoboulus' βούλα, 'counsel', as one which is marked as being to do with *kleos*. As far as the perpetuation of a name and an utterance through time is concerned, that is to say concerning *kleos*, Cleoboulus is foolish.

Secondly, we can think about performance: whether or not we have it complete, how does this song of Simonides communicate with an audience?[41] It seems to presuppose knowledge—at least the possibility of such knowledge—of the Midas epigram, and this knowledge must come from oral tradition. Ford suggested a kind of sympotic capping, where a performance of Simonides' song could follow a performance of the epigram.[42] Imagining this kind of performance, or any performance to an audience familiar with the epigram, clarifies the rhetoric. The implicit claim of the epigram, to perpetual *kleos* associated with the endurance of the monument, is not merely mistaken but stupid: we know the epigram, but *the very fact that we know it* shows that this is not about the endurance of the statue or of the inscription. We can see for ourselves that this is not how *kleos* works. To see that Cleoboulus is wrong does not require the wisdom of a sage: anybody who can 'trust in his own wits' can see for himself. The paradox that this epigram, while basing its claims to endurance on the longevity of the monument, actually endured through *oral* tradition is at the root of Simonides' response to it.


## CALLIMACHUS AND SIMONIDES

Simonides' own clever response to the poetics of inscribed commemoration should inform our reading of Callimachus' Simonides. That is to say, it should provide an answer to my initial question about the way in which the voice of the dead poet comes alive in the 'Tomb of Simonides'. The elegy thematizes the relationship between voice, writing, and memory—and presents us with a puzzle: how should we make sense of its 'voice'? As we read, we find that the voice

---

[41] Ford (2002), 105 agrees with Campbell (1967), 393 that this is a complete song, which seems to me uncertain.
[42] Ford (2002), 106.

represents Simonides himself, as an epitaph might represent the voice of the dead man. But Simonides' narrative forbids that we understand this as an epitaph: he describes the fate of his own tombstone, built into the tower by Phoenix, who paid no attention to the inscription.[43] Writing is not only a feature of the stone (γράμμα) but even features as part of the content of the epitaph (τὰ περισσά in 9 refers to the 'extra letters' of the alphabet: other sources also attribute alphabetic innovations to Simonides).[44] This, though, is a talking inscription, a γράμμα... λέγον, which can no longer be read on stone, or speak through the voice of the passer-by so often invoked in inscriptions.

Callimachus' *Aitia* is a collection of 'origins': each elegy gives the *aition*, 'origin', of a practice or custom. It is not easy to identify the *aition* in this elegy. The question which it most obviously raises is, again: where is this voice coming from? We need an *aition* for the poem itself. Andrew Morrison suggests the possibility that we have an *aition* for the fact that Simonides' tomb no longer exists, and cites my suggestion that the elegy might serve as an *aition* for the lack of poetic epitaphs for Simonides from the Hellenistic period.[45] Now, however, I wonder: how lost *is* Simonides' epitaph? Simonides tells us of its content in indirect discourse, which feels very close to—but still distinct from—quotation: 'the inscription which said that I, the son of Leoprepes, was lying here, the holy man from Ceos, who first invented the extra letters... and the art of mnemotechnics'. Harder's choice to translate κεῖσθαι as 'lying *here*' is telling: she should, I think, have written 'lying *there*', but she is responding to the sense that the *ipsissima verba* of this epitaph are lying just beneath the surface—one *wants* to rewrite the poem into direct speech, and to recover the epitaph itself. The impression, as a result, is that this epitaph is not really lost: Simonides, as befits an expert in memory, can still recall its contents, and Callimachus has him do so. Within the world of the poem, the destruction of the tombstone has *not* obliterated the memory of the inscribed poem, any more than it destroyed the epigram of Midas: it is teasingly and paradoxically present after all.[46]

---

[43] Cf. Bing (1988a), 67–8; Morrison (2013), 290–2; Harder (1998), 96–8.

[44] Testimonia 39, 78 in Poltera (2008). Irrespective of the question whether 6 refers to Phoenix or to 'the Phoenician', the name evokes 'Phoenician letters' (e.g. Hdt. 5.58), again thematizing writing: Bruss (2004), 64.

[45] Morrison (2013), 298–9 with n. 41.

[46] Cf. the sophisticated reading at Garulli (2007), 256 on the relationship between the destruction of the stone and the survival of Simonides' voice; for Bing (1988a), 70,

I conclude, therefore, that Callimachus' elegy should be read as a successful reception of a Simonidean poetics of inscribed poetry and of epitaph in particular, in the light of what I have suggested about such a poetics in my interpretation of Simonides 581.[47] Simonides' imagined tomb and epitaph are in their way a site of memory, but above all a site for reflection about memory, and about Simonides' own reflections on the same topic. Through Callimachus' elegy we are looking, from a temporal distance, at a poetics where the dead must be buried, and their burial must be marked; where tombs and inscriptions matter and where the relationship between text, context, materiality of monuments, and the preservation of tradition is an object of intense interest; but where the inscribed text can become independent of the monument and float free, commemorating the man and the tomb even if the inscription no longer exists.[48] And yet . . . the epitaph is somehow present *and* absent. We can read με κεῖσθαι in indirect discourse, but the 'original' words—did the epigram say ἐνθάδε κεῖμαι, or ἐνθάδε κεῖται, 'I lie here' or 'Simonides lies here'?[49]—are lost to us, even if we feel that they are not lost to 'Simonides', that he, the master of memory, would have been able to repeat the poem word for word. Perhaps it is for that step—across the distance in time between Simonides and Callimachus—that we need Callimachus and his poetic power to give back to Simonides his own voice.[50]

---

the 'incorporation' of the epitaph by indirect discourse corresponds to the incorporation of the stone into the tower, and 'points up the mediated, oblique quality of the relationship between Callimachus and his remote predecessor'—and surely it does; yet Callimachus' elegy *also* presents Simonides' voice directly. Cf. Acosta-Hughes (2010), 177 for reflections on the relationship between Simonidean and Callimachean memory and voices here.

[47] Cf. Garulli (2007), describing and interpreting an allusive relationship between Callimachus' elegy and Simonidean fragments, including the response to Cleoboulus.

[48] Cf. Bruss (2004) and Garulli (2007), 255–6 on the complex relationship between writing, orality, and voice in Callimachus.

[49] The relationship between voices is subtly but significantly different according to whether we imagine Simonides' epitaph as expressed in the first or the third person: I am grateful to Regina Höschele for stressing this to me.

[50] For the impetus to write this chapter and for their patience along the way I am grateful to the editors of this volume and organizers of the conference in Durham, and also to Lilah Grace Canevaro for organizing the workshop 'Reading Greek Literature through Objects' (Edinburgh, September 2014); my thanks also to other participants at both events for comment and discussion.

# 3

## Ennius' *imago* between Tomb and Text

### Francesca Martelli

The tomb of the poet in ancient Greece and Rome tells a story of circuitous substitutions. As the tomb or gravestone substitutes for the dead person whose absence it marks,[1] so its most common function for the poet is to mark the redundancy (and impossibility) of this material form of proxy in favour of literary modes of memorial.[2] With this gesture of refusal comes the displacement of a series of related phenomena, both concrete and abstract, as the tomb—which should anchor the deceased in historical time by delimiting his/her life's span—provides instead a site for inscribing his/her ongoing life in literary history. Death may mark the poet's separation from the realm of the living, but it also completes the process of his/her incorporation into the virtual community of poets who will sustain his/her position within this alternative realm. This paradox is one that many ancient poets, Greek and Roman, draw on in their own 'epitaphs',[3] where they defy the idea of death in the very text that is designed to mark it, by using this genre to advertise their relationships with the literary predecessors

---

[1] Cf. Vernant (1990), 40–1 on the grave stele or funeral statue as corporeal substitute for the dead.

[2] For the poet, it is, then, not so much a substitute, as the negative imprint of a substitute. The fact that the idea of the poet's tomb rests, more often than not, on a text transmitted on paper, only further inverts this process of substitution, insofar as it confronts us with how much more fitting a surrogate this insubstantial record of a tomb is for a figure who 'lives' on the page: see the discussion by Rawles, Chapter 2 in this volume.

[3] Cf. Rossi (2001), 81–101 for discussion of this subgenre of Hellenistic epigram, examples of which include *AP* 7.718 (Nossis); *AP* 7.415 (Callimachus); *AP* 7.715 (Leonidas). Also *AP* 7.417–9 and 421 (Meleager). For a description of the epitaphs of Naevius, Plautus, and Pacuvius as a continuation (or counterpart) of this Hellenistic subgenre, see Dahlmann (1962), 77–100.

who make up that eternal community.[4] They borrow from inscriptional epitaph the genealogical claims that are a prerogative of this genre, yet underscore how very different the kinds of genealogy of which they boast are. The story of the poet's tomb as written through the genre of his self-epitaph is therefore one that sidelines the prerogatives of historical record in its promotion of the poet's place in literary history, even as it makes this point by drawing on, and flouting, the tomb's historical pretensions. As such, it proffers a useful touchstone for exploring how historical and literary-historical considerations circulate from one discursive sphere to the other,[5] and showcases all kinds of Greenblattian axioms about the poetics of history (and its materialities) and the historicity (and material debts) of literary poetics.

There can be few better examples of the literary historical bias of poets' epitaphs than the famous 'epitaph' on himself attributed to Ennius,[6] even if it is the fortunes of this text in subsequent literary history, as much as its own debts and influences, which impress this bias on modern readers (*var.* 17–18 Vahlen):

> nemo me lacrimis decoret nec funera fletu
>   faxit. cur? volito vivos per ora virum.

> Let no one cover me with tears nor my funeral rites with
>   weeping. Why? I flit living over the mouths of men.

While this text bears no trace of having been designed for inscription on stone, its boast of the pervasive reach and immortality of the poet's fame alludes to the finitude and fixity of lithic epitaphs in its very

---

[4] This is perhaps even more explicit in the case of epitaphs composed by poets *for other poets*: for discussion of the literary genealogies inscribed into the former by the poets of the Hellenistic period, see Bing (1988a), 59–72, as well as several chapters in this volume, especially 1, 2, 7, 9, 10, and 14.

[5] The fact that, like many types of epigram to come out of the Hellenistic world, this genre adapts motifs found in real inscriptions for the alternative publication setting of the papyrus roll (and, in many cases, anthology) further reinforces this tension between literary and historical discursive spheres.

[6] The text is transmitted three times in Cicero's extant works: once at *Tusc.* 1.34 alongside another distich attributed to Ennius (*var.* 15–16 Vahlen), and again at *Tusc.* 1.117 and at *Sen.* 73. Aside from naming Ennius as the author of this text, Cicero gives no other detail regarding the original function or context for which it was written. Scholars have suggested that Cicero took it either from Varro's *Imagines* or from the *De poetis*, and have consequently inferred that Varro himself may be responsible for its composition. Cf. esp. Dahlmann (1962), 68 for discussion. Suerbaum (1968), 208 n. 611, and 336; Lausberg (1982), 276; and Ramsby (2007), 26–7 are among the critics who assume this text to belong to the genre of epitaph.

defiance of those properties. The statement is, as we have come to expect of a literary epitaph, informed by the words of a distinguished literary predecessor: more specifically, a famous passage of Theognis, in which the Greek poet proclaims his power to confer immortality by giving his beloved wings.[7] Given that it is with distichs like this one that Ennius is credited with having introduced elegiacs to Latin verse,[8] the allusion here to one of Greece's best-known *elegists* is a highly self-conscious choice. With this gesture, Ennius nods to his Greek literary heritage while at the same time marking his own foundational status as the originator of Latin elegy.[9] The generic niceties of Ennius' allusion are, however, effaced by the subsequent literary tradition, which uses his distich as a template for statements of literary immortality of virtually every genre. Quoted and requoted in hexameters and lyric meters as well as in elegiac couplets,[10] Ennius' epitaph writes the script of literary immortality for all Latin poets (of the Augustan era, at least). The history of this text's reception thus affirms the truth of its original claim (that the author lives on because his words continue to circulate on the lips of men), while effacing the generic particulars of that claim, in a manner that befits Ennius' identity as the father of *all* Latin poetry.[11] In this way, it is made to operate as a vector for the entire Latin literary tradition, inscribing

---

[7] Theognis 237–40: σοὶ μὲν ἐγὼ πτέρ' ἔδωκα . . . εἰλαπίνῃσι παρέσσῃ | ἐν πάσαις πολλῶν κείμενος ἐν στόμασιν ('I have given you wings . . . you will be present at every feast, lying on the lips of many'). The substitution of first-person verb forms for Theognis' original second-person verbs, transmutes the Greek poet's offer of fame to another into an acceptance of that fame, as if Ennius were speaking as Theognis' beloved. The allusive relationship between poets is cast here as between *erastēs* and *eromenos*, despite the fact that Ennius has transferred an erotic statement from sympotic elegy to a funereal context, where it is made to speak to a different kind of longing.

[8] Such was the view of later antiquity, at least (Isidore *Origines* 1.39.14): *hic autem vix omnino constat a quo sit inventus, nisi quia apud nos Ennius eum prior usus est* ('But there is hardly any agreement as to who invented elegiacs, except that Ennius was the first among us Latin speakers to use it').

[9] For a cursory discussion of the impact of Ennius' epitaphs on the formation of Latin elegy, see Ross (1969), 137–9. Ennius' probable invention of Latin elegiacs is frequently overshadowed by his more celebrated invention of the Latin hexameter, and remains a neglected area in discussions of the 'origins' of Latin elegy.

[10] Cf. Verg. *G.* 3.9 (also *G.* 4.226 with Thomas (1988) vol. II, ad loc.; and *Aen.* 12.235); Hor. *Carm.* 2.20; Hor. *Carm.* 3.30 (with Woodman (1974); and Nisbet and Rudd (2004) ad loc.); Prop. 3.1.23–4; and Ov. *Met.* 15.875–9 (with Hardie (2002), 94–7).

[11] On the casting of Ennius as *pater* of Roman poetry by the Augustan poets, see Prinzen (1998), 265–6 n. 24; and Goldschmidt (2013), 33.

the genealogical dynamics of literary succession (and, therefore, sub-stitution) across the whole field of Latin literature.[12]

The fortunes of this epitaph in subsequent literary history enshrine Ennius' place at the head of one kind of 'family'. Yet this text is not the only one from antiquity to use ideas of the tomb in order to articulate Ennius' position in Roman cultural history. The same poet is the subject of an alternative story of entombment, one that places him in a different category of family altogether, and which speaks to a different set of substitutions. This story, which is first attested in Cicero, maintains that a statue of the poet was placed in the tomb of the Scipiones in order to honour the fame that his poetry lent their deeds in life.[13] For Cicero, as for many of the later writers who report it, this act comes to emblematize the reciprocity entailed in the correct working of cultural capital in Republican Rome.[14] In its consideration of the debts owed to the material enablers and honor-ands of this poet's literary output, this story brings out the material aspect of the poet's tomb as well as, if not better than, any other, and highlights the socio-economic dimensions of what that material sta-tus means. In doing so, it situates Ennius on a completely different kind of historical axis to that seen operating through his epitaph, and

---

[12] As symbolic father of this tradition, Ennius might be said to instantiate this principle of substitution for other reasons too: in Lacanian thought, the paternal function or *nom-du-père* authorizes the subject's entry into the Symbolic, and, above all, provides him/her with access to the processes of substitution, or metaphoric functioning, which mobilize the play of signifiers within the Symbolic. In identifying Ennius as father of the Roman literary tradition, the later poets make him the figure who instantiates their virtual order of existence in literary history, an order of reality that maps neatly onto the Lacanian Symbolic, insofar as it operates entirely in metaphorical relation to other, more concrete historical narratives.

[13] Cicero *Arch.* 9.22: *carus fuit Africano superiori noster Ennius; itaque etiam in sepulcro Scipionum putatur is esse constitutus ex marmore. at iis laudibus certe non solum ipse qui laudatur sed etiam populi Romani nomen ornatur* ('Our Ennius was held dear by the elder Africanus, and so a marble statue of him is reputed to have been placed even in the tomb of the Scipiones. Yet we may be sure that the praise he bestowed upon his patron lends adornment not only to its theme, but also to the name of the Roman people'). Cf. Zetzel (2007), 8–9 on the imprint that Cicero leaves on this story as a consequence of his using it in defence of Archias.

[14] Cf. also Valerius Maximus 8.14.1: *Superior Africanus Ennii poetae effigiem in monumentis Corneliae gentis collocari voluit, quod ingenio eius opera sua illustrata iudicaret...* ('The elder Africanus wanted the portrait of the poet Ennius placed among the monuments of the Cornelian clan because he judged that by Ennius' genius his own performances had been illuminated ... ').

thus provides an unlikely corrective to the literary historical bias of the story of (non-)entombment which that text tells.

There is, then, a fundamental tension between Ennius' famous 'epitaph' and the other story that comes down to us from antiquity concerning his entombment, one that speaks to the tensions that the tombs and epitaphs of poets always encapsulate—and with special force. It is worth pausing here to ask how far this dichotomy holds up when put under pressure. For cultural capital of the kind found circulating between Ennius and Scipio, in Cicero's version of the story, only works in practice by drawing the feats of the statesman into the poet's aesthetic prerogatives and hierarchies as well as vice versa. Some renderings of the story enact this side of the exchange in the dynamics of their telling, and, when they do so, provide a channel for the interests of literary history and of other historical narratives to compete and circulate. With this in mind, I turn to Livy's account of the story, where it is used not primarily to comment on the poet's status in the wider cultural economy, but, as Mary Jaeger has shown, to articulate something significant about his role in shaping history.[15] It arises at a critical point in the narrative of Scipio's death and trial when the historian's usual methods and sources break down completely, as he confronts the difficulty of locating in history a figure whose legend resists accurate historical record (Livy 38.56.1–4):

> multa alia in Scipionis exitu maxime vitae dieque dicta, morte, funere, sepulchro, in diversum trahunt, ut cui famae, quibus scriptis adsentiar non habeam. non de accusatore convenit: alii M. Naevium, alii Petillios diem dixisse scribunt, non de tempore quo dicta dies sit, non de anno quo mortuus sit, non ubi mortuus aut elatus sit; alii Romae, alii Literni et mortuum et sepultum. utrobique monumenta ostenduntur et statuae; nam et Literni monumentum monumentoque statua superimposita fuit, quam tempestate disiectam nuper vidimus ipsi, et Romae extra portam Capenam in Scipionum monumento tres statuae sunt, quarum duae P. et L. Scipionum dicuntur, tertia poetae Q. Ennii.

> Much else is said, especially about the end of Scipio's life, his trial, his death, his funeral, his tomb, all so contradictory that I find no tradition, no written documents, which I can accept. There is no unanimity as to

[15] Jaeger (1997), 133–76. See also Miles (1995), 59–61 for a similarly appreciative appraisal of the poetics of this passage, in contrast to the dissatisfaction expressed by Luce (1977), 95; Walsh (1961), 133; and Frank (1930), 193 with regard to its dearth of historical information.

his accuser: some say that Marcus Naevius accused him, others the Petilli; there is no agreement as to the time when he was prosecuted nor as to the year when he died nor as to where he died or was buried; some say that both death and burial took place at Rome, others at Liternum. In both places tombs and statues are shown; for at Liternum there is a tomb and a statue placed upon the tomb, which I myself saw recently, shattered by a storm, and at Rome, outside the Porta Capena, in the tomb of the Scipiones, there are three statues, two of which are said to represent Publius and Lucius Scipio, the third, the poet Quintus Ennius.

The proliferation of stories and rumours surrounding Scipio's death is, according to Jaeger's reading, an inevitable consequence of the extent of his fame, which in turn owes much to the tribute of poets. The juxtaposition of different types of evidence that Livy invokes in this passage—eyewitness account[16] and hearsay, respectively—are a reminder of the differences between history and poetry, to which the historian famously draws attention in his preface,[17] but which seem to break down completely here. The presence of Ennius' statue in the account provided by hearsay leads Jaeger to read this version of Scipio's death and burial as presenting a poetic substitute for the gap left in the alternative version by the damaged statue that personal autopsy provides by way of historical evidence.[18] According to this reading, Livy's account of the Scipiones' decision to honour Ennius with a statue in their family tomb says as much about the energies circulating between poetic texts and other categories of historical record, as it does about the circulation of prestige between poet and patron (even if the dynamics of exchange and substitution involved in both these processes do resemble each other in many ways).

The set of displacements between poetry and history that we see operating at this point in Livy's narrative do not stop here. As a coda

[16] Briscoe (2008) ad loc. notes that this is the sole instance of a claim to autopsy found in the extant books of Livy. Cf. also Marincola (1997), 102 n. 198 on the significance of this solitary instance.

[17] Livy *praefatio* 6: *quae ante conditam condendamve urbem poeticis magis decora fabulis quam incorruptis rerum gestarum monumentis traduntur, ea nec adfirmare nec refellere in animo est.* At the start of Book 6, Livy promises to turn away from his reliance on poetic *fabulae* and offer a clearer account of the following phase of Roman history, on the implicit grounds that he has access to written documents for this period.

[18] Jaeger (1997), 170: 'Here, as in the preface, poetry, represented by the statue of Ennius, serves as a marker for the absence of history, since the problematic evidence of Africanus' final days provides Livy with examples of deeds that are "glorious because of poetic stories rather than intact reminders of achievements"'.

to Jaeger's reading, I want to suggest how they continue to circulate as the rest of Chapter 56 unfolds, by magnifying a detail that feeds into the narratives of cultural capital which Ennius and Scipio generate between them in this the final chapter of Scipio's life. The honour that the Scipiones paid to Ennius by erecting a statue to him in their family tomb is clearly enhanced by the accounts that come down to us of Scipio's own attitude toward self-memorialization: in particular, about his refusal to have statues of himself put up in Rome during his lifetime in an era when this practice was otherwise in vogue.[19] Our earliest and most significant piece of evidence for this attitude comes, in fact, from this very chapter in Livy's history.[20] And it is worth asking whether or not this detail, too, is open to the kinds of poetic substitution that Jaeger points to in the earlier part of this narrative.

Towards the end of Chapter 56, in a passage no less hedged with disclaimers concerning the reliability of his sources,[21] Livy includes the report of a speech allegedly delivered by Tiberius Gracchus at Scipio's trial, in the course of which Gracchus chastises Scipio's recent behaviour by recalling his exemplary past. Alongside Scipio's refusal of extraordinary powers, Livy includes a further detail about his refusal of honorific statues (Livy 38.56.12):

[Tiberius Gracchus] castigatum enim quondam ab eo populum ait, quod eum perpetuum consulem et dictatorem vellet facere; prohibuisse

[19] Cf. Gruen (1992), 121–3 for discussion of the 'reverse snobbery' of Scipio's self-effacing gesture, at a time when the aristocratic practice of setting up honorific statues to oneself was otherwise prevalent in Rome. Ancient sources are perhaps more inclined to credit modest motives behind the gesture: in *Epist.* 86.3, for example, Seneca relates Scipio's reluctance to be commemorated through conspicuous physical monuments to the variant tradition of his death and burial, not in the family tomb at Rome, but in exile at Liternum, and attributes motives of modesty to both these gestures of withdrawal. Yet the modesty expressed by Scipio's burial at Liternum is in turn complicated by a further story, attested by Valerius Maximus and Appian, according to which Scipio's *imago* was placed in the *cella* to the temple of Jupiter Optimus Maximus following his death. This account brings the chain of displacements and substitutions that we find operating in the story of Ennius' statue in the tomb of the Scipiones full circle.
[20] Valerius Maximus also testifies to Scipio's refusal of honorific statues at 4.1.6, in a passage which may, however, derive from Livy.
[21] Prior to his account of Gracchus' speech, Livy not only highlights its inconsistencies with other documentary evidence available for the details of Scipio's trial (including a speech attributed to Scipio himself), but even questions the authenticity of the speech itself (Livy 38.56.5): *nec inter scriptores rerum discrepat solum, sed orationes quoque, si modo ipsorum sunt quae feruntur, P. Scipionis et Ti. Gracchi abhorrent inter se.*

statuas sibi in comitio, in Rostris, in curia, in Capitolio, in cella Iovis poni; prohibuisse ne decerneretur ut imago sua triumphali ornatu e templo Iovis optimi maximi exiret.

For [Tiberius Gracchus] said that the people had once been rebuked by Scipio because they wanted to make him perpetual consul and dictator; that he forbade statues to himself to be erected in the Comitium, on the Rostra, in the Curia, on the Capitoline, in the cell of Jupiter; that he prevented also a decree that his image in triumphal dress should appear to be coming out of the temple of Jupiter Optimus Maximus.

The fact that this speech is strongly marked as a contested source should alert us to the possibility of encountering here a similar set of displacements to those that we saw at an earlier moment of contestation in this chapter in Livy's narrative. Indeed, it is this very detail concerning Scipio's refusal of both extraordinary powers and honorific statues that has led some scholars to view the speech as a whole as a much later invention—perhaps even an anti-Caesarian forgery, designed to rebuke Caesar for accepting honours that Scipio had turned down.[22] In view of this, we may well ask what makes Scipio in particular such a plausible example for this gesture of refusal.

Many scholars believe that Ennius himself alludes to the aspect of Scipio's self-image that we find 'evidenced' in this passage, in a fragment commonly assigned to the *Scipio*, his trochaic poem commemorating the statesman's achievements (*var.* 1 Vahlen):[23]

> \<o tum\> quantam statuam faciet populus Romanus \<tibi,
> Scipio\>, quantam columnam, \<claro\> quae \<praeconio\>
> res tuas gestas loquatur.

Then what a statue the Roman people will erect for you, Scipio, what a column, to proclaim your deeds with public fanfare.

But could it not be the other way around? Could it not be that Ennius' poem (or the sentiment it expresses) lurks behind Livy's version of Tiberius Gracchus' speech, informing if not inspiring the detail about Scipio's refusal of honorific statues? Ennius' poetry is, after all, shot through with references to the inadequacy of physical forms of

<hr/>

[22] Cf. Mommsen (1864–79), 502–10; Walbank (1967), 56; and Briscoe (2008) ad loc. for the suggestion that the speech should be dated to Caesar's dictatorship and may have been designed to attack him for accepting the very honours that Scipio had refused.
[23] Cf. Goldberg (1995), 17; and Courtney (1993), 26–7 for this view.

commemoration, not just at the start of *Annales* 16,[24] but indirectly, too, in his epitaph. It is therefore perfectly possible that either Scipio or Livy or the anti-Caesarian forger of Gracchus' speech—or all three—may be taking inspiration from the poet when constructing this particular aspect of the statesman's self-image. Here too, then, the discourses of historiography and poetry are entangled. Poet honours statesman by drawing the refusal of honorific statues that becomes part and parcel of his self-image into his own narratives of literary immortality, just as the statesman's family honours the poet by erecting a statue to him in their tomb. Livy's text not only records the processes of displacement at work in the circulation of prestige, it enacts them, too, by drawing the poet's tropes and aesthetic preroga- tives into his historical narrative.

As other scholars also point out, the tomb of the Scipiones is a particularly suitable monument on which to focus a discussion of poetry, since the *elogia* inscribed on it also transformed Hellenistic epigram into a specifically Roman genre.[25] However we construe the cultural affiliations of these inscriptions—as part of a narrative of rising Hellenism[26] or of dogged Roman conservatism[27]—the influ- ence of Hellenistic literary epigram on these texts is hard to deny, and makes them a touchstone for considering how the energies proper to

---

[24] The juxtaposition, near the start of Ennius' *Annales* 16, of 404–5 Vahlen (*reges per regnum statuasque sepulcraque quaerunt, / aedificant nomen, summa nituntur opum vi*) and 406 Vahlen (*postremo longinqua dies confecerit aetas*), suggested by both Vahlen and Skutsch, would amount to a familiar Pindaric rejection of physical monuments.

[25] This, of course, holds true whether or not we subscribe to the view promoted by Wölfflin (1892), 188–219 that Ennius or Pacuvius may have composed the Scipionic *elogia*. The hypothesis has been dismissed by most subsequent scholars—including Degrassi (1965), Zevi (1970), and Coarelli (1972), who all date the earliest of these *elogia* to a period that would predate Ennius' involvement with the Scipiones.

[26] The epitaphs (which comprise some of our earliest extant Roman inscriptions) are held by many scholars to present a narrative of the rising Hellenism of mid- Republican Rome, as the tombs of each generation of Scipiones reveal an increasing awareness of Hellenistic literary forms. Cf. Coarelli (1972), 38–62 for a summary version of the arguments behind this chronology; and Van Sickle (1987) on the epitaphs' poetic debt to Hellenistic models.

[27] Ramsby (2007), 25 points to the long persistence of the traditional Saturnian metre to argue that the narrative of rising Hellenism which the Scipionic inscriptions represent is one heavily qualified by a Roman conservatism. The Italic origins of the Saturnian metre, once disputed by e.g. Cole (1969), 47, on quantitative grounds, have since been convincingly reaffirmed by the accentual approach of Mercado (2012). Cf. also Parsons (1999), 135; and Freeman (1998), 86, who both locate its origins in other indigenous Italic metres.

specific media circulate between one another. Another way of plotting
that process is to look to the literary texts inspired by the *elogia*, and
here again an epitaph attributed to the poet Ennius offers a helping
hand. *ILLRP* 309 and 310, the epigrams inscribed on the tombs of
Scipio Barbatus and his son, are cited by Lausberg as the two most
important sources for the phrasing of the other famous self-epitaph
attributed to Ennius:[28]

> aspicite o cives senis Enni imaginis formam.
>   hic vestrum panxit maxima facta patrum.

> Gaze, fellow citizens, on the contours of aged Ennius' image:
>   he set to verse your fathers' greatest deeds.

This text, commonly viewed as a composition of Varro's, written for
publication beneath an image of Ennius in his (Varro's) *De poetis*,
cannot, as almost all scholars emphasize, belong alongside the statue
of the poet said to have been placed in the Scipiones' tomb,[29] but does
surely allude to this story, as rather fewer scholars seem prepared to
allow. Aside from its allusions to the Scipionic *elogia*, the reference to
the public visibility of the poet's *imago*, and to the *patres* whose deeds
he set to verse, all point to the tomb of the Scipiones as an appropriate
context for envisaging this poet's portrait. At the same time, the
publication of this epitaph in a literary anthology of similar tributes
bears witness to the new cultural contexts made available for hon-
ouring poets at this stage in Roman cultural history. It anticipates the
practice, soon to become widespread, of erecting busts of authors in
the public libraries at Rome that held their works. This, surely, is to be
seen as a form of entombment—one that situates the *imago* of the
poet alongside those of his literary forebears in a space that recognizes
their identity as a group, much like the tomb of the Scipiones, or,
indeed, as the atrium in a Roman household collects the *imagines* of a
family's ancestors. The formation of a Roman literary canon is what

---

[28] Lausberg (1982), 276 lists the following parallels between Ennius *var.* 15–16
Vahlen and the Scipionic *elogia*: Ennius' address to the *cives* (which is not Greek) finds
a parallel in the *vos* used in *ILLRP* 309, the epigram on Barbatus (*consul censor aidilis
quei fuit apud vos*, where *vos* implies 'citizens'). Further parallels include the paratactic
introduction of a statement with *hic* in both *Ennius var.* 15–16 Vahlen and *ILLRP* 310,
the (older?) inscription on Barbatus' son (*consul censor aedilis hic fuit a[pud vos]*, / *hic
cepit Corsicam Aleriamque urbem* . . . ).

[29] Suerbaum (1968), 210–14; Badian (1972), 154–5; Coarelli (1972), 76; and
Goldberg (1995), 17–18.

enables this development.[30] But it is worth considering how the story of Ennius' statue being placed in the Scipiones' tomb presides over this cultural practice in a manner that befits his status as the father of that literary canon, even as it still stands as a rebuke to the breakdown in reciprocity governing the procedures of symbolic capital in the privatized world of imperial rule. What scope for the circular mechanisms of cultural prestige arise when the library replaces the statesman's tomb as the place to honour a poet? The fact that one important library on the Palatine was annexed onto the first emperor's house does complicate this process, as I argue below.

Imperial authors cannot help but see the story as an illustration of their own cultural disenfranchisement. This at least is how Ovid, our sole poetic witness to the story, takes it when he recalls it in order to draw a line between the practice of honouring poets like Ennius in the past and the neglect that poets receive in his own day (*Ars amatoria* 3.405–14):

> cura deum fuerant olim regumque poetae:
>     praemiaque antiqui magna tulere chori.
> sanctaque maiestas et erat venerabile nomen
>     vatibus, et largae saepe dabantur opes.
> **Ennius emeruit, Calabris in montibus ortus,**
>     **contiguus poni, Scipio magne, tibi.**
> nunc hederae sine honore iacent operataque doctis
>     cura vigil Musis nomen inertis habet.
> sed famae vigilare iuvat: quis nosset Homerum,
>     Ilias aeternum si latuisset opus?

Poets once were held dear by gods and kings, and choirs of old won great rewards. Sacred was the majesty and venerable the name of the poet, and lavish the wealth bestowed on him. **Ennius, sprung from Calabrian hills, won a place, great Scipio, by your side.** Today the ivy lies unhonoured, and wakeful toil devoted to the learned Muses bears the name of idleness. But wakeful preserving of the poet's fame brings rewards: who would know of Homer, if his immortal *Iliad* had lain hidden?

Later in his career, in the *Tristia*, Ovid quotes the epitaph of Ennius that forbids mourning with an almost obsessive frequency. Yet he invariably converts the epitaph's prediction of literary immortality

---

[30] Horsfall (1993) turns this relationship around, by presenting the emergence of libraries in Rome as an important spur to the formation of a Roman literary canon.

into an expression of self-doubt,[31] in ways that are normally viewed as a reflection of his own state of literary decline, and which transform the *Tristia* as a whole into an extended self-epitaph, one that encourages rather than forbids weeping. But it is an echo of the other self-epitaph attributed to Ennius that articulates the cultural flipside of this feeling of disempowerment, and which places it squarely in the hands of imperial control. *Tristia* 1.7 opens by telling the reader how to react to its author's *imago* in ways that cannot but recall the *imago* mentioned in the other epitaphic distich attributed to Ennius (*var.* 15–16 Vahlen). The difficulty is that Ovid's *imago* belongs neither in a public library, nor speaks to the kind of broad civic demographic that Ennius' portrait addresses, but to a privatized readership consisting of personal friends:

> Siquis habes nostris similes **in imagine** vultus,
>   deme meis hederas, Bacchica serta, comis.
> ista decent laetos felicia signa poetas:
>   temporibus non est apta corona meis.
> hoc tibi dissimula, senti tamen, optime, dici,
>   in digito qui me fersque refersque tuo,
> effigiemque meam fulvo complexus in auro
>   cara relegati, quae potes, ora vides.

'Whoever you may be who possess **a portrait** of my features, remove from my locks the ivy, the chaplet of Bacchus. Such fortunate symbols are suited to happy poets; a wreath does not become my times/temples.' Hide the fact, yet feel it, too, that this is said to you, my best of friends, who carry me about on your finger, and, clasping my image on the yellow gold, see the dear face – all that you can see of an exile.

The privacy of one commemorative context, inside the homes and private libraries of his readers, gives way to the even more private intimacy, as Ovid envisages a portrait of himself inscribed on a ring worn by a dear friend: the *public* library, where Ovid should be envisaging his *imago*, is conspicuous for its omission. And the location of the poet's portrait is, of course, a metonymic reflection of the location of his texts: Ovid's exile poetry bears important witness to the kinds of selectivity and censorship practised by the custodians of Rome's public libraries, and to how that censorship had privatized the consumption of literature in Rome under the Caesars. The *Ex Ponto*,

---

[31] See, for example, *Tr.* 3.14.21–4 and *Tr.* 5.7.25–30.

for example, opens by drawing a distinction between the official reading fora sanctioned by the Roman state and the private homes of the enclosed circle of addressees in which Ovid's own works circulate (1.3–10):

> si vacat, hospitio peregrinos, Brute, libellos
> excipe, dumque aliquo, quolibet abde modo.
> **publica** non audent intra **monimenta** venire,
> ne suus hoc illis clauserit auctor iter.
> a, quotiens dixi 'certe nil turpe docetis:
> ite, patet castis versibus ille locus!'
> non tamen accedunt, sed, ut aspicis ipse, latere
> **sub Lare privato** tutius esse putant.

If you have leisure, Brutus, give harbourage and guest-room to these overseas booklets, lodge them wherever you can: they dare not enter **a public library**—for fear their author has closed this route to them. Ah, how often I've said, 'You surely teach nothing disgraceful: go, that place lies open to chaste verses!' Yet still they don't approach such places, but as you can see, think it safer to hide in **a private household**.

If the public library, with its capacity to select and exclude, serves not just to reflect the current state of the Roman literary canon, but to construct an official version of that canon, Ovid's own sense of exclusion from this space raises questions about his place in certain versions of Latin literary history. The lists of named canonical poets that we find littered throughout his works, particularly memorably at the end of the *Ex Ponto* (4.16), where Ovid closes his oeuvre by incorporating his own name into a 'canon' of virtual unknowns, might be explained against this development: uncertain of whether he or his contemporaries will be incorporated into the canon-forming library, his only option is to construct his own version as a corrective to that produced by the censorious library-owners (or their agents) and disseminate it in the one way he can, that is to say, privately.[32]

If the library is a literary family tomb—or atrium—from which some would-be canonical poets are excluded by the censors, it proves

---

[32] There is a parallel between the self-serving mode of selection seen both on the part of the imperial public librarians and in Ovid's literary canon in *Pont.* 4.16, and the forms of selectivity that could be put to work in choosing which ancestral *imagines* to put up in one's atrium. See Flower (1996), 206 on Cicero *Fam.* 9.21. Genealogy presents itself as immune to the processes of selection and substitution found in other historical narratives, but is in fact just as open to them.

to be somewhat more flexible in its capacity to extend to others, and it is here that we see the idea of the poet's tomb as a site for the circulation of cultural prestige coming full circle. In his discussion of 'visual supplementation' in Roman public libraries,[33] David Petrain draws our attention to one individual whose portrait did make it into the Palatine library following his death, thus making him part of the canon or family of Roman authors commemorated therein: Germanicus Caesar, whose posthumous honours included having his likeness embossed on a bronze shield and being placed in the library alongside several authors memorialized there in similar fashion, in order to honour the literary endeavours undertaken in his lifetime.[34] Just as Ennius was thought to have been honoured by having his statue set up in the tomb of the Scipiones, so two centuries later a prominent statesman and one of Caesar's heirs would be honoured by having his portrait set up alongside other poets and authors in the space that entombed their *imagines*. While poets could be excluded from the library, statesmen could still derive honour by being allowed to share the commemorative space normally preserved for the poets' guild. This bears witness to the ongoing desire to make cultural capital continue to circulate between poets and statesmen, this time in the library—the space that has taken over as the site of the poets' entombment. What better sign of the prestige-conferring benefits of Latin poetry within the cultural economy of imperial Rome than that a Caesar should want to share the tomb of the poets?

---

[33] Petrain (2013), 340–5.

[34] The source for this set of honours is, as it happens, an important witness to Germanicus' literary endeavours: cf. *Pont.* 4.8.67–72, where, in a somewhat backhanded compliment, Ovid acknowledges the prince's poetic ambitions, but denies him a place in his own literary canon with the claim that higher offices have made him a more fitting subject for poetry than a composer of it.

# 4

# A Portrait of the Poet as a Young Man

## The Tomb of Quintus Sulpicius Maximus on the Via Salaria

*Valentina Garulli*

On 20 September 1870, Italian artillery bombarded the ancient walls of Rome for a few hours, until a breach opened between Porta Pia and Porta Salaria. The event marked the capture of Rome, the unification of the Kingdom of Italy, and, as several textbooks grandly put it, the end of papal secular power. To this day, all major Italian cities and many smaller localities boast a street named after the event: *XX settembre*. The attack also had other consequences. The Porta Salaria was so badly damaged that it had to be demolished in 1871: out of the debris emerged the tomb of an ancient Roman poet, Quintus Sulpicius Maximus, who—we can reconstruct from the inscription on the monument itself—died in 94 CE and lived for only 'eleven years, five months, and twelve days'. Had the tomb not been discovered, we would know nothing of this young poet. Yet inclusion in this volume, generally dedicated as it is to poets whose oeuvres are known, is justified, since Maximus' most important composition—a monologue delivered by Zeus in Greek hexameters—is inscribed on the very monument that commemorates his death.

The Latin prose inscription that accompanies Maximus' hexameter poem reveals that the boy took part in the most prestigious imperial competition, the so-called Capitoline Games (*ludi Capitolini*), which were established by the emperor Domitian, and included contests in gymnastics, equestrian sports, music, and poetry. The contest in which Maximus competed took place in 94 CE, during the third

edition of the Capitoline Games. The inscription further reveals that
Maximus competed against fifty-two Greek poets. These competitors
were probably adults, or at least older than Maximus, since the Latin
inscription tells us that he could arouse his listeners' sympathy by
his excellent performance coupled with his tender age.[1] This means
that he must have performed in an open division of the games. We
cannot tell whether he and the other participants were expected to
improvise their lines, or whether they were given time to compose
on a subject assigned in advance. The fact that such a long poem
was inscribed on the tombstone and that Maximus is portrayed as
holding a papyrus scroll may suggest that he wrote down his poem at
some point, perhaps immediately before his performance. Be that as
it may, Maximus was charged with versifying on the following subject:
'the words that Zeus might have used in reproaching Helios for having
entrusted his chariot to Phaethon'. Maximus did not win the com-
petition, but 'departed with honour' (*cum honore discessit*). In other
words, he won honourable mention, in recognition of an outstanding
performance in relation to his age.[2]

The tomb was set up by his parents in the cemetery near the Via
Salaria, shortly after his death, and was later built into the third-
century eastern tower of the Porta Salaria, the gate by which the Via
Salaria linked the city to the countryside.[3] After the bombardments of
1870, and the dismantlement of the third-century gate in 1871, a new
gate designed by architect Virginio Vespignani was built in 1873, and
dismantled again in 1921, in order to facilitate the flow of traffic
through the city. Today, Piazza Fiume is located on the site where the
Porta Salaria used to be. The tomb of Quintus Sulpicius Maximus
was removed from its original location to the Museo della Centrale

---

[1] Literary and epigraphic sources mention some young Roman poets who com-
peted in the games; however, there seems to be no evidence about a separate boys'
category: see White (1998), 90 n. 17 and Manieri (2014), 148.

[2] See Henzen (1871), 104–5.

[3] One of the most influential archaeologists of Rome, Rodolfo Lanciani, com-
mented on the public interest following the demolition of the ancient walls and gate
in 1871, complaining that the place 'had changed, and not for the better'. Since his day,
a lot more has changed in this area, and most certainly 'not for the better'. Some
excavations before and after 1871 were important in terms of reconstructing the
archaeological context of our tomb. From 1695 to 1741 excavations in the vineyard of
the Naro family, between the Porta Salaria and the Porta Pinciana, revealed 26 graves of
praetorians and 141 civilian tombs. Later, in 1887, along the new Corso d'Italia, 855
tombs were discovered in the course of nine months: Nocita (2012).

Montemartini, Musei Capitolini (inv. NCE 2963), and was replaced *in situ* by a plaster cast, which overlooks the busy road (Figure 4.1).[4]

The Parian marble altar has a central niche enclosing a statue: Maximus is portrayed in a frontal pose and, despite his young age, wears a tunic covered by a toga. This is the formal dress of a Roman citizen,[5] and, along with other formal indicators such as the *tria nomina* emphasizing his Roman identity,[6] offers a visual reminder of the man Maximus was expected to become. The poem Maximus composed is carved on both sides of the portrait niche, except for the last three lines, which are inscribed on the partially unfolded scroll held by the statue in its left hand. In the inscribed area below the niche are engraved a Latin prose dedication and, under this, in two columns, two Greek epigrams in elegiacs. The altar 'is crowned with a triangular pediment decorated with a wreath with long fluttering ribbons; the acroteria are in the shape of two half palmettes. The niche with a rounded top is cut into the upper part of the front of the altar with a disregard for the borders of the frame [ . . . ]. An *urceus* [jug] is engraved on the right side of the monument, on the left side there is a *patera [libation bowl]*'.[7]

Given the interest and importance of this example of an ancient poet's tomb, in the present chapter I aim to fulfil two goals. The first is to provide a reliable edition of the inscribed text of the monument accompanied by an English translation.[8] The second is to add some interpretative comments directed towards the main concerns of this volume. The monument deserves fuller discussion than I can provide here, and it is therefore with interest and anticipation that I note

---

[4] Another excellent reproduction is located in the Museo della Civiltà Romana, instructively displayed with letters painted in red as they would have been in the original. The monument measures 165 cm high, 85 cm wide, 68 cm deep; Greek letters are 1/1.7 cm high and Latin letters 1.4/1.9 cm: Moretti (1979); Nocita (2012).

[5] However, see Henzen (1871), 113–4 and Kleiner (1987), 164.

[6] See Wallace-Hadrill (2008), 41–57.

[7] On the funerary libations at the tomb, see Platt's discussion at pp. 44–6. Nocita (2012) adds: 'according to Kleiner, the base has a plain marble plaque that was once covered with another epitaph, although the inscriptions on the altar are so extensive that an additional epitaph was probably superfluous.'

[8] Unlike reproductions, photographs, and even videos of the monument, which are also easily available online, editions of the inscribed text are less easily accessible. Some publications offer only the Latin inscription, others publish only the Greek poems. Nocita's excellent edition, which presents all the texts, was published in the *Bullettino della Commissione Archeologica Comunale di Roma* in 2000 and is not always easily available.

**Figure 4.1.** Cast copy of the tomb of Quintus Sulpicius Maximus, first century CE, Piazza Fiume.

PURL: https://commons.wikimedia.org/wiki/File:QS_Maximus_memorial_stone.JPG.

Kathleen Coleman's current work on a book manuscript based on her 2010 Jerome Lectures entitled 'Q. Sulpicius Maximus, Poet, Eleven Years Old'.[9] The hope of this chapter is to ensure that this fascinating

---

[9] The preliminary results of that research are published in Coleman (2015).

tomb contributes to our understanding of the tomb as a material site of literary reception, and more specifically as a site where the tension between literary and material survival can be clearly felt.[10]

## THE INSCRIBED TEXT

*ab anaglypho ad sinistram*[11]

Κ(οΐντου) Σουλπικίου | Μαξίμου καίριον· | τίσιν ἂν λόγοις |
χρήσαιτο Ζεὺς | ἐπιτιμῶν Ἡλίῳ, | ὅτι τὸ ἅρμα ἔδωκε | Φαέθοντι.

Ἡμετέρου κόσμοι|ο φαεσφόρον ἁρμε|λατῆρα
οὐχ ἕτε|ρον πλὴν σεῖο θεοὶ | ποίησαν ἄνακτες· |

---

[10] In what follows, corpora of inscriptions and standard epigraphic resources will be written out in full at the first citation and subsequently cited according to the abbreviations used in Bérard et al. (1989–). *Guide de l'épigraphiste*. Paris, 4th edn. In addition, *IGRR = Inscriptiones Graecae ad res Romanas pertinentes*, I (R. Cagnat-P. Jouguet-J. Toutain), III (R. Cagnat-G. Lafaye), IV (G. Lafaye), I, III–IV, Paris (1911) (I), (1906) (III), (1927) (IV); *PIR*[2] VII/2 = *Prosopographia Imperii Romani. Saec. I, II, III*, consilio et auctoritate Academiae Scientiarum Berolinensis et Brandenburgensis cur. W. Eck, VII/2, Berolini-Novi Eboraci (2006); *SupplItal = Supplementa Italica. Imagines. Supplementi fotografici ai volumi italiani del CIL*, G.L. Gregori-M. Mattei (eds), *Roma (CIL, VI)*, I. Musei Capitolini, Rome (1999).

[11] For a select bibliography on this monument, see Visconti (1871); Sauppe (1871); Ciofi (1871; 1872); Henzen (1871); Parker (1877), pl. X (Latin prose inscription only); Kaibel (1878), no. 618; *C(orpus) I(nscriptionum) L(atinarum)* VI 33976 (G. Henzen-C. Huelsen) and p. 3906 (C. Huelsen); Cougny (1890), 133–4 no. 2.267; *I(nscriptiones) G(raecae)* XIV (2012) (G. Kaibel); Dessau (1902), no. 5177 (Latin prose inscriptions only); *I(nscriptiones) G(raecae) ad R(es) R(omanas pertinentes)* I 350–2 (Cagnat); Peek (1955) 591–4 no. 1924; Gordon (1958), 144–5. no. 153 (Latin prose inscription only); McCrum and Woodhead (1966), 42 no. 64 (Greek and Latin prose inscriptions only); Vérilhac (1978), 115–21 no. 78; Moretti (1979), 189–93 no. 1336; Kleiner (1987), 162–5 no. 45; Fernández Delgado and Ureña Bracero (1991); Döpp (1996), Greek poem only; Rawson (1999), 90 and 98 (Latin prose inscription only); Nocita (2000); *Supplementum Epigraphicum Graecum* L (2000) no. 1060; *E(pigraphic) D(atabase) R(ome)* no. 107864 (Giulia Tozzi, 12/05/2014); see also Altmann (1905), 219–20 no. 285; Platner and Ashby (1929), 486–7; Lugli (1938), 340–1; Mustilli (1939), 97 no. 1; Marrou (1964), 130 no. 151; Helbig (1966), 512 no. 1734; Gercke (1968), 33 R31; Toynbee (1971), 267–8; Boschung (1987), 113–4 no. 957; Reggiani (1990), 84–6; Caldelli (1993), 70–1, 126 no. 07; Bernsdorff (1997); *Suppl(ementa) Ital(ica)* no. 19 (Mariangela Alfiero); Caruso (1999); *P(rosopographia) I(mperii) R(omani)*[2] VII/2 372 no. 1012. Many images of the inscriptions and of the monument are available: see e.g. Visconti (1871), 16–21 and pl. 1–2; Henzen (1871), 102 and 106–11 (facsimile of the inscriptions); Parker (1877), pl. X; *CIL* VI 33976 (facsimile of the inscriptions); *IG* XIV 2012 (facsimile of the inscriptions); Altmann (1905), 219 fig. 180; Mustilli (1939), pl. LVI; Gordon (1958), pl. 64b; *ad IGUR* III 1336; Boschung (1987), pl. 56 no. 957; Kleiner (1987), pls XXVII.3, XXVIII.1–2; Reggiani (1990), 86 fig. 87; Caldelli (1993), pl. IV; *SupplItal* 19.1–4; Caruso (1999), 499 fig. 153; Nocita (2000), figs 1–5; *EDR* 107864.

τίπτε κακόφρονα θῆ|κες ἐφ᾽ ἀψίδεσσιν Ὀ|λύμπου
υἱέα καὶ | πώλων ἄφατον τά|χος ἐγγυάλιξας, |
ἡμετέρην οὐδ᾽ ὅσ|σον ὑποδ(δ)είσας ἐπα|ρωγήν;                          5
οὐ τάδε πιστὰ | θεοῖς σέο δήνεα· ποῖ Φα|έθοντος
εὐσταθὲς | ἅρμα φορεῖτο; τί σου | πυρὸς ἀκ<α>μάτοιο |
φλὸξ ἄχρι καὶ θρόνον | ἦλθεν ἐμὸν καὶ ἐπ᾽ εὐ|ρέα κόσμον;
μίγνυτο | καὶ κύκλοισιν ὑπερ|μενὲς ἄχθος ἀπ᾽ εἴ|λης·
Ὠκεανὸς χέρας | αὐτὸς ἐς οὐρανὸν ἠέρ|ταζε·                          10
τίς ποταμῶν | οὐ πᾶσαν ἀνεξηραί|νετο πηγήν;
καὶ σπό|ρος ἐς Δήμητρα κα|ταίθετο, καί τις ἄπλα|τον |

_ab anaglypho ad dextram_

ἀζαλέην ἔκλαυσε παρὰ | δρεπάναισι γεωργός, |
σπείρων εἰς ἀχάριστα | μάτην θ᾽ ὑπὸ κυφὸν ἄρο|τρον
ταῦρον ὑποζεύ|ξας ὑπό τ᾽ ἀστέρα βουλυ|τοῖο                          15
κάμψας ἄρρενα γυ|ῖα σὺν ἀχθεινοῖσι βόεσ|σιν·
γαῖα δ᾽ ὑπέστενε πᾶ|σα κακόφρονος εἴνεκα | κούρου·
καὶ τότ᾽ ἐγὼ πυ|ρὶ φέγγος ἀπέσβεσα. | μηκέτι παιδὸς |
μύρεο λυγρὸν ὄλεθρον, | ἑοῦ δ᾽ ἔχε φροντίδα κόσ|μου,
μή ποτε χειρὸς ἐμῆς | φλογερώτερον ἔγχος ἀθροί|σῃς.                  20
γίνωσκ᾽ οὐρανίοιο | Διὸς νόον· οὐ μὰ γὰρ αὐτὴν
Ῥεί|ην ἄλλο τ<ι τ>οὐδὲ κακώτερον | ἴδεν Ὄλυμπος· |
κόσμος ἐμὸς σὴ πίστις ἔφυ με|γακυδέος ἔργου.
οἰχέσθω τὰ | πάροιθε, τὰ δ᾽ ὕστερα φροντί|δι κεῦθε·
οὐ σὸς ἔφυ· πώ|λων γὰρ ἀπείριτον <ο>ὐ σθένος | ἔγνω,              25
ῥυτήρων οὐδ᾽ ἔσχε | πολυφραδὲς ἔργον ἀνύσσαι. |
ἔρχεο νῦν, πάλι κόσμον ἐποί|χεο, μὴ τεὸν εὖχος
ἀλλο|τρίαις παλάμαισι πόρῃς | ἀμενηνὰ πονήσας· |
μούνῳ σοὶ πυρόεντος | ἐπειγομένῳ κύκλοιο |
ἀντολίη καὶ πᾶσα καλὸς | δρόμος ἔπλετο δυσμή· |                       30
σοὶ τόδε πιστὸν ἔδωκε | φέρειν νόος ἄφθιτον εὖχος. |
φείδεο γῆς καὶ παντὸς ἀρι|πρεπέος κόσμοιο,
ἴσχε δρό|μον μεσάταισιν ἐπ᾽ ἀψίδεσ|σιν Ὀλύμπου·
ταῦτα πρέ|ποντα θεοῖς, ταῦτ᾽ ἄρκια· μαί|εο, δαῖμον,
μιλίχιον πά|λι φέγγος· ὁ σὸς παῖς ὤλεσε | πουλύ·                    35
καὶ τὸν ἀπειρέσιον | μέγαν οὐρανὸν αὐτὸς <ὅ>δευε, |
ἥμισυ μὲν γαίης νέρθεν, | τὸ δ᾽ ὕπερθε τανύσσας· |
οὕτω γὰρ πρέψει ἐτεὸν φάος | Οὐρανίδαισι,
καὶ φωτῶν | ἀκάκωτος ἀεὶ λειφθήσε|ται εὐχή{ι},
πρηυμενῆ | δ᾽ ἕξεις Ζηνὸς νόον· ἢν δ᾽ ἐτέ|ρη τις |                  40
λείπηται σέο | φροντὶς ἀταρβ[έ]|ος, ἴστορες αὐτο[ὶ] |
ἀστέρες, ὡς πυ[ρό]|εντος ἐμοῦ μ[έ]|νος αἶψα κεραυνο[ῦ] |
ὠκύτερον πώ|λων σε, θεός, δέ|μας ἀάσε[ι]εν.

3 θῆκ<α>ς Henzen, Cougny : θῆκε σ᾽ Ciofi ‖ 4 ἐγγυάλιξας Sauppe : ἐγγυαλίξας Visconti, Henzen, Henzen-Huelsen, Vérilhac ‖ 5 ὑποδ<δ>είσας Peek | ἐπα<γ>ωγήν Eitner (teste Döpp) ‖ 7 φόρει; τὸ τίς οὗ πυρὸς Ciofi | *AKMATOIO* lapis : ἀκ<α>μάτοιο Visconti, Henzen, Kaibel, Henzen-Huelsen, Cougny, Cagnat, Peek, Moretti, Vérilhac, Döpp, Nocita ‖ 9 κύκλοισι Cougny | ἀπ᾽ εἴλης Sauppe : ἀπειλῆς Visconti, Henzen ‖ 10 χέρας αὐτὸς vel χέρα καὐτὸς Kaibel[2], Peek ‖ 12 ἄ<μαλα>ν dub. Sauppe ‖ 18 καίτοι ἐγὼ Sauppe ‖ 19 *OΛEOPON*, leg. Visconti | σοῦ Sauppe, Henzen : σὺ Visconti ‖ 20 ἀθρήσῃς con. Kaibel[2] : ἀθροιήσῃς Cougny : ἀείσῃς Sauppe ‖ 22 *AΛΛOTPIOYΔE* lapis, corr. Visconti : ἀλλοτρί᾽ οὐδὲ Ciofi ‖ 25 *CY* lapis, corr. Visconti ‖ 27 ἔτι οἴχεο Ciofi ‖ 30 καλοῦ δρόμου dub. Sauppe ‖ 33 ἐ<ν> ἀψίδεσσιν Sauppe cl. v. 3 ‖ 34 μαίε<τ>ο, δαίμ<ω>ν Visconti : μ[ήδ]εο δαίμ<ω>ν Sauppe ‖ 36 *EΔEYE* lapis, corr. Visconti ‖ 38 πρέψειε τεὸν Visconti, Ciofi, dub. Henzen, Kaibel[1], Cougny, Döpp : πρέψει τε τεὸν Sauppe ‖ 41 λείπεται σευ Cougny, λείπεται σεο Nocita ‖ 42 suppl. Visconti : ἀστέρες, ὡς πυρόεντος ἐμοῦ μένος αἶψα περαίνῃ Ciofi ‖ 43 ὠκύτερον πώλων σ[ε θ]εός δέμας – – – Vérilhac : *ΩKYTEPONΠΩ|ΛΩN . . . . . . ΔE|MΛC . . . . . AKMH*, ὠκύτερον πώλων, (παιδὸς) δέμας (ἤλασεν) ἀκμῆ Visconti : *ΛΩΛECN ΩKYTEPONΠΩ|ΛΩNCΩKOC-KYTEPONΠΩ|ΛΩNCΩKOCΔE|MΛCΛΩΛECN* Kaibel[2] : ὠκύτερον πώλων . . . . . δέμας . . . . . . Kaibel, Henzen-Huelsen, Cougny, Cagnat : ὠκύτερον πώλων . . . . . . . . . . . . . . Ciofi : ὠκύτερον πώλων παιδὸς (?) δέμας [ὤλεσεν] ἀκμῆ Henzen : ὠκύτερον πώλων σε τεόν τε δαμάσσεται ἅρμα Sauppe

*sub anaglypho*

Deis Manibus Sacrum. | Q(uinto) Sulpicio Q(uinti) f(ilio) Cla(udia) Maximo, domo Roma, vix(it) ann(os) XI, m(enses) V, d(ies) XII. | hic tertio certaminis lustro inter Graecos poetas duos et L | professus favorem, quem ob teneram aetatem excitaverat, | in admirationem ingenio suo perduxit et cum honore discessit. Versus | extemporales eo subiecti sunt, ne parent(es) adfectib(us) suis indulsisse videant(ur). | Q(uintus) Sulpicius Eugramus et Licinia Ianuaria parent(es) infelicissim(i) f(ilio) piissim(o) fec(erunt) et sib(i) p(osterisque) s(uis).

Eugram(m)us *Kaibel[2]*

Ἐπιγράμματα.

Μοῦνος ἀπ᾽ αἰῶνος δυοκαίδεκα παῖς ἐνιαυτῶν
  Μάξιμος ἐξ ἀέθλων εἰς Ἀίδην ἔμολον·
νοῦσος καὶ κάματός με διώλεσαν· οὔτε γὰρ ἠοῦς,
  οὐκ ὄρφνης μουσέων ἐκτὸς ἔθηκα φρένα.
λίσσομαι ἀλλὰ στῆθι δεδουπότος εἵνεκα κούρου,            5
  ὄφρα μάθῃς σχεδίου γράμματος εὐεπίην,
εὐφήμου καὶ λέξον ἀπὸ στόματος τόδε μοῦνον
  δακρύσας· εἴης χῶρον ἐς Ἠλύσιον·
ζωούσας ἔλιπες γὰρ ἀηδόνας, ἃς Ἀιδωνεὺς
  οὐδέποθ᾽ αἱρήσει τῇ φθονερῇ παλάμῃ.            10

Βαιὸν μὲν τόδε σῆμα, τὸ δὲ κλέος οὐρανὸν ἵκει,
  Μάξιμε, Πιερίδων ἐξέο λειπομένων,
νώνυμον οὐδέ σε Μοῖρα κατέκτανε νηλεόθυμος,
  ἀλλ᾽ ἔλιπεν λήθης ἄμμορον εὐεπίην.

οὔτις ἀδακρύτοισι τεὸν παρὰ τύμβον ἀμείβων     15
ὀφθαλμοῖς σχεδίου δέρξεται εὐστιχίην.
ἄρκιον ἐς δόλιχον τόδε σοι κλέος· οὐ γὰρ ἀπευθὴς
κείσεαι, οὐτιδανοῖς ἰδόμενος νέκυσι,
πουλὺ δὲ καὶ χρυσοῖο καὶ ἠλέκτροιο φαεινοῦ
ἔσ(σ)ετ᾽ ἀεὶ κρέσσων ἣν ἔλιπες σελίδα.     20

1 δύο καὶ δέκα Visconti, Henzen, Kaibel[1], Cougny ‖ 3 ἀπώλεσαν Henzen-Huelsen ‖ 4 οὔτ᾽ ὄρφνης expectaret Kaibel[1], Cougny ‖ 7 εὐφήμ<ει> Visconti ‖ 10 φθονερᾷ Henzen-Huelsen ‖ 12 Πιερίδων Visconti | ἐξέο (i.e. ἐκ σέο) Kaibel, Cagnat, ἐ(κ σ)έο Visconti, ἐ<κ σ>έο Henzen, Cougny : ἐξ ἔο Ciofi[1] ‖ 14 ἄλλο λίπεν Ciofi[1] ‖ 17 δολιχὸν Visconti : δόλιχον Cougny, Nocita ‖ 18 καίσεαι Henzen-Huelsen | εἰδόμενος Visconti, <ε>ἰδόμενος Henzen, Henzen-Huelsen, Kaibel[2], Cagnat ‖ 20 ἔσ<σ>ετ᾽ edd. pll. | κρέσσ<ο>ν Visconti

## TRANSLATION (BY BARBARA GRAZIOSI)

The extemporaneous verses of Quintus Sulpicius Maximus: the words Zeus might have used, reproaching Helios because he gave his chariot to Phaethon.

The sovereign gods made you alone and no other
The light-bearing charioteer of our well-ordered world,
Why then did you set your bad-minded son upon the vaults of
    Olympus
And gave him the unspeakable speed of the horses,
Not at all fearing my power?     5
These plans of yours are not loyal to the gods: where did the
    well-built chariot
Of Phaethon travel? How could the flame of your unquenchable
    fire
Reach to my very throne, and engulf the broad universe?
From the heat the mighty mass mixed with the spheres,
And Ocean himself raised his hands to heaven;     10
Which river was not completely dried up from the source?
And the seed sown for Demeter burnt down, and the farmer
Mourned by his sickles the parched unapproachable land
In vain he sowed the thankless soil; in vain
He yoked his oxen to his curved plough, bending his manly
    limbs     15
Behind his heavy oxen, under the evening star.
The whole earth groaned on account of that bad-minded boy,
And I at last put out his fame with fire. Do not lament

The dire death of your child, but consider your world
Lest you earn from my hand an even more burning spear.     20
Know the mind of heavenly Zeus. By Rheia, Olympus
Never saw anything worse than this.
My world was in your charge, a grand task,
But let bygones be bygones, keep in your mind the future
He was not your son. He did not realize the boundless strength
  of your horses     25
And he did not master the tricky skill of the reins.
Go now, travel the world again, lest by belabouring weak
  thoughts
You hand over to other hands your glorious task.
The sunrise and the sunset and the whole beautiful course is for
  you alone
As you hasten along your fiery orbit.     30
The divine mind entrusted this to you as your glorious task.
Spare the earth and the whole beautiful universe,
And steer a middle course through the vaults of Olympus.
This is what befits the gods, and what is right. Take up, divine
  spirit,
Your sweet light again—your son has done much damage—     35
And travel yourself the boundless great sky again,
Aiming halfway between earth below and what is above.
That way eternal light will ever suit the descendants of Uranus,
the prayer of men will always be left without complaint,
and you will always have the mind of Zeus well disposed
  towards you.     40
But if some other purpose is left in you, reckless one,
The stars themselves be witness that the strength of my flaming
  thunderbolt
Will, swifter than your horses, destroy your countenance, god.

Sacred to the Deified Dead. In memory of Quintus Sulpicius Maximus, the son of Quintus, of the Claudian tribe. Rome. He lived eleven years, five months, and twelve days. In the third edition of the contest, performing as one among fifty-two Greek poets, he turned the good will he had aroused because of his young age into admiration because of his talent, and left with honours. Lest his parents may seem to have been unduly influenced by their affection for him, his extemporaneous verses have been inscribed here. Quintus Sulpicius Eugramus and Licinia Ianuaria, his unfortunate parents, erected this tomb for their most pious son, for themselves, and for their descendants.

Epigrams

Uniquely, though I was but a twelve-year-old boy,
    I, Maximus, left the Games and went into Hades.
Disease and exhaustion destroyed me: never at dawn
    Or in the evening I set my mind outside the realm of the Muses.
Pause here, I pray you, for the sake of this poor boy,        5
    and see the beauty of this extemporaneous poem,
and speak with pure lips through falling tears,
    this single prayer: 'Go to the Elysian land.
For you have left here living nightingales,
    which Hades shall never seize with his envious hand.'      10

This is only a small memorial, but the fame shall reach heaven,
    Maximus, the fame of the Pierian poetry left behind by you.
Fate that has no pity, did not obliterate you without a name,
    But left behind beautiful verse that takes no share in oblivion.
Nobody who comes to your tomb will look without tears.      15
    at the beautiful rows of your impromptu composition.
This glory is secure, for you, for a long time; you do not lie
    Here unknown, like the dead of no account.
The column of poetry you left behind will forever be
    Far more precious than gold and shining amber.[12]

## LITERATURE AND THE TOMB AS MEANS
## OF SOCIAL ADVANCEMENT

Maximus died too early to benefit from his success at the Capitoline
Games. The circumstances of his death are described in the first
epigram placed under his portrait: 'sickness and tiredness consumed
me, for I devoted myself to the Muses night and day' (3). The epigram
suggests that his victory and his death had the same cause: extreme
hard work in the pursuit of literature. In a short piece for *BBC
Magazine*, Mary Beard suggests that this is a case of 'the "pushy
parent" syndrome in ancient Rome'.[13] The parents further explain

---

[12] I would like to thank Barbara Graziosi for the translation she provided. For an
earlier and freer English version see Nelson (1903), 385–7.

[13] Beard (2012).

that they wanted the poem by which Maximus won honourable mention to be engraved on the monument so that nobody would think that their love for their son had made them overstate his talent. They had to go to great expense to set up such a visible and rich monument in honour of their son's poetic performance and in memory of his life.

Maximus is referred to as a Roman freeborn citizen (that is to say, with his full name, the name of his father, and the name of his tribe), but his father's name (*Quintus Sulpicius Eugramus*) suggests that he was of Greek origin. This must be why Maximus mastered the Greek language almost perfectly. In particular, the lack of any reference to Eugramus' and Licinia's fathers and the cognomina *Eugramus* and *Ianuaria* reveal that they were ex-slaves, freed by their owners.[14] Maximus' family gives an excellent example of social mobility in Roman society.[15] We may, for instance, usefully compare their case with that of Horace's parents, about a century earlier: the celebrated poet of Augustan Rome was also the son of a freedman,[16] and judging from Horace's own depiction in *Satires* 1.6.65–99, his father was clearly also a 'pushy parent'.[17]

In light of their circumstances, we should not be surprised that Maximus' parents were concerned with their son's education and success: 'a celebrity poet in the family would certainly have done wonders for their finances. And at a less glamorous level, in a world without pensions or social security, they really needed some children to look after them in old age.'[18] Certainly, Maximus' monument indicates that his parents had to be freed slaves of considerable means: not only had they invested in their child's education, but they also erected a lavish memorial for him. Indeed, in terms of function, the monument was meant to perform for them what they expected their son to achieve through poetry—had he lived. At the level

---

[14] See Henzen, ad *CIL* VI 33976: *mater pueri libertina videtur fuisse Licinii alicuius [...]: itaque fortasse non casui adtribuendum est, quod monumentum hoc stetit non procul a sepulcro gentilicio Liciniorum*; see also Henzen (1871), 114.

[15] On the 'fluid and competitive nature of Roman imperial society which supposedly reached exceptional levels of social mobility', and especially on the sons of freedmen, who 'enjoyed *ingenuitas*, which was an absolute quality that could be neither gradated nor forfeited', see Mouritsen (2011), 261–78: 277 and 265 respectively; Mayer (2012), 43–4.

[16] See Mouritsen (2011), 265–74.

[17] I would like to thank Barbara Graziosi for this observation.

[18] Beard (2012).

of social analysis, then, the boy's life and the monument celebrating his death can both be interpreted as means of social advancement for his family.


## MAXIMUS' POEM

The poem in forty-three hexameters laid out on either side of Maximus' statue, and flowing into the papyrus scroll he holds in his hand, is conceived as a monologue uttered by Zeus reproving Helios for entrusting his chariot to his young son Phaethon. Zeus asks Helios how he could have allowed his foolish child to drive the chariot, while the gods had charged him, and nobody else, with this task. Since Phaethon was about to destroy the world by burning it, Zeus had to kill him. The first part of the speech describes the destruction of the world, while in the second part Zeus gives some new instructions to Helios.

Maximus' poetic performance reminds us of the rhetorical exercises called *progymnasmata*, known to us from papyri and rhetorical handbooks: these must have featured prominently in the type of education Maximus received. In particular, Maximus' poem can be regarded as the earliest example of the rhetorical exercise called *ēthopoiia* ('character-drawing') in verse.[19] The episode of Phaethon was well known from literature and art,[20] and Maximus would have known from memory several sources from which he could draw relevant material when composing his lines.[21] At this level, the theme and execution of the poem are easily explicable, and in line with what we can infer about Maximus' social and educational circumstances. The context in which the poem is displayed, however, raises more

---

[19] See Agosti (2005), 36–7. Quintilian 3.8.49–54 describes these exercises as the hardest (*difficillima*) and the most useful (*utilissima*).

[20] On Phaethon's myth in funerary monuments, see Zanker and Ewald (2008), 86–90.

[21] As Agosti (2005), 36 n. 10 and 37 observes, Maximus appears to know Ov. *Met.* 1.747–2.400 and makes extensive use of archaic epic poetry. The quality of Maximus' poem has been criticized by modern scholars (see Nocita (2000), 96 and Manieri (2014), 148 n. 7) but, as Kathleen Coleman points out, 'it really is not all that bad a poem [ . . . ] especially when you consider that he had to make it up on the spot': Potter (2010). For the implications of the theme involving the king of the gods in an age of autocracy, see Coleman's lectures: Potter (2010).

interesting (and difficult) questions of interpretation—which ultim-
ately have to do with the relationship between literature and life.

Phaethon's father is squarely blamed for the death of his young
son: he should not have entrusted his chariot to him, or indeed given
free rein to his flight towards heaven. Phaethon flew too close to
Olympus and Zeus therefore struck him down. The supreme god
gives advice to the bereaved father: his son, he claims, was a 'bad-
minded boy' (κακόφρονος . . . κούρου, line 17) and should not be
mourned. In fact, Helios should consider the ordered universe, the
κόσμος, and fear lest Zeus strike him down, too, for failing to curb the
ambition of his son and for mourning him. The father should 'know
the mind of heavenly Zeus' (γίνωσκ᾽ οὐρανίοιο Διὸς νόον, line 21), and
the remainder of the poem goes on to ventriloquize Zeus's thoughts.
The deceased Maximus can compose a whole poem about a bad boy
who tried to rise above his station, and while this, perhaps, confirms
him as the *filius piissimus* lamented by his parents in the Latin
inscription, it also suggests some uncomfortable parallels between
Phaethon and Maximus himself. Both boys died at a young age.
Both attempted to do something extraordinary in relation to their
age and status.

The challenge of interpretation is to steer a course between literature
and life, between claiming literary artifice for the whole monument or
simply invoking real-life 'coincidence'. Manieri rightly argues that the
subject assigned to Maximus fits the political agenda of the Capitoline
Games. The emperor Domitian presided over them, as the representa-
tive of Jupiter on earth.[22] He had, moreover, rebuilt the temple of Jupiter
after it had been destroyed by fire; so the subject of the poem seemed
designed to praise the emperor for repairing the damage made by
'Phaeton'.[23] It is also possible, and even likely, that the subject was
chosen to fit the personality and age of the contestant: it seems safe to
assume that competitors were assigned different themes for their com-
position, and that having the boy Maximus perform a poem in which a
father was rebuked for the reckless behaviour of his son would have
been pleasing to the audience.[24]

Once the poem was inscribed on the tomb, however, it could also
be read in relation to the other inscriptions presented on the monu-
ment, and not just, as Manieri does so well, in terms of its original

[22] Manieri (2014), 153–4.    [23] Manieri (2014), 158–9.
[24] Manieri (2014), 155 and n. 6.

agonistic setting. The contrast between a good and a bad boy, but also the dangers of giving free rein to ambition, remained important issues in the new setting, too. There seems to be little doubt that the poem inscribed was, essentially, the poem performed at the Games—even if it may have been revised before inscription. It seems, then, most reasonable to take an approach to the interpretation of the monument that acknowledges how literary production affects perceptions of the poet's life, but also how the author's life and death, in turn, frame interpretation of his poetry. The epigrams at the bottom of the monument further explore these dualities.

## THE EPIGRAMS

While the hexameter poem on the subject of Phaethon's death is explicitly attributed to Maximus, the two funerary epigrams on his tomb have no explicit author. We can assume that they were not composed by Maximus himself, given that they refer to his death—though, of course, as several contributors to this volume emphasize, it was customary to imagine that poets composed their own epitaphs.[25] Still, a second poet must have been at work here. He might have been a relative (Maximus' father?) or a professional working in an epigraphic workshop. In this case, the second poet might have also revised the poem on Phaethon, adjusting it for the written and definitive version—as many have supposed.[26] The second line of the first epigram, 'I, Maximus, left the Games and went into Hades' (Μάξιμος ἐξ ἀέθλων εἰς Ἀίδην ἔμολον) may be taken precisely as an attempt to put an end to that kind of speculation: Maximus died straight after the Games, and his composition was already there, fully formed. Viewers of the monument can read for themselves a written

---

[25] See especially Graziosi and Goldschmidt, Introduction, pp. 1–17 and Laird, Chapter 12, pp. 255–6.
[26] Several scholars have suspected as much, arguing that the literary merit of the verses was due to Maximus' father, who rewrote the poem after the extemporaneous verses of the son. The Phaethon poem does indeed display varied and sophisticated vocabulary, twelve of the forty-three lines are dactylic verses (6, 7, 8, 17, 18, 19, 20, 26, 27, 31, 36, 42), thirty-one are spondaic hexameters, two are irregular verses (5 and 10): Nocita (2012). See also Caldelli (1993), 70–1. As suggested above, there may also be a reworking of the Phaethon poem at the level of content, given the suggested parallels (and differences) in the stories of Phaethon and Maximus himself.

version of his extemporaneous composition (line 6)—and they can understand, through reading the poem, that the parents did not aggrandize his talents. This is something that the parents themselves mention as a motivation for putting up his verses, as stated in the Latin inscription: 'Lest his parents may seem to have been unduly influenced by their affection for him, his extemporaneous verses have been inscribed here' (*Versus extemporales eo subiecti sunt, ne parent(es) adfectib(us) suis indulsisse videant(ur)*).

For all that parental aggrandizing of the verses is denied, the epigrams at the bottom of the monument enact a transfer of agency from the young poet to those who commemorate him. The first epigram is delivered in the first person, by Maximus himself, though the poem ends with the envisaged prayers of those who mourn him. The second is addressed to him in the second person by those who are concerned with the poetry he composed, and the way it has become a monument.

In the first epigram, Maximus laments his own death and explains its cause: 'Disease and exhaustion destroyed me: never at dawn / or in the evening I set my mind outside the realm of the Muses' (νοῦσος καὶ κάματός με διώλεσαν· οὔτε γὰρ ἠοῦς, / οὐκ ὄρφνης μουσέων ἐκτὸς ἔθηκα φρένα, lines 3–4). So here again is an obvious contrast to be drawn with Phaethon, that 'bad-minded son/boy' (κακόφρονα ... υἱέα and κακόφρονος ... κούρου, lines 3–4 and 17 of the hexameter poem), who instead of applying his mind to literary matters, drove his father's chariot with a child's wild abandon and ignorance of the consequences. The monument presents other contrasts: Phaethon scorched the earth and prevented plants from growing and farmers from harvesting (16–17); Maximus, for his part, left a lovely, well-ordered world where the nightingales sing forever, and cannot be stopped by Hades (9–10, note the pun ἀηδόνας ... Ἀιδωνεύς): a reminiscence of Callimachus *Epigram* 2.5–6 Pf. (= AP 7.80.5–6).[27] More generally, as Montiglio points out in this volume (pp. 226–33), several Greek epigrams on the tombs of poets insist on the regenerative powers of nature, as a means of reflecting on the regenerative powers of poetry. Here we have an example of that theme: Hades cannot stop the nightingales from singing forever, though he did put an end to Maximus' career as a poet. Thus, while Zeus killed Phaethon in order

---

[27] See Garulli (2012), 356.

to ensure the regular working of nature, Hades snatches the studious Maximus from a delightful world, where nightingales never stop regenerating and singing, and are thus immune to Hades.

The second epigram, addressed to Maximus, reflects on other kinds of immunity. It describes Maximus' poetic achievement as a 'papyrus column', a σελίς (20). Above the epigram, Maximus is portrayed as holding a papyrus scroll in his hands, which preserves the last lines of his poem: this creates a visual continuity between the inscribed columns of the altar and the stone σελίς of the fictional, stone papyrus held by Maximus. The central (and most visible) part of the massive altar therefore provides us with an important key to understanding the monument in its entirety: the tomb lends the materiality of the stone to the poet himself, his text, and its reception.[28]

In Maximus' funerary monument several messages combine: visual representation interacts with text and, to some extent, architecture. More than any other, this tomb can be regarded as a textual space as well as a material site. In fact, inscribed texts cover almost the entire surface of the stone. The scroll and the marble, here, are one and the same. What is more, only a minor part of these texts belong to the funerary genre. The tomb in fact combines a varied discourse *on* the poet (including commemorative inscriptions and a portrait) and the actual work *of* the poet: it is a vehicle not only of commemoration but also of transmission, since Maximus' tomb functions not only as a monumental site but also as a book made of stone.

### THE MATERIAL RECEPTION OF LITERATURE

Visual and narrative representations of the poet coexist with his text. Reading the image and reading the text are thus connected enterprises. Portraits generate an intellectual process by which the viewer is asked to 'read' the author's work through the interpretation of specific details of physiognomy, expression, and gesture. Maximus' portrait is a material projection of the poet as *togatus*, that is to say as a young man and a Roman citizen. Did Maximus' father make him wear the toga before the usual age on the occasion of the Games? Or is

---

[28] For the competition between portrait and poem, see e.g. Mart. 7.84.

this an anticipation of what Maximus would have become? Whether Maximus actually wore his toga or not, this representation intends to emphasize the status of Maximus as a Roman citizen, who simultaneously had an excellent command of Greek.

The bilingualism of the monument matches the visual impact of the portrait (the Roman toga, the papyrus inscribed with Greek letters). The layout and lettering are accurate and well balanced, the letters lunate. The inscribed text is displayed on the stone with varying letter sizes. The most legible part of the inscription is the Latin prose dedication, which provides the reader with the necessary information on the dead person. The largest letter size is used for the traditional *adprecatio* to the Manes, the souls of dead ancestors, and for Maximus' anagraphic data: this message, in Latin, is addressed to all readers.

A smaller letter size is used for the Greek verses, that is to say, the poem and the epigrams. The latter are inscribed on the base, immediately below the Latin prose inscription: they must therefore have been more legible, since they were closer to the ground than the poem. The epigrams are also introduced by a heading, carved with larger letters, declaring the literary genre of the following texts ('Epigrams'). The different size of the letters indicates that all those who could read the Greek alphabet were informed about the nature of the following lines, even if only a minority took the trouble to read the epigrams. The poem itself seems to have been reserved for an even smaller and selected minority of readers, since it was placed at a distance from the ground.

Layout and language mark different levels of reading and engagement:[29] monolingual Latin readers could know who the boy was and what he did, and visualize him as a young poet. Bilingual readers could also reflect on the short but glorious life of Maximus, and even appreciate Maximus' poetic work, finding in his portrait a visual counterpart to Maximus' representation as sketched in the inscriptions. Text and portrait complete and support each other, depending on the reading level of the viewer.

The overall effect of Maximus' monument must have been, and still is, impressive: he was commemorated through a unique combination of text and image. As we have seen, Maximus' parents wished the viewers of the monument not only to remember their son, but specifically to remember him as a poet. This ambition sheds light on the

---

[29] See Bing (2009), 169–74.

social and cultural value of poetry, on the role played by intellectuals in public life, and on the importance of culture as a means of social advancement. In order to have its intended effect, the tomb is both a celebrative and a funerary monument: it celebrates a moment of glory,[30] and simultaneously commemorates a dead boy, making his performance in the Games representative of his whole life. The usual procedure is therefore reversed: the monument usually celebrates a whole life, and the person's death gives the occasion for that celebration. In our case, a specific occasion in life stands for the whole, and a *poeta unius carminis, unius diei* ('a poet of one poem and one day') is represented as a poet for ever more.[31] The monument thus gives permanence to the transience of poetic recitation (*versus extemporales*), just as it transforms the living voice into inscribed letters, and the absent dead into physical image and portraited presence. The continuation of the text between stone and roll is part of this game, alluding to the process of moving from the dead subject to monument, from voice to stone, from specific occasion to eternity, from the discourse of the poet to a discourse about the dead poet, from poetry to monument. Within such a game, the papyrus roll plays an intermediary part between voice and stone, and helps to keep together the poet's life, work, and memory.

Maximus' parents achieved their aim. While countless streets, avenues, and squares celebrate the day on which the Porta Salaria came under artillery fire, there is one short street in Rome that celebrates the poetic discovery revealed in the debris. Not only is a replica of the monument commemorating the young Maximus still *in situ*, facing a busy crossroads in central Rome, but the street sign of Via Sulpicio Massimo remembers the boy as a 'giovinetto romano, poeta e oratore del I sec.'.[32]

---

[30]  Potter (2010): 'The monument of Maximus was characteristic of a culture that delighted in monumentalizing the ephemeral [ . . . ]. The monument itself fits into a context that includes all manner of commemorative art connected with games of various sorts, erected by men who wished their few days of fame as sponsors of the events to be remembered forever.'

[31]  See Marrou (1964), 130 n. 151: 'le petit défunt est donc ici représenté en train de déclamer son poème'.

[32]  'Roman boy, poet and orator from the first century CE'.

# 5

## Ovid's Tombs

### Afterlives of a Poetic *corpus*

*Nora Goldschmidt*

'But who knows the fate of his bones, or how often he is to be
buried? Who hath the oracle of his ashes, or whither they are to
be scattered?'

(Thomas Browne, *Hydriotaphia, Urne-buriall*, 1658)

Sometime during the thirteenth century, two *clerici* were visiting
Ovid's tomb 'in the territory of Tomis' (*in terra Thomitana*).[1] They
were debating the best and worst lines the poet had composed, when
suddenly Ovid's disembodied voice replied from beyond the grave:
the best verse he ever wrote was *est virtus placitis abstinuisse bonis* ('it
is a virtue to abstain from good things that give pleasure', *Heroides*
17.98), and the worst was *omne iuvans statuit Iupiter esse pium*
('Jupiter established that whatever gives pleasure is good', cf. *Heroides*
4.133). Taken out of context these quotations dramatize opposing
interpretations of Ovidian poetry: the first was regularly cited in the
Middle Ages to support the moral interpretation of Ovid's works;[2] the
second seems a typically Ovidian avowal of the very opposite senti-
ment. In one fell swoop and in his very own words, the self-
constructed poet of pleasure is confirmed as a dour proto-Christian

---

[1] The story is preserved in two manuscripts: Freiburg, University Library, MS. 380
(= Bischoff (1952)), and British Library, London, MS. Harley 219 (= Wright (1842),
43–4; 225). See also Trapp (1973), 42–3 and Dimmick (2002), 274–5.
[2] Trapp (1973), 42.

in medieval mode: 'the disembodied voice has become a species of Echo, capable only of reproducing the sentiments of its interlocutors.'[3] But when the two clerics begin to pray for Ovid's soul, the poet's voice suddenly calls out again: *nolo 'pater noster': carpe, viator, iter!* ('I don't want "Our Father": traveller, be on your way!'). Spoken from the depths of his tomb, the poet's parting words might be taken literally: as one of the two manuscript versions of the anecdote explains, Ovid was already damned and knew perfectly well that prayer would not help him, and so refused the Christian intervention offered him from beyond the grave.[4] But the poet's refusal can also be understood as a more sweeping rejection by the author to accept the posthumous reception being imposed upon him.

Centred on the tomb of the poet, this anecdote stages a power struggle inherent in any act of literary reception: meaning may 'always already' be created at the point of reception, and hence be devolved onto readers,[5] yet Ovid, more insistently than most other poets, attempted to control his own reception by encoding it into his oeuvre. He not only gave explicit instructions for his own afterlife in his texts, but also revisited his earlier works in a series of auto-receptions, which, taken together, set up a reception model for posterity that ensured the author 'is always already extended'.[6] Ovidian receptions are typically confined within the parameters set by Ovid's texts: a retelling of an episode from the *Metamorphoses*, for example, however recherché, can essentially be read as a posthumous episode begun by Ovid himself, which 'extends' the Ovidian text—and the author in the text—within the textual system which Ovid's literary *corpus* has already established. By contrast, the poet's tomb can function as a site of intervention where the balance of power between the text and its receiver is destabilized. Tombs of the poets constitute a point where authors die and readers are born, a place where the author, through his talismanic (or purported) physical presence can

---

[3] Dimmick (2002), 275.

[4] The Freiburg MS notes that 'we must believe that the voice speaking from the tomb was the voice of the devil, trying to deprive Ovid of the sanctified status he had so long enjoyed': according to one tradition, Ovid had been converted to Christianity towards the end of his life by St John the Evangelist and later became known as 'St Naso': Trapp (1973), 43–4; Dimmick (2002), 275.

[5] Martindale (1993), 3.

[6] On Ovid's revisions as extension of the authorial self, see Martelli (2013), 4.

lend authority to new interpretations, and yet can no longer *quite* speak for himself.

Characteristically, Ovid himself seems partly to have anticipated this. After his relegation from Rome in 8 CE, his works display an increasing concern with the afterlife of his physical body, over which, stranded in Tomis, he would have no control after death. The poet's solution, in the *exilica*, is to redouble his efforts to co-opt the biological body into the body of work, insistently and explicitly equating his material *corpus* with his written texts. For example, he puns repeatedly on *corpus* ('body'/'body of work').[7] He calls his books his 'flesh and blood' (*viscera mea*),[8] and in the opening of the *Tristia*, the book roll is introduced as an *ersatz* body: it can go to Rome while the poet remains in exile: *tu tamen i pro me* (1.1.57), 'go for me', as the poet prays that he might become identical with his book roll (*di facerent possem nunc meus esse liber*, 1.1.58). In *Tristia* 3.3, attention seemingly shifts to the poet's material corpse, asking that his bones be sent back to Rome when he dies, and adding an epitaph to be inscribed on his marble tomb:

> ossa tamen facito parva referantur in urna:
>> sic ego non etiam mortuus exul ero.
> [ . . . ]
> atque ea cum foliis et amomi pulvere misce,
>> inque suburbano condita pone solo;
> quosque legat versus oculo properante viator,
>> grandibus in tituli marmore caede notis:
> HIC EGO QVI IACEO TENERORVM LVSOR AMORVM
> INGENIO PERII NASO POETA MEO
> AT TIBI QVI TRANSIS NE SIT GRAVE QVISQVIS AMASTI
> DICERE NASONIS MOLLITER OSSA CVBENT.

But see that my bones are brought home in a little urn: then I'll not remain exiled even in death. [ . . . ] So mingle my ashes with sweet dried herbs and spikenard, bury them close to the City, and inscribe these lines in big letters on my marble tombstone for the passer-by to read with hurried glance: I WHO LIE HERE, NASO THE POET, WHO ONCE PLAYED WITH

---

[7] *corpus* = literary work: e.g. *Tristia* 2.535 (*Aeneid*); 3.8.35–6; *Tristia* 3.14.7–10: Hexter (1999), 345 n. 15; cf. 331; Farrell (1999); Hardie (2002), 298–9 with n. 40. Walker (1997), 200 sees 'the multiple meanings of *corpus*, used to denote the physical body of the poet Ovid, but also the body of Ovid's literary works' as uniquely characteristic of the exile elegies.

[8] *Tristia* 1.7.19–20; cf. Farrell (1999), 141.

TENDER LOVES, HAVE PERISHED AS A RESULT OF MY OWN
GENIUS. PASSER-BY, IF YOU HAVE LOVED, DO NOT DISDAIN TO
SAY: 'LET THE BONES OF NASO LIE SOFT.'

(*Tristia* 3.3.65–6; 69–76)

Having composed his epitaph, the poet suddenly changes tack:[9]

> hoc satis in titulo est. etenim maiora libelli
> et diuturna magis sunt monimenta mihi,
> quos ego confido, quamvis nocuere, daturos
> nomen et auctori tempora longa suo.

So much for an epitaph. My books make a better and more enduring
monument: although they have hurt him, I trust that they will bring their
author a name and a long life.

(*Tristia* 3.3.77–80)

Reiterating the declaration at the end of the *Metamorphoses* that his
works, his 'better part' (*pars . . . melior*, 15.875), will give him life after
death (*vivam*, 15.879), Ovid once again puts ultimate faith in his texts.
And yet, inevitably—as reception would bring to the fore—the literary
'tomb' Ovid so carefully constructed (*diuturna monimenta*, 3.3.78)
fails wholly to contain the poet's physical *corpus*, leaving a space for
posthumous fractures in the textual universe the poet created.

In practice, since no-one ever found out where Ovid was truly
buried, his body *did* disappear, dissolving into a textual absent pres-
ence within the poet's self-constructed poetics of illusion.[10] Yet rather
than simply accepting the diffusion of Ovid's physical remains into
the realm of radical textuality, a reception history has emerged in
which the material tomb has taken centre stage, destabilizing the
reception of the text which the Ovidian textual *corpus* painstakingly
attempted to control.[11] This chapter focuses on three case studies in
which the literary and material receptions of the poet's *corpora* interact
to tell an alternative story to the master-plot of reception which Ovid
encoded in his texts: the first is a poem, the pseudo-Ovidian *De vetula*;
the second a painting, Johann Heinrich Schönfeld's *Sarmaten am*

---

[9] Even here—in the most direct treatment of the tomb in Ovid's works—the poet's
body is subsumed into the text: unlike most epitaphs of poets, Ovid's auto-epitaph is
embedded within the author's published poetry book, fusing, at the level of the written
page, the poet's literary and biological bodies.

[10] Cf. Hardie (2002) *passim* on the absent presence of the author.

[11] For an excellent broad survey of the fascination with Ovid's tomb, see Trapp
(1973), with Pansa (1924), 87–95.

*Grabe Ovids*, and the last an archaeological discovery, the alleged 'tomba di Ovidio', now better known as the Mausoleum of the Nasonii in Rome. Building on anxieties inherent in Ovid's poems, each of these examples uses the figure of the tomb (real or imagined) to destabilize the dynamics of reception by exploiting or overwriting the hermeneutic gap created by the material fact of the poet's physical remains. In doing so, they utilize—even as they unravel—the equation of physical and biological *corpora* established in Ovid's works in order to take control of the Ovidian text in reception.

## DE VETULA: OVID'S MISSING CORPUS

At some point in the thirteenth century—during the height of the medieval craze for Ovid, when the two *clerici* were wandering in the vicinity of Tomis—a three-book hexameter poem known as *De vetula* ('On the Old Woman') was allegedly discovered in a recently excavated tomb supposedly containing the remains of Publius Ovidius Naso. Presented in Ovid's own voice, the poem was hailed as his long-lost autobiography from exile.[12]

At first sight, *De vetula* presents a relatively conventional form of reception, 'extending' the Ovidian canon through creative dialogue with Ovid's texts. The poem has a complex intertextual relationship with the Ovidian textual *corpus*, 'out Oviding Ovid' in its metaliterary play,[13] and, at one level, it can be read as yet another 'revision' of the original Ovidian texts. The 'Ovid' of the first two books is a recognizable figure from the *Amores* or *Ars amatoria*. Book 1 tells of how the poet spent his youth given over to love (*quando vacabat amori*, *De vetula, prefatio* 5) and Book 2 of how he fell in love with one particular *puella* only to be tricked at an assignation: the old woman of the title waits for him in bed instead of his girl. The *puella* and the poet finally get together twenty years later, but this time they

---

[12] *De vetula* is traditionally dated to around 1250: Robathan (1968), 8, and must have been published between 1222 and 1268: Hexter (2011) 307 n. 110. Authorship has been attributed to Richard Fournival, though the evidence is not conclusive: for full discussion, see Klopsch (1967), 78–99; Robathan (1968), 6–10; Hexter (2011), 307 n. 110. On *De vetula*, see esp. Lehmann (1927), 13–15; Klopsch (1967); Robathan (1968); Hexter (1999) and (2011), 305–8; Godman (1995).

[13] Hexter (1999) 340.

are both old, and this is the catalyst to the 'transformation' of the third and final book (*qua re mutavit, De vetula, prefatio* 6). Taking a cue from the original Ovid, Book 3 then revisits the *exilica* to tell the 'true' story of Ovid's new life in exile, devoted to study and reflection, and presenting him effectively as an enlightened proto-Christian. The poem was known by the alternative title *De mutatione vitae Ovidii* (*On the Transformation of Ovid's Life*),[14] and the whole conceit is in some ways set up as the final transformation which Ovid proper, in the opening of the *Tristia*, instructed to be added as a 'revision' to his epic: this story of Ovid's life in exile, so the poem implies, is the final revision to the *Metamorphoses* which the 'original' Ovid had prescribed.[15]

*De vetula* can therefore be seen as a sequel to the Ovidian textual *corpus*, supplementing, but not replacing, the original work. But the assumption of the balance of power in that relationship is overturned in the fiction of the poem's discovery, the book found sealed in the long-lost tomb. This 'discovery' is foregrounded in the poem's multi-levelled frame. A prose introduction is followed by a verse preface by the 'editor' Leo, 'pronotary of the holy palace of Byzantium', with a further preface by the *auctor* 'Ovid' (*prefatio ipsius auctoris*). The prose introduction explains the circumstances of the poem's discovery:

. . . quando videlicet rex Colcorum dictum librum invenit in quodam sepul-cro extracto de cimiterio publico sito in suburbio Dioscori civitatis, que caput est sui regni, misit Constantinopolim, ubi erat copia Latinorum, pro eo, quod Armenici nec Latinam linguam intelligunt nec apud se interpretes huius tunc habebant.

. . . When the king of the Colchians found the book in a certain tomb excavated from the public cemetery situated in a suburb of the city of Dioscorus, the capital of his kingdom, he sent it to Constantinople, where there were many 'Latins', because the Armenians did not understand Latin and had no inter-preters at that time who did.

(*De vetula, introitus*)

According to most medieval accounts, Ovid was buried in exile in Tomis, a place variously identified as an island or a region in Colchis

---

[14] Robathan (1968), 13.
[15] For Ovid's instructions that his own 'metamorphosis' (his unhappy fate in Tomis) be added to the *Metamorphoses*, see *Tristia* 1.1.119–22. On Ovid's revisions, see Martelli (2013).

at the mythical end of the ancient world, via an over-reading of *Tristia* 3.9.33–4, where Ovid etymologizes Tomis from the Greek τομή, 'cutting', associating it with Medea (from Colchis), who cut her brother into pieces: hence the discovery here by the 'king of the Colchians', who then sends the book to be deciphered by the 'Latins' at Constantinople.[16]

A second preface, in verse, explains that Ovid had the poem buried with him in the hope that his bones—and the poem along with them—would one day be sent back to Rome, fulfilling the wish he expressed in *Tristia* 3.3 (*si saltem contingeret ossa referri*, pref. 11; mirroring Ovid's own desires that his bones be brought back home, **ossa** *tamen facito parva* **referantur** *in urna*). *De vetula* is transmitted with a further frame, an academic introduction (*accessus*), in the voice of an anonymous scholar, which is likely to have been part of the original composition.[17] This adds more details, including the fact that the codex was found 'recently' (*nuper*) during excavations in the public cemetery 'near the town of Tomis' (*iuxta oppidum Thomis*), buried at the head of Ovid's tomb inside an ivory capsule (*capsella eburnea*), 'unconsumed by age' (*nulla vetustate consumptus*), and that the tomb itself was marked by an inscription in Armenian translating to Latin as *hic iacet Ovidius ingeniosissimus poetarum* ('here lies Ovid, the most gifted of poets'), explaining the identification of the tomb by the Latinless locals.[18]

The idea of the book in the tomb has a long history in lending fake texts the air of authoritative discoveries,[19] but in this Ovidian example, both long-lost tomb and pseudepigraphic text are simultaneously 'discovered'. Lying next to the reputed body of the poet himself, the 'fake' takes on the status of 'original'—and perhaps even usurps it. In its immediate reception context, the ruse perpetrated by

[16] For the medieval geography of Tomis, see Trapp (1973), 45. On this movement 'reversing Ovid's banishment from urbane Rome to unlettered Tomis', see Heyworth (2009), 2.

[17] Godman (1995), 105.

[18] For the text, see Robathan (1968), 42–3. On the so-called *capta Troia accessus*, see Klopsch (1967), 19 n. 4: Ghisalberti (1946), 36 n. 5, 50–1, appendix 1. Godman (1995), 105 makes a compelling case for combined original authorship of all the prefatory material, despite repetition of information: 'the different personae of Leo, author, and exegete play related roles in the sophisticated game'.

[19] The trope frames Dictys' chronicle of the Trojan War and is a recognizable topos of medieval literature: Horsfall (2008–9); Klopsch (1967), 22–35.

*De vetula*, despite its self-conscious anachronisms, was fundamentally successful: the 'forgery designed to draw attention to its suspect character' was dutifully accepted into the Ovidian canon.[20] Petrarch would later express his suspicions ('like putting peacock eggs under hens', *ut gallinis pavonum ova subiciunt*),[21] but most of the poem's early readers, including figures such as Roger Bacon and the younger Dante, were more than willing to participate in the fiction of Ovidian authorship.[22] *De vetula* was popular (around thirty-nine Latin manuscripts survive with excerpts and fragments in others); it circulated in a well-known French translation by Jean Le Fèvre (*c*.1320–after 1380) and even reached non-literate audiences in the form of exempla in medieval pulpits.[23]

Because Ovid, in his authentic texts, was obsessed with burial and because he drew such a close parallel between his body and his body of work, the idea of the literary text buried with the poet could easily pass as an Ovidian invention, the natural culmination of the book/body duality that Ovid himself had inscribed. But the close physical contact with the poet's putative bones lent this text an extra air of independent authenticity: Ovid wanted this to be his last word, we are to believe, but, since his bones had hitherto remained undiscovered, the poem had not—yet—filtered into the canon (as 'Leo' explains in the preface, 'since no one had taken care to return the bones, the poem was not at all read nor taken into circulation', *sed quia nullus eis curavit de referendis / nec fuit autemptim lectus nec habetur in usu*, *De vetula, prefatio* 13–14). Despite his best efforts, the original 'Ovid' never quite managed to bring his physical and biological *corpora* in such close proximity. Now, with the new text aligned so closely with the imagined materiality of the poet's bones—however brazen the fakery might be—*De vetula* could become a serious contender for Ovidian authorship. The poet's tomb therefore destabilizes the hermeneutic primacy of the Ovidian 'original' so that it is no longer clear which is the 'fake' and which the 'original', which the 'receiver' and which the 'received'.

---

[20] Godman (1995), 111.    [21] *Rerum senilium* 2.4.
[22] See Robathan (1968), 1–3 on the early reception of the poem.
[23] The poem continued to be printed into the fifteenth century. For the textual history, see Klopsch (1967) and Robathan (1968). For ecclesiastical uses in sermons, see Wenzel (2011), 161.

## TOMB RAIDERS: JOHANN HEINRICH SCHÖNFELD'S 'SARMATEN AM GRABE OVIDS'

Just as Ovid had predicted, his texts continued to 'live' in reception, extending the author through the continuation and supplementation of his work. But the parallel unruly appetite for the poet's absent material *corpus* whose fate he could not control flourished, too. Rumours circulated that Ovid's tomb had been sited within distant living memory: it was a magnificent marble vault decorated with poetry set on engraved plates, or else a humble tumulus with the name 'Publius Ovidius Naso' cut roughly into the surrounding stones.[24] From the second half of the sixteenth century, imaginary archaeology gave way to 'eyewitness' accounts from thanatourists who claimed to have seen the tomb with their own eyes and read the Latin (or sometimes Polish) inscription on its stone surface.[25]

At some period before 1662, the Swabian painter Johann Heinrich Schönfeld (1609–*c*.1683) produced a painting of the tomb of Ovid, *Sarmaten am Grabe Ovids (Sarmatians at the Tomb of Ovid)* (Figure 5.1).[26] Schönfeld had begun his artistic career painting conventional religious or mythological scenes, several of which were inspired by Ovid's *Metamorphoses*. But, after a period of exile and travel during the 1630s and 1640s in Rome and Naples, he developed a parallel preoccupation with the image of the ancient tomb, often in association with plunder and decay.[27]

---

[24] Trapp (1973) 47; 48–9. Concurrent stories were also in circulation about the discovery of 'Ovid's pen', which Queen Isabella of Hungary held in 1540: Trapp (1973), 48. Such stories were partly based on Ovid's own mention of the local people's admiration for him and his compositions in the vernacular language: e.g. *Ex Ponto* 4.9.97–104; Pansa (1924), 87–8.

[25] Trapp (1973), 47–5; 57.

[26] Mentioned briefly by Trapp (1973), 57–8. On the painting, see also Voss (1964), 24; Pée (1971), 132–3. For Schönfeld, see esp. Voss (1964); Michaud (2006); Zeller, Waike, and Kaulbach (2009); Trepesch, Müller, and Sedelmeier (2010). At least three versions of the painting existed: one in the Royal Collection purchased by Charles II in 1662; another (probably a copy: Pée (1971), 132), now in Budapest, and a third, which tells its own story of exile and loss: previously in Voss' own collection, it was confiscated by the German police in 1935, handed over to the Soviet authorities after the Second World War, and is now lost: Voss (1964), 24; Pée (1971), 132–3.

[27] Notably the *Schatzgräber* ('Treasure hunters') series, painted in the 1630s, 1650s, and 1660s, several of which are set in ruined ancient tombs: see esp. Weick (2009). Key examples include *Hebung eines Schatzes vor einem Grabmal* (*c*.1633, Rome), the pair *Schatzgräber* (*c*.1655, Friedrichshafen), set at a grave which may be Cicero's (so Weick (2009), 119), and *Schatzgräber vor einem antiken Grabmal* (*c*.1654/5,

**Figure 5.1.** Johann Heinrich Schönfeld, *Sarmaten am Grabe Ovids (Sarmatians at the Tomb of Ovid)*, (c.1653). Oil on canvas, 110 × 93.5 cm.
Royal Collection Trust/© Her Majesty Queen Elizabeth II 2017.

In Schönfeld's painting, Ovid's crumbling tomb is seen centre right, flanked by an urn (Ovid's *parva urna* from *Tristia* 3.3, perhaps) and a damaged fluted column. The partially visible inscription on the stone repeats that of *Tristia* 3.3.73–6:

Kremsmünster). See also, e.g., the tomb-themed *Philosoph am Grabe Alexander (Philsopher at the Tomb of Alexander the Great)*: an etching from the original survives from the 1650s in Augsburg, with further examples in Stuttgart and Vienna (Trepesch, Müller, and Sedelmeier (2010), 110).

HIC EGO QVI IACEO TENERORVM LVSOR AMORVM
INGENIO PERII NASO POETA MEO
AT TIBI QVI TRANSIS NE SIT GRAVE QVISQVIS AMASTI
DICERE NASONIS MOLLITER OSSA CVBENT
I WHO LIE HERE, NASO THE POET, WHO ONCE PLAYED WITH
TENDER LOVES, HAVE PERISHED AS A RESULT OF MY OWN
GENIUS. PASSER-BY, IF YOU HAVE LOVED, DO NOT DISDAIN TO
SAY: 'LET THE BONES OF NASO LIE SOFT.'

Around the tomb, describing a semicircle, we see five male figures.
The foremost, a rich red cloak on his back and a quiver of arrows
hanging from his right hip, gestures towards the tomb; another,
decked out in robe and beads, concentrates on the inscription and
attempts to write down what he sees as two others look intently over
his shoulder. A hunting dog appears in the bottom right-hand corner;
in the background stands a horse, and a further figure, turned to the
left, gazes out into the distance.

There were several early modern accounts of expeditions to hunt
down Ovid's missing tomb in the depths of the Black Sea region of
south-eastern Europe with which Schönfeld's painting may be in
dialogue. An account of 'Polish, Livonian and other Histories' by
Lorenz Müller, for example, published in 1585 and reprinted in a
number of editions, described a detour the author took while on
military campaign against the Tartars: a 'Volhynian nobleman' led
him—after six days on horseback across unchartered wastes—to the
long-lost 'tomb of Ovid', which was in such a state of disrepair that
they needed to use gunpowder to blacken up the letters of the stone
inscription.[28] Traces of accounts like these haunt Schönfeld's paint-
ing. The three central male figures are marked out by the half-shaved
haircut popular in the period among 'Sarmatist' Polish aristocracy,
who had adopted a set of habits and dress that linked them to an
invented tradition of 'Scythian' origin in the region. The horse in the
background suggests a long search for the tomb, and, in the version
purchased by Charles II of England in 1662, a figure standing to the
right of the horse (who may once have represented the European
thanatourist, perhaps) has mysteriously been erased from the canvas.
But unlike these accounts of the tomb which tended to feature a fake

---

[28] Müller (1595), 78–80; Trapp (1973), 52–3.

epitaph as standard (repeated in various descriptions of the tomb find),[29] Schönfeld goes back for his inscription to Ovid's auto-epitaph in *Tristia* 3.3, bringing literary reception into dialogue with the imagined materiality of the physical tomb. In the *Tristia*, Ovid had, unusually, embedded his auto-epitaph within a poetry collection, fusing the tomb with the text on the published page, and thereby ensuring that the biological body of the poet could be co-opted into the *diuturna monumenta* of his poetry. Schönfeld decouples the epitaph from the oeuvre, firmly situating the tomb in material reality and in the thematics of decay. The painting echoes Nicolas Poussin's popular *Et in Arcadia ego* (the second version from around 1638 also depicts four figures contemplating an inscription on a classical sepulchral monument), which may partly explain the appeal that led to the royal purchase in 1662 and triplicate copies. But Schönfeld's painting is significantly darker than Poussin's, transferring Ovid's epitaph— imagined in the Roman *suburbanum* and embedded comfortably in the eternally replicable book roll—to the material reality and geographical and cultural alterity of the decaying tombstone.

At the end of the *Metamorphoses*—a poem Schönfeld had used as a source for some of his earlier mythological paintings—Ovid, conflating his body with his text, famously expressed confidence that he would be read (*legar*) 'wherever Rome's power extends over the conquered world' (*quaque patet domitis Romana potentia terris, / ore legar populi, Metamorphoses* 15.877–8). But who, now, is in posthumous control of that reception? For Ovid, 'Tomis' was set in the borderlands of the Roman Empire. Schönfeld's updated 'Tomis', located in modern Constanţa and the broader region of Wallachia in which it was imagined, was now in the borderlands not of the Roman Empire but the Ottoman Empire. This was, for Schönfeld and his contemporaries, a place of cultural multiplicity, contestation, and ambiguity, where various cultures around eastern Europe interacted with Ottoman forces. Sarmatism, the national self-invention of the Polish *szlachta*, had partly absorbed Ottoman influence, which helps to explain the attire of Schönfeld's 'Sarmaten'.[30] But there is a much more complex dialogue about cultural ownership and contestation underwriting the painting and its early reception. Despite their distinctive hairstyles, to his contemporaries and near contemporaries,

[29] Trapp (1973), 50–1.      [30] Hosking and Schöpflin (1997), 144.

Schönfeld's oriental 'Sarmaten' could suggest themselves more imme-
diately as Ottomans: in the early inventories of the example pur-
chased by Charles II, for instance, the men around the tomb are
explicitly identified as Turks.[31] The Ottomans were to be defeated
at the very gates of Vienna in 1683 around the time of the painter's
death, and Schönfeld's 'Sarmaten', with their opulent robes and
feathers, could easily be read as culturally ambiguous figures repre-
sentative, in part, of the encroaching East. Ovid may have tried to
control the reception of his textual and physical bodies by implicating
the two with the continuity of the Roman Empire, but, in the longer
term, those certainties would be unravelled. As Schönfeld's painting
brings to the fore, the tomb is a site of reception that destabilizes the
certainties about posterity which a written text may try to prescribe.
Like the physical body of the poet, the question of who can have
cultural ownership over his written texts or the contexts in which they
can 'mean' or fail to mean is more plural and less certain than Ovid,
in his works, could ever predict or control. The issue is complicated
further by that fact that Ovid's written text itself is inscribed on the
stone memorial. Standing at the tomb, Schönfeld's Sarmatians (or are
they Turks?) are engaged in an act of reading that quite literally brings
together Ovid's literary and physical bodies, yet it is far from clear
whether they can understand what it is that they are reading. The
painting thus presents us with an unresolvable trade-off: the educated
viewer of the painting can understand the meaning and significance
of the words on the tomb, but is faced with the essential absence of the
poet's body, while the 'Sarmatians' are in the right place—they have
found Ovid's missing *corpus*—but they do not seem to understand
what it is that they have discovered.

## 'LA TOMBA DI OVIDIO'

Ovid's missing *corpus* was not always consigned to the dark border-
lands of the East. Other accounts of the poet's tomb fulfilled his

[31] The painting is described as 'A ruin, with five Turks taking a description of it'
according to the 1688 inventory (Bathoe (1758), 78). A later entry from 1705–10
keeps the Turks but substitutes the Roman poet with a Greek philosopher: 'a scene[?]
with five Turks taking the Inscription of Aristotle's Tomb': 'A List of her Majesties
Pictures in Kensington, Hampton Court and Windsor Castle', p. 15). I am very
grateful to Alex Buck at the Royal Collections Trust for this information.

original wish that his body be buried in Rome. According to one story, the poet's bones had been shipped back home where they were buried in secret.[32] Boccaccio knew an alternative version which told how the poet had made it back to the city alive, only to be suffocated on his return by the enthusiastic crowds who came to welcome him home.[33] These stories of homecoming found their archaeological corollary when, a few decades after Schönfeld's painting, in March 1674, a purported 'tomb of Ovid' was discovered during roadworks in Rome, cut into the rock face next to the ancient Via Flaminia. Much of the archaeological detail of the tomb has now disappeared, including many of the richly depicted frescoes the workmen had discovered.[34] But the crucial account by Giovanni Pietro Bellori, first published in 1680 as *Le pitture antiche del sepolcro de' Nasonii* and accompanied by detailed engravings of the original wall paintings by Pietro Santi Bartoli, survives in a number of editions.[35]

The Bellori-Bartoli account helps us to reconstruct the missing archaeological record, but it also documents the reception history of another kind of absence: that of Ovid's body. Inside the tomb, an inscription declared that 'Q. Nasonius Ambrosius' had built the structure and dedicated it to himself and to his household:[36]

> D M
> Q. NASONIVS AMBROSI
> VS. SIBI ET SVIS FECIT LI
> BERTIS. LIBERTABVSQVE
> [ET N]ASONIAE VRBICE
> [CONI]VIGI SVAE. ET COL
> [LI]BERTIS SVIS. ET
> POSTERISQVE. EOR

---

[32] Ghisalberti (1946) 24; 58.

[33] Ghisalberti (1946), 35; Trapp (1973), 44–5. For Ovid's Roman tomb, cf. Smiles in this collection (pp. 314–16) for J. M. W. Turner's *Ancient Italy—Ovid Banished from Rome*, in which the poet's sarcophagus is visible in the foreground of the painting at the very scene of his exile.

[34] Three panels were removed early on by, Don Gaspare Altieri, who had been adopted by Pope Clement X to be installed in his own villa: Trapp (1973), 67–8; Joyce (2002), 182. The British Museum holds six of the murals, including an illustration of the *Rape of Persephone*, probably removed from the tomb around the same time: Trapp (1973), 68.

[35] For the volume, see Trapp (1973), 62–7; Leach (2001); Joyce (2002), 182–6; Thomas (2003). On Bellori, see esp. Bell and Willette (2002); on Bartoli as preserver of antiquity, see Thomas (2003), 5–6.

[36] *CIL* VI 3 22882.

TO THE GODS OF THE DEAD, QUINTUS NASONIUS AMBROSIUS
CONSTRUCTED THIS FOR HIMSELF AND HIS FAMILY AND HIS
FREEDMEN AND WOMEN AND FOR HIS WIFE NASONIA URBICA
AND HER FREEDMEN AND WOMEN AND THEIR DESCENDANTS.

The tomb is now seen as having no connection to the poet Ovid and
is usually dated to the Antonine period or the early to mid third
century CE.[37] Bellori, too, acknowledged that there was no concrete
evidence that P. Ovidius Naso was ever buried here: he admitted that
the poet probably died far away in Tomis.[38] But for Bellori, this was,
nevertheless, the 'tomb of Ovid'. Getting around the nomen/cogno-
men problem with some deft argumentation, he believed that, in
this tomb, the Nasonii were honouring their most important liter-
ary son generations after his death.[39] The tomb, in other words, was
a cenotaph, with Ovid's missing *corpus* as the absent presence at
its heart.

Dismissing criticism from his sceptical rivals (whom he called
'Aristarchi moderni'), Bellori used Ovid's text to fill in the absence
of his body.[40] He started with the location, reading the tomb as a
posthumous realization of the burial instructions Ovid had embedded
in his texts and quoting Ovid's description of his Roman garden in
*Ex Ponto* 1.8.43–6 in order to localize the tomb in or near Ovid's villa
at the fork of the Via Flaminia and the Via Clodia in the Roman
*suburbanum* where the poet said he wanted to be buried in *Tristia* 3.3.[41]
Inside the tomb, the identification with Ovid fundamentally affected
the way Bellori read the iconography. Although (as the 'Aristrarchi
moderni' complained), many of the images cannot be connected to
Ovid, some of the mythological images on the walls can be read as clear
vignettes from Ovid's works, most notably the abduction of Proserpina

---

[37] For the current scholarly consensus on the tomb, see esp. Messineo (2000);
Feraudi-Gruénais (2001), 66–73 (with extensive bibliography); Borg (2013), 59–65.
The tomb is traditionally dated to the Antonine period; for the later date (on the basis
of decorative style and lack of cremations), see Feraudi-Gruénais (2001), 73; Borg
(2013), 62.

[38] Bellori (1680), 12–13.

[39] Bellori argues that the family nomen had been changed by a later descendant in
honour of the famous Ovid (whose cognomen was Naso), citing an example from
Macrobius to back up his conclusion: (1680), 13–14.

[40] Bellori (1680), 14; for details of the detractors, see Trapp (1973), 65–7.

[41] Bellori (1680), 13–14, citing two other scholars (Cluverius and an enigmatic
'Bossius').

(now in the British Museum) narrated in *Metamorphoses* 5,[42] and
Europa carried off by Zeus in the guise of a bull as her female com-
panions look on, described in *Metamorphoses* 2 and *Fasti* 5, which
Bellori quotes directly to explain the image.[43]

In some ways, therefore, the tomb, in Bellori's hands, 'extends' the
author in relatively conventional ways through a posthumous reread-
ing of his works, reversing the dynamic of Ovid's original fusion of
his biological body into his text by co-opting, instead, the text into
the physical fabric of the tomb. Bellori also embeds the author into the
newly discovered material culture in more fundamental ways. His
overall view of the iconography is that the whole represents the trans-
lation of the soul to Elysium, where (as Virgil described in *Aeneid* 6)
poets, in particular, live on after death. The gist of Bellori's interpret-
ation of afterlife-themed iconography is still seen as compelling by
some,[44] but not the way in which he linked it to Ovid, or read the
crucial wall painting in the principal niche (Figure 5.2).[45]

The image depicts (from right to left) a veiled woman being led by
Mercury towards two figures crowned in laurel, a standing man with
left hand raised beside a seated woman, who is resting one hand on a
cithara and holding a long tibia in the other. To most modern
scholars, the scene represents the return of Eurydice led by Mercury
to Orpheus and his seated mother, the Muse Calliope, or maybe a
*pepaideumenos* of some kind, perhaps even a poet.[46] For Bellori,
however, it was very specifically the poet Ovid himself, with his
favourite Muse Erato by his side, being led by Mercury to the Elysium
fields. Again, Bellori uses Ovid's textual *corpus* to make up for the
missing body: he quotes the invocation to Erato in *Ars amatoria*
2.15–16, and identifies the woman on the right via Ovid's own
'autobiographical' clues as 'Perilla', the enigmatic figure known only
from *Tristia* 3.7 as the poet's protégée in the art of poetry.[47]

---

[42] Bellori (1680), 44–5 on plate 12 chooses to quote Claudian rather than
Ovid here.

[43] Bellori (1680), 48 on plate 17, quoting Ovid, *Fasti* 5.605–10. Cf. Ovid, *Meta-
morphoses* 2.836–75.

[44] See, e.g., Borg (2013), 246.        [45] Bellori (1680), 11–16 on plate 5.

[46] For the pervasive modern interpretation, see Feraudi-Gruénais (2001), 68 with
further references. Borg (2013), 244, although unpersuaded by the identification with
Ovid, suggests the wreathed male figure may depict 'a *pepaideumenos*, perhaps a poet',
and that the scene 'might be modelled on ideas of Elysium as the abode of the best poets'.

[47] *nata* (3.7.18). For Perilla, see Ingleheart (2012).

**Figure 5.2.** Pietro Santi Bartoli, engraving from the principal niche of the 'tomba di Ovidio', in Giovanni Pietro Bellori and Pietro Santo Bartoli, *Le pitture antiche del sepolcro de' Nasonii nella via Flaminia* (Rome, 1680), Tavola V.

As papal antiquarian and a notable biographer, Bellori was able to claim a major archaeological discovery that also allowed him to write the final chapter of Ovid's biography, a chapter Ovid himself could never have had the foresight to compose.[48] The tomb could now be seen as 'a Museum and Parnassus of the Shades' ('Museo, e Parnasso dell'Ombre'), in which the dead poet could have a tangible afterlife: 'instead of dark Cypresses', Bellori says, 'immortal laurels spring; instead of sounds of lamentation, harmonious notes resound'.[49]

---

[48] Bellori was particularly celebrated for his *Lives of the Modern Artists* (*Vite de' pittori, scultori et architetti moderni*), published in 1672, hailed as a seventeenth-century equivalent to Vasari: Joyce (2002), 186. Some of the broader scholarly techniques used in the earlier work are repeated in *Le pitture*: Leach (2001), 74; Joyce (2002); Thomas (2003).

[49] Bellori (1680), 7: 'nella vaghezza delle Pitture . . . & nella memoria di colui & alle Muse, che fu tanto grato ad Apolline' . . . 'in vece di atri Cipressi, spunta Lauri immortali, e risuona canore note più tosto che lamentevoli accenti.' The cypress is traditionally a tree of death. A laurel (the poet's tree) famously grew at Virgil's tomb.

Ovid imagined his afterlife at the end of the *Metamorphoses*—typically conflating the physical with the verbal—as a fundamentally textual existence (*ore legar populi*, 'I will be read on the lips of the people', 15.878). Bellori's version of the tomb reverses the balance of that existence from textual to material: it is in the imagined latent presence of the body of the author in the archaeological record, rather than in the exclusively textual record of the page or on people's mouths, that the poet now 'lives'—an afterlife emphatically secured by the archaeologist rather than the 'original' deceased author. Despite Ovid's attempt to inscribe the body into the text, the poet's reception thus took on a new material 'life', long after the wall paintings themselves had disappeared.[50] For the many thanatourists who would come to visit the tomb, or imagine it in the comfort of their own homes on the strength of Bellori's book and Bartoli's engravings—including Laurence Sterne who appears to have had several of Bartoli's prints of 'poor Ovid's tomb' decorating his study—the poet's afterlife found material form in the landscape of Rome.[51]

## THE SEARCH CONTINUES

Ovid may have attempted to effect 'the fusion of textual and biological bodies'[52] in order to exert complete posthumous control over his afterlife but, in the end, there is a disjunction between the textual and the physical that has been impossible to ignore. Spanning different times and media, the examples discussed here highlight a parallel story of Ovidian reception, in which the idea of the material 'fact' of the poet's biological *corpus* intervenes in the traditional dynamics of reception. There is, then, another story to tell about the reception of Ovid, one in which the body of the poet is decoupled from the body of the work even as it engages in creative dialogue with it. Ovid could never quite inscribe his physical *corpus* into his textual *corpus*: and

[50] Thomas (2003), 2–3 quotes a Grand Tour guidebook from 1722 recommending the tomb on the strength of the fame of the book's engravings, even though the wall paintings themselves had been 'utterly lost': 'that noble treasury of antique painting . . . so well known by the prints of Peter Sancta Bartoli'.
[51] For Sterne, see Trapp (1973), esp. 70. Watercolours of the prints could be ordered from Bartoli and his son, and were popular with English travellers in particular: Trapp (1973), 67.
[52] Hardie (2002), 37.

**Figure 5.3.** Piața Ovidiu (Ovid Square), Constanța, Romania, with Ettore Ferrari's statue of the poet (1887).
© iStock: 496476311.

it is around that fundamental absence that an alternative reception history has been staged.

Like the texts through which Ovid declared that he would 'live', the reception history of Ovid's tomb has continued well beyond *De vetula*'s conceit of the book in the tomb or the tomb 'read' from the book in Bellori and Bartoli. Modern 'Tomis', Constanța in Romania, is today home to a bronze statue of the poet by Ettore Ferrari (Figure 5.3). Erected in 1887 when Romanian nation-building was at its height, the statue (like Schönfeld's painting) is accompanied by Ovid's auto-epitaph from *Tristia* 3.3, strongly implying that this monument in modern Tomis is meant to be a substitute for the poet's tomb (*HIC EGO QVI IACEO, Tristia* 3.3.73).[53] Ovid left his

---

[53] The implication is even more obvious if we consider that an exact copy of the statue, minus the epitaph, is located in Ovid's birthplace, modern Sulmona.

mark on the memory cultures of east-central Europe, not only in tombs such as those discovered by Schönfeld's Sarmaten, but lakes, towers, and marshes claimed and contested for centuries as Ovidian sites by the inhabitants.[54] The idea that Romania, in particular, was Ovid's true burial place has been hard to shake off. In 1931—as the *Daily Telegraph* reported—a local archaeologist claimed to have discovered Ovid's skull.[55] The archaeological search has since been abandoned,[56] and yet, recently, the National Bank of Romania issued a set of coins depicting the statue minted in 2008 in commemoration of the bimillennium of Ovid's exile to the region.[57] If we wish, we can still hold in our hands an image of Ovid issuing from his purported 'grave'.[58]

[54] Trapp (1973), 56.
[55] *Daily Telegraph*, 29 July 1931; the sarcophagus in which it was found later proved to be Hellenistic: Claassen (2008), 230.
[56] Claassen (2008), 232.
[57] The coin was minted in copper (1 Lei), silver (5 Lei), and gold (100 Lei): <http://www.bnro.ro/EmisiuniDetails.aspx?idd=445&WebPageId=1164>.
[58] I am very grateful to Alex Buck, James Koranyi, and audiences at Chicago, Liverpool, and St Andrews, where earlier versions of this chapter were presented.

# II

# The Poet as Character

# 6

# Earth, Nature, and the Cult of the Tomb

## The Posthumous Reception of Aeschylus *heros*

### Emmanuela Bakola

One of the key themes in this volume is the close association of poets with the landscapes which posthumously house (or are imagined to house) their bodies. In fictional funerary epigrams, travelling accounts, and stories, especially from the post-classical period, images of nature are used to capture how the poets are perceived by posterity. Nature is sometimes more important than man-made commemorative structures.[1] Perhaps the most telling example, discussed by Graziosi in this volume, is that of Orpheus. From torrential streams to rivers flowing underground, from caves emanating oracular knowledge to nightingale song, many and varied natural elements are imagined as operating at the poet's various imaginary resting places and, even more importantly, echoing the perceived character of the Orphic oeuvre.[2] Although Orpheus might be considered an exceptional case, since his poetry had the reputation of breathing life into nature as early as the classical period,[3] other sources suggest that he might not be so special in his posthumous connection to nature and landscape. As Montiglio observes, the vituperative character of Hipponax' iambic poems is captured in the poetic rendition of the vegetable growth at his burial

---

[1] See especially Platt, Chapter 1; Graziosi, Chapter 8; Moniglio, Chapter 10; and Hanink, Chapter 11 in this volume.

[2] *AP* 7.9 = n. 2.1379–86 G-P; Paus. 9.30.6–12; Diog. Laert. 1.5; Phanocles fr.1; Hygin. *Poet. astr.* 2.7. See Graziosi in this volume, pp. 172–94.

[3] For example, Simon. fr.567 *PMG*, Aesch. *Ag.* 1629–32, Eur. *IA* 1211–15, Eur. *Bacch.* 560–4.

site, which is capable of growing only stinging thorns and acerbic fruit to match the character of his poetry.[4] In other funerary epigrams of the *Palatine Anthology*, the perceived 'sweetness' of Sophocles' lyrics is captured by the image of live bees making honey and adorning his tomb,[5] and Anacreon's association with Dionysiac inspiration is reflected in the image of a vine that moistens the ground and nurtures the buried poet and his poems.[6]

The material connection of poetic personalities, styles, and oeuvres with elements of nature and landscape through the poeticization of burials is intriguing, and one rightly wonders about its rationale and origins. Unfortunately, since we have only a small fraction of these poets' works and of the responses by later authors and audiences, we can make little detailed observation. Nevertheless, recent advances in the study of the poets' biographical traditions, especially as concerns the value of comedy as a source,[7] give us reasonable confidence that as a general tendency, this kind of reception echoes elements from the poets' own oeuvres, their poetic personas, or early responses to their work. In the present volume, for example, Montiglio astutely proposes that the lush vegetation which is envisaged to adorn poets' tombs in the *Palatine Anthology* echoes their privileged poetic connection with Dionysus, which often originates in their oeuvres and is attested in other sources including Old Comedy.[8]

Another route which may shed light on the poets' posthumous association with landscape is the proliferation of poets' hero cults in the post-classical period. Tomb cults of poets and the narratives that surrounded them flourished especially from the Hellenistic period onwards.[9] As Hanink observes, the places where the poets are buried

---

[4] *AP* 7.536 (Alcaeus of Messene 13 G-P). See Montiglio in this volume, pp. 226–7.

[5] *AP* 7.36 (Erycias). See Platt, pp. 46–7 in this volume and Montiglio pp. 229–30.

[6] *AP* 7.24 ('Simonides' 3 G-P). See Montiglio pp. 227–8.

[7] Lefkowitz' thesis (1981, 2nd edn 2012) about the fictionality of ancient biographies as mere readings of the poets' works has been nuanced further, and the study of comedy has been instrumental to this: see, for example, Biles (2002); Bakola (2008); Rawles (forthcoming), Introduction and chs 4 and 5. While the biographical anecdotes are not necessarily 'historical' in a strict sense, many are not arbitrary and, provided the right methodology is used, they can offer valuable glimpses into early reception and literary criticism.

[8] For Dionysus and poetic inspiration, and comedy's use of the idea, see pp. 127–9 below. See also Montiglio p. 233.

[9] See Kimmel-Clauzet (2013).

create a root system that nourishes the Greek landscape.[10] These observations may provide some explanation for the proliferation of portrayals of poets' tombs through nature imagery in the aforementioned post-classical sources. One purpose of this chapter is to explore the religious dimension of the tombs of the poets: in this respect, it is important to note that hero cults were saliently connected with the preservation and promotion of fertility, prosperity, and well-being—or their opposites, if the apportioned honours failed to be observed.[11] The poet becomes a 'character' in posthumous accounts of his life; at the same time, his position after burial enlivens his connection to the earth: it is this relationship between biographical reception and religious cult that this chapter seeks to illuminate.

An example of how oeuvre, poetic self-presentation, and hero cult may together contribute to a poet's posthumous connection with natural elements is provided by the Mnesiepes Inscription, an important source for the cult of the iambic poet Archilochus.[12] According to this inscription, after Archilochus' death in Paros, the fertility of the land and its people was blighted. This was remedied only after the Parians instituted a hero cult for the poet, building the Asclepieion and worshipping him alongside other divinities including Dionysus. This tradition has rightly been connected to the poetic appropriation of Dionysus and natural powers as sources of inspiration in Archilochus' own work, famously suggested by fr.120W:

ὡς Διωνύσου ἄνακτος καλὸν ἐξάρξαι μέλος
οἶδα διθύραμβον οἴνῳ συγκεραυνωθεὶς φρένας.

I know how to initiate a fine song for Lord Dionysus,
a dithyramb, after my mind is thunderstruck with wine.[13]

In this chapter, I turn to a different poet who, as I try to demonstrate, was also associated posthumously with the materiality of nature: Aeschylus. I argue that fifth-century audiences were familiar with the idea that Aeschylus was worshipped as a hero profoundly connected to the landscape that held his remains. I also suggest that this connection was underpinned by elements which ultimately derive

---

[10] See below, p. 250.     [11] See below, pp. 136–8.
[12] On the cult of Archilochus on Paros and its date in the sixth century, see Clay (2004), 9–39, including 10–24 on the Mnesiepes inscription, which dates from the third century BCE. Cf. Nagy (1989), 64–5. For a critique of Clay, see MacPhail (2005).
[13] See Clay (2004), 9–39. See also below, pp. 131–2.

from Aeschylus' own works. Key to my argument about Aeschylus' hero cult is one of the most interesting but least explored testimonies about the poet's afterlife and reception in antiquity, namely the *Life of Aeschylus* §10–11. This testimony suggests that, after Aeschylus' death, his tomb in Gela, Sicily, became the site of formal cult, attracting regular pilgrimages by members of the tragic profession:

καὶ σφόδρα τῷ τε τυράννῳ Ἱέρωνι καὶ τοῖς Γελῴοις τιμηθεὶς ἐπιζήσας τρίτον ἔτος γηραιὸς ἐτελεύτα [ ... ] ἀποθανόντα δὲ Γελῷοι πολυτελῶς ἐν τοῖς δημοσίοις μνήμασι θάψαντες ἐτίμησαν μεγαλοπρεπῶς, ἐπιγράψαντες οὕτω·

> Αἰσχύλον Εὐφορίωνος Ἀθηναῖον τόδε κεύθει
> μνῆμα καταφθίμενον πυροφόροιο Γέλας·
> ἀλκὴν δ᾽ εὐδόκιμον Μαραθώνιον ἄλσος ἂν εἴποι
> καὶ βαθυχαιτήεις Μῆδος ἐπιστάμενος.

εἰς τὸ μνῆμα δὲ φοιτῶντες ὅσοις ἐν τραγῳδίαις ἦν ὁ βίος ἐνήγιζόν τε καὶ τὰ δράματα ὑπεκρίνοντο.

Having been greatly honoured by the tyrant Hieron and the citizens of Gela, he lived a further two years and died an old man [ ... ] After his death, the citizens of Gela gave him a lavish public burial and honoured him magnificently by writing the following epitaph:

> This memorial holds Aeschylus the Athenian, son of Euphorion,
>   who died in grain-bearing Gela.
> The grove of Marathon could speak of his famous courage
>   and the Mede with thick long hair who knows of it.

And whoever was professionally involved in tragedy, when they visited his memorial, would offer sacrifices and perform his plays.[14]

I explore this testimony in the light of Aristophanes' *Frogs,* one of the earliest forms of Aeschylean reception, which, I argue, lends substantial value to it. My method is based on a re-examination of the Aristophanic play's spatial semantics, especially concerning the portrayal of 'Aeschylus' as a chthonic force and his 'resurrection' in the play's finale. I argue that *Frogs* shows an awareness that the poet was associated with fertility in contemporaneous literary-critical discourses. I then demonstrate that this posthumous association, which is found both in the *Frogs* and in the *Life of Aeschylus,* is especially connected with the land that was imagined as holding his

---

[14] Radt, *TGrF* III, test. 1, 10–11. For recent analyses, see Wilson (2007), 356–71; Kowalzig (2008) 130; Poli-Palladini (2013), 285–96. See also below, n. 48.

bones. In the final part of this chapter, I explore possible connections between theatre and earth cults, and reflect on how Aeschylus' hero cult may fit into this scheme.


## ARISTOPHANES' *FROGS:* ATHENS' CULTURAL STERILITY, 'AESCHYLUS', AND HIS *ANODOS* FROM THE DEPTHS OF THE EARTH

*Frogs* is one of the most valuable sources for the ancient reception of Aeschylus' tragedy. Although excellent works have been published on the subject,[15] little attention has been paid to how the play's performative dimensions might augment our understanding of the Aristophanic 'Aeschylus'. *Frogs* starts with the description of death and sterility on earth: all the good poets have died and among those who have remained, no one is sufficiently sexually potent to inseminate Lady Tragedy and produce noble theatrical offspring. The emphasis on sterility and the need for potency[16] is illustrated especially clearly in this key (and famous) speech by:

> Δι.: ἐπιφυλλίδες ταῦτ' ἐστὶ καὶ στωμύλματα,
> χελιδόνων μουσεῖα, λωβηταὶ τέχνης,
> ἃ φροῦδα θᾶττον, ἢν μόνον χορὸν λάβῃ,
> ἅπαξ προσουρήσαντα τῇ τραγῳδίᾳ.
> γόνιμον δὲ ποιητὴν ἂν οὐχ εὕροις ἔτι
> ζητῶν ἄν, ὅστις ῥῆμα γενναῖον λάκοι.
> Ἡρ.: πῶς γόνιμον;

Dionysus: Those are cast-offs and empty chatter, choirs of swallows, wreckers of their art, who maybe get a chorus and are soon forgotten, after they piss just once inside Lady Tragedy. But if you look for a potent poet, one who could utter a lordly phrase, you won't find any left.

Heracles: What do you mean 'potent'?[17]

(*Frogs* 92–8)

---

[15] For the most recent treatments, see Griffith (2013), 100–49 and Hunter (2009), 1–52. A bibliographical list on the Aristophanic 'Aeschylus' of *Frogs* can be found in Scharffenberger (2007), 231.

[16] For an analysis of the meaning of *gonimos* ('potent') at *Ran.* 92–8, see Sfyroeras (2008), 307–9.

[17] Aristophanes' texts and translations follow Henderson.

Dionysus, god of the theatre and of the life-giving forces of nature, wants to address this cultural sterility. He sets off on a journey to the underworld aiming to restore potency to Athens, connecting it, for now, mistakenly with Euripides. Dionysus' *katabasis*, 'his descent into the underworld', alludes heavily to *katabasis* narratives like those of Orpheus, Heracles, Theseus, and Dionysus himself,[18] and concludes with the antidote for sterility and death: namely a resurrection, an *anodos*, celebrated with a torch-lit procession. The following verses, the very last of the play, are pronounced by Pluto and the chorus as Aeschylus is accompanied to the world above:

> Πλ.: φαίνετε τοίνυν ὑμεῖς τούτῳ
> λαμπάδας ἱεράς, χἄμα προπέμπετε
> τοῖσιν τούτου τοῦτον μέλεσιν
> καὶ μολπαῖσιν κελαδοῦντες.
> Χο.: πρῶτα μὲν εὐοδίαν ἀγαθὴν ἀπιόντι ποιητῇ
> ἐς φάος ὀρνυμένῳ δότε δαίμονες οἱ κατὰ γαίας,
> τῇ δὲ πόλει μεγάλων ἀγαθῶν ἀγαθὰς ἐπινοίας.
> πάγχυ γὰρ ἐκ μεγάλων ἀχέων παυσαίμεθ᾽ ἂν οὕτως
> ἀργαλέων τ᾽ ἐν ὅπλοις ξυνόδων. Κλεοφῶν δὲ μαχέσθω
> κἄλλος ὁ βουλόμενος τούτων πατρίοις ἐν ἀρούραις.

Pluto: Now display your sacred torches in this man's honour and escort him forth, hymning his praises with his own songs and melodies.

Chorus: First, you gods below earth, grant to the departing poet a fine journey as he ascends to the sunlight, and to the city grant fine ideas that will bring fine blessings. For, that way, we may have an end of great griefs and painful encounters in arms. Let Cleophon do the fighting, and any of those others who wants to fight in his native soil!

(*Frogs* 1524–33)

The theme of 'space above, space below' and the journey between the two (*katabasis, anodos*) are clearly central to the play. If we observe this spatial scheme and the ideas it embodies, as well as the language and imagery of these passages (especially ascending into light, 1529; being accompanied by torches, 1524; bringing along blessings from below, 1530; putting an end to suffering and stopping wars, 1533),

---

[18] For Dionysus' *katabasis* in the *Frogs* and its rich ritual and mythic background, see Bowie (1993), 228–38; Lada-Richards (1999), 53–5, 78–86; Griffith (2013), 174–7, 191–8. For heroic *katabaseis*, see most recently, Felton (2007), 94–6. For Dionysus' *katabaseis* and returns and their role in his myth and cult, see Bowie (1993), 145–7; Detienne (1986).

we cannot but agree with Lada-Richards, who in her book on the rite-of-passage structure of the *Frogs* argues that Aeschylus' return to Athens is presented as an *anodos*, and, specifically, like the (archetypal) *anodos* of Persephone, whose ascent from the world of the dead after her abduction by Hades restores fertility and life to a blighted land.[19]

The concept of *anodos* is known to us mostly from the *Homeric Hymn to Demeter* and from the numerous *anodoi* of mystic rituals and vase paintings. To the Greeks (whether the term *anodos* was used or not),[20] the very concept of an upwards movement would have also been known from manifold other narratives and cult.[21] In general, *anodoi* of chthonic powers are movements from the depths of the earth which symbolically capture the processes of generation, growth, and restoration of life. Beyond Persephone/Kore, other divinities who are most often shown as enacting this movement include Pandora, Gaia, and Semele; the pattern is extended, as far as we can see, from drama especially to personified abstractions, like Peace, and resurrected heroines, like Alcestis.[22] As Bérard has shown, movement through space is the most important element in this narrative pattern: just as death and the cessation of fertility is represented through a downwards motion, so its regeneration is represented through an upwards motion.[23]

Despite the clarity of the spatial pattern and the accompanying effect of the restoration of fertility and life in the *Frogs*, the term *anodos* and especially its association with the processes of the earth are not used in scholarship (outside Lada-Richards) to describe Aeschylus' resurrection. Nor has there been an exploration of what this would mean for the perception of Aeschylus in antiquity. It is possible that the reluctance to use this term is due to the fact that *anodoi* are more commonly understood in their relation to gender

---

[19] Lada-Richards (1999), 106–7.

[20] For the term, see Bérard (1974), 22–4. Regardless of the term used, the pattern is common and recognizable.

[21] For *anodoi* and their defining characteristics, especially in drama, see Olson (1998), xxxv–xxxvii and Lada-Richards (1999), 106–14. For *anodoi*, space, and movement in iconography, see Bérard (1974), *passim*. More generally on the topic, see also Ferrari (2004); Sfameni Gasparro (2000); Simon (1989); Sutton (1975). For the numerous busts of Persephone and Demeter, see Hinz (1998); Bell (1981), 30.

[22] For the so-called *anodos* dramas, see Foley (1992).

[23] See Bérard (1974), 21–30 for the structuralist methodology concerning movement. See also Lada-Richards (1999), 106–7.

than to space. There is a tendency to assume that *anodoi* concern
female deities or heroines, especially in drama.[24] As a result, the
regeneration pattern of the *Frogs* is usually understood in terms of
either an extended literary metaphor, or in connection with the rite
of passage undergone by the initiand Dionysus and/or the initiand
Aeschylus (at least, that is, by those who accept the existence of
this pattern).[25]

Nevertheless, as I suggested earlier, it is the spatial movement that
captures the essence of *anodoi*, not gender.[26] Chthonic movements
were understood to be enacted by all the earth's powers, including
*male* powers. In iconography and literary texts, we can see male
characters enacting upwards movements from the depths of the
earth and thereby capturing the processes of (re)generation and
growth: most often Dionysus and Erichthonius, but also cult heroes.[27]
However, before turning to what Aeschylus' resurrection might mean
if it is described as *anodos*, I need to reflect further upon the essence
of this movement. In particular, I need to clarify the special *identity* of
the powers that are portrayed as emerging from the depths of the

---

[24] Most publications do not exclude the possibility of male *anodos*. However, the
pattern is often thought to concern female powers alone, for several reasons: the
archetypal *anodos* is that of Persephone; the *anodos* is connected to the restoration of
fertility; and the iconographical evidence concerns a disproportionate number of
females: see Bérard (1974), 25; Foley (1992), 314 n. 43; Simon (1989); Olson (1998),
xxxvii; Ferrari (2004). For examples of male *anodos*, see below, n. 27.

[25] Bowie (1993), 228–38; Lada-Richards (1999), *passim*; for a critique, see Griffith
(2013), 190–1.

[26] *Anodoi* as ascents from the earth can also be represented through *horizontal*
movements and journeys, see Bérard (1974), 25–6, 28.

[27] For Dionysus' *anodoi* in iconography, see Bérard (1974), 44, pl. 3–5; see also
Taplin (2013) on the 'Cleveland Dionysus' (Cleveland Museum of Art 1989.73). For
Erichthonios (where the upwards movement captures Athenian autochthony through
the process of birth and generation), see Bérard (1974), 34–8 and Shapiro (1998).
Amphiaraos' epiphany in Carcinus' homonymous play is presented like an *anodos*;
see Aristotle *Poet.* 1455a and cf. Green (1990); contra Davidson (2003). Pausanias
1.15.3 notes that on the 'Battle of Marathon' painting in the *Painted Stoa*, the hero
Theseus was represented as if rising out of the earth (Θησεὺς ἀνιόντι ἐκ γῆς εἰκασμένος;
cf. Plu. *Per.* 35). On the famous 'Basel Dancers' vase (Basel, Antikenmuseum BS 415),
see Schmidt (1967), 70–8: the *eidolon* of a male figure is shown rising from his tomb
(note the bust convention, which shows upwards movement, and the smaller size of
the *eidolon*). The *eidolon* of an armed hero is also shown rising from his tomb on a
fifth-century Attic *askos* lid (Boston, 13.169). Although these figures have not been
considered in relation to the *anodos* pattern outlined here, the *anodos* of the cult hero
Darius in Aeschylus' *Persians* 681–93 (cf. Henrichs (1993), 166; Bakola (2014), 16–25)
shows that *anodoi* can also take place from tombs while evoking the processes of
generation and growth.

earth. Not all characters, of course, can embody this movement. In the case of Aristophanes' 'Aeschylus', however, there is something that makes him particularly suited for such a movement, certainly more so than his—also dead—opponent 'Euripides': this is the fact that for fifth-century audiences, 'Aeschylus' was associated with the concept of fertility.

## 'AESCHYLUS', NATURE, AND EARTH: THE POET AS 'POWER BELOW'

It has long been shown that Old Comedy, primarily *Frogs* but also other plays, depicts Aeschylean poetry not just as old, but also as Dionysiac and natural.[28] In *Frogs* particularly, Aeschylus' poetry is described in terms of a 'natural' force flowing forth with a raw, overwhelming power. Especially telling are lines 816–17, 852–3, 859, 886–7, 1005, and 1257–61 of *Frogs*, where the poet is imagined as a gushing stream of water, a storm of hail, a $Βακχεῖος\ ἄναξ$, 'a lord possessed and inspired by Bacchus', and as possessed by inspirational mania. Furthermore, Aeschylean inspiration resembles a mystic, religious process, hence the poet's evocation of Demeter's mysteries. Other sources, which also reflect an influence from comedy, present 'Aeschylus' as losing himself in a trance and composing in a state of intoxication.[29] This nexus of ideas, including the flowing, the natural, the liquid, the intoxicated, the powerfully raw, was associated generally with the concept of the Dionysiac,[30] and was linked not just with 'Aeschylus' but also with 'Cratinus'. 'Cratinus' aligned his poetry not just with that of the great tragic poet, but also with that of 'Archilochus'. It was Archilochus, in fact, who, in the surviving sources, first likened the effect of intoxication that inspires the most beautiful dithyramb to a force of nature with strong Dionysiac associations, namely that of a

---

[28] See Lada-Richards (1999), 235–47, 277–8; Bakola (2008), 16–20 and (2010), 24–9 on Cratinus fr.342; Griffith (2013), 18–19 and 123.

[29] Ath. I 22ab; cf. Ath. 10.428f–9a, Plu. fr.130, Plu. *Quest. Conv.* 1.5.1, 622E and 7.10.2.715D, Lucian *Dem. enc.* 15, Eust. *Od.* 1598.58.

[30] For the association of Dionysus with 'liquid power' in general, as well as, more widely, with nature and its regeneration, see Daraki (1985), 34–58; Otto (1965), 152–70.

thunderbolt (fr.120W, above).[31] On the opposite side of the popular imagination, Euripidean poetry (and the poetry of the new poets more generally) was depicted as coming not from nature, but from learning, meticulous study and analysis of sources, technical innovation, experimentation, and artistic virtuosity, something which, in *Frogs*, is captured by the use of scientific instruments and tools.[32] To put these observations in a wider context, the Aristophanic construction of the Aeschylean poetic style builds upon the ubiquitous polarity of Greek thought 'nature-culture'.

If the construction of 'Aeschylus' as 'Dionysiac' and as an embodiment of nature's flowing and gushing energies is taken into account, we can make better sense of the outcome of the play and the *anodos* language that describes the playwright's resurrection. Due to his connection with the underworld and his ability to move from one world to another, Dionysus is probably the deity most closely associated with the spatial movement of *anodos*, both in narrative accounts and in iconography.[33] However, this is not to suggest that 'Aeschylus' is portrayed as an alter ego of Dionysus. The Dionysiac is part of a much richer nexus of representation. 'Aeschylus', as I argue, is represented as a chthonic power in both a more wide-ranging and a more specific way.

One key indication is given by the way Dionysus addresses 'Aeschylus' just before he produces his judgement. He tells him:

> . . . ἀλλ' ἐνθένδ' ἀνίει τἀγαθά
>
> You send up your blessings from here
>
> (*Frogs* 1462)

---

[31] For the links between 'Archilochus', 'Aeschylus', and 'Cratinus', see Bakola (2010), 16–80 and *passim*. For the Dionysiac associations of the thunderbolt, see Mendelsohn (1992), 114–24.

[32] See especially the *Frogs* prelude to the *agōn* (814–29; analysed below) and 796–803; in general, on 'Euripides" association with technical ability, craft, and technology as opposed to 'Aeschylus" connection with nature, natural inspiration, and Dionysus, see Bakola (2008), 8–20. The imagery of tools is used in *Thesmophoriazousae* 53–7 (for Agathon) and *Clouds* 184–214 (for the 'new', sophistic learning, which was popularly associated with 'Euripides'). This contrast has its origins in the long-standing polarity 'poetry as divine inspiration' and 'poetry as artefact', attested at least as early as Alcaeus fr.204.6, Alcman 39 *PMG*, Solon fr.1.2, and especially Pindar *O.* 2.86–8.

[33] See above, n. 27. Structuralist studies of Dionysus are particularly thorough on this, especially Bérard (1974), 44; Segal (1982), 48–50; and Daraki (1985), 118–57.

As the use of the verb ἀνίει ('send forth', as from the depths of the earth) suggests,[34] 'Aeschylus' is addressed as a power capable of administering blessings from the place where he lies dead. The same chthonic energy of bringing good things up is evoked, as we saw, at the very end of the play, but in a different manifestation: there, the entire upwards movement of 'Aeschylus' is thought to bring blessings to the *polis*.

However, there is more to the portrayal of 'Aeschylus' as a 'power below'. Rich evidence is provided by the choral ode that closes the journey, in the *Frogs*, and opens the *agōn* by introducing the two poets:

> ἦ που δεινὸν ἐριβρεμέτας χόλον ἔνδοθεν ἕξει,
> ἡνίκ᾽ ἂν ὀξύλαλον παρίδῃ θήγοντος ὀδόντα
> ἀντιτέχνου· τότε δὴ μανίας ὑπὸ δεινῆς
> ὄμματα στροβήσεται.

> ἔσται δ᾽ ἱππολόφων τε λόγων κορυθαίολα νείκη
> σχινδαλάμων τε παραξόνια σμιλεύματά τ᾽ ἔργων,
> φωτὸς ἀμυνομένου φρενοτέκτονος ἀνδρὸς
> ῥήμαθ᾽ ἱπποβάμονα.

> φρίξας δ᾽ αὐτοκόμου λοφιᾶς λασιαύχενα χαίταν,
> δεινὸν ἐπισκύνιον ξυνάγων βρυχώμενος ἥσει
> ῥήματα γομφοπαγῆ πινακηδὸν ἀποσπῶν
> γηγενεῖ φυσήματι.

> ἔνθεν δὴ στοματουργὸς ἐπῶν βασανίστρια λίσπη
> γλῶσσ᾽ ἀνελισσομένη φθονεροὺς κινοῦσα χαλινοὺς
> ῥήματα δαιομένη καταλεπτολογήσει
> πλευμόνων πολὺν πόνον.

*Surely fearful wrath will fill the heart of the mighty thunderer* when he sees the sharp talking tusk of his rival in art being whetted; *then with fearful fury will his eyes whirl about.*

We'll have helmet-glinting struggles of tall-crested words, we'll have linchpin-shavings and chisel-parings of artworks as a man fends off a thought-building hero's galloping utterances.

*Bristling the shaggy-necked shock of his hirsute ridge of mane, his formidable brow frowning, with a roar he will hurl utterances bolted together, tearing off timbers with his earth-born blast.*

---

[34] For the uses of ἀνίημι as 'send forth' from the depths of the earth, see LSJ s.v. I. See especially Ar. *Heroes* fr.504; A. *Pers.* 650; S. *OT* 270, 1405; A. *Th.* 413; h. *Cer.* 333.

Then the smooth tongue unfurling, mouth-working tester of words, slipping the reins of envy will sort out those utterances and parse clean away *much labour of lungs.*

(Frogs 814–29)

If read collectively, the majority of the images that concern 'Aeschylus' represent the poet as a terrifying thundering monster blasting destructive winds which emanate from the depths of the earth. As his incontrollable fury swells from below, it turns into a stormy force and showers boulders that shatter the opponent's creations (*Frogs* 814–17; 822–5).[35] Although this portrayal of Aeschylus encompasses elements from several mythological descriptions of divine powers and monsters,[36] as well as epic images of battles, in its basis undoubtedly lies the mythical imagery of Typhoeus, Typhon, or Typhos, the primitive force of winds, smoke, and blasts, and the last representative of the Earth in Hesiod's narrative concerning the chthonic challenge to Zeus' order.[37] In fact, only twenty lines after the ode, the association of 'Aeschylus' with Typhos is made explicit when Dionysus calls for a sacrifice of a black victim, a common sacrifice to a chthonic power,[38] in order to appease him:

> ἄρν᾽ ἄρνα μέλανα παῖδες ἐξενέγκατε·
> Τυφὼς γὰρ ἐκβαίνειν παρασκευάζεται.
>
> A lamb, boys, bring out a black lamb!
> Typhos is preparing to emerge!
>
> (Frogs 847–8)

Why is the imagery of Typhos, the mythical source of devastating storm winds, chosen for the characterization of 'Aeschylus'? Several possibilities present themselves: is the poet meant to be understood as chaotic, furious, and fiery, a 'nasty old man' or a loud-thundering

---

[35] For the association of 'Euripides' with 'culture', and especially technology and tools (i.e. technical poetry), see above, n. 32.

[36] See Dover (1993), 291–5; Scharffenberger (2007), *passim*.

[37] For a discussion of Typhoeus in these terms, see Clay (2003), 125–8. For the figure of Typhoeus, see Gantz (1993), vol. 1, 48–51.

[38] Scullion (1994), 111 for more bibliography; cf. Dover (1993), 298. Although the distinction between Olympian and chthonic sacrifice is now acknowledged to be a lot more complex than initially thought, it is still useful; see, for example, the essays in Hägg and Alroth (2005) and Ekroth (2007). Black victims have a tendency to be associated with powers that fall in the chthonian rather than the Olympian category, and the sacrifice alluded to in *Frogs* fits well with Typhos' earth-born origins.

demagogue?[39] The imagery of winds in the ode is prominent, and one might add to the possible interpretations the almost pervasive and near-daimonic role of winds in Aeschylean tragedy, especially in the *Oresteia* and the *Seven*.[40] However, although these may play an important part, there is surely more to the interpretation of 'Aeschylus' as Typhos.

## THE GIGANTIC BODY IN THE SICILIAN EARTH: 'AESCHYLUS' AND SICILY

There are two important elements which call for consideration: first, the poet/raw force of nature has been roused to incontrollable *wrath*. It is this wrath that is meant to be appeased through the propitiatory sacrifice of a black victim suggested by Dionysus (*Frogs* 847–8). Wrath is a major dramatic motif in the characterization of the Aristophanic 'Aeschylus', as many scholars have remarked.[41] The intertextual background of the 'Aeschylean' wrath has so far only been considered in relation to the angry Achilles of *Myrmidons* and its literary model, the *Iliad*. However, in the ode just mentioned, wrath has a more elemental character. It seethes from below: it is earth-born (*Frogs* 825) and threatens elemental havoc (*Frogs* 814–17; 823–5). Arguably, a parallel even more appropriate than the epic and tragic Achilles is the description of Typhoeus in *Theogony* 824–46. There, Hesiod represents Typhoeus' chthonic wrath with imagery including fire, thunder, bellowing sounds, bulls, and typhoons.

The second important point, closely related to the wrath seething from below, is that, in fifth-century sources (and possibly even as early as Hesiod),[42] Typhos' elemental force is imagined as lurking

---

[39] For these interpretations, see Dover (1993), 18 and Sharffenberger (2007), *passim*.

[40] Scott (1966); Peradotto (1964), 382–8; Thalmann (1978), 32–8.

[41] *Frogs* 843–4, 844–5, 851–5. Cf. Tarkow (1982); Dover (1993), 18; Sharffenberger (2007).

[42] See *Theog.* 859–61: φλὸξ δὲ κεραυνωθέντος ἀπέσσυτο τοῖο ἄνακτος / οὔρεος ἐν βήσσῃσιν ἀιδνῆς παιπαλοέσσης, / πληγέντος. 'A flame shot forth from that thunder-bolted lord in the mountain's dark, rugged dales (or: on Etna's rugged dales: cf. Tzetzes in *Lyc.* 688, who at 860 cites the variant Αἴτνης), as he was struck'. However, see West (1966), ad loc.

within the specific locality of the island of Sicily. From Pindar's odes to the pseudo-Aeschylean *Prometheus* trilogy, the threatening power lurking under the ground of Sicily and causing the terrifying explosions of Mount Etna is imagined in terms of a gigantic male body lying under the island: the body of the chthonic Typhos. In *Pythian* 1.18–24, for example, Pindar says that 'Sicily weighs upon his [i.e. Typhos'] shaggy chest, and a skyward column constrains him, snowy Etna, nurse of biting snow all year round, from whose depths belch forth holiest springs of unapproachable fire; during the days rivers of lava pour forth a blazing stream of smoke, but in times of darkness a rolling red flame carries rocks into the deep expanse of the sea with a crash'.[43] In *Prometheus Bound* 363–72, the equally striking description of Typhos under Sicily is especially illuminating: the poet's imagination merges earth-born blasts of wind and issues of smoke, fire, and boulders in the figure of this power.[44] And, once again, Typhos is imagined like an enormous male body lying under the Sicilian earth and powering its volcano.

If we accept that Aristophanes imagines 'Aeschylus' to be like Typhos, how can we reconcile the character's chthonic wrath and threatening forces with his portrayal in Aristophanes as a force of fertility, blessing, and well-being, which we entertained earlier? Are these aspects not essentially contradictory? In fact, the whole picture can be understood as remarkably consistent. Aeschylus' construction as a force of the earth capable of restoring fertility and life to a blighted *polis*, and as a power lying in the depths of the Sicilian soil, who may be roused to anger and capable of destruction can be read as two complementary sides of the same entity *if 'Aeschylus' is understood to be a chthonic power*. In Greek religion and cult, chthonic powers were generally perceived to have both productive and destructive energies. They were understood to be responsible for all growth and life that comes from below, but also, if their anger was aroused, for sterility, disease, and death.[45]

---

[43] Cf. Pindar *O.* 4.6–7.

[44] For Typhos in *Prometheus Bound* as modelled on Hesiod, see Solmsen (1949), 132; Griffith (1978), 119. For a description of Typhos and his association with Etna, see also Pseudo-Apollodorus, *Bibl.* 1. 39 and 1.44.

[45] For the powers associated with the earth, and their connection with growth and death alike, see Parker (2005), ch. 18, esp. 423–4, who discusses visual sources, too (cf. Parker (2011), 82). Cf. Henrichs (1991), 162–9, 192–3, 195–201, and *passim*; Burkert

As argued earlier, the association of Aeschylean inspiration with natural powers and flowing energies is an important factor in this portrayal. However, Aeschylus is attested to have had an even more specific link to chthonic powers known for such abilities—at least in one strand of ancient reception—namely, hero cult.[46] This link is provided by the *Life of Aeschylus* §10–11 testimony, quoted at the beginning of this chapter. According to this testimony, soon after his death the poet was offered *enagismata*, the sacrifices traditionally made to chthonic deities and heroes. The wording suggests that after Aeschylus' death, his tomb in Gela, Sicily, became a site of formal cult, attracting regular pilgrimages by members of the tragic profession.[47] Scholars hold radically different views on the historicity of this account, ranging from outright rejection to wholesome acceptance to complete silence.[48] However, the connection with Typhos that is

(1985), 200–1, 206–8, who emphasize ambivalence: as guardians and watchers of the use of the earth, chthonic powers can be either punitive or rewarding.

[46] As chthonic powers, beyond their energy of blessing (manifested in epiphanies or things 'sent up from below'), cult heroes have a destructive facet, which is an eternally present possibility in case the hero does not receive the customary cult, and which can manifest in wrathful phenomena of nature, sterility, disease, or death. For the two complementary facets of heroic powers, see Snodgrass (1982); Burkert (1985), 206–8; Kearns (1989), 7 and *passim*; Henrichs (1991), 192–3; Johnston (1999), 29, 153–5; Parker (2005), 447–51; Currie (2005), 46, 118–19. Nagy's decades of research on hero cult show that, through their death, heroes partook in the cosmic/natural order (*dikē*) and served it by rewarding the just with flourishing fertility, health, and wealth, and punishing the unjust with illness, starvation, and destruction: (1979), 189–96; (1990a), 177; (2013), 345–52 and *passim*. See also Rohde (1925), 127–38. Among the ancient sources, the following may be mentioned: Ar. fr. 322; S. *OC* 389–415, 457–64; E. *Heracl.* 1026–44; *Alc.* 995–1005; Hdt.1.67–8, 1.167; Paus. 1.34.4, 8.23.7, 8.9.3, 9.18.5, 9.30.9–11, 9.38.3–5; Plu. *Cim.* 19. Ekroth (2002) questions the special nature of the heroic sacrificial ritual, showing its overlaps with divine cult, but does not disconnect hero cults from the earth, and issues of fertility, health, and protection of life. On hero cults, see further Farnell (1921); Visser (1982); Seaford (1994), 114–20; Antonaccio (1995).

[47] Cf. Wilson (2007), 356–71; Kowalzig (2008), 130; Poli-Palladini (2013), 285–96. For ἐναγίζειν and hero cult, see Parker (2005) and Ekroth (2002), 74–128. Φοιτάω, 'to visit regularly/repeatedly', suggests the existence of a regularly organized (annual?) festival, as Kowalzig (2008), 130 rightly suggests.

[48] An outright sceptical view has been expressed by many scholars who work on biographical traditions in antiquity and have endorsed Lefkowitz' thesis about the provenance of poetic biographies (1981, 2nd edn 2012): e.g. Kimmel-Clauzet (2013); Kivilo (2010), 222–3; Pelliccia (2009); Burnett (1983), 18–19. Contra Currie (2005), 129–30. Clay (2004); Hendrickson (2013); and Pelling (2002), 143–70 adopt a nuanced position on the value of ancient biographies. Many studies of Aeschylus' biography and early reception do not discuss the *Life* account at all: e.g. Hanink and Uhlig (2016); Sommerstein (2010); Herington (1967). Cf. Sommerstein (2008),

suggested here through the evidence of *Frogs* opens up an alternative and more productive route to examine the validity of this testimony. The imagery of the gigantic body lying in the soil of Sicily, which Aristophanes evokes through the image of Typhos, accords perfectly with the ancient imagination of heroes as bodies of larger-than-life proportions lying in the soil of the locality which is connected with their worship.[49] Thus, by imagining 'Aeschylus' through the evocation of Typhon as a larger-than-life body that operates from the depths of the Sicilian earth in both benevolent and destructive ways, I believe that Aristophanes engages creatively with the fact that the poet had a hero cult in Sicily.

The hypothesis that Aristophanes evokes Aeschylus' hero cult in *Frogs* also accords with the fact that cult heroes were imagined as essentially, and powerfully, active in their place of burial. Narratives from across antiquity report cult heroes causing illnesses or disasters, blessing the land with abundant vegetation, emanating knowledge—oracular or otherwise—or mysteriously blocking an enemy's attack.[50] Aeschylus' representation by Aristophanes as the force that powers a volcano acquires special significance in this respect, also because it ties in with Aeschylus' poetic association with fertility.[51] Therefore, the volcanic power of Typhos contains brilliant potential to capture the double function of 'Aeschylus' as cult hero.

Aeschylus' association with Etna was, moreover, strengthened by the commissioned composition and production of *Aetnaeae* in

xvii–xviii; Rosenmeyer (1982), 376, Guardì (1990); Griffith (1978); Culasso Gastaldi (1979). On the other side of the spectrum, some scholars have accepted the testimony about Aeschylus' cult as essentially reliable: Clay (2004), 3, 81, 95; Wilson (2007); Kowalzig (2008); Poli-Palladini (2013), 285–96. Corroborating evidence in this case should probably include the huge popularity of myths from Aeschylean dramas on tragedy-related vase painting in Sicily especially. This suggests that Aeschylus was appreciated in fifth- and fourth-century Sicily in a way that he was not in Athens. See Kossatz-Deissmann (1978); Taplin (2007); Nervegna (2014), 172–6. (I thank Eric Csapo for this last observation.)

[49] See, most famously, Herodotus 1.68.3 on the bones of Orestes. Cf. Hdt. 2.91.3 and 4.82. Phlegon of Tralles (*FGrHist* 257 F 36 11–19) collects data on gigantic bones. See also Ekroth (2007), 110.

[50] For a survey and analysis of various sources, see Visser (1982); cf. Nagy (1979) 189–96; Nagy (1990a) 177.

[51] For the fertility of the volcanic ash falling from Mount Etna, especially in relation to viniculture, see Strabo 6.2.3. For a modern analysis of volcanic soil properties, see Shoji, Nanzyo, and Dahlgren (1994), esp. ch. 8. Such properties were known in antiquity.

Syracuse in the 470s. In fact, the *Aetnaeae* provides a particularly exciting link between Aeschylus and the volcano. Scholars associate the play with a specific eruption in the 470s: this event was used by Hieron in order to evacuate Catana and refound it as Aetna, and the new foundation was then celebrated with Aeschylus' production of *Aetnaeae*. The play, moreover, engaged with imagery and cult connected with a volcanic phenomenon. This was the cult of the Palici, native Sicilian cult heroes who were worshipped at the site of boiling craters or volcanic thermal springs, and imagined, as fr.6 of Aeschylus' fragmentary play suggests, to perform exactly the motion of emerging from below:

A. τί δῆτ᾽ ἐπ᾽ αὐτοῖς ὄνομα θήσονται βροτοί;
B. σεμνούς Παλικούς Ζεύς ἐφίεται καλεῖν.
A. ἦ καὶ Παλικῶν εὐλόγως μενεῖ φάτις;
B. πάλιν γὰρ ἥκουσ᾽ ἐκ σκότου τοδ᾽ εἰς φάος.

A. So what name will mortals give them?
B. Zeus ordains that they be called the holy Palici.
A. And will the name of Palici be appropriate and permanent?
B. Yes, for they have come back (*palin*) from the darkness to this realm of light.[52]

This is not to suggest, of course, that Aeschylus' hero cult in Gela was historically connected with the volcano by the Sicilians. Rather, Aeschylus' association with Etna, through the commissioned production of *Aetnaeae*, helped Aristophanes to present the tragedian as a chthonic power of both blessing and destruction, just like Etna itself.[53]

Furthermore, if the function of cult heroes is considered in spatial terms, the representation of Aeschylus' ascending into the light in the finale of *Frogs* makes even better sense. It is arguable that a hero's epiphany might be imagined in terms of a 'motion from below', in other words, an *anodos* motion. If 'Aeschylus' is imagined as 'lying' in the Sicilian earth, the successful effect of hero cult may be imagined as an upwards movement, an epiphany, or a resurrection, with results in

---

[52] For Aeschylus' *Aetnaeae*, see most recently Poli-Palladini (2013), who reviews earlier scholarship; for the role of the Palici in the play, see Poli-Palladini (2013), 292–5, 302–6, and 319–21; for the earth cult of Palici generally, see Croon (1952).

[53] Some scholarship emphasizes the sociopolitical function of hero cults, whether in regards to the élite, the individual, or the community, e.g. Brelich (1958); Bérard (1982); Seaford (1994), 110–14, 180–8; Currie (2005). This, however, should not obscure an essential aspect of hero cults, namely that they were also believed to promote well-being, prosperity, fertility, and health—or, conversely, harm those who failed to offer proper worship.

promotion of fertility and protection of life. This is what 'Aeschylus' is expected to do in the finale of the *Frogs*. The concluding choral utterance, expressing the hope that the poet's *anodos* will bring blessings, end wars, protect the value of life, and, above all, grant (artistic) fertility to Athens, is telling of the reinvigorating effect that the emergence of the poet hero in his native land is imagined to bring:

> πρῶτα μὲν εὐοδίαν ἀγαθὴν ἀπιόντι ποιητῇ
> ἐς φάος ὀρνυμένῳ δότε δαίμονες οἱ κατὰ γαίας,
> τῇ δὲ πόλει μεγάλων ἀγαθῶν ἀγαθὰς ἐπινοίας.
> πάγχυ γὰρ ἐκ μεγάλων ἀχέων παυσαίμεθ' ἂν οὕτως
> ἀργαλέων τ' ἐν ὅπλοις ξυνόδων. Κλεοφῶν δὲ μαχέσθω
> κἄλλος ὁ βουλόμενος τούτων πατρίοις ἐν ἀρούραις.

First, you gods below earth, grant to the departing poet a fine journey as he ascends to the sunlight, and to the city grant fine ideas that will bring fine blessings. For that way, we may have an end of great griefs and painful encounters in arms. Let Cleophon do the fighting, and any of those others who wants to fight on his native soil![54]

(*Frogs* 1528–33)

We should not miss the Aristophanic twist, however: in the *Frogs*, the hero 'Aeschylus' is not shown to rise in the locale of his burial, the 'grain-bearing Gela' of Sicily (as his posthumous epigram cited by the *Life of Aeschylus*, l. 2, puts it). He rises in Athens, his native land. This is the land whose fertility he is expected to restore. This observation has further implications regarding the poet's posthumous reception, and connects it with some significant, but often overlooked, dimensions of dramatic festivals both in Sicily and in Athens: their connections with earth and fertility cults.

## THE COMPETITION FOR 'AESCHYLUS' BLESSINGS: THEATRE AND EARTH CULTS

By representing the poet as a cult hero enacting an *anodos* epiphany in the land of Athens, the *Frogs* reappropriates 'Aeschylus' and

---

[54] Lada-Richards (1999), 327–9 closes with the insight that Aeschylus' address at *Ran.* 1526–33 foreshadows his heroization, but does not relate this to any historical account. Cf. Poli-Palladini (2013), 308–16, who finds many elements suggestive of Aeschylus' heroization in the *Frogs*, but does not consider the ode that likens 'Aeschylus' to the Typhos.

makes him into the property of the Athenians. Undoubtedly, this Aristophanic twist reflects Athenian competitiveness towards the Sicilians who had claimed him through his emigration, burial, and cult. This provides significant supporting evidence to the validity of the *Life* testimony, which we can now appreciate in a more secure light. For if, as *Frogs* suggests, Aeschylus was posthumously perceived by Athenian audiences as cult hero, it is significantly more likely that he actually was. Corroborating evidence for the historical validity of the *Life* testimony is also provided by recent research on the cults of other dramatic poets, especially Sophocles and Euripides. Indeed, in recent years, the evidence which has been accumulating about the tragedians' hero cults suggests that all three canonical tragic poets enjoyed a hero cult by the end of the fifth century.[55]

Competitiveness may also be traced in the representation of the poet in the *Frogs* finale specifically as a source of blessing. In contrast to the early construction of 'Aeschylus' as a wrathful 'power below' threatening to strike from the depths of the Sicilian earth (*Frogs* 814–29), the final image of the poet in *Frogs* is that of a benevolent power. The very last words of the play, πατρίοις ἐν ἀρούραις 'on his native soil', show that the resurrection of Aeschylean poetry is perceived as potentially beneficial not just on the level of politics, but also on the level of the general well-being of land and people. Thus, although the land of Sicily did become a second homeland for the poet in the last years of his life and housed his remains, ultimately—Aristophanes seems to suggest—it is the land of Athens that benefits from his status as hero.

This brings me to the final part of this chapter, and to a specific question. How should we read the emerging conclusion that the powers granted to a poet like Aeschylus would extend beyond artistic benefits into seemingly unrelated areas, such as fertility and well-being of land and people? From a modern perspective, the connection between performance of poetry and chthonic cults seems remote, especially as we are used to thinking of theatrical festivals and the patronage of Dionysus, in connection to civic cult.[56] However, an

---

[55] For Sophocles' hero cult in Athens as *Dexion* in relation to the cult of Asclepius, see Clay (2004), 78–79 and, for the sources, 151–2. See also Currie (2005), 5, 182. Contra Lefkowitz (2012) 84–6. For Euripides' hero cult in Salamis, see *SEG* 47, 282; Gell. 15.20.5. See also Lolos (2013), (2003), (2000).

[56] Responding to the view that tragedy has nothing to do with Dionysus (e.g. Taplin (1978), 162), contributors to the celebrated *Nothing to do with Dionysus?* volume argue for a variety of civic functions in connection with the god.

unprejudiced examination of the evidence suggests links which cannot be easily ignored. It has long been observed that, in Sicily, the spaces that hosted theatrical performances were almost uniformly connected with chthonic cults. The cult of Demeter and Persephone, but also those of other deities with a chthonic character, like the Nymphs, Pan, and the dead, figure prominently at the island's theatrical sites. The most striking example is the ancient theatre in Syracuse where the cults of Demeter and Persephone are richly attested from the second quarter of the fifth century, as is the cult of the Nymphs.[57] The same phenomenon is also attested in Akragas, Heloros, Monte Iato, Morgantina, and Akrai (albeit our earliest evidence for these theatres is not as early as for Syracuse).[58] Furthermore, as we are often reminded, the patron gods and recipients of drama in Sicily are primarily Demeter and Kore. Hinz, Kowalzig, and other scholars have plausibly argued for a connection between the spread of the theatre, the promotion of the cults of the two goddesses, the presentation of Sicily as the 'breadbasket' of the Mediterranean, and the agricultural policies of the Deinomenid tyrants (and of subsequent states later on).[59]

These observations apply not only to a Sicilian context. Sources for the performance of poetry in mainland Greece yield considerable evidence for the connection between performance and chthonic/ fertility cults, or cults which promote the well-being and prosperity of land and people. It has, of course, long gone out of fashion to talk about the fertility functions, or even origins, of the festivals which hosted dramatic performances in Attica, namely the Great Dionysia, the Lenaia, and the Dionysia in the demes of Attica.[60] The burgeoning research into the civic functions, finances, and overall organization of the theatrical festivals has contributed enormously to the appreciation of their civic and secular dimensions, but has also suppressed other

---

[57] Hinz (1998), 100–2; Todisco (2002), 29, 184–6; Wilson (2007), 354; Kowalzig (2008), 131–2.

[58] Hinz (1998), 55–69; Todisco (2002), 29, 168, 169, 172, 175, 178, 181; Wilson (2007), 354; Kowalzig (2008), 131–2; MacLachlan (2012); Csapo and Wilson (2015), 331, 339, 383. Wilson (2007), n. 15 comments that 'to these we may add the *Thesmophorion* by the recently excavated theatre in Cyrene'.

[59] Kowalzig (2008); Hinz (1998), 19–28.

[60] Cf. especially James (1961); Pickard-Cambridge (1968), 42–3. For the Rural Dionysia, the argument has recently been revived by Habash (1995) and Jones (2004), ch. 4.

elements. The perception of these festivals by audiences, as attested in ancient sources, suggests that we might be missing a significant part of the picture.[61]

The very connection of the agricultural calendar with the theatrical festival calendar is a fact that we cannot deny, and one that has been explored to the same depth as the connection with civic business.[62] The recent interest in the deme theatres of Attica has, paradoxically, made more palpable the connection—in terms of physical proximity, but also convergence of occasion—between performance spaces and fertility cults. The theatres in Eleusis and Thorikos, which hosted vibrant performance festivals in the fifth century BCE, were adjacent and prominently connected to chthonic cult sites: the former, with its likely location on the south side of the Eleusis acropolis,[63] was spatially connected with the most famous site of the cult of Demeter and Persephone in the Greek world; and the latter with the cult of the dead in the necropolis immediately adjacent. Possibly even more striking is the fact that the silver mines, where the Thoricians extracted the silver from their earth, were immediately next to the theatre.[64] In the deme Ikarion, the theatre and festival were also attached to a prominent hero cult: the cult of Icarius, who was venerated for his reception of wine from the god, and worshipped for the institution of viniculture. The connection is suggested by the collocation of funds for the cult of Icarius on a stele with a decree dealing with the running of the local Dionysia, dating to around 450 BCE.[65]

Even the Great Dionysia cannot escape from fertility associations. Recently, Eric Csapo made a convincing case for the connection of the *pompē* in the Great Dionysia with comic theatre.[66] The *pompē* has always been understood as a procession which celebrates Dionysus as one of the great life-bringing forces and which teems with symbols of fertility (although Csapo refrains from talking about the procession in

[61] See especially *Acharnians* and *Peace*: both plays connect the dramatic festivals with the regeneration of life. For *Acharnians,* the agrarian ideals as core concerns of the Rural Dionysia and the connection of the phallic procession to the theatre, see Jones (2004), 125–7, 142–7; and Habash (1995). The connection of the dramatic festivals with well-being, fertility, and prosperity is suggested by *Peace* 520–729, esp. 528–38. Overall, it is significant that the Trygaios, a character who embodies the theatre (cf. Hall 2006) accomplishes the *anodos* of the chthonic divinity Peace, which brings along fertility, well-being, wealth, *and* the revival of the Dionysia.

[62] One of the least known treatments is James (1961).

[63] See Wilson (forthcoming a).   [64] See Wilson (forthcoming b).

[65] See Wilson (2015) and (forthcoming c).   [66] Csapo (2013).

these terms). The overlaps that Csapo points out between the outlook of the *pompē* and that of comedy are significant. Perhaps the most revealing parallel for what has been observed here is the connection of the cult of Asclepius with the Athenian theatre, both in terms of space and in terms of occasion.[67] Again this suggests an ancient connection between drama and other concerns which we, with our modern preconceptions, are not used to associating with it, such as health and well-being. Mitchell-Boyask's 2008 book on the relationship between the cult of Asclepius and Athenian drama is one welcome recent development on the subject.

How may this contextualization of earth cults and theatre help us envisage Aeschylus' own hero cult? If we trust the *Life* testimony, we are entitled to imagine the organization of a formal cult for the poet by the community of the Geloans shortly after his death. The account in the *Life* moreover attests to travelling, pilgrimage, and *theoria* by Aeschylus' worshippers, and suggests the organization of a dramatic festival in the poet's honour. As in all hero cults, for the individuals and the community enacting their worship, the anticipated effects would have certainly extended beyond the ideology of the state. Effects as basic as protection, well-being, and prosperity are always part of cult-hero worship, and the *Life* description of pilgrimage in honour of Aeschylus seems to inscribe the poet with the status of a patron of the tragic trade.[68]

Further evidence from Old Comedy and, in particular, from Cratinus' *Plutoi* ('Wealth-Gods'), suggests a fifth-century understanding of Aeschylus as a poet preoccupied with the deep space of the earth, and with chthonic powers that can offer blessings as well as potential destruction. This, of course, tallies with the treatment of space and natural imagery in Aeschylus' own plays.[69] Should we link the prominence of the earth and its resources in Aeschylus' oeuvre, and

---

[67] Mitchell-Boyask (2008), ch. 7.

[68] For cult heroes as patrons of professionals, see Farnell (1921), 71–2, 87–90, 153, 219, 268; Kearns (1989), 36–43.

[69] See Bakola (2013), (2016). These publications argue that Aeschylean tragedy reflects deeply on the space that hosts and sustains humanity and on how humanity relates back to this space. Certain concepts and images which are key and appear repeatedly, such as 'wealth'—generated by human activity but also by natural growth—are conceptualized collectively as the earth's resources. Space in Aeschylus, in other words, is largely a generative space. What humans do with these resources, how they use and abuse them, and how these uses and abuses affect the relationship between themselves and natural space are issues that capture the poet's reflections on

more specifically the interest in deep spaces (the sea, caves, the earth's fertile and terrifying depths, the underworld), to his posthumous status as 'power below'? In the context of this volume, this case looks stronger than ever.

The exact chronological relationship between the cult of Aeschylus in Sicily, the performance of his plays, his portrayal in Aristophanes' *Frogs*, and his association with Typhon and the volcano Etna may remain open for further input and discussion; what seems to me beyond doubt is the alignment between some key preoccupations of Aeschylean drama, his presentation in fifth-century literary critical discourses, his construction as cult hero in his second homeland Gela, and his presentation in fifth-century comedy.[70]

the relationship between humans and the cosmos, and lie at the very heart of Aeschylean tragedy.

[70] I would like to thank Eric Csapo, Barbara Graziosi, Nora Goldschmidt, and the two anonymous readers for their comments and suggestions which helped improve this chapter. The research for this chapter was facilitated by a Leverhulme Early Career Fellowship and a Visiting Research Grant, CHS, Harvard.

# 7

## Tombs of Poets' Minor Characters

### Peter Bing

Imagine that you are in New York City, at the corner of Broadway and Wall Street in Lower Manhattan, peering into the churchyard of historic Trinity Church (founded 1696). A brief stroll into the grassy, tree-shaded yard brings you past graves of such famous figures as Alexander Hamilton and steamboat pioneer Robert Fulton. Nearby is a large brownstone slab, lying flat on the ground and unadorned except that it is scored with a strange rectangular depression (filled in at some point with concrete), below which is inscribed a name: Charlotte Temple. During the nineteenth, and well into the twentieth, century, this tomb was the chief attraction of the graveyard, a site of pilgrimage frequented especially by women, who (according to plentiful contemporary accounts) shed tears over the stone and left offerings of flowers. Who was the grave's occupant? She was in fact a fiction, the heroine of America's first novel to become a bestseller, Susannah Haswell Rowson's *Charlotte Temple: A Tale of Truth*, published in 1791 (Figure 7.1).[1]

In its time, the book was a sensation, a scandalous bodice-ripper framed as a cautionary tale 'for the perusal of the young and thoughtless of the fair sex',[2] whose title character, the fifteen-year-old daughter of an English nobleman of humble means, is lured to America by the handsome soldier, Montraville, through promises of love and marriage. Upon arriving in New York, he sets her up in a suburban cottage, not as his wife but as his mistress, leaving her pregnant and nearly destitute

---

[1] Here cited according to Rowson (1905).
[2] Rowson (1905), vol. 1, 3, Author's Preface.

**Figure 7.1.** The author at Charlotte Temple's Tomb, 13 May 2015.
Photograph: Peter Bing.

while himself marrying a wealthy New York socialite. Soon, Charlotte is evicted from her cottage and forced to wander the snowy streets of New York. She dies in a hovel shortly after giving birth. As to Montraville, we learn that he was conscience-stricken at the news of Charlotte's death, and that 'to the end of his life was subject to severe fits of melancholy, and while he remained at New York, frequently retired to the churchyard, where he would weep over the grave, and regret the untimely fate of the lovely Charlotte Temple.'[3] With Montraville's frequent, rueful visits to the graveyard, Rowson offers a text-internal paradigm for her audience, modelling the tearful response of her readers—though she could hardly have anticipated how it would inspire sorrowful pilgrimages to a 'tomb' of Charlotte Temple.

The author herself insists that she heard her tale from 'an old lady who had personally known Charlotte', and has thrown over it only 'a slight veil of fiction, and substituted names and places according to my own fancy'.[4] Almost from the start, therefore, readers conjectured about the real-life identities of the characters,[5] and a veritable cottage industry in Charlotte Temple tourism quickly arose, turning not just the heroine's alleged tomb but several possible locations for her cottage into popular sightseeing destinations.[6]

There was scepticism already in the nineteenth century. In an article entitled 'Who Was Charlotte Temple?' in the *Leslie's Popular Monthly* of November 1890 (pp. 600–6), John Flavel Mines, writing under his nom de plume, Felix Oldboy, wittily dissects the novel's presumed historicity, comparing the search for Charlotte Temple *Realien* to the literary tourism of the ancient world. 'Some cities', he says, 'claimed Homer dead, and as many old houses were from time to time pointed out as the place where the unhappy girl lived while in New York' (602).[7] Like the heroine herself, her tombstone too—according to Mines—must be fictitious, a metafiction, as it were: her name was probably inscribed after the fact on one of the cemetery's many 'waifs and strays' (603), displaced from their proper settings during the chaotic period of 1839–46 when Trinity Church was demolished

---

[3] Rowson (1905), vol. 2, 127.          [4] Rowson (1905), vol. 1, 3.

[5] The 1905 edition includes a fascinating 'historical and biographical introduction' to the novel of nearly a hundred pages by the prominent journalist and editor Francis W. Halsey, who assumes that the novel's characters represent real-life individuals. Charlotte, for example, was equated with a certain Charlotte Stanley, and Montraville with the author's cousin, Colonel John Montrésor.

[6] This, although the novel studiously avoids mention of any particular street or known structure in the city. The novel's devotees, however, sought even to connect its other characters with specific settings—for example, locating the resting place of the repentant Montraville in an unmarked tomb on Wards Island in the East River. Cf. Mines (1890), 605–6.

[7] For instance, to celebrate its centennial in 1886, the 7th Street Methodist Episcopal Church published a map of the village as it had earlier been at the turn of the century, showing the location of Charlotte's house at the corner of Astor Place and Lafayette Street: cf. Mines (1890), 602.

and rebuilt.[8] And in fact, Trinity Church officials confirmed Mines' suspicions as recently as 2008, when they raised the slab to investigate what was beneath and found . . . nothing.[9]

'Men and women are fond of creating such delusions for themselves', says the sceptical Mines (605), who clearly disapproves of the phenomenon. More positively, we might see in Charlotte's 'tomb' a perfect instance of the aestheticist axiom that 'Life imitates Art far more than Art imitates Life'[10]—or what Tim Whitmarsh has called 'the power of the mimetic arts to approximate to, capture, or even create reality',[11] that is, its potential for so engaging and stimulating the imaginary of some in its audience that for these the boundary between art and life dissolves and the literary creation becomes 'real'. In such circumstances, they may feel (among other things) the urge to interact with fictional characters,[12] to commune with them by retracing their steps and linger over places where they 'lived' and 'died'.[13] They may even, as the mournful acts inspired by *Charlotte Temple* reveal, offer up tears and sepulchral honours—to a fictional character.[14]

---

[8] At that time, Mines suggests, the brownstone slab might have lost its identifying 'brass tablet, or memorial of lead', originally set in that rectangular hollow still visible on the stone. Might not a workman involved in the construction, 'either as a means of covering the loss or moved by a sentimental idea, . . . have carved out the name "Charlotte Temple"?' (604).

[9] Cf. Hughes (2008).        [10] Wilde (1891), 31–2, 39, and 54.

[11] Whitmarsh (2009), 227.

[12] In this it resembles the participatory ethos of modern 'fan culture' as embodied, for instance, by Trekkies, fans of the *Star Trek* series, who do not just passively consume the popular series, but emulate and extend its fictional world, creating and performing their own responses. On this phenomenon, see Jenkyns (1992).

[13] Among the many modern instances of literary tourism connected with the lives and deaths of fictional characters, consider Juliet's 'tomb' in Verona <http://www.open.ac.uk/blogs/literarytourist/?p=49>; Sherlock Holmes' apartment at 221b Baker Street; the tombstones in Juliette, Georgia, commemorating Buddy Threadgood and Ruth Jamison, characters from the book and movie *Fried Green Tomatoes*, or the online *Game of Thrones* graveyard, where you can leave flowers on the 'tombs' of favourite characters who have been killed off <http://www.slate.com/articles/arts/television/2014/04/game_of_thrones_deaths_mourn_dead_characters_at_their_virtual_graveyard.html>.

[14] Wilde (1891), where a speaker describes how the death of fictional characters may provoke grief far more intense than that caused by the demise of an actual person: 'A steady course of Balzac reduces our living friends to shadows, and our acquaintances to the shadows of shades . . . One of the greatest tragedies of my life is the death of Lucien de Rubempre. It is a grief from which I have never been able completely to rid myself. It haunts me in my moments of pleasure. I remember it when I laugh . . . [Balzac] created life, he did not copy it.'

In this chapter, I want to focus on the act of commemorating the tombs of *ancient* literary characters, particularly minor ones, in the Hellenistic age. Such acts may be related to what I termed 'the memorializing impulse' in an earlier essay,[15] that is, a trend originating in the fourth century BCE, but coming to full flower only in the following centuries of the Hellenistic era, in which people created memorials of various kinds for important figures of the poetic past— whether this involved setting physical monuments like statues or the buildings of hero cult, or whether it comprised textual commemoration (scholarship like the *Pinakes* of Callimachus, or poetic homages as in the countless fictitious epitaphs for past literary greats). But while that earlier essay traced these different threads in the Hellenistic urge to preserve, commemorate, and master the literary heritage concerning its *poets*, here I want to extend that discussion to the veneration of those poets' (fictional) *characters*—in particular the lesser figures of their *oeuvres*—as interred in their graves.

One might think that the enduring fixity of tombs would make these easy targets of scholarly investigation. Yet tombs of literary characters turn out to be strangely and appealingly elusive, moving targets as it were, since it is hard to tell in any given instance whether we are dealing with a real-life monument—perhaps inspired by literature (as with the tomb of Charlotte Temple, a case of Life imitating Art), perhaps itself generating literature—or on the other hand, whether we have to do purely with poetic invention. The alternatives are hard to disentangle because ancient interest in the literary dead and their tombs proves to be decidedly intricate.

On the one hand, that interest entails the enduring reality, or at least the ongoing influence, of hero cult.[16] Such cult, typically centred on the tomb of a given hero, and hence of largely local significance,

---

For a famous instance of how an ancient audience could respond to a literary creation as 'real', see the tradition transmitted in the *Life of Aeschylus* (p. 2 ll. 10–13 Page) that the sight of Aeschylus' chorus of Furies in his *Eumenides* 'so terrified the people that children in the audience fainted and embryos were aborted'.

[15] Bing (1993).

[16] I take as my working definition of hero cult that used by Walter Burkert (1985), 203: 'the hero is a deceased person who exerts from his grave a power for good or evil and who demands appropriate honor . . . A hero cult involves setting apart one particular grave, known as a *heroon*, from other burials by marking off a special precinct, by bringing sacrifices and votive gifts, and occasionally by building a special grave monument.' Still fundamental is Rohde (1921), 146–99. See also Kearns (1989), 1–7.

was a given of daily life in communities across the Greek world from the eighth century on.[17] And even in its earliest manifestations, it is precisely storybook figures, characters from Homeric epic such as Agamemnon at Mycenae, Agamemnon and Cassandra at Amyclae, Menelaus and Helen at Sparta, or Odysseus in the Cave of the Nymphs on Ithaca, who comprise the earliest archaeologically traceable instances of hero cult.[18] Here, scholarship on such cult has been bedevilled by a chicken-and-egg problem (a bedevilled egg?): did pre-existing cult influence the depiction of the heroes of epic song (with Art thus imitating Life),[19] or did epic on the contrary shape the development of hero cult (Life imitating Art)? Many scholars since Farnell have seen literature, that is epic, as a crucial engine of hero cult's formation.[20] Thus Burkert, for example, plausibly argues that 'the worship of heroes from the eighth century onwards must . . . be derived directly from the influence' of this genre, and 'Families and cities took pride in being able to connect their traditions with the heroes of epic.'[21] Ten years ago, moreover, in his book, *Archilochos Heros*, Diskin Clay reminded us that the practice of hero cult only expanded and grew more prominent in the Hellenistic age, with

[17] See Graf (2003).
[18] For an overview, see Antonaccio (1994), esp. 398–9 with n. 50, and in greater detail Antonaccio (1995). Antonaccio (1994), 399–400 notes that archaeological evidence suggests that hero cult did not necessarily have to be situated at the site of the hero's grave—contrary to most literary testimony, which typically situates it in that context.
  On the early date of Odysseus' cult, see Coldstream (1976), 16–17 ('perhaps this is a rare case where the cult of a Homeric hero grew up quite independently of epic influence, in memory of a local ruler'), Malkin (1998), 94–119 ('Dedicating tripods at that cave constituted—in addition to an offering—a ritual imitating what Odysseus had done . . . the similarity of the finds to the text of the *Odyssey*—costly tripods placed in a cave—is too close to deny any Odyssean connection. Everything points to a deeply significant identification involving exceptional dedications.' p. 98). See, however, Antonaccio (1995), 152–5, who believes the connection of the cave with Odysseus is a Hellenistic phenomenon.
[19] Thus to F. H. Stubbings 'it seems certain that this shrine [*sc.* the Polis Bay cave in Ithaca with its twelve ninth-/eighth-century tripods] helped to inspire the description of the Cave of the Nymphs in the *Odyssey*', moreover 'it is even possible to see in the bronze tripods the "originals" of those which Odysseus in the poem brings home from Phaeacia', in Wace and Stubbings (1962), 419. See, however, the witty response of Heubeck and Hoekstra (1989) ad 13.217–18.
[20] Farnell (1921), 284–342. See further Coldstream (1976); Burkert (1985), 203–8. For a trenchant assessment of older scholarship, along with an attempt to down-date the rise of hero cult to the late sixth century BCE, see Bremmer (2006), 15–20. For a recent discussion of the hero as a concept in cult, cf. Mangoldt (2013), 4–14.
[21] Burkert (1985), 204.

heroic honours increasingly bestowed on the *newly* dead and even on the living.[22]

Such cult was undoubtedly one important aspect of the Hellenistic veneration of the poetic dead, often serving as implicit backdrop for many purely literary epigrams that function as epitaphs for a poet's characters—even where no cult for those specific characters existed. But that is only one part of the picture. For Hellenistic esteem for the literary heritage and its entombed cast of characters possessed a further aspect: it could also manifest itself purely as literature, that is, as poetry inspired by poetry, Art by Art, with no real-life component in ritual or cult. It is along the boundary between these two aspects, at its sometimes indistinct frontier, that the peculiarly Hellenistic quality in the commemoration of poets' (fictional) characters comes into focus. That is especially so when we look beyond the major figures of epic (those mentioned above who were early recipients of cult) and examine the bit-players of the literary tradition.

Let us start with the collection of sepulchral epigrams known as the 'Aristotelian' *Peplos*, a work of the fourth century BCE—that is, at the threshold of the Hellenistic age—which combines prose accounts about epic heroes (mainly from Homer) with forty-eight elegiac distichs posing as the inscriptions on their tombs.[23] In a recent study of the *Peplos*, Kathryn Gutzwiller connects it with hero cult, arguing that 'these epitaphs are designed for those who were not present at a heroic grave, perhaps originally to an entire civic body united by a local cult but also, or eventually, to a broader, Panhellenic audience asked to recognize local claims to the hero.'[24] She contends with good reason that the *Peplos* itself provided a narrative frame for individual epitaphs,[25] confirming the existence of cult for many of its heroes. In particular, she finds a crucial link to the practice of hero cult in epitaph #15 on Idomeneus and Meriones:

> Κνωσσίου Ἰδομενῆος ὁρᾷς τάφον· αὐτὰρ ἐγώ τοι
> πλησίον ἵδρυμαι Μηριόνης ὁ Μόλου.

---

[22] On this development, see Clay (2004); Jones (2010), esp. ch. 6; and Alcock (1991), 457–8.

[23] For the text of the distichs, see Bergk (1853), whose numbering I use.

[24] Gutzwiller (2010b), 226. As Gutzwiller states (231), 'the purpose of these epigrams . . . [was] to validate and commemorate a heroic status disseminated Panhellenically through Homeric poetry.'

[25] Gutzwiller (2010b), 228–30.

> You see the tomb of Idomeneus of Knossos. But I
> am placed nearby, Meriones the son of Molos.

This distich is quoted by Diodorus Siculus (5.79.4) in a passage probably derived from the *Peplos*, which is immediately followed by the comment (also plausibly present in the *Peplos*) that 'these, then, the Cretans especially honour in ritual, make sacrifice to, and pray to as manifest heroes, calling on them as helpers in the perils of war' (τούτους μὲν οὖν ὡς ἥρωας ἐπιφανεῖς τιμῶσιν οἱ Κρῆτες διαφερόντως, θύοντες καὶ κατὰ τοὺς ἐν τοῖς πολέμοις κινδύνους ἐπικαλούμενοι βοηθούς). Citing corroborating testimony for cult linked to many heroes of the *Peplos,* Gutzwiller concludes that 'in all likelihood, the other epitaphs were accompanied, in their *Peplos* context, by similar statements about cult practices.'[26]

Yet the *Peplos* also, and very pointedly (it seems to me), includes numerous epitaphs on notably minor Homeric characters, many of whom appear only once in the epic,[27] and for whom we have no corroborating evidence of cult. Is it enough to say, as Gutzwiller does (228), that 'the epitaphs for more minor heroes likely provide indication of cult activity simply not recorded in any other surviving source'? I think not. For in some cases, the obscurity of the tomb's occupant and his very lack of cult seems to be the point. Thus Prothoos, son of Tenthredon (#28 ~ *Il.*2.756), leader of the Magnesians, appears as follows:

> Σῶμα μὲν ἐν πόντῳ Προθόου Τενθρηδόνος υἱοῦ
> κεῖται· ἀνοίκτιστον δ' οὔνομα τύμβος ἔχει.

> The body of Tenthredon's son Prothoos lies
> in the sea, but the tomb holds his unmourned name.

As we learn, Prothoos perished at sea, where his body remains (Σῶμα μὲν ἐν πόντῳ . . . / κεῖται, lines 1–2); his tomb is thus a cenotaph, holding only his name (οὔνομα τύμβος ἔχει, line 2). Sepulchral epigram conventionally distinguishes, as here, between the lifeless remains of

---

[26] Gutzwiller (2010b), 230.

[27] Typically, they turn up in the catalogue of ships, cf. Nireus (#17 ~ *Il.*2.671–2), the most beautiful of those who came to Troy (not second to Achilles in the *Peplos* as he had been in Homer); Agapenor (#30 ~ *Il.*2.609), leader of the Arcadians; Gouneus (#32 ~ *Il.*2.748), leader of those around Dodona, who appears without patronymic even in Homer; Thalpios and Polyxeinos (#36 ~ *Il.*2.620), leaders of the Epeians; Pheidippos and Antiphos (#39 ~ *Il.*2.678), leaders of the Koans.

the deceased and the persistence of a name. Yet what is striking, and surprising, in our distich is that Prothoos' name is characterized as '*unmourned*' (ἀνοίκτιστος, line 2).[28] This seems to highlight from the standpoint of the later tradition the hero's very insignificance. Most importantly, such a characterization is quite antithetical to hero cult, where mourning rites were normal, indeed a hallmark: 'Crying and wailing are often attested (which would be impossible in rituals for the gods . . . )'.[29] The 'unmourned name' thus pointedly belies any link to a real-life ritual context. Rather, it seems as though the *Peplos*-poet chose to bestow funereal honours of a purely literary kind, expressly without cult, even on such marginal figures.[30] Unlike in epic, here at least they get equal space in a simple couplet, the lesser with the greater, a purely poetic tribute set beside—and thus accentuated by—the honours for greater heroes revered in cult.[31]

Minor epic characters can, of course, also be prominent recipients of cult: think only of Protesilaos, whose cult's renown extends from the closing pages of Herodotus (9.116–20) to Philostratus' *Heroikos*. Or again, the children of Medea: secondary figures in literature, yet

---

[28] Differently, see now Martins de Jesus (2015), 56. Lycophron, one of the few other authors to mention Prothoos and his father (*Alex.* 899–900), focalizes the '*unmourned*' state from the perspective of the dead man: Prothoos was one of those shipwrecked off the coast of Libya, 'who torn on the rocks will bewail their unburied destiny' (ἀκτέριστον ἐν πέτραις / αἰῶνα κωκύσουσιν ἠλοκισμένοι, lines 907–8). That is, he portrays the deceased as eternally absorbed in shrieking (κωκύειν, typically used of female mourners, cf. LSJ s.v., here in a perpetual present tense made more emphatic by αἰῶν, which may connote an endless span of time), engaged in the very ritual lament for the dead that would normally fall to the mourners at a funeral. The distich from the *Peplos*, by contrast, at least grants to 'Prothoos' (i.e. to his name) a tomb. See also Apollodorus (*Epit.* 6.15, cited in the scholia to Lycophron, line 902), who says by contrast that he was shipwrecked off Cape Caphareus in Euboea and that his men were swept on to Crete, where they settled.

[29] See Graf (2003). In keeping with this practice is the so-called Seal of Posidippus (*SH* 705.12–20 = 118.12–20 AB), where the poet urges his audience apropos the recent establishment of a shrine for Archilochus on Paros 'to give to the Parian nightingale a mournful flood, with fruitless tears streaming from the eyes, and groaning' (lines 18–20: ἀλλ᾿ ἐπὶ μὲν Παρ<ί>ηι δὸς ἀηδόνι λυγρὸν ἐφ.[ / νᾶμα κατὰ γληνέων δάκρυα κεινὰ χέω[ν / καὶ στενάχων).

[30] Indeed, one might say that a cenotaph can function as the very emblem of a purely literary epitaph, in all of which the body is on some level missing. On cenotaphs and their metapoetic significance, see Bruss (2005), 97–167.

[31] Perhaps this represents a distillation and rebalancing of the Iliadic habit of including 'obituary notices' for the deaths of minor characters, cf. Griffin (1980), 140–3; cf. also Schein (1984), 72–6 on the deaths of 'little heroes who exist merely to be killed' (p. 72).

conspicuous in ancient sources through their hero cult at Corinth.[32]
An epigram by Gaeticulus (*AP* 7.354 = *FGE* pp. 58–9), probably
writing early in the first century CE, sheds interesting light on their
worship:[33]

Παίδων Μηδείης οὗτος τάφος, οὓς ὁ πυρίπνους
    ζᾶλος τῶν Γλαύκης θῦμ᾽ ἐποίησε γάμων,
οἷς αἰεὶ πέμπει μειλίγματα Σισυφὶς αἶα,
    μητρὸς ἀμείλικτον θυμὸν ἱλασκομένα.

This is the tomb of Medea's children, whom fire-breathing
    jealousy at the wedding of Glauke turned into sacrificial victims,
they to whom the land of Sisyphus sends appeasement offerings forever,
    to placate the unappeasable wrath of their mother.

The θύματα (ritual victims) that Medea's offspring became, and the
μειλίγματα the Corinthians always send, clearly refer to the children's
cult, which other sources explain as the Corinthians' response to a
plague that befell the city following their murder.[34] Yet it is note-
worthy that Pausanias (2.3.7) explicitly says that 'following the
Roman sack of Corinth [146 BCE], when the indigenous Corinthians
were killed off, these rites were no longer performed for them by the
city's new settlers, nor did their children any longer cut off their hair
or wear the black clothing' (Κορίνθου δὲ ἀναστάτου γενομένης ὑπὸ
Ῥωμαίων καὶ Κορινθίων τῶν ἀρχαίων ἀπολομένων, οὐκέτι ἐκεῖναι
καθεστήκασιν αὐτοῖς αἱ θυσίαι παρὰ τῶν ἐποίκων οὐδὲ ἀποκείρονταί
σφισιν οἱ παῖδες οὐδὲ μέλαιναν φοροῦσιν ἐσθῆτα). In Pausanias' time,
then, as in Gaeticulus', the cult no longer existed. Thus this epitaph—
despite its emphasis on the permanence of the veneration (αἰεὶ
πέμπει, line 3)[35]—in all likelihood does not refer to current, or even
recent practice. Rather, it reflects Gaeticulus' engagement with writ-
ten sources, antiquarian sources at a remove from the thing itself.
It is thus a text commemorating texts *about* the cult of Medea's

---

[32] The establishment of their cult is referred to already in Euripides' *Medea*
1377–83, but seems to have gone back earlier, cf. Mastronarde (2002), 50–1. Cf.
generally Pache (2004), 9–48.
[33] The poem is missed by Pache (2004) in her otherwise exhaustive survey of the
sources.
[34] So e.g. Parmeniscus, a student of Aristarchus, cited by Didymus in the scholia to
Euripides' *Medea* 264, quoted by Mastronarde (2002), 50–1.
[35] The permanence expressed in αἰεὶ is echoed by the Corinthian land itself, αἶα.

children—literature imitating literature, with secondary reference to past historical reality.[36]

Lesser literary figures such as Medea's children in Gaeticulus, or Prothoos son of Tenthredon in the *Peplos*, certainly embody Hellenistic and later tastes for the bit-players of the poetic past. But in both these examples we are still dealing with a generation of heroes remote in time, hallowed in the Greek imagination by their role in epic. Hesiod locates them in an age prior to our own.[37] Is the gesture of commemoration different when Posidippus, instead of composing an epitaph for an epic hero—an Achilles or an Agamemnon—writes a poem in sepulchral style for a character from Sappho? With that question in mind, let us look at his epigram for Doricha, the hetaira of Egyptian Naucratis, reputedly a fellow-slave of Aesop and lover of Sappho's brother Charaxus (Athen.13.596c = 17 G-P = 122 AB):

Δωρίχα, ὀστέα μὲν σὰ πάλαι κόνις ἦν ὅ τε δεσμός
χαίτης ἥ τε μύρων ἔκπνοος ἀμπεχόνη,
ἧι ποτε τὸν χαρίεντα περιστέλλουσα Χάραξον
σύγχρους ὀρθρινῶν ἥψαο κισσυβίων·
Σαπφῶιαι δὲ μένουσι φίλης ἔτι καὶ μενέουσιν          5
ᾠδῆς αἱ λευκαὶ φθεγγόμεναι σελίδες.
οὔνομα σὸν μακαριστόν, ὃ Ναύκρατις ὧδε φυλάξει
ἔστ' ἂν ἴηι Νείλου ναῦς ἐφ' ἁλὸς πελάγη.

Doricha, your bones were dust long ago, and the ribbon
    of your hair, and the perfume-breathing shawl,
wherewith you once enfolded charming Charaxus,
    skin to skin, until you took hold of the morning cups.
But the bright resounding papyrus columns of Sappho's dear
    song abide, and will yet abide.
Most blessed is your name, which Naucratis will thus preserve
    as long as a ship sails out from the Nile across the salt sea.[38]

---

[36] One might consider it almost an inversion of the perspective on hero cult described by Henrichs (1993), 165 for Sophoclean tragedy. There, 'the cult hero is thus seen *in statu nascendi* against the implicit but unmarked background of existing hero cult in the audience's present.' Here, by contrast, cult heroes appear as eternal recipients of veneration in a hero cult that a learned audience may recognize as past and no longer existing in its own present.

[37] The fourth in his scheme of five, the ἀνδρῶν ἡρώων θεῖον γένος, οἳ καλέονται / ἡμίθεοι (*WD* 159–60).

[38] I follow Austin and Bastianini's Greek text, with translation adapted.

158     *Peter Bing*

The liaison between the Naucratite courtesan and Charaxus first certainly appears in Herodotus (2.134–5), who reports that she was set free by him at great price and that the poetess often rebuked him for his affair in song (ἐλύθη χρημάτων μεγάλων ὑπὸ ἀνδρὸς Μυτιληναίου Χαράξου τοῦ Σκαμανδρωνύμου παιδός, ἀδελφεοῦ δὲ Σαπφοῦς τῆς μουσοποιοῦ... ἐν μέλεϊ Σαπφὼ πολλὰ κατεκερτόμησέ μιν, 2.135). The historian calls her Rhodopis, rather than Doricha, and traditions diverge as to whether these two represent separate individuals.[39] Strabo (17.1.33) expressly equates Doricha and Rhodopis,[40] a position Denys Page explains by suggesting that 'Rhodopis' was the hetaira's nickname.[41] Athenaeus (13.596b–c), however, from whom we have the epigram of Posidippus, says that Herodotus mistakenly conflated Doricha with that Rhodopis, who had dedicated spits as a tithe at Delphi (Herodotus 2.135.4).[42] Doricha does indeed appear in Sappho's poetry (fr.15.11, maybe also fr.7.1), though until now not explicitly linked with Charaxus;[43] our epigram

---

[39] Lidov (2002) argues that Rhodopis and Doricha only came to be identified with one another in the Hellenistic biographical tradition for which Posidippus is our earliest source. Yatromanolakis (2007), 337 plausibly sees that assimilation as already having taken place in oral traditions prior to Herodotus: 'Given the available sources about Rhodopis and Dorikha, it would be safer to argue that in the context of much talking and singing about Rhodopis in men's meeting places and sympotic contexts (to which κλεινή, ἀοίδιμος, and περιλεσχήνευτος point in Herodotos' narrative), Sappho's Dorikha, probably represented by the poet as a harmful lover for Kharaxos, was assimilated into the culturally vibrant figure of Rhodopis.' See also his critique of Lidov at p. 325 n. 175.

[40] '[The hetaira], whom Sappho the poetess of songs calls Doricha, who became the beloved of her brother Charaxus while he travelled on business bringing Lesbian wine to Naukratis, but whom others name Rhodopis' (ἦν Σαπφὼ μὲν ἡ τῶν μελῶν ποιήτρια καλεῖ Δωρίχαν, ἐρωμένην τοῦ ἀδελφοῦ αὐτῆς Χαράξου γεγονυῖαν, οἶνον κατάγοντος εἰς Ναύκρατιν Λέσβιον κατ' ἐμπορίαν, ἄλλοι δ' ὀνομάζουσι Ῥοδῶπιν).

[41] Page (1955), 49 n. 1.

[42] Lidov (2002), 221 suggests that Athenaeus (13.596b–c), who says by contrast that Doricha, not Charaxus, was the target of Sappho's abuse 'must have misunderstood the antecedent of the gender-neutral Ionic pronoun in Herodotus' concluding phrase, κατεκερτόμησέ μιν'.

[43] This despite recent publication of important new Sapphic fragments, notably the 'Brothers Poem' (cf. Obbink (2014)), which fill out the picture of Charaxus' merchant seafaring, including worries that he 'return with a full ship' (ἀλλ' ἄϊ θρύλησθα Χάραξον ἔλθην / ναΐ σὺν πλήαι, lines 1–2), and a proposed prayer to Hera, 'that he should bring his ship back home safely to port' (πόλλα λίσσεσθαι βασίληαν Ἥραν / ἐξίκεσθαι τυίδε σάαν ἄγοντα / νᾶα Χάραξον, lines 6–8). For further new fragments, cf. Burris, Fish, and Obbink (2014). For discussion, see West (2014); Ferrari (2014). The latter plausibly argues that the new 'Brothers Poem' should be taken together with the newly augmented Sappho fr.5 and fr.15 as charting the

explicitly affirms that presence (lines 5–7), describing her ties to Charaxus in intimate detail.

In his epigram, Posidippus commemorates Doricha dead, adopting the rhetoric and language of epitaph. The speaker addresses the deceased as a passer-by might on reading her name on a tombstone.[44] The sepulchral aspect appears also in how the poem contrasts the body's impermanence with the persistence of *kleos*:[45] Doricha's bones have long since turned to dust, as have the clothes that adorned her body, yet her name (οὔνομα, line 7) will live on.[46] Similarly, the demonstrative adverb ὧδε in line 7 seems at first sight (if not ultimately) to suggest a funerary context, as it often appears in epigrams for monuments in the deictic sense 'here', i.e. on this monument (as e.g. at Posidippus 74.14 AB, etc.), a colouring that is only reinforced by its combination with φυλάξει (line 7): in inscribed epitaphs, the body's transience is frequently offset by the tomb, the departed's surviving family, or her community—in this case Naucratis—'guarding' or 'preserving' (φυλάσσειν) the remains and memory of the deceased (*CEG* 120.1, 487.4, *GV* 1764.6, *AP* 7.64.1). Finally, by labelling her name 'most blessed', μακαριστόν (line 7), Posidippus uses an epitaphic term of praise, μάκαρ, to describe Doricha's special eminence in death, one consistent with a hero's. For as Lattimore puts it, 'the μάκαρες are those whose lot after death is blessed, and these in turn

travels and travails of her brother Charaxus from the standpoint of Sappho back in Mytilene. The 'Brothers Poem' describes worries for Charaxus' safe return; fr.5 offers a prayer to the Nereids for a safe sea journey home of a brother (unnamed in the surviving fragments), and that 'he may wipe out those mistakes he once made, . . . and that he may free from painful torments those whose hearts he exhausted before'; fr.15 envisions a further journey, expresses the hope that he '[may wipe out] those mistakes he once made', and the wish to Aphrodite that Doricha (named at fr.15.11 beyond any serious doubt) not be able to boast about a renewed erotic liaison. Ferrari is right to underline the intertextual link, identified by Fränkel, between fr.5.5 ὄccα δὲ πρόcθ' ἄμβροτε πάντα λῦca[ι and fr.15.5 ὄccα δὲ πρ] όcθ' [ἄμ]βροτε κῆ[να –', where both lines seem to refer to Charaxus' misadventures with Doricha.

[44] Such direct address of the deceased goes back to the sixth century (*CEG* 127 = *GV* 1384). See further Peek's section IV 2, 'an den Toten gerichtete Rede', in *GV* 1384–1563. For literary variations on such address, see Callimachus' epigrams on Timonoe (*AP* 7.522 = 40 G-P = 15 Pf.) and Menekrates (*AP* 7.725 = 42 G-P = 61 Pf.).

[45] See Peek's 'Kontrastierender Typus' 7b ('Leib – Seele, Leib – Nachruhm') in *GV* 1754–84.

[46] Recall the σῶμα / οὔνομα contrast in the distich for Prothoos from the *Peplos* (p. 154).

would be approximately the same as the ἥρωες.' μακαριστόν, in other words, suggestive of quasi-heroic status.[47]

The post-Sapphic prose tradition concerning Doricha/Rhodopis, it should be stressed, focuses precisely on her tomb. Thus according to Herodotus, 'some of the Greeks' claim—incorrectly—that she built one of the very pyramids of Giza (Τὴν [sc. πυραμίδα] δὴ μετεξέτεροί φασι Ἑλλήνων Ῥοδώπιος ἑταίρης γυναικὸς εἶναι, οὐκ ὀρθῶς λέγοντες, 2.134), monuments whose function, as the historian elsewhere notes (2.124.4), was sepulchral. The pyramid came, it seems, to be commonly referred to as 'the hetaira's tomb', a characterization that remained popular into Imperial times: Strabo repeats it (17.1.33),[48] as does Diodorus Siculus (1.64.14)[49] and Pliny the Elder *(Naturalis historia* 36.17.82).[50] Tradition thus arrogates to its own purpose a real-life monument, grafting onto it the legend of a Naucratite hetaira, and creating thereby a metafiction, as with the 'tomb' of Charlotte Temple[51]—this, despite that tradition's thorough debunking at the hands of Herodotus (no more successful in this than the sceptic

---

[47] Lattimore (1962), 52. Lattimore goes on to say 'the term μάκαρ was a regular epithet of the gods, and it may well be that the authors of such epithets had the idea vaguely in mind that to survive in paradise after death meant the same thing as to become deified.' See also M. L. West's note on μάκαρες θνητοί at Hesiod *Op.* 141. For the superlative μακαριστόν to mark the very special dead in Posidippus, cf. 47.5 AB.

[48] 'It [sc. the pyramid] is called the tomb of the hetaera, which came about through her lovers' (λέγεται δὲ τῆς ἑταίρας τάφος γεγονὼς ὑπὸ τῶν ἐραστῶν).

[49] 'This pyramid some call the tomb of Rhodopis the hetaira, whose building they say some of the governors, who became her lovers, constructed together out of love for her' (ταύτην δ' ἔνιοι λέγουσι Ῥοδώπιδος τάφον εἶναι τῆς ἑταίρας, ἧς φασι τῶν νομάρχων τινὰς ἐραστὰς γενομένους διὰ φιλοστοργίαν ἐπιτελέσαι κοινῇ τὸ κατασκεύασμα).

[50] *haec sunt pyramidum miracula, supremumque illud, ne quis regum opes miretur, minimam ex iis, sed laudatissimam, a Rhodopide meretricula factam. Aesopi fabellarum philosophi conserva quondam et contubernalis haec fuit, maiore miraculo, tantas opes meretricio esse conquisitas.*

[51] This metafiction evidently raised the question how an hetaira, who already in Herodotus embodied the special allure of Naucratite courtesans, would have come to have her tomb so far from that city, in one of the great pyramids near Memphis. Strabo (17.1.33) tells a tale designed to answer that very question, as it mediates between the Naucratite locale in which Doricha plied her trade and her far-off burial in the pyramid. The story resembles Cinderella's: 'once upon a time while Doricha was bathing, an eagle snatched the hetaira's sandal away from one of her serving girls and, as it flew above the king, let it fall onto his lap, as he was dispensing justice in Memphis. Struck by the beautiful shape of the sandal and the unexpectedness of the occurrence, the king at once sent into the countryside to discover the woman to whom it belonged: she was found in the city of Naucratis, and brought to the king, who made her his wife. At her death she received the tomb mentioned before' (Μυθεύουσι δ' ὅτι λουομένης αὐτῆς ἓν τῶν ὑποδημάτων αὐτῆς ἁρπάσας ἀετὸς παρὰ τῆς θεραπαίνης

Mines in dissuading those who came to venerate Rowson's heroine at her 'grave'). Given Posidippus' sepulchral language, then, and the parallel tradition about 'the hetaira's tomb'—a monument certainly inspiring a sense of awe and power befitting a hero cult, even if evidence for that is lacking[52]—we might be tempted, with Rosenmeyer, to imagine that in his epigram 'the poet apparently stands in front of Doricha's tomb, addressing her directly', and that—following Strabo— we should identify that tomb with the pyramid.[53]

On closer inspection, however, it is doubtful that the poem has anything at all to do with a tomb or even a monument. There is no hint that the speaker is standing in front of the mighty pyramid near Memphis; the only locality mentioned is Naucratis; that is the place envisioned by the epigram as maintaining the memory of its long-dead subject, and it does so *not* by means of a memorial. For with its opening word, Doricha (line 1)—that οὔνομα that it proclaims will be preserved (line 7)—the poem signals that the hetaira's survival will not depend on a physical monument but on her representation in language, that is, on her poetic *kleos*.[54] For, as I have argued else-where,[55] the demonstrative adverb ὧδε in line 7 should not in fact be construed as having its deictic sense 'here', as would be likely in an epitaph; rather, ὧδε refers back to the ability of the papyrus scroll to bestow permanence on its subject (μένουσι . . . ἔτι καὶ μενέουσιν / . . . αἱ

---

κομίσειεν εἰς Μέμφιν καὶ τοῦ βασιλέως δικαιοδοτοῦντος ὑπαιθρίου, γενόμενος κατὰ κορυφὴν αὐτοῦ ῥίψειε τὸ ὑπόδημα εἰς τὸν κόλπον· ὁ δὲ καὶ τῷ ῥυθμῷ τοῦ ὑποδήματος καὶ τῷ παραδόξῳ κινηθεὶς περιπέμψειεν εἰς τὴν χώραν κατὰ ζήτησιν τῆς φορούσης ἀνθρώπου τοῦτο, εὑρεθεῖσα δ' ἐν τῇ πόλει τῶν Ναυκρατιτῶν ἀναχθείη καὶ γένοιτο γυνὴ τοῦ βασιλέως, τελευτήσασα δὲ τοῦ λεχθέντος τύχοι τάφου. Cf. similarly Aelian, *VH* 13.33).

[52] Remember, however, that Doricha's fellow-actors in the biographical narrative known already to Herodotus [2.134], Sappho, and Aesop, *were* recipients of such cult. For Sappho, see Aristotle, *Rh.*1398b 11–17 (citing Alcidamas), with Kimmel-Clauzet's assessment (2013), 198 of the force of the verb τετιμήκασι in this passage as referring concretely to cultic honours (τετιμήκασι . . . καὶ Μυτιληναῖοι Σαπφῶ καίπερ γυναῖκα οὖσαν), cf. also Clay (2004), 150–1. For Aesop, see Clay (2004), 127–8.

[53] Rosenmeyer (2006), 23 with n. 43.

[54] Note that Herodotus, too, stresses that it is her name (οὔνομα) that is on the lips of all Greeks (οὕτω δή τι κλεινὴ ἐγένετο ὡς καὶ οἱ πάντες Ἕλληνες Ῥοδώπιος τὸ οὔνομα ἐξέμαθον, 2.135.5), the object of song (ἀοίδιμος, like Archidike, another Naucratite hetaira), and of talk in every male club (περιλεσχήνευτος; cf. LSJ s.v.). See Yatromanolakis (2007), 312–37, who stresses how the terms Herodotus uses to describe the fame of the hetaira's affair with Charaxus point to the performance setting of Sappho's songs at symposia.

[55] Bing (2009), 262–3.

λευκαὶ φθεγγόμεναι σελίδες, lines 5–6), and therefore means that it is 'thus', i.e. 'through the medium of the scroll', that Naucratis will preserve the hetaira's name. Precisely by evoking conventions of sepulchral verse, then, the poem throws into stark relief its salient point: our epigram attests to an encounter with the notorious concubine in literature, not at her tomb, and it is poetry (Sappho's song, Posidippus' epigram)—i.e. literature, and not monuments—that will keep alive the literary figure, Doricha.[56]

The poem itself gives us a taste of how literature breathes life into such a figure. For even as it points to her corpse's bones, it reanimates the hetaira's carnal allure and titillates the reader by evoking intimate articles of her clothing—a hair band and a shawl that smells of myrrh—and how she used the latter to enfold Charaxus (περιστέλλουσα, line 3). In literature, copulating couples conventionally cloak themselves,[57] and such cloaking is also familiar from depictions in vase painting.[58] Here, however, the action is particularly provocative: Doricha performs what is usually represented in literature and art as a male gesture. Further, she presses against her lover 'skin to skin' (σύγχρους, line 4). And when, following περιστέλλουσα and σύγχρους, we learn that 'you clasped' (ἥψαο, line 4), a reader might expect the sexual sense of ἅπτω, 'have intercourse with' (LSJ s.v. III 5). If so, what Doricha clasped—the κισσύβια or cups of verse 4—comes as a humorous surprise, *para prosdokian*. Altogether, Posidippus makes the hetaira a vivid erotic presence even in death. It is in that sense, perhaps, that her name will live on as 'most blessed' (οὔνομα σὸν μακαριστόν, line 7), through the written legacy of Sappho—despite that poet's hostility to her in song.[59] As P. T. Barnum may have put it, 'there's no such thing as bad publicity'.

---

[56] G-P, on the contrary, describe the epigram as 'on a monument at Naucratis to the hetaira Doricha' (introduction to XVII) and suggest that ὧδε, 'whether *thus* (as seems more likely) or *here*, seems to indicate some form of memorial to Doricha' (on line 7). In the same vein most recently see Ferrari (2014), 10 n. 18): 'The encomiastic tone of the epigram is well explained if it was commissioned to the poet of Pella on the occasion of the erection of a commemorative monument for the hetaira, to which ὧδε in l.7 deictically alludes.'

[57] Cf. Alcibiades' attempt to seduce Socrates in Plato *Symp.* 219b by covering the two of them with his himation; cf. also Ascl. *AP* 5.169.3–4 = 1 G-P.

[58] Dover (1989), 98–9.

[59] I wonder whether Posidippus could have been referring with his μακαριστόν to Sappho fr.15.1], a μάκαι[ρα, which occurs in the very song containing our only certain naming of Doricha (fr.15.11). As fr.15.9 is plausibly addressed to Kypris, the feminine μάκαι[ρα is usually construed as referring to the goddess as part of a prayer for 'good

Thus even as it evokes epitaphic convention and possibly suggests its subject's quasi-heroic standing (with increasingly prominent Hellenistic hero worship possibly lurking in the background), Posidippus' epigram is determinedly unconcerned to commemorate the tomb of a real-life individual; it aims rather, as literature, to engage with and celebrate a lesser literary figure, a 'name' (οὔνομα), rather than an actual person, known to us from the poetry of Sappho. Perhaps we should similarly read a series of Hellenistic poems in which Archilochus' characters, the daughters of Lycambes, speak from their Parian grave to defend their reputations, after being driven to suicide by their maker's verbal assaults—though here one should add that these poems do not merely engage with a fixed Archilochean tradition (as Posidippus did with Sappho); they seek by emulation to *extend* it. The poems start in the third century BCE, and the idea evidently became popular enough that we find examples also from subsequent centuries.[60] Here, however, no trace of an actual tomb exists, no metafictional artefact of the collateral tradition like the burial place of Medea's children or a pyramid dubbed 'the hetaira's tomb'. It is, rather, purely a literary figment. Archilochus himself, by contrast, is one of our best-attested cases of real-life Hellenistic hero cult.[61] And his cult forms an important backdrop to our reading, even in these playful poems, self-consciously literary *jeux d'esprit*, that give voice to Lycambes' interred daughters. Consider the epigram by Meleager as an example (*AP* 7.352 = 132 G-P):

> Δεξιτερὴν Ἀίδαο θεοῦ χέρα καὶ τὰ κελαινά
> ὄμνυμεν ἀρρήτου δέμνια Περσεφόνης,
> παρθένοι ὡς ἔτυμον καὶ ὑπὸ χθονί· πολλὰ δ᾽ ὁ πικρός
> αἰσχρὰ καθ᾽ ἡμετέρης ἔβλυσε παρθενίης
> Ἀρχίλοχος· ἐπέων δὲ καλὴν φάτιν οὐκ ἐπὶ καλά

---

sailing' (]ευπλο.·, fr.15.2). That reconstruction is extremely uncertain, however, and we should at least consider whether Sappho's μάκαι[ρα might already refer to Doricha.

[60] The earliest instance comes from a late-third-century BCE fragmentary papyrus containing a poem in iambic tetrameter catalectics using Ionic forms, that is, emulating the style of Archilochus (*SH* 997 = P. Trinity Coll. Dublin 193a). It is imitated soon after in an epigram of Dioscorides of the second century BCE (*AP* 7.351 = 17 G-P), which is copied in turn by an epigram of Meleager (*AP* 7.352 = 132 G-P). Cf. Rosen (2007), 472–4.

[61] For the Hellenistic cult of Archilochus, see Clay (2004) and most recently Kimmel-Clauzet (2013), 223–30.

ἔργα, γυναικεῖον δ᾽ ἔτραπεν ἐς πόλεμον.
Πιερίδες, τί κόρῃσιν ἐφ᾽ ὑβριστῆρας ἰάμβους
ἐτράπετ᾽, οὐχ ὁσίῳ φωτὶ χαριζόμεναι;

By the right hand of Hades the god and the dismal bed
  of unspeakable Persephone, we swear
that we are truly virgins even under the earth. But that bitter man
  spewed out many shameful things against our virginity,
Archilochus. And he turned his poems' pretty phrases not to pretty
  deeds, but to war against women.
Why, Muses, did you turn his violent iambs against
  girls and gratify an unholy man?

Here, these previously subsidiary figures speak for themselves, turn-
ing Archilochus' self-righteousness against him in what Ralph Rosen
has called 'this imaginary "anti-iambus"'.[62] In Meleager's witty con-
ceit, the virgins seize the mantle of iambic poet: it is they now who
invoke the Muses (virgins too, supposedly) and exploit the power of
verse for attack (lines 7–8). First, after solemnly affirming their own
innocence and accusing Archilochus of slander, they demolish his
well-known boast of prowess as both warrior and poet—'I am the
servant of lord Enyalios and skilled in the lovely gift of the Muses' (1 W):
in fact, they declare, he engages in womanish warfare, γυναικεῖον . . .
πόλεμον (line 6);[63] his words may be pretty, yet his deeds are des-
picable (ἐπέων δὲ καλὴν φάτιν οὐκ ἐπὶ καλά / ἔργα, lines 5–6). To be
sure, Archilochus enjoyed heroic status and cult at this time, but
Lycambes' daughters seem simultaneously to point to and dispute
that status when they describe him merely as φώς, and emphatically
οὐχ ὅσιος, not 'hallowed' (line 8). Indeed, by complaining that the
Muses gave *charis* to such a man (χαριζόμεναι, line 8), they may refer
to the very anecdote about Archilochus' *Dichterweihe* inscribed on
the wall of his Parian shrine, i.e. his moonlight encounter with the
goddesses in the countryside where, in exchange for his cow, they
offered him a fitting price (αὐταὶ δώσουσιν αὐτῶι τιμὴν ἀξίαν),[64]

---

[62] Rosen (2007), 474.

[63] Indeed, the daughters may (as Regina Höschele suggests to me) turn Archilo-
chus' own language against him with the adjective γυναικεῖον, which appears just once
in the surviving fragments, when Archilochus exhorts fellow-citizens to push away
their 'womanish grief', γυναικεῖον πένθος (13.10 W): from their perspective, he
engages in the very womanish behaviour he warned others against.

[64] Mnesiepes inscription, *SEG* 15.517 col.2.33.

apparently a lyre, the symbol of his art. The daughters' final word, χαριζόμεναι, is a parting iambic shot, for given the well-known erotic connotation of χαρίζομαι (LSJ s.v. I 3; cf. s.v. χάρις III 2), it insinuates with a sharp iambic jab that the Muses' exchange consisted of something more than a lyre, namely of sexual favours.[65] Does the plural imply that all nine had their way with him?[66] Finally, Jennifer Larson has identified a common story type in connection with Greek heroine cult, 'The Wrongful Death of the Heroine'.[67] For all of the poem's literariness, its status as Art about Art, could it be that the wrongful deaths of Lycambes' virgin daughters evoke for an ancient audience the prospect of their eventual heroization and ritual appeasement (as we saw in the case of Medea's children)? The Parian poet may have considered the case closed, but—what a surprise!—his story is not over: our epigram not only engages his fictional world, it appropriates and extends it. Take that, Archilochus!

Engaging with and elaborating such a world is (I think) also what my final examples are concerned with, two sepulchral epigrams transmitted under the name of Erinna. This fourth-century poetess was the author of the *Distaff*, a hexameter lament of some three hundred verses mourning Baucis, the narrator's childhood companion, who died

---

[65] The daughters of Lycambes thus take up the mocking banter that Archilochus had engaged in with the Muses on the Mnesiepes inscription: προσελθόντα σκώπτειν, τὰς δὲ δέξασθαι αὐτὸν μετὰ παιδιᾶς καὶ γέλωτος (*SEG* 15.517 col.2.30–1).

[66] As Jerzy Danielewicz suggests to me, the idea of having sex with all nine Muses recalls the tradition about the singer Thamyris. According to Asclepiades of Tragilus (schol. to Eur. *Rhesus* 916 = *FGrHist* 12 F 10), 'When the Muses came to Thrace, Thamyris asked to move in with them, saying that for the Thracians it was customary for one man to couple with many women. The Muses, in response to his invitation, proposed that they hold a contest in song: if they won they would do what they wanted with him, but if he won he would take as many women as he wanted' (ἀφικομένων δὲ τῶν Μουσῶν εἰς Θράκην τὸν μὲν Θάμυριν μνείαν ποιήσασθαι πρὸς αὐτὰς ὑπὲρ τοῦ συνοικεῖν ἀπάσα<ι>ς, φάσκοντα τοῖς Θραιξὶ νόμιμον εἶναι πολλαῖς τὸν ἕνα συνεῖναι· τὰς δὲ προκαλεσαμένοι ἐπὶ τούτωι ποι[εῖς]θαι τὴν δι' ὠιδῆς ἄμιλλαν ἐφ' ὧι, ἐὰν μὲν αὐταὶ νικήσωσιν, ὅτι ἂν θέλωσιν αὐτὸν ποιεῖν, εἰ δὲ ἐκεῖνος, ὅσας ἂν αὐτὸς βούληται, τοσαύτας λήψεσθαι γυναῖκας). See also Apollodorus' *Library* 1.3.3. Perhaps the notion of coupling with all nine Muses suggests the genesis of boasts by other poets (φιλόμουσοι, all!) of their ability to have sex nine times in a row? See Höschele (2006), 134 who cites the *novem continuas fututiones* of Catullus 32.8, Philodemus' ἐννέα at *AP* 11.30.1 = 27 G-P = 19 Sider, Ovid's *exigere a nobis angusta nocte Corinnam/ me memini numeros sustinuisse novem* at *Amores* 3.7.25–6, and also the *Life of Aesop* (ch. 75), where Aesop satisfied his mistress nine times in a row (ἐπετέλει τὸ πάθος ἕως ἐννέα), but failed on his tenth attempt.

[67] Larson (1995), 131–44.

shortly after her wedding.[68] Here, we are no longer dealing with a dead poetic figure of the heroic age, however minor; nor again with characters hallowed by centuries of popular and scholarly reception, like Doricha or Lycambes' daughters. Rather, Baucis inhabits the contemporary world of Erinna's βαιὸν ἔπος, her 'little epic',[69] 'an alternative world', as Gutzwiller calls it, 'the world of a woman's life as seen by a woman'.[70] Here, a first-person narrator, named 'Erinna' in the text (line 38) and described as nineteen years of age at the time of her friend's death (line 37), grieves for her girlhood friend, recalling their games, their dolls, the wool-working in their homely setting, etc., all described in an admixture of Doric (which may evoke earlier lyric threnody,[71] if not the poet's native dialect[72]) and Aeolic (perhaps a nod to Sappho), even as it diverges starkly from traditional epic language. Hellenistic poets greatly admired the poem's artfulness and innovation, embracing its 'alternative world', and seeing in it an important precursor of their own literary values.[73] The two epigrams which I examine here (*AP* 7.710 = 1 G-P = F°5 Neri, and *AP* 7.712 = 2 G-P = F°6 Neri), like Erinna's hexameter poem itself, commemorate the death of Baucis (as indeed do the two different epigrams discussed by Platt in the first chapter of this volume, pp. 26–9):

> Στᾶλαι καὶ Σειρῆνες ἐμαὶ καὶ πένθιμε κρωσσέ,
> ὅστις ἔχεις Ἀΐδα τὰν ὀλίγαν σποδιάν,
> τοῖς ἐμὸν ἐρχομένοισι παρ' ἠρίον εἴπατε χαίρειν,
> αἴτ' ἀστοὶ τελέθωντ' αἴθ' ἑτεροπτόλιες·
> χὤτι με νύμφαν εὖσαν ἔχει τάφος, εἴπατε καὶ τό·
> χὤτι πατήρ μ' ἐκάλει Βαυκίδα, χὤτι γένος
> Τηνία, ὡς εἰδῶντι, καὶ ὅττι μοι ἁ συνεταιρίς
> Ἤρινν' ἐν τύμβῳ γράμμ' ἐχάραξε τόδε.

[68] Parts of fifty-four verses from the poem's end have survived on a papyrus, PSI 1090, cf. the editions of Lloyd-Jones and Parsons in *SH* 401 and (with exhaustive commentary) Neri (2003).
[69] Thus Antipater of Sidon in a celebratory epigram (58.2 G-P = *AP* 7.713.2).
[70] Gutzwiller (1997a), 204.    [71] See Fantuzzi and Hunter (2004), 29.
[72] West (1977), 117: 'The Doric element is meant to convey that she is an ordinary person, a homely little Telian maid.'
[73] She is celebrated in epigrams of Asclepiades *AP* 7.11 = 28 G-P, Anon. *AP* 7.12, Leonidas or Meleager *AP* 7.13 = 98 G-P, Antipater of Sidon *AP* 7.713 = 58 G-P, and Anon. *AP* 9.190. For her poem's appeal to Hellenistic authors, see Gutzwiller (1997a), 204 and 210; Sens (2003).

Stelae and my Sirens and the mournful urn,
  you who enclose the little ash of Hades,
say farewell to those passing my grave,
  whether local townsmen or from other cities;
say also that the tomb holds me, a bride; and say this too:
  that my father called me Baucis, and that by race
I was from Tenos, so they may know, and that my comrade
  Erinna caused this writing to be engraved on the tomb.

Νύμφας Βαυκίδος εἰμί, πολυκλαύταν δὲ παρέρπων
  στάλαν τῷ κατὰ γᾶς τοῦτο λέγοις Ἀίδᾳ·
"Βάσκανος ἔσσ᾽, Ἀίδα." τὰ δέ τοι καλὰ σάμαθ᾽ ὁρῶντι
  ὠμοτάταν Βαυκοῦς ἀγγελέοντι τύχαν,
ὡς τὰν παῖδ᾽ Ὑμέναιος ἐφ᾽ αἷς ἀείδετο πεύκαις,
  τᾶσδ᾽ ἐπὶ καδεστὰς ἔφλεγε πυρκαϊᾶς,
καὶ σὺ μέν, ὦ Ὑμέναιε, γάμων μολπαῖον ἀοιδάν
  ἐς θρήνων γοερὸν φθέγμα μεθαρμόσαο.

I belong to Baucis the bride. As you pass the much-lamented
  stele, say this to subterranean Hades:
'You are spiteful, Hades.' To the viewer, these beautiful letters
  will announce the most cruel fate of Baucis:
that with the torches to which the Hymen song was sung,
  her father-in-law cremated the girl on this pyre.
For your part, Hymenaeus, you changed the tuneful marriage song
  to the anguished wail of lament.

By at least *c.*100 BCE, Erinna had come to be known not only as the author of the *Distaff* but as a poet of epigram: Meleager includes her among the authors of his *Garland* (AP 4.1.12 = 1.12 G-P). Yet critics have long harboured doubts as to whether our two epigrams can truly be by Erinna.[74] My sense is that they are best taken as *responses* to the *Distaff*, products of admiring readers who have written themselves into Erinna's fictional world. Whether or not they are by the same authors, the two epitaphs seem carefully keyed to one another like

[74] The most forceful expression of these doubts regarding the two epigrams' authenticity were voiced by West (1977), 114–15. For a judicious assessment, see Neri (2003), 85–8, 431–8: He concludes (p. 88) that 'Resta l'impressione che esse siano nate nello stesso *milieu* e con la stessa funzione dei *testimonia* epigrammatici . . . : breve "dossologia" di Erinna . . . ma non opera schiettamente erinniana.' For the view that they are both genuine, see e.g. Wilamowitz-Moellendorff (1913), 228–30; Luck (1954), 170–2 with n. 14.

*Parallelgedichte* on an actual monument:[75] the first, spoken by Baucis, culminates by dwelling on Erinna, the dead girl's συνεταιρίς (line 7), poet of the *Distaff*; the second, voiced by the tomb, appears to summarize Erinna's epic (ὠμοτάταν Βαυκοῦς ἀγγελέοντι τύχαν, line 4, etc.).[76] The striking σφραγίς at the close of the first epigram, where Erinna is named as the epigram's author (καὶ ὅττι μοι ἁ συνεταιρίς / Ἤρινν' ἐν τύμβῳ γράμμ' ἐχάραξε τόδε, lines 7–8), may indeed suggest, as Neri puts it, that 'con questa "firma", un eventuale falsario poteva cercare di dare maggiore credibilità alla propria composizione.'[77] In any case, the epigrams seem at least as concerned to commemorate Erinna and her poem as Baucis. From that perspective, it is notable that both epigrams so immerse themselves in that 'alternative world of a woman's life as seen by a woman' that they essentially write out the men: Baucis' male relatives, though mentioned, are left anonymous: each appears solely in his societal 'function', the father in the first poem (πατήρ, line 6), the father-in-law in the second (καδεστάς, line 6). Their anonymity and the concomitant focus on the female sphere bespeak a sympathetic response to Erinna's work,[78] a *literary* response: Art inspired by Art.

The epigrams respond, moreover, by filling a void in the narrative of the *Distaff*, that is, they not only engage the poem's 'alternative world', but extend its reach. Erinna had lamented in the *Distaff* that 'it is not permitted for my feet to leave the house / nor for my eyes to gaze upon your corpse, nor to wail / with my hair uncovered' (οὐ [γ]άρ μοι πόδες ....[.].[ ]ἄπο δῶμα βέβαλοι, / οὐδ' ἐσιδῆν φαέ.[σσι ἔχω νέ]κυν, οὐδὲ γοᾶσαι / γυμναῖσιν χαίταισιν, lines 32–4). As though to compensate, the epigrams bring Erinna to the site of Baucis' tomb (παρ' ἠρίον in line 3 of the first poem) as author of its inscription

---

[75] This is not to say that there are not incongruities which may point to multiple authors: the first poem evokes plural stelae (στᾶλαι, line 1), the second only a solitary marker (στάλαν, line 2). This led Schneidewin to emend the first to singular στάλα (followed by Gow and Page), others such as Dilthey (1869), 28–30 to consider only that epigram genuine, while taking the second for a later imitation. In this he is followed, e.g., by Gutzwiller (1998), 77 n. 81.

[76] Thus also Neri (2003), 87.          [77] Neri (2003), 431.

[78] West (1977), 115, on the other hand, suggests that 'the reason [for the absence of the names] is that the author or authors of the epigrams did not know the names... [but] knew only what was known throughout Greece from the *Distaff*: the wedding, the death, and Erinna's friendship.' As we possess only fragments of fifty-four out of three hundred verses, however, we cannot know that the men were not named elsewhere in the poem.

(Ἤρινν' ἐν τύμβῳ γράμμ' ἐχάραξε τόδε, line 8)[79] and even at the pyre where her corpse was burned (τᾶσδ' . . . πυρκαϊᾶς, line 6 in the second poem). Indeed, the poetess' own words are perpetually repeated there, for the rebuke that passers-by are asked to hurl at Hades in the second poem ('You are spiteful, Hades', 'Βάσκανος ἔσσ', Ἀίδα', line 3) is likely a quote from the *Distaff*:[80] the words are cited as the poetess' own in an epigram on Erinna by Leonidas or Meleager (ἦ ῥα τόδ' ἔμφρων / εἶπ' ἐτύμως ἁ παῖς· 'Βάσκανος ἔσσ', Ἀίδα.' *AP* 7.13.3–4), as discussed by Platt on pp. 27–8. The cue in our epigram that leads us back to the *Distaff* as the source for this reproach is ἔσσ', the only Aeolic form in this otherwise Doric epigram.[81]

It is worth adding that Erinna's presence at Baucis' tomb was further actualized by Meleager, since, as Regina Höschele points out at pp. 207–8, he likely juxtaposed within his *Garland* our epigrams for Baucis with others in sepulchral style commemorating Erinna.[82] Their 'tombs' stood side by side in his anthology. In that setting, as Höschele argues (p. 207), 'Erinna's portrayal as Baucis' συνεταιρίς in the sphragis to 7.710, . . . retrospectively takes on an additional layer of meaning: the two are comrades (συνεταιρίδες!) closely joined not just in life but also in death.'

Like the examples we have studied before, then, these two epigrams commemorating Baucis (a character from literature, not from life) are a kind of metafiction, reactions to, and spin-offs from, an urtext. In the course of this chapter we have seen how such metafictional responses to dead figures from literature take a variety of forms. Sometimes, as with the 'tomb' of Charlotte Temple and of the Naucratite hetaira, they appear as physical monuments in the real world; in other instances, like the tomb for Medea's children, they relate to written or oral traditions *about* such monuments, long after the structures themselves have vanished; at other times again, as with the epigrams

---

[79] At first, we might be tempted to imagine Erinna herself 'carving' the text onto the tomb, though on reflection we should probably read χαράσσειν in a causative sense.

[80] Thus already Hartung (1857), 113–14, who includes it as his fr.7 of Erinna. See also West (1977), 115; Sens (2003), 83; Neri (2003), 152–3 who lists it as Erinna F 2.

[81] Neri (2003), 86. West (1977), 115 and Neri (2003), 86 also emphasize the awkward redundancy of Ἀίδᾳ / . . . Ἀίδα (lines 2–3) in successive clauses, which they take as a further sign that the epigram is the work of an inept imitator, not of Erinna herself. I would also point out that those clauses are metrically identical, producing a monotonously sing-song quality to the lines.

[82] Höschele in this volume, pp. 195–215.

on Doricha and Lycambes' daughters, they take their inspiration *as* literature largely *from* literature—though in each of these preceding types we may also find greater or lesser reference to the cult of literary heroes (no surprise, given that in these texts we are typically concerned with the tombs of established cultural icons, and with a genre—epigram—that was historically connected with actual monuments). In the case of the epigrams on the tomb of Baucis, we approach most closely to a kind of metafiction inspired by, and remaining part of, a purely fictional world. In this they resemble what Mark Payne has studied in connection with metafictions in, and in response to, Theocritean pastoral—another 'alternative world', like that of the women evoked by Erinna.[83] Through poems like the epitaphs for Baucis, readers enter that world, writing themselves into its fictional scenery; they engage with its characters and their concerns; through emulation, they even extend its reach. In this instance, they go so far as to take on the guise of its author, Erinna—the ultimate homage to a literary model.

---

[83] Payne (2007), 21: In metafiction, readers 'participate imaginatively in the creation of a world even as they are simultaneously made aware that this world is an invention . . . by endeavoring to become a fictional subject, the impersonator attempts to make present in his own life what is properly located in a fictional world.' Pastoral fiction 'lies just across the border from reality. When we aspire to it, we seem to inhabit its world for a while, and, when we have done so, we will . . . long to return there.'

# 8

## Still Singing

### The Case of Orpheus

*Barbara Graziosi*

Orpheus is a prominent character in ancient literature and art. Several stories about him resonate through the sources and still have remarkable vitality today.[1] Ibycus, the earliest extant author who mentions him, reveals that Orpheus was already 'of famous name' in the sixth century BCE (ὀνομακλυτὸν Ὀρφήν).[2] A relief from Delphi, a metope from the Sicyonian treasury dated to 570–560 BCE, depicts Orpheus with a lyre in hand, next to the Argo: he is evidently about to embark on the ship, joining Jason and the other Argonauts in their quest to retrieve the Golden Fleece.[3] As well as telling stories about him, several ancient sources present Orpheus as the author of mystic texts. Aristophanes mentions him together with Musaeus, Hesiod, and Homer, in a passage that treats them all as authors, and succinctly defines their oeuvres: 'Consider how useful our noble-minded poets have been from the beginning. Orpheus revealed to us the mysteries

---

[1] Orpheus features prominently in medieval and modern literature, art, music, ballet, theatre, and film. I quote just one work per genre, an exercise that demands restraint: *Sir Orfeo*, an anonymous Middle English narrative poem of the eleventh century; *Orfeo ed Euridice*, painted by Titian *c.*1508; Gluck's opera *Orfeo ed Euridice* (1762); the ballet *Orpheus*, created by choreographer George Balanchine to music by Stravinsky (1948); *Orpheus Descending,* a play by Tennessee Williams (1957); and *Black Orpheus*, a 1959 film by Marcel Camus. Reid (1993) provides a much longer, yet by no means complete list of post-classical works featuring Orpheus.

[2] Ibycus 306 *PMG* = *Orph.* 864 II Bernabé.

[3] Marble metope depicting Orpheus by the Argo, Sicyonian treasury: Archaeological Museum of Delphi 1323 = Orpheus no. 6 *LIMC*.

and abstinence from murder, Musaeus taught us cures from illnesses
and oracles, Hesiod working the land, the seasons for fruits, and
ploughing; and then, as for godlike Homer, for what did he acquire
honour and fame besides this, that he taught useful things: drawing up
troops, brave deeds, the arming of men?'[4]

Given the abundance and variety of ancient engagements with
Orpheus, there may be good pragmatic reasons, as well as more prob-
lematic intellectual ones, for keeping Orpheus the mythical character
and Orpheus the author of religious texts firmly apart. It has become
a commonplace of scholarship to declare, at the beginning of a study
on Orpheus, whether it is going to deal with one or the other. Thus,
in the first chapter of *Orpheus: The Myth of the Poet,* Segal declares:
'The "poetic" Orpheus inevitably overlaps with the founder of Orph-
ism, but it is the Orpheus of the poetic tradition that this chapter
discusses.'[5] Guthrie, to give a reverse example, dismisses depictions of
Orpheus in poetry on the first half of the first page of *Orpheus
and Greek Religion,* in order to address himself to the origin and
meaning of Orphic texts, rituals, and beliefs: 'It is when we try to be a
little less poetic and a little more historical that we find our difficulties
beginning.'[6] The difficulties Guthrie mentioned in 1952 are still keenly
felt: the study of ancient Orphism is a controversial and rather esoteric
field of enquiry, shaped by a select number of devoted scholars, who
argue with each other over what beliefs and practices may have con-
stituted 'so-called Orphic ways of life'.[7] Burkert explains: 'the problem
of Orphism has become one of the most hotly disputed areas in the
history of Greek religion. The lack of sound and ancient sources,
imprecise concepts, and hidden Christian or anti-Christian motiv-
ations on the part of the interpreters have created a tangled web of
controversies.'[8]

It may seem foolhardy to attempt an intervention in this field, let
alone combine it with an interpretation of Orpheus as a figure in
poetry, given the wealth and complexity of ancient sources, and of

---

[4] *Frogs* 1030–6 = *Orph.* 547 I Bernabé.       [5] Segal (1989), 1.
[6] Guthrie (1952), 1.
[7] Ὀρφικοί τινες λεγόμενοι βίοι: Plato, *Laws* 782c–d = *Orph.* 625 I Bernabé.
Santamaria (2012) offers an overview of publications that appeared in the first decade
of the third millennium alone. For a broader account of scholarship on Orphism from
the Renaissance to the twenty-first century, see Edmonds (2013), 51–68. On the issue,
see also below, p. 186.
[8] Burkert (1985), 296.

modern scholarship on them. The justification for writing a short study of a large subject is that I aim to make a simple point, namely that Orpheus the character and Orpheus the author coincide, very precisely, at his tomb.

## ORPHEUS THE CHARACTER

There are three main stories about Orpheus' accomplishments in life that deserve attention in the context of my argument. One has already surfaced: Orpheus joined Jason and the Argonauts on their expedition to retrieve the Golden Fleece. The earliest extant text that mentions this feat is Pindar, *Pythian* 4.176–7, which emphasizes Orpheus' exceptional qualities as a singer. Apollonius of Rhodes, in the Catalogue that opens his *Argonautica*, goes as far as granting Orpheus first place in his list of Argonauts. He elaborates on 'the bewitching power of his lyre' (*Arg.* 1.31) and concludes that he joined the expedition because a prophecy stated that he would be 'a helper in facing the challenges to come' (*Arg.* 1.32–4). This prompted ancient readers to ask an obvious question, as a scholium to line 1.23 testifies: 'It is a matter of enquiry why Orpheus, who was not strong, sailed with the heroes. It is because Chiron, who had mantic powers, prophesied that, if Orpheus went with them, they would be able to sail even past the Sirens.'[9] As Meuli argued, it is probable that the prophecy already featured in an early epic *Argonautica,* in which each Argonaut had an individual power suited to meeting a specific challenge along the way.[10] Orpheus, because of his exceptional talent as a singer, would be able to overcome the Sirens' song with his own.[11]

The second famous story associated with Orpheus is that he was able to enchant even animals, plants, and stones with the sweetness of his song. Apollonius mentions this power, specifically in relation to the oaks he was supposed to have moved from Pieria to Thrace, but in this case, too, the story is much older. The earliest extant source

---

[9] Schol. ad 1.23, pp. 8–9 Wendel = *Orph.* 896 I, 907, and 1010 II Bernabé, translation based on S. Burges Watson, *Living Poets* (Durham, 2015): <https://livingpoets.dur.ac.uk/w/Scholion_to_Apollonius_of_Rhodes,_Argonautica>.

[10] Meuli (1921), 2–24; see also West (2005), 45 who argues that Apollonius relied on the early epic *Argonautica* in his account of Orpheus and the Sirens.

[11] The episode is told in *Arg.* 4.891–919.

that mentions Orpheus' power to enchant nature is Simonides, in a fragment of Franciscan beauty (567 *PMG* = *Orph.* 943 Bernabé):

τοῦ καὶ ἀπειρέσιοι
πωτῶντ᾽ ὄρνιθες ὑπὲρ κεφαλᾶς,
ἀνὰ δ᾽ ἰχθύες ὀρθοὶ
κυανέου ᾽ξ ὕδατος ἄλ-
λοντο καλᾶι σὺν ἀοιδᾶι.

And countless birds
flew over his head,
and fish leapt straight out
of the dark water,
at his beautiful song.

Orpheus' capacity to charm animals, plants, and stones features also in tragedy and is, unsurprisingly, a popular theme in ancient art.[12]

The third and most famous story about Orpheus—but also the least well-attested in early sources—is his *katabasis*, his descent into the underworld with the aim of bringing his wife Eurydice back to life. It is likely that Euripides alludes to this myth in his earliest tragedy, the *Alcestis*, though even that can be disputed.[13] The *Alcestis* tells the story of a different husband, Admetus, who allows his wife Alcestis to die in place of him. Early on in the play, Admetus expresses his (moderate) regret at the situation: had he Orpheus' 'song and music' to charm Persephone and her husband, he would of course descend into the underworld and bring his wife back to life; but unfortunately he does not, so Alcestis should busy herself in the underworld and ensure there is a comfortable home ready for him there, when he, too, meets his end.[14] The wording of the passage may allow for the possibility that

---

[12] In tragedy: Aesch. *Ag.* 1629–30 (= *Orph.* 946 Bernabé); Eur. *Iphig. Aul.* 1211–14 (= *Orph.* 948 Bernabé) and *Bacch.* 560–4 (= *Orph.* 947 Bernabé). For representations in ancient art, see Orpheus nos 89–163 *LIMC*.

[13] Jane Harrison did: (1908), 601–5.

[14] Eur. *Alc.* 357–64 (part of which = *Orph.* 680 and 980 Bernabé):

εἰ δ᾽ Ὀρφέως μοι γλῶσσα καὶ μέλος παρῆν,
ὥστ᾽ ἢ κόρην Δήμητρος ἢ κείνης πόσιν
ὕμνοισι κηλήσαντά σ᾽ ἐξ Ἅιδου λαβεῖν,
κατῆλθον ἄν, καί μ᾽ οὔθ᾽ ὁ Πλούτωνος κύων
οὔθ᾽ οὑπὶ κώπῃ ψυχοπομπὸς ἂν Χάρων
ἔσχον, πρὶν ἐς φῶς σὸν καταστῆσαι βίον.
ἀλλ᾽ οὖν ἐκεῖσε προσδόκα μ᾽, ὅταν θάνω,
καὶ δῶμ᾽ ἑτοίμαζ᾽, ὡς συνοικήσουσά μοι.

Euripides refer only to Orpheus' musicality rather than the whole story of his descent into the underworld, but it seems more likely that it implies a contrast between the loving husband Orpheus, who goes into the underworld in order to save his wife from death, and the selfish king Admetus, who allows his wife to die in place of him. The more interesting observation is that the passage emphasizes Orpheus' capacity to retrieve his wife from the underworld, rather than his failure to do so. This detail has been much debated in scholarship, from Wilamowitz (who argued for an original happy ending to Orpheus' *katabasis*) to Jane Harrison (who insisted that, in early depictions of Orpheus, *'there is no Eurydice'* to be seen).[15]

The content and antiquity of the myth of Orpheus and Eurydice continues to attract debate, for two main reasons. The first concerns the study of religion and, more specifically, Orpheus' likely early association with male groups, rather than heterosexual love.[16] The second concerns the evaluation of literary and artistic merit—a matter that is still often framed in terms of originality. Was the tragic Orpheus, the lover who turns back to look at his wife while still in Hades, and thus loses her forever, Virgil's creation?[17] Or was Virgil reworking a theme already established in classical Greece and, for example, beautifully expressed in the so-called 'Orpheus relief'?[18]

Amid all the uncertainty some points can, I think, be made with a degree of confidence. The first is that 'no extant version is unequivocal about the success of Orpheus' mission' to retrieve his wife.[19] The second is that there is, indeed, some equivocation: it would be too blunt to declare, with Heath, that Orpheus' mission was always, and

[15] The happy ending was championed, e.g., by Wilamowitz-Moellendorff (1932), 193 and, as influentially, by Linforth (1941), 16–21. Harrison (1908), 602 rightly notes the absence of Eurydice in early representations of Orpheus: her italics. On the myth of Orpheus and Eurydice before Virgil, see also Heurgon (1932) and Bowra (1952). For a more recent summary of the scholarly debate on this issue, see Heath (1994).

[16] For Orpheus' early association with male groups, see Graf (1987) and Bremmer (1991). The story of the Thracian women who tore Orpheus apart, discussed below on pp. 177 and 191, is best explained as a hostile reaction to his homosexuality; see Lissarrague (1994) for a good interpretation of the visual evidence.

[17] Lee (1996), for example, insists on an original 'happy ending' for Orpheus and Eurydice in order to demonstrate Virgil's originality and brilliance.

[18] For two opposing interpretations of the so-called 'Orpheus relief', see Touchette (1990) and Heath (1994). The relationship between a Greek 'original' of *c.*420 BCE and several surviving Roman versions makes interpretation particularly difficult.

[19] Burges Watson (2013b); see also Sansone (1985).

in all sources, 'a failure'.[20] The reference in the *Alcestis* to Orpheus'
music—and its usefulness in terms of rescuing a wife from the
underworld—has already been discussed. We also know of a comedy
by Antiphanes (fourth century BCE) entitled *Orpheus*: too little of it
survives to reconstruct the plot;[21] but, given the popularity of the
*katabasis* in comedy,[22] it is possible that the play staged a happy
outcome, much like Euripides' own tragicomic *Alcestis*, which ends
with Heracles snatching the dead heroine from Hades and handing
her back to her husband.

Plato explicitly links the main characters in these plays: we read
in the *Symposium* that Alcestis was truly brought back to life, on
account of her devotion and courage, whereas the gods only showed
Orpheus an image of his wife, and never handed over the woman
herself, because he was a coward and contrived a means of descending
into the underworld alive, rather than accepting death like Alcestis.[23]
The trouble here is that the account offered in the *Symposium* may
not be the only, or even the most widely accepted, version of the story.
Orpheus and his followers are also treated with hostility in other
Platonic dialogues,[24] so it is possible that the passage in the *Symposium* is an attempt to discredit Orpheus and cast doubt over his power
to grant life after death. Isocrates, a near contemporary of Plato's,
states unproblematically that Orpheus 'used to lead the dead out of
Hades'.[25] He describes a general ability, rather than mention a specific
rescue—but it seems that, at some point in the classical period,
Orpheus' power to charm even the gods of the underworld inspired
a story about his wife.[26]

Other myths and cults associated with life after death, most famously those concerned with Demeter and her daughter at Eleusis, also
involve a lovely young wife in Hades and her partial, ambiguous
return to the living. Some have argued that the name Eurydice,
which is made up of the two elements: *eury* ('broad') + *dikē* ('justice')

---

[20] Heath (1994).       [21] See Antiphanes, fr.178 KA = *Orph.* 631, 1149 Bernabé.
[22] See also Bakola, Chapter 6 in this volume.
[23] Pl. *Symp.* 179d = *Orph.* 983, 1037 I Bernabé.       [24] See below, p. 181.
[25] Isocr. *Busiris* 8.
[26] Paus. 10.30.6 (= *Orph.* 999, 1047, 1065 II Bernabé) describes a painting by
Polygnotus (*c.*460 BCE) in which Orpheus is depicted making music in the underworld,
but in which Eurydice does not feature. For her first appearances in the ancient
sources, see Sansone (1985).

and is first attested in the late second or early first century BCE,[27] seems 'more appropriate for a judging queen of the dead than for a woman rescued from death'.[28] But this seems problematic: it is a well-attested name for ordinary mortal women.[29] No matter how Eurydice enters the story, association with cult helps to explain the ambiguity we find in surviving literary and artistic accounts of Orpheus' *katabasis*. After all, rebirth, reincarnation, and more generally life after death are uncertain possibilities, laden with despair and hope—and shrouded in mystery.

Just as Eurydice (almost) makes it out of the underworld, so Orpheus never (quite) dies. A lost tragedy by Aeschylus, the *Bassarai*, known to us principally from a summary in pseudo-Erathosthenes, tells the story of how the women of Thrace tore the singer apart in the course of Bacchic rites in honour of Dionysus, because they were offended by his exclusive devotion to Apollo.[30] After he was killed, the Muses collected Orpheus' limbs and buried them in Libethra, near Mount Olympus, where his head would henceforth deliver oracles.[31] A beautiful hydria, dated to 440–430 BCE, depicts a naked man consulting the head of Orpheus in the presence of six Muses.[32] Other authors used the story of the severed head as an *aition* for the power of poetry. According the Hellenistic poet Phanocles, Orpheus' head, nailed to his lyre, floated from Thrace all the way to Lesbos, where both head and instrument were buried: 'from that day on, songs and lovely lyre-playing have held sway over the island'.[33]

An epigram attributed to the Hellenistic poet Damagetus, otherwise known exclusively as an author of epitaphs, poses as an inscription on the tomb of Orpheus in Libethra. It summarizes several feats attributed to him that have already featured here and adds one that

---

[27] The name, in the form Εὐρυδίκεία, is first attested in the 'Epitaph for Bion', [Moschus] 3.124 = *Orph.* 986 Bernabé. For a good discussion of Orpheus' anonymous bride in the early sources, see Fontannaz (2008), 50–1, who also offers a sane perspective on the doubtful exception of one version of the 'Orpheus relief'.

[28] Lee (1996), 7.

[29] As confirmed by the Lexicon of Greek Personal Names: <http://www.lgpn.ox.ac.uk/>.

[30] [Eratosthenes] *Cat.* 24 (p. 29.3 Olivieri = 577.10 Maass) = *TrGF* vol. 3, p. 138 Radt = *Orph.* 536, 1033 I, 1070, and 1074 I Bernabé.

[31] See Burges Watson (2013a) on the play as an *aition* for the oracle. On the *Bassarai* more generally, see West (1990); Di Marco (1993); Seaford (2005); and Burges Watson (2015). On Orpheus' severed head as the source of oracles and its alternative burial in Lesbos, see Faraone (2004).

[32] Basel, Antikenmuseum BS 481 = Orpheus no. 68 *LIMC*.

[33] Fr.1.21–2. Powell = *Orph.* 1054 Bernabé.

finds no parallel elsewhere: Orpheus allegedly invented the elegiac verse used in this and countless other epitaphs.[34] Here he becomes the predecessor of all those who inscribe poems on tombs, including the author of the epigram, thus helping the dead carry on singing from their grave (*AP* 7.9 = Damagetus n. 2, 1379–86 G-P = *Orph.* 1071 Bernabé):

Ὀρφέα Θρηϊκίησι παρὰ προμολῇσιν Ὀλύμπου
τύμβος ἔχει, Μούσης υἱέα Καλλιόπης,
ὧι δρύες οὐκ ἀπίθησαν, ὅτωι συνάμ' ἕσπετο πέτρη
ἄψυχος, θηρῶν θ' ὑλονόμων ἀγέλη,
ὅς ποτε καὶ τελετὰς μυστηρίδας εὕρετο Βάκχου
καὶ στίχον ἡρώιωι ζευκτὸν ἔτευξε ποδί,
ὃς καὶ ἀμειλίκτοιο βαρὺ Κλυμένοιο νόημα
καὶ τὸν ἀκήλητον θυμὸν ἔθελξε λύρηι.

This tomb holds Orpheus, by the Thracian foot of Olympus, the son of the Muse Calliope, whom oaks did not disobey, in whose company soulless stone followed, and the herd of beasts who dwell in the forest. He once also discovered the mystical rites of Bacchus and fashioned the verse that is yoked together to the heroic metre. He even bewitched with his lyre the grave mind and charmproof heart of implacable Clymenus (i.e. Hades).

What it might mean to state, on a tomb, that the deceased managed to animate even 'soulless stone' and bewitch Hades with his music is a question that links Orpheus the character with Orpheus the author—the subject to which I now turn.


## ORPHEUS THE AUTHOR

Spectacular discoveries in the second half of the twentieth century have, in large measure, confirmed what scholars had previously argued on the basis of less direct evidence, namely that actual texts attributed to Orpheus circulated in the late sixth and fifth centuries BCE. A papyrus, discovered in Derveni in 1962, between the slabs of a tomb, proved the existence of a theogonic poem in hexameters attributed to

---

[34] This is how I understand line 6. Gow and Page (1965), ad 5–6 agree.

Orpheus and dated to about 500 BCE.[35] The papyrus itself preserves part of an allegorical commentary on this poem: the aim of it is, we are told, to elucidate a 'hymn', also called 'a poem alien and enigmatic to human beings', by which 'Orpheus wanted to express not contentious riddles, but great things in riddles'.[36] In this poem, the papyrus continues, Orpheus 'legislated not for the many', but for the 'pure in hearing'.[37] The context of this extraordinary find is suggestive: the papyrus was not included among the many objects buried together with the deceased inside his tomb, but was rather burned together with his body on a funeral pyre.[38] Once the cremated remains of the body had been collected and placed inside the grave, the half-carbonized papyrus was swept on top of the grave together with other debris from the pyre. Perhaps the commentary was deemed useful in performing, or explaining, rites for the deceased but, in any case, was not considered something the deceased himself would need to have close at hand inside his grave.[39]

Other inscribed objects of a comparable nature have, however, been found inside various tombs—and in close physical contact with the deceased: thin sheets of gold (*lamellae*), bearing instructions on how to handle the journey into the underworld, have been discovered close to or on the chest of buried bodies, sometimes rolled up inside a small container and worn as amulets. One of the earliest (and longest) was discovered in the cemetery of Hipponion in Calabria, in 1969, rolled up and placed on the breast of a buried woman. It dates to *c.*400 BCE and opens with a clear statement, 'This is the work of Memory', before offering instructions on what to do once in Hades: 'Stay away from a spring of black water, on the right-hand side, next to a white cypress, at which the souls of the dead go and

[35] West (1983), 18.
[36] Derveni papyrus, column VII, lines 2 and 5–7, my translation. The text was published in its entirety, almost fifty years after its discovery, in Kouremenos, Parássoglou, and Tsantsanoglou (2006). It is also available online here: <http://dp.chs.harvard.edu/index.php?col=1&ed=KPT>. See also Bernabé (2007), 171–269.
[37] Derveni papyrus, column VII, lines 10–11, my translation. Text as in Kouremenos, Parássoglou, and Tsantsanoglou (2006).
[38] Given that the bottom half of the papyrus burned away, while the charred top half blew off and survived, it can be conjectured that the rolled papyrus was placed in the hand of the deceased, before his body was set on fire. Betegh (2004), 56–73 offers a good account of the find.
[39] Calame (1997) 79–80 makes some useful remarks about the possible use of the papyrus, contrasting it to the *lamellae* discussed below.

refresh themselves', and proceed instead straight to 'a cold stream flowing out of the lake of Memory'.[40] The guardians of that stream should be asked for permission to drink of the water: 'Tell them "I am the child of Earth and starry Sky. I am parched with thirst and I am perishing. But give me quickly cold water to drink from the lake of Memory."'[41] Permission will be granted, the amulet confirms, and 'you too, drinking, will thread on the holy path on which thread other renowned initiates and revellers' (μύσται καὶ βάκχοι).[42] These instructions can be usefully put in dialogue with a passage in Plato's *Cratylus*, according to which 'some people claim that the body (*sōma*) is the tomb (*sēma*) of the soul because the soul is buried there for the time being; while others say that it is correctly called 'a sign' (*sēma*) because the soul signifies whatever it wants to signify by means of the body. I think it is most likely that the followers of Orpheus gave the body its name, with the idea that the soul is being punished for something, and that the body is an enclosure or prison in which the soul is securely kept (*sōzetai*), as the name *sōma* itself suggests, until the penalty is paid; for, on this view, not even a single letter of the word needs to be changed.'[43]

Other gold *lamellae* bear instructions that resemble those found in the Hipponion grave and some suggest the idea of redemption, that is to say of paying the penalty for unjust deeds through a series of reincarnations. None of these *lamellae* are explicitly attributed to Orpheus, but they do bear some similarity with the text and context of the Derveni papyrus, the Platonic testimony just quoted, and other explicitly Orphic materials. Recurrent themes include a distinction between those who are initiated and those who are not; specific theogonic views about the nature of the world and of the deceased's place in it (note 'I am the child of Earth and starry Sky', in the *lamella* from Hipponion, and the theogonic import of the poem elucidated in the Derveni papyrus); continuity of life after death for the initiate, reincarnation, purification, atonement, and various references to Bacchic revels. The latter have fuelled extensive discussion about the relationship between Orpheus and Dionysus—which, as has already emerged, was also the subject of Aeschylus' *Bassarai*.[44]

---

[40] The text, first published by Pugliese Carratelli (1974), changed substantially in subsequent editions. I translate Bernabé's text: *Orph.* 474, lines 1–5.

[41] *Orph.* 474, lines 10–12, Bernabé.      [42] *Orph.* 474, lines 15–16, Bernabé.

[43] Plato, *Crat.* 400c = *Orph.* 430 I, 667 Bernabé.      [44] See above, p. 177.

That relationship is illuminated by a third set of remarkable discoveries: several small inscribed bone plaques, dated to the fifth century, were found in Olbia, on the north shore of the Black Sea.[45] These set out various mystical oppositions: 'Peace—War: Truth— Falsehood: Dion', says one; 'Life—Death—Life: truth: Dio—*Orphik*[?]' sets out another. 'Dion' and 'Dio' are, in this context, most naturally taken as abbreviations for Dionysus; '*Orphik*[?]' may be taken to be a reference to Ὀρφικ[οί] (i.e. 'followers of Orpheus'), but could also refer to Orphic rites, as Parker suggests, or even to Orphic revelations, i.e. texts.[46] We have, then, confirmation of what could already be inferred from Aeschylus' play, namely that Orpheus and Dionysus were closely connected in accounts concerned with death, and life after death.

Now, apart from similarities of theme, all these discoveries share one important feature, which can easily escape notice in our literate age: they rely on the technology of writing, sometimes with the specific aim of preserving memory beyond death. Euripides confirms that Orpheus was associated not just with alternative forms of religion, and Bacchic revelling, but specifically with books. In the *Hippolytus*, Theseus, who believes his wife Phaedra committed suicide because she was raped by the puritanical Hippolytus, accuses the young man of great hypocrisy: 'You go on posturing and, with your vegetarian diet, make a display of your food; you go on and revel (βάκχευε), taking Orpheus as your master and honouring the vapours of many books!'[47] Plato likewise complains about wandering priests who present themselves at the doors of wealthy households, or even persuade whole cities 'with a hubbub of books by Musaeus and Orpheus', promising 'purity from wrongdoing through sacrifices and the pleasures of play, effective both during life and also after death, which they call initiations'.[48]

[45] Discussion in West (1983), 17–18; the latest editions are *Orph*. 463–6 Bernabé and Graf and Johnston (2007).

[46] See Parker (1995), 485. Bernabé reads Ὀρφικοί in *Orph*. 463, signalling uncertainty only in the apparatus. Graf and Johnston (2007), 185–6 provide a line drawing of the tablet and insist that the last letter could be a ν rather than an ι because the edge of the tablet is damaged.

[47] See Eur. *Hipp*. 948–57 = *Orph*. 627 Barnabé. The lines translated here are 952–4.

[48] Plato, *Resp*. 364e–365a = *Orph*. 573 I, 693, and 910 I. The phrase 'through sacrifices and pleasures of play' (διὰ θυσιῶν καὶ παιδιᾶς ἡδονῶν) has been much debated. The sacrifices associated with Orpheus are not taken to involve animal sacrifice, especially given that Plato elsewhere associates 'the Orphic life' with vegetarianism

A speech generally attributed to Alcidamas (fourth century BCE) confirms the connection between Orpheus and literacy.[49] In fact, it goes as far as claiming that Orpheus, rather than Palamedes, invented the alphabet. An epigram supposedly inscribed on the tomb of Orpheus in Thrace is adduced in support of this assertion:

Γράμματα μὲν δὴ πρῶτος Ὀρφεὺς ἐξήνεγκε, παρὰ Μουσῶν μάθων, ὡς καὶ ἐπὶ τῶι μνήματι αὐτοῦ δηλοῖ τὰ ἐπιγράμματα·

Μουσάων πρόπολον τῆιδ' Ὀρφέα Θρῆικες ἔθηκαν,
ὃν κτάνεν ὑψιμέδων Ζεὺς ψολόεντι βέλει
Οἰάγρου φίλον υἱόν, ὃς Ἡρακλῆ' ἐδίδαξεν,
εὑρὼν ἀνθρώποις γράμματα καὶ σοφίην.

Orpheus was the first to introduce writing, having learnt it from the Muses, as the epitaph on his tomb demonstrates:

> The Thracians buried Orpheus here, the minister of the Muses
> Whom lofty-ruling Zeus slew with the smoking thunderbolt,
> The dear son of Oeagrus, who taught Heracles
> Having discovered writing and wisdom for mankind.[50]

The claim contained in this epitaph did not go unchallenged: Androtion, an Attidographer writing in the fourth century BCE, focused precisely on Orpheus' Thracian origin, and the well-known illiteracy of his people, in order to dismiss the notion that he was truly the inventor of letters.[51] This objection should, I think, be contextualized in terms of specific debates about the authority and authenticity of Orphic texts, which I discuss below.[52] Before entering into detail, however, a more general observation needs to be made: the spread of literacy in the fifth century BCE encouraged the use of written texts

---

(*Laws* 782c–d = *Orph.* 625 I Bernabé.). The 'pleasures of play' may be a reference to the Bacchic revels mentioned in other sources: see Parker (1995), 483–4 and below, pp. 183, 192–4 on the treatment of animals.

[49] O'Sullivan (2008) doubts the attribution of the *Ulysses* to Alcidamas and its classical dating, but I am not entirely convinced by his arguments. In any case, the attribution matters little for my argument: the epigram quoted in the *Odysseus* was known in the fourth century, as confirmed by Androtion.

[50] Alcidamas, *Ul.* 24 = *Orph.* 1027, 1030 II, 1046 I, 1073 I Bernabé; text and translation: Muir (2001), 30–1.

[51] *FGrHist* 324 F 54a and 54b = *Orph.* 1028 Bernabé. For the view that Androtion was responding specifically to Alcidamas, see Harding (1994), 181. O'Sullivan (2008) does not consider this.

[52] Jones (2015), in his summary and interpretation of the two Androtion fragments, agrees.

as a means of challenging mainstream polytheism and promoting alternative forms of religion. The practice of attributing texts to Orpheus flourished in this context and continued for many centuries, as several later Orphic hymns testify.[53]

As to the reasons why mystic texts were often, if by no means exclusively, attributed to Orpheus, Parker offers two initial answers: 'As the greatest singer known to myth, and one who visited the underworld in person, he was ideally qualified to sing of the fate of the soul.'[54] It seems to me, however, that two more considerations deserve attention. The first links Orpheus' harmonious relationship with animals to the vegetarianism of his followers—a connection that not even Edmonds, in his avowed 'new-age' reading of Orphism, contemplates.[55] To be sure, he points out that 'abstinence from the eating of meat . . . has a much higher cue validity for association with the name of Orpheus' than, for example, theories about the transmigration of the soul.[56] However, he then devotes his monograph to dismantling the idea of a coherent, Orphic set of 'doctrines', claiming, for example, that the list of foibles Theseus ascribes to Hippolytus is 'neither coherent nor accurate', but rather constitutes a general 'rejection of the world'.[57] I share Edmonds' scepticism about the coherence of Orphic doctrine, but do not believe that the alternative is a descent into utter vagueness. Coherence is provided, in my view, not by a coherent set of beliefs but by the figure of Orpheus—and it is this figure that scholars of religion, including Edmonds, have tended to neglect.[58] Our sources associate Orpheus not just with vegetarianism, but with the avoidance of bloodshed and, specifically, animal sacrifice.[59] These stances form a coherent picture, especially when considered in relation to Orpheus' mythical ability to charm animals and, as I argue below, make his voice heard through them.[60]

---

[53] Fayant (2014) offers the most recent edition and translation of Orphic hymns (into French); see also West (1983) and Morand (2001), as well as, of course, Bernabé (2004–7).

[54] Parker (1995), 484.     [55] Edmonds (2013), 5.

[56] Edmonds (2013), 219.

[57] Edmonds (2013), 208 and 6, quoting Redfield (1991), 106.

[58] Graf and Johnston (2007), 165–84 are a welcome exception, though their emphasis is quite different from the arguments presented here.

[59] See e.g. Aristoph. *R.* 1030–6, quoted above, and Hor. *Ars* 390–1, discussed below.

[60] See p. 189.

The second consideration links Orphic authorship to Orpheus' earliest known appearance in myth, namely as an Argonaut. According to mythical chronology, Orpheus was at least one generation older than the heroes who fought at Troy; while Homer must certainly have been younger, since he sang of their great deeds. Similar considerations apply to Hesiod, since he, too, mentioned the Trojan expedition.[61] As a result, followers of Orpheus could claim access to older and more authoritative insights than those contained in the poetry of Homer and Hesiod—the most influential authors in shaping mainstream Greek views of the gods.[62] This point about mythical chronology may seem rather bookish—but, as the Derveni papyrus and other sources demonstrate, Orphic wisdom was, in point of fact, bookish.[63]

The diffusion of the new technology of writing, in combination with an author of mythical antiquity, created the perfect storm. Our sources show that, as soon as Orphic texts began to circulate, they were denounced as forgeries. Herodotus claimed that rites called 'Orphic' and 'Bacchic' were in fact 'Egyptian' and 'Pythagorean'.[64] He also insisted that Homer and Hesiod are the earliest Greek authorities on the gods: 'It was Hesiod and Homer who first explained to the Greeks the birth of the gods, gave them their names, assigned them their honours and spheres of expertise, and revealed their appearance. The poets who are said to have been earlier than these men were, in my opinion, later.'[65] The remark is most naturally taken as an attack on the antiquity of Orpheus and Museaeus and perhaps, more specifically, of the poems attributed to them.[66] Plato attributes

---

[61] The most interesting reference, also because it fuelled the idea that Hesiod was a contemporary of Homer's and had competed against him in poetry and wisdom, is *Op.* 648–62, cf. Bassino (2017).

[62] On the importance of Homer and Hesiod in shaping Greek views of the gods, see Hdt. 2.53.2–3, quoted below. Their influence is confirmed by the fact that Plato attempts to mount 'a wholesale rejection of traditional Greek polytheism' (Roochnik (2009), 165) by criticizing select lines from the poems of Homer and Hesiod in the second book of the *Republic*.

[63] Calame (1997), 80 goes as far as arguing that the man buried at Derveni experienced 'an initiation not so much ritual as scholarly'. I see no reason to deny it could have been both.

[64] Hdt. 2.81.2 = *Orph.* 45 Bernabé. A family of Herodotean manuscripts omits reference to 'Bacchic' and 'Egyptian' rites, but this hardly affects my argument: Orphic attribution is certainly denied.

[65] Hdt. 2.53.2–3.

[66] Given Orpheus' participation in the Argonautic expedition, it would have been difficult for Herodotus to deny that he belonged to an earlier generation than Homer.

to Orpheus several lines of poetry, some of which match the Derveni papyrus—but also, as has already emerged, speaks disparagingly of a mass of books that go under the names of Orpheus and Musaeus.[67]

Aristotle mentions two views that, he claims, can be found 'in the books said to be by Orpheus': the first is that the body is like a net that contains the soul; the second is that the soul floats through the air and then enters the body as breath.[68] These views are clearly meant to explain the transmigration of the soul to and from animal as well as human bodies, but Aristotle makes a characteristic objection: 'not all classes of animal breathe (this fact has escaped the notice of the holders of this view).'[69] In short, Aristotle does not endorse the views that others attribute to Orpheus and, it seems, denies the historicity of Orpheus altogether. This last inference can be made on the strength of Cicero, who draws a reluctant line between Orpheus the figure of the imagination and Orpheus the author (*De natura deorum* 1.107 = *Orph.* 889 I and 1101 IV Bernabé):

> Orpheum poetam docet Aristoteles numquam fuisse, et hoc Orphicum carmen Pythagorei ferunt cuiusdam fuisse Cercopis; at Orpheus, id est imago eius, ut vos vultis, in animum meum saepe incurrit.

> Aristotle teaches that the poet Orpheus never existed, and the Pythagoreans say that this Orphic poem was the work of a certain Cercops. But Orpheus, or rather his image, as you would have it, often comes to my mind.

Doubt and speculation about Orpheus' oeuvre continued for many centuries, culminating in a bewildering series of entries in the *Suda*: the Byzantine encyclopaedia lists no less than seven authors named Orpheus, and attributes to each a different set of works. Moreover, the entry for the original, Argonautic Orpheus names several other poets who, we are told, in fact composed the poems that were then

---

Several other fifth-century and later sources present Orpheus as an ancestor of Homer; see e.g. Gorgias fr.25 DK, with Graziosi (2002), 82. What seems to have worried Herodotus was the alleged antiquity not of Orpheus himself, but of the religious insights attributed to him.

[67] Cf. Pl. *Leg.* 715e (*Orph.* 31 III Bernabé) and Derveni papyrus, column 17, line 12: for discussion of this and other quotations of Orphic texts in Plato, see Edmonds (2013) 15–16.

[68] Aristotle, *De gen. anim.* 2.1, 734a16 (= *Orph.* 404 Bernabé) and *De anima* 1.5, 410b27 (= *Orph.* 421 I Bernabé).

[69] Aristotle, *De anima*, 1.5, 410b30–411a1.

fraudulently attributed to him. It is no easy task to sift through the information provided in the *Suda*, but the survival of so many names of Orphic authors proves a simple fact: great effort went into exposing Orphic texts as forgeries and naming the culprits.

Given the state of the ancient evidence, it is unsurprising that modern editors of Orphic texts—that is to say, texts that were attributed to Orpheus in antiquity—have great difficulty in establishing what to include in their editions. In the most recent attempt to collect *Orphica*, Alberto Bernabé edits all texts explicitly attributed to Orpheus together with a vast range of other 'similar' materials.[70] The very title of his monumental edition, *Orphicorum et Orphicis similium testimonia et fragmenta*, points to a problem of definition. It seems that Bernabé's criteria for inclusion derive from an understanding of Orphism as a religious movement defined by a set of doctrines: the duality of body and soul, salvation through purification of the soul over a cycle of reincarnations, and the ultimate union of the purified soul with the divine. This makes him vulnerable to the charge that he relies on 'the implicit model of doctrinal Christianity to define Orphism'.[71] In one of his recurrent attacks on Bernabé, Edmonds articulates a different approach: he starts with the name 'Orpheus', identifying texts and rituals explicitly attributed to him, then broadens his Orphic category to include 'even material that is not sealed with the name of Orpheus but is classified as extraordinary in the same ways as other evidence that does bear Orpheus' name'.[72] This extension resembles Bernabé's method, but the result is different. Rather than a set of doctrines, Edmonds identifies a stance: Orpheus, in his view, is associated with 'extraordinary purity or sanctity', or 'extreme antiquity' (or 'strangeness' and 'perversity' in hostile accounts).[73] In Edmonds' definition, Orphism becomes less doctrinal and more rhetorical: the result of different religious experts competing for authority by invoking the name of Orpheus.

As even this short summary of the latest controversies suggests, the current scholarly debate about Orphic poetry aims to make a contribution to the study of Greek religion. The aim of my intervention, by contrast, is to demonstrate that progress can be made by considering,

---

[70] Bernabé (2004–7).
[71] Edmonds (2013), 68. The whole study of Orphism is peppered with such accusations.
[72] Edmonds (2013), 8.    [73] Edmonds (2013), 7.

much more closely than has been done so far, the relationship between Orpheus the character and Orpheus the author—a relationship best understood by visiting his tomb.


## STILL SINGING

The best guide to ancient Greece is surely Pausanias: when looking for the tomb of Orpheus, he does not disappoint.[74] Prompted by a statue of Orpheus in Helicon, Pausanias remembers the tomb of the singer 'in the region below Mount Pieria and in the city of Dion' and gives precise indications about where to find it: 'if one goes out of Dion and advances along the road towards the mountain for about twenty stades, there is a pillar on the right and a monument on top of the pillar—a stone urn—and the urn holds the bones of Orpheus, so the inhabitants say' (9.30.7). Nearby, a river flows underground: this, according to local informants, is because the women who tore Orpheus apart wanted to wash their hands in it afterwards, but 'the river plunged into the earth, so as not to provide its waters for purifying the murder' (9.30.8). At this point, Pausanias recalls another story that an informant in Larisa, near Mount Olympus, told him about a different tomb of Orpheus in Libethra where, Pausanias insists, he was originally buried. An oracle warned the inhabitants that if the bones of Orpheus were ever exposed to the sun, a boar would destroy their city. They did not take much notice of this because they considered that a boar could not possibly destroy a whole city and that, in any case, boars have 'more courage than strength' (9.30.9). One day, however, the story goes on (9.30.10):

ποιμὴν περὶ μεσοῦσαν μάλιστα τὴν ἡμέραν ἐπικλίνων αὑτὸν πρὸς τοῦ Ὀρφέως τὸν τάφον, ὁ μὲν ἐκάθευδεν ὁ ποιμήν, ἐπήιει δέ οἱ καὶ καθεύδοντι ἔπη τε ἄιδειν τῶν Ὀρφέως καὶ μέγα καὶ ἡδὺ φωνεῖν. οἱ οὖν ἐγγύτατα νέμοντες ἢ καὶ ἀροῦντες ἕκαστοι τὰ ἔργα ἀπολείποντες ἠθροίζοντο ἐπὶ τοῦ ποιμένος τὴν ἐν τῶι ὕπνωι ὠιδήν· καί ποτε ὠθοῦντες ἀλλήλους καὶ ἐρίζοντες ὅστις ἐγγύτατα ἔσται τῶι ποιμένι ἀνατρέπουσι τὸν κίονα, καὶ κατεάγητε ἀπ᾽ αὐτοῦ πεσοῦσα ἡ θήκη καὶ εἶδεν ἥλιος ὅ τι ἦν τῶν ὀστῶν τοῦ Ὀρφέως λοιπόν.

[74] Paus. 9.30.7–12, which partly coincides with *Orph.* 934 II, 1066, 1055, 532 II = 682 Bernabé.

A shepherd fell asleep around midday while leaning against the tomb of Orpheus, and it happened that while he was sleeping he sang verses of Orpheus in a loud and sweet voice. Those who were grazing their flocks or ploughing nearby each left their tasks and gathered to hear the song of the sleeping shepherd. And pushing one another and quarrelling about who would be nearest to the shepherd they over-turned the pillar and the urn fell down from it and was broken, and the sun saw whatever was left of the bones of Orpheus.

The very next day the river *Σῦς* ('Boar'), 'one of those torrential rivers around Mount Olympus', destroyed the city of Libethra. At that point, the people of Dion 'took the bones of Orpheus to their city' (9.30.11) and, according to Pausanias, placed them in a tomb fashioned exactly like the one in Libethra: a column with an urn on top.

The story of the shepherd who starts singing 'the poems of Orpheus' when he falls asleep on the tomb of the ancient singer suggests that Orpheus is very much alive, and full of music, inside his grave—and also that he can utter his verses through the mouths of others. These others need not, in fact, be human beings like the shepherd: Pausanias also claims that, according to the Thracians, 'the nightingales who have their nests on the tomb of Orpheus sing more sweetly and loudly' than ordinary ones (9.30.6). All this suggests a rather diffuse model of authorship, in which Orphic song emerges from stones and animals.[75] Rationalizing critics like Herodotus and Aristotle may try to dismiss Orphic poems as late forgeries, but this is not the only way to understand them—and, I suggest, may not have been how the 'forgers' themselves understood what they were doing. For them, it may have been a matter of being 'pure of hearing', as the Derveni papyrus puts it, of being able to hear the song of Orpheus even as it emerged from a stone, a nightingale, or the cosmos itself.

Pausanias gives, I think, an interesting account of how Orphic authorship worked for those who credited it, as opposed to those intent

---

[75] The story of the shepherd sleeping against the tomb bears some similarity with the 'magnetic' model of poetic inspiration described by Plato in *Ion* 533d–534a, when discussing the relationship between the performing rhapsode, the poet Homer, and the Muse. The differences between that account of Homeric authorship and the under-standing of Orphic authorship I have outlined are, however, at least as telling as the similarities. Homeric poetry does not emerge from nature, animals, or rocks—and is not as closely linked to specific places and landscapes. Unlike Homer's, Orpheus' oeuvre focuses on the workings of nature and on the transmigration of the soul into different bodies, whether human or animal. There is a correspondence, in other words, between content and creation of the oeuvre. The closest parallel to this story is, to my knowledge, the account of a shepherd falling asleep near the tomb of a follower of Pythagoras and hearing a voice singing; see Iamblichus, *Life of Pythagoras* 28.148.

on exposing it as an elaborate scam. His story is by no means an isolated testimony: it tallies with other, much earlier (and indeed later) evidence. Euripides' *Alcestis*, as well as containing the earliest allusion to Orpheus' rescue of his wife (if this is how we should interpret lines 357–64), also refers to 'Thracian tablets inscribed by the voice of Orpheus'.[76] The reference is most naturally taken to imply a process akin to that described in Pausanias. A beautiful red-figure cup in the Fitzwilliam Museum dated to *c*.420 BCE, and therefore chronologically close to the *Alcestis* (438 BCE), depicts the severed head of Orpheus facing a scribe with tablet and stylus in hand.[77] There is good reason to believe that Aeschylus' *Bassarai* ended with the prediction that the buried head of Orpheus would, in future, deliver oracles, as has already emerged.[78] The late antique *Orphic Argonautica* recalls that myth: its concluding lines suggest that it may itself be such an oracle.[79] Even this short survey shows that the buried Orpheus carried on singing, long after death.

The tombs of Orpheus, and the narratives they inspire, recall key Orphic themes. Animals and stones are drawn to Orpheus' music, and in turn his voice can be heard through them. The landscape speaks of rituals of purification (the river flowing underground), and of places of transmigration, where Orpheus can speak through the voice of others, or of nature itself. Most importantly, we have here a poet who sings long after death and an oeuvre linked to reincarnation. The case of Orpheus may be extreme, but it is true more generally that the oeuvre shapes stories about the author. Comparisons can be made between the case of Orpheus (which is generally treated as *sui generis*) and that of other poets. It seems relevant, for example, that Homer, too, was considered the author of several poems which were, in some contexts, exposed as forgeries composed by later descendants and followers.[80] At the other end of the spectrum, papyri attributed

---

[76] Euripides, *Alc.* 969–71: Θρήισσαις ἐν σανίσιν, τὰς / Ὀρφεία κατέγραψεν / γῆρυς; but see the whole passage 962–72 = *Orph.* 812 and 919 Bernabé.

[77] Red-figure cup, Fitzwilliam Museum, Loan Ant.103.25 = Orpheus no. 70 and Apollon no. 872 *LIMC*. Online image here: <http://webapps.fitzmuseum.cam.ac.uk/explorer/index.php?oid=89338>.

[78] See p. 177.

[79] The poem, delivered in the first person by Orpheus and addressed to his disciple Musaeus, concludes with the protagonist entering the cave where he was first conceived, evoking the possibility of reincarnation but also raising the question of how he can speak from there: *Orphic Arg.* 1373–6.

[80] See Graziosi (2002), ch. 5.

spells and incantations to legendary figures of the past, such as the magician Pitys of Thessaly: again, the case of Orpheus may not be so different. As for speaking from the grave, it seems important that the tombs of poets are associated, more generally, with singing nightingales and lush vegetation.[81] Poetry, like nature, regenerates.[82]

When he was alive, Orpheus went to Hades and charmed 'even the grave mind and charmproof heart of implacable Clymenus'; now that he is dead his voice still sings for us in the world of the living. As we hear the song—whether it emanates from a shepherd, nature itself, or one of the Orphic books mentioned in our sources—the figure of Orpheus presents itself: *imago eius ... in animum meum saepe incurrit*, as Cicero puts it. It is in that sense, above all, that the poet remains alive.


## VIRGIL'S NIGHTINGALE

Scholars of Greek religion generally warn against being unduly influenced by depictions of Orpheus in Virgil, Ovid, and the later Western tradition. Jane Harrison is eloquent on the subject: 'the modern commentator thinks of Orpheus as two things—as a magical musician, which he *was*, as passionate lover, which in early days he was *not*. The commentator's mind is obsessed by "Che faro senza te, Euridice?" [sic].'[83] Over a hundred years after her seminal *Prolegomena to the Study of Greek Religion*, her complaints are echoed in the most up-to-date investigations of Orphism: Edmonds, for example, criticizes the Roman poets for 'extracting every bit of sentimental pathos from his love story', at the expense of focus on 'Orpheus the author'.[84] It has already emerged, I hope, that closer attention to depictions of Orpheus in literature and art can help understand how Orphic authorship worked. In this final section, I would like to suggest the reverse, namely that attention to Orpheus as a religious

[81] See Garulli on nightingales, Chapter 4 in this volume, pp. 88, 91, 98–8, and Montiglio on bees, wax, Sophocles' tomb, and plant imagery in general, and its association with the Dionysiac in particular: Chapter 10 in this volume.

[82] See Bakola, Chapter 6 in this volume, on poetry and nature as powers that regenerate 'from below', and Hanink, Chapter 11 in this volume, on Pausanias' sense that the poets' tombs constitute a deep 'root system', p. 250.

[83] Harrison (1908), 602. It is amusing that Harrison herself does not seem to have been too mesmerized by Gluck's opera: she misquotes the lyrics of Orfeo's famous aria, 'Che farò senza Euridice'.

[84] Edmonds (2013), 24.

authority can enhance our reading of poetry. I do so by focusing on one example, which is also arguably the most influential depiction of Orpheus: *Georgics* 4.454–527.

Virgil draws from several earlier Greek traditions when fashioning his version of the myth. If literary achievement is to be based on 'originality', then it can be argued that he is the first known poet to present Orpheus' failed rescue of Eurydice as the reason for his eventual death. My point here, however, is to recognize not only Virgil's innovations, but his fine ear for Orphic themes.[85] We read in the *Georgics* that Orpheus almost succeeds in rescuing his wife: 'already, stepping forward, he had overcome all challenges; and the restored Eurydice, walking behind him, was reaching the breezes above' (4.485–7). He loses her because of a 'sudden madness', a tragic failure that makes him turn back and look at her. After his bereavement, Orpheus wanders over icy northern steppes, 'widowed fields' (*arva . . . viduata*, 4.518) as barren as himself. He rejects 'Venus and marriage' (4.516) and, for this reason, the Thracian women tear him apart in their Bacchic rites. There is no explicit reference, in Virgil's version, to Orpheus' homosexuality, but his barren love is contrasted with the rites of the fertile 'mothers' who kill him (*matres* 4.520).[86] His severed head, tossed into the river Hebrus, revolves in its currents all the way down stream. His tongue, already cold, cries out 'Eurydice!', and the riverbanks carry and repeat his call (*'Eurydicen' toto referebant flumine ripae*, 4.527).[87]

Virgil knew that Orpheus carried on singing after death. The concluding lines devoted to his myth make that clear, but the voice of nature and the voice of Orpheus also blend in an earlier passage, in which Virgil likens the bereaved Orpheus to a nightingale.[88] The laments of the singer and the bird emerge from places of seclusion and darkness (*rupe sub aeria . . . gelidis . . . sub antris . . . populea sub umbra*, 'under a high rock' . . . 'in ice-cold caves' . . . 'under the shade of a poplar'). They echo each other and fill the air (4.508–15):

---

[85] On how the Augustan poets innovate in relation to one another, and specifically by engaging with Orpheus, see Heslin (2018), chs 4 and 5.

[86] A point I owe to Segal (1989), 48.

[87] Mynors (1990), ad 523–7 argues that *toto . . . flumine* should be taken as an allusion to the *aition* about the special musicality of Lesbos: 'all the way', he translates, 'down the swift Hebrus to the Lesbian shore'.

[88] Mynors (1990), ad 511–15 rightly points out, on the strength of Paus. 9.30.6, that nightingales are specifically associated with Orpheus' power to sing even after death. More generally, on nightingales as symbols of poetry, see Call. *Ep.* 2.5–6, and Rosati (1996) for further references and discussion.

rupe sub aeria deserti ad Strymonis undam
flesse sibi, et gelidis haec evolvisse sub antris
mulcentem tigres et agentem carmine quercus:
qualis populea maerens philomela sub umbra
amissos queritur fetus, quos durus arator
observans nido implumes detraxit; at illa
flet noctem, ramoque sedens miserabile carmen
integrat, et maestis late loca questibus implet.

He wept under a rock near the empty waters
of Strymon, and in the ice-cold caves developed his song
charming tigers and making the oak trees follow him.
As a nightingale he sang, that suffering under a poplar's
shade laments the young she has lost, whom a harsh ploughman
Has noticed and snatched from the nest unfledged; and the nightingale
Weeps all night on a branch, repeats the pitiful song
And fills the place far and wide with her sorrowful calls.

Now, the *durus arator*, the 'harsh ploughman' of this simile, is no
vegetarian: surely, he snatches the fledglings in order to eat them.
His figure recalls that of the *iratus arator*, the 'angry ploughman' who,
earlier in the poem, cuts down and uproots a whole forest, dispersing
the birds who have their nests in it, in order to turn it into arable land
(2.207–11). The simile of the nightingale, at the end of the poem,
elaborates on that earlier passage, focusing our attention on the
relationship between man and nature, which is the main subject of
the *Georgics*.[89]

That Virgil knew Orpheus as a founder of cults which rejected
animal sacrifice and championed vegetarianism is all but certain: his
friend Horace described the Thracian singer in precisely those terms
(*Ars Poetica* 391–3):[90]

silvestris homines sacer interpresque deorum
caedibus et victu foedo deterruit Orpheus,
dictus ob hoc lenire tigres rabidosque leones;

Orpheus, the priest and interpreter of the gods,
deterred the savage race of men from slaughters and impure diet;
for this reason he was said to soothe tigers and furious lions.

---

[89] On the importance of the final myth of Orpheus for the *Georgics* as a whole, see
the seminal studies by Griffin (1979) and Conte (2007).

[90] Brink (1971), ad loc. would like to restrict the phrase *victu foedo* to cannibalism,
but that seems to me too narrow a reading; Rudd (1989), ad loc. rightly notes that
*caedibus* points most naturally to the killing of animals; *victu foedo* would then most
naturally refer to the 'revolting meal' after a killing.

That literary scholars have failed to realize the relevance of Orpheus as a religious authority when interpreting the *Georgics* has everything to do with the artificial separation between Orpheus the author and Orpheus the character.[91] A better understanding of the link between the two not only improves our understanding of Orphism, as I argued above, but also turns us into better readers of Virgil, since the simile of the nightingale is of some consequence for the interpretation of the *Georgics* as a whole—and even of Virgil's understanding of himself as poet.

Richard Thomas, in his Cambridge 'Green and Yellow' commentary on the *Georgics*, writes of the simile: 'Orpheus, who traditionally controls nature, has through a failure of emotion become identified with the victim of the ethics which earlier in the poem represent that same control.'[92] The problem with this interpretation of both passage and poem is that Orpheus never controlled nature in the manner Thomas suggests: he never moved oaks from one place to another in order, say, to clear land for ploughing. His power to move them is directly linked, in the text, to his bereavement: it is precisely when he cries out like a nightingale (that is to say, after, according to Thomas, he experiences a 'failure of emotion') that his song enchants tigers and moves oak trees. The more difficult question is whether Virgil seeks to control nature in the manner Thomas suggests—or, to put it differently, where the voice of the poet stands in relation to the nightingale and the ploughman. The *Georgics* teach productivity: the angry farmer who turns 'lazy woods' (*nemora . . . ignava*, 2.208)

---

[91]  Mynors (1990) ad 509–10, for example, suggests that 'caves' may be understood as 'valleys' in *gelidis haec evolvisse sub antris*, which I translated as 'in the ice-cold caves developed his song'. The phrase, however, may allude to a tradition of Orphic utterances emerging from caves, on which see the vases and texts discussed on p. 189 with n. 75 above. The Virgilian passage seems to have caused difficulties also in antiquity: the variant *astris*, less well attested, represents the *lectio facilior*. As for the term *evolvisse*, some have suggested that it refers to the unrolling of papyrus and hence the practice of writing down Orphic utterances. It seems to me that it should be related to *volveret* in line 525 (of Orpheus' severed head revolving in the currents and still singing).

[92]  Thomas (1988), vol. II, ad 511–15. Segal (1989), 46 is closer to my reading, but still works with the opposition of man versus nature: 'The second and third lines (512–13) are especially significant, for the bird is seen as a victim of man's vigilant and unfeeling work upon nature, a victim of the *durus arator*. Hence Orpheus, through the bird simile, reveals a perspective on the world different from that of Aristaeus. He shows us the relation between man and nature from the point of view of nature, not man. Through him animate nature, given a voice, renders back the nature-centred, not the man-centred view of things.' I find this still too schematic: the lament speaks of human *and* animal pain, poet *and* nightingale, sterile *and* reproductive love.

into arable land is commended. And yet Virgil also hears the song of Orpheus and the cry of the nightingale, and we hear both through him.

In a poem lamenting the death of a common friend, Horace sees Virgil as Orpheus (*Odes* 1.24): it is in the desire to call back the beloved that the Roman poet resembles the Thracian singer, who resembles the nightingale. There is no need, here, to return to a two-voice theory of Virgilian poetry, to the supposed opposition between the land-farming, empire-building aspects of the *Georgics* and a melancholy strain beneath.[93] The voices merge. There is no special individuality to the song of loss: we all hear it and we all sing it. It is everywhere and it mesmerizes. At the same time, there is still, of course, the need to live, eat, be productive, farm the land, write poems, build empires.

It is true that in the concluding *sphragis*, the 'signature' that seals the *Georgics* (4.559–66), Virgil ascribes the task of war and the promise of future glory to Augustus, whereas he looks back to the past, and specifically to the young, inactive Virgil flourishing in the countryside, in order to define himself as the poet of the *Bucolics*. He, too, sings from the shadows: *sub tegmine fagi* (4.566, cf. Orpheus and the nightingale above: *rupe sub aeria . . . gelidis . . . sub antris . . . populea sub umbra*). These echoes suggest that the fate of the individual, the proud defin-ition of 'life and work', is not all that matters—nor is the *sphragis*, the signature, the epigraph, and the final individuating epitaph. There is also death, in its general applicability to all the living. There is the poet singing of nature, and there is also nature singing through the poet. In the transition between the two, there is Orpheus—both author and character.[94]

[93] The 'two voices theory' of Virgilian criticism takes its name from Parry (1963); it is also identified with the 'Harvard school', which proved to be influential in Europe as well: see e.g. Lyne (1987). For a brief introduction to the theory, see Thomas (2014).

[94] I would like to thank Nora Goldschmidt, Johannes Haubold, Peter Heslin, Phil Horky, and Ioannis Ziogas for their comments on this chapter: it is a pleasure and a privilege to be able to rely on their expertise and have it so close at hand, in the Department of Classics and Ancient History, Durham University. I am also very grateful to the volunteers of academia.edu, specifically Tomasz Mojsik, Jay Reed, Adrian Pay, and Karel Thein, who offered high-quality feedback on an earlier draft of this chapter. Robert Parker, whose lectures on both Greek religion and Augustan poetry I attended as an undergraduate, provided long-term inspiration and also specific comments which substantially improved this chapter.

# III

# Collecting Tombs

# 9

## Poets' Corners in Greek Epigram Collections

### Regina Höschele

#### THE CREATION OF POETS' CORNERS

When Edmund Spenser, author of *The Faerie Queen*, died at Westminster in 1599, it must have seemed only natural that the poet be granted his final resting place in the nearby abbey. As William Camden, a contemporary historian, reports, the funeral procession was led by fellow poets, who cast songs of mourning along with their pens into his grave.[1] This vision of a throng of poets accompanying the hearse and filling Spenser's tomb with odes of farewell is a powerful one. So intriguing did it prove that, centuries later, in 1938, his grave was opened in the hopes of unearthing the interred manuscripts and quills. One is, after all, easily tempted to imagine Shakespeare among the mourning poets.[2] Could it be that buried here lay evidence destined to confirm, once and for all, Francis Bacon as the author of Shakespearean drama? Word of the impending tomb-opening spread as far as Australia, where a local newspaper well captures the general atmosphere of excitement: 'The idea is enough to set the world aquiver with expectation—and far too disturbing to

---

[1] Camden (1627), 172: *Poëtis funus ducentibus, flebilibus carminibus et calamis in tumulum conjectis.*
[2] For poets possibly present at the funeral (not including Shakespeare), cf. Hadfield (2012), 395.

dwell upon.'[3] But, alas, neither elegies nor pens nor, for that matter, Spenser's body were found.[4]

Even if the poems did not materialize *in situ*, Camden's account memorably features a poet's tomb as the locus for the gathering of verse by multiple authors commemorating the deceased. Though most epitaphs on ancient poets by Hellenistic and later epigrammatists exist only in the imaginary space of the written page, not in any concrete location so alluring to the literary pilgrim,[5] the tombs they evoke constitute a similar site for poetry and poetic variation. The *Palatine Anthology* presents us with whole series of epitaphs on literary greats written from the perspective of later generations who honour their archaic and classical predecessors through the erection of textual memorials, over and over again.[6] As Peter Bing has argued, these epitaphs—along with (fictional) inscriptions for statues of the poets—emblematize the sense of rupture that Hellenistic writers felt vis-à-vis the literary past, a sense of remoteness combined with the intense desire to bridge the gulf across time and space.[7] Recent studies have well shown how the imagined tomb can serve as a place of active engagement with literature, where epigrammatists vie to capture a poet's essential qualities in the limited space of a few lines. Responding not just to the oeuvre of the deceased but also to previous variations on the theme, such epitaphs frequently reflect on aesthetic principles and metaliterary issues. After all, this is where

---

[3] *The Adelaide Advertiser*, Wednesday, 26 October 1938, p. 24.

[4] Eagle (1956) gives an account of the meagre findings, concluding, 'There really was little to report as Spenser's tomb was not found, and the digging was in the wrong place' (p. 283). See also Prendergast (2015), 126–47.

[5] To be sure, numerous cities housed tombs of poets, some of which even served as cultic sites (most prominently the *Archilocheion* on Paros); cf. Clay (2004), Jones (2010), 41–5, and Kimmel-Clauzet (2013). However, most epitaphs on poets transmitted by the *AP* are literary fabrications.

[6] Some epitaphs are also written for authors of a more recent past or contemporary with the poets, such as Heraclitus (Callimachus, *AP* 7.80), Sositheus (Dioscurides, *AP* 7.707), Machon (Dioscurides, *AP* 7.708), or Erinna (see below).

[7] Cf. Bing (1988a), 50–90: 'such fictitious epitaphs may have fulfilled a need to deal with the fact that the old poetic world (and its movers) in some fundamental sense no longer existed' (p. 59). This could result in what Bing (1993), 620 called 'the memorializing impulse', a desire to set monuments for the greats of the literary past. See, too, Bing (1988b) on Theocritus, *AP* 9.599 about a statue of Anacreon, which calls attention to its own artificiality; on this poem, cf. also Rossi (2001), 279–85. Klooster's (2011), 24–41 analysis of poets' epitaphs closely follows Bing's.

poets memorialize paradigmatic members of their own tribe, where Art contemplates Art.[8]

If we turn our gaze from the individual tomb to assemblies of epitaphs, we are faced with a form of literary history 'writ in stone'. For not only may we observe interactions between epitaphs on a single author, but the graves of different poets can likewise enter into a dialogue. Where, we might ask, were epitaphs on poets positioned within epigram books and what significance was attached to their location? Since we cannot examine the original collections (what we have are essentially anthologies of anthologies), the question might be rephrased thus: what can we still tell with a reasonable amount of certainty about the epitaphs' placement, and what conclusions may we draw about their function within the context of a book roll? In what follows, I would like to review the various scholarly hypotheses concerning the epitaphs' positioning and further reflect on the dynamics engendered by the assembly of sepulchral poems on a papyrus scroll.

But before taking a closer look at the ancient material, let us return once more to Westminster Abbey, a fascinating real-world equivalent to the literary graveyards of Greek epigram. Though the location of Spenser's tomb is no longer known, we do know that it was deliberately chosen and that the choice was to be a consequential one. As people seem to have felt that, with Spenser, England had lost its greatest poet since Chaucer, they decided to lay him to rest in close proximity with the author of *The Canterbury Tales*, who had been buried in the abbey in 1400.[9] In his guide to the tombs of 'kings, queens, noblemen and others', Camden records the text of a Latin epitaph, no longer extant, that once marked Spenser's tomb:[10]

---

[8] Cf. e.g. Rosen (2007) on Archilochus and Hipponax; Barbantani (1993), 47–66 and Gutzwiller (2014) on Anacreon; Sens (2003) on Erinna; Barbantani (2010) on Ibycus, Stesichorus, and Simonides. See, moreover, Prioux (2007), 3–74 on statues of Anacreon and Philitas; Neger (2012) and Mindt (2013) on poets in Martial's epigrams.

[9] Chaucer owed his burial there not to his poetic achievements but to the fact that he, as a former government official, was tenant of the garden of the Lady Chapel of Westminster Abbey. Cf. Pearsall (1995), who discusses the politics behind the transfer of Chaucer's tomb from its initial location in the abbey to its south transept in 1556.

[10] Camden (1600), without pagination. The only other witness to this text is the antiquarian John Dart (died 1730), who, with reference to Camden, quotes the epitaph in English, cf. Dart (1723), 75.

Hic prope Chaucerum situs est Spenserius, illi
  Proximus ingenio, proximus ut tumulo.
Hic prope Chaucerum, Spensere poeta, poetam
  Conderis, et versu quam tumulo propior.
Anglica, te vivo, vixit plausitque poesis,
  Nunc moritura timet, te moriente, mori.

Here, next to Chaucer, Spenser lies, closest to him in genius, closest to him in
his tomb. Here, next to Chaucer, you, Spenser, are interred, a poet next to a
poet, closer to him in your verse than in your tomb. While you were alive,
English Poetry lived and gave applause, now that you are dead, she's about to
die and fears to.

The poetic affinity between Chaucer and Spenser is made manifest
through the tombs' physical collocation.[11] In fact, the union was to
start a long-lasting trend. For over the following decades more and
more poets came to be buried in what is nowadays known as the
'Poets' Corner'.[12] Many of the finest representatives of English litera-
ture are interred here, while countless others are honoured through
statues, busts, stone slabs, or window panels. Already in 1711, Joseph
Addison noted in his essay 'Thoughts in Westminster Abbey', that 'In
the Poetical Quarter I found there were poets who had no monu-
ments, and monuments which had no poets.'[13]

The impulse to thus commemorate a nation's most prominent
writers as well as other luminaries is widespread—halls of fame such
as the Regensburg Valhalla, the Florentine Basilica of Santa Croce,
also known as the *tempio dell'itale glorie*,[14] or the Pantheon in Paris
are notable examples. In 2002, the latter received the remains of
France's most popular author, Alexandre Dumas père, who until

---

[11]  The poem imitates the epitaph composed by Pietro Bembo for Jacopo Sannazaro,
who is buried in the vicinity of Virgil's tomb: *Da sacro cineri flores; hic ille Maroni /
sincerus musa proximus ut tumulo.* Cf. Hendrix's discussion in this volume, p. 287.

[12]  For a list of poets buried there by 1723, cf. Hadfield (2012), 396. William Basse's
poem on Shakespeare's death offers an amusing reflection of this trend by asking
Spenser, Chaucer, and Beaumont 'to make room / for Shakespeare in your threefold,
fourfold tomb' (lines 3–4), to which Ben Jonson reacts in his 1623 eulogy of the bard:
'My Shakespeare, rise: I will not lodge thee by / Chaucer, or Spenser, or bid Beaumont
lie / a little further to make thee a room: / Thou art a monument without a tomb' (lines
19–22).

[13]  First published in *The Spectator* 26 on 30 March 1711; a modern scholarly edition
is provided in *The Spectator, Vol. 1*, ed. by Donald F. Bond, Oxford 1987, 108–11.

[14]  The fame of Santa Croce is augmented by Ugo Foscolo's poem *Dei sepolcri*
(1806), which celebrates the eternalizing power of tombs and poetry alike: see further
the Introduction to this volume, pp. 14–15.

then had been buried in his hometown of Villers-Cotterêts. Actors dressed as characters from his novels formed part of the procession that led his coffin—escorted by none other than four musketeers—from the Senate to the Pantheon. Significantly, President Jacques Chirac concluded his eulogy by commenting on Dumas' placement next to his *frères en littérature*:

> When the bronze doors of the Pantheon will close, Alexandre Dumas shall, at long last, find his place next to Victor Hugo and Emile Zola, his brothers in literature, his brothers in dedication, his brothers who have marked and, from their quill, made the History of the Republic by defending—with as much persistence as genius—Freedom, Equality, and Brotherhood. The Republic, too, has its musketeers.[15]

Not only was the transfer of Dumas' body, then, staged as a revue of his oeuvre, the coffin conducted by embodiments of his most famous creations, but, on a figurative level, he himself was turned into a musketeer and reunited with his very own Athos and Porthos.

### DIOSCURIDES' POETIC NECROPOLIS

These modern examples of a poet's interment, one as heavily symbolic as the other, nicely parallel the ways in which the tombs of poets are marked and invested with meaning in ancient epigram collections: here, too, boundaries between literature and reality are blurred, tombs are transferred to different locations, poetic affiliation is expressed through physical proximity, and literary characters are imagined as mourning for their creator. Several of precisely these elements are operative in a pair of epigrams by Dioscurides, with which I would like to begin my considerations. In the first (*AP* 7.37 = 22 G-P, see also pp. 224–5), a satyr expresses his grief over the death of Sophocles, who is praised for refining satyr drama and bringing the genre of tragedy to perfection. Resting in his hands is the mask of a character in mourning, which is said to represent either Sophocles' *Antigone*

---

[15] 'Lorsque les portes de bronze du Panthéon se refermeront, Alexandre Dumas trouvera enfin sa place aux côtés de Victor Hugo et d'Emile Zola, ses frères en littérature, ses frères en engagement, ses frères qui ont marqué et fait de leur plume l'Histoire de la République en défendant avec autant d'acharnement que de génie la Liberté, l'Egalité et la Fraternité. La République aussi a ses mousquetaires.'

or his *Electra*, each the very pinnacle of tragic art. Both these plays feature female protagonists lamenting at a grave: their sorrow for the death of a kinsman is thus symbolically transformed into mourning for the poet who had brought them to life and is framed by the grief-stricken voice of another poetic creation, the satyr standing on the poet's tomb. One is instantly reminded of the costumed characters escorting Dumas to his final resting place.

It has long been noted that this epigram is meant to be read together with the epitaph on the Alexandrian dramatist Sositheus (*AP* 7.707 = 23 G-P), a member of the tragic Pleiad, who is commended for having restored satyr drama to its original form, i.e. for having reversed the modernizing trend initiated by Sophocles.[16] The two epitaphs are closely intertwined through a series of verbal and thematic resonances.[17] Of greatest significance for our purposes is the beginning of Sositheus' epitaph, which is likewise spoken by a satyr and explicitly refers back to its Sophoclean counterpart:

> Κἠγὼ Σωσιθέου κομέω νέκυν, ὅσσον ἐν ἄστει
> ἄλλος ἀπ' αὐθαίμων ἡμετέρων Σοφοκλῆν,
> Σκίρτος ὁ πυρρογένειος·

'I, too, Scirtus the red-bearded, am watching over a dead body, Sositheus, just as one of my brothers in the city is watching over Sophocles . . .'

As Bing observed, in genuine inscriptions such a cross reference would only be comprehensible if the two monuments stood in close proximity to each other, and yet precisely such physical closeness is denied by the text itself, which points to Sophocles' tomb 'back in the city' (i.e. Athens), as opposed to Sositheus' grave out in the countryside. He concludes: 'Their sequential connection—κἠγώ, "I too" (1)—is that between neighbouring texts *on the page*.'[18] Fictional though the monuments may be, the poems' textual juxtaposition has the same function as the placement of Spenser's tomb next to Chaucer's, or Dumas' reinterment alongside Hugo and Zola: it highlights their literary affiliation, while the close rapport between the playwrights is further underlined by the kinship of the two satyr-brothers.

Even if the two epigrams nowadays appear in different parts of *AP* 7 (separated by some 670 poems), there can be little doubt that they were

---

[16] Cf. Gabathuler (1937), 86; G-P, II, 254; Bing (1988a), 39–40; Fortuna (1993); Gutzwiller (1998), 259–60.

[17] For a detailed discussion, cf. Höschele (2010), 130–3.     [18] Bing (1988a), 40.

conceived as 'companion pieces' and originally stood side by side.[19] In fact, they seem to have formed part of a longer series on playwrights, which trace the development of drama from its beginnings to the Hellenistic age.[20] A sequential reading leads us from 1) tragedy's πρῶτος εὑρετής, Thespis (7.410 = 20 G-P), to 2) Aeschylus, who is said to have elevated 'Thespis' invention' (7.411 = 21 G-P) to greater heights, and from there to 3) Sophocles (7.37 = 22 G-P), who brought the genre to its apex. The latter's epitaph precedes, as we have seen, 4) the one on Sositheus (7.707 = 23 G-P), which in turn is followed by 5) an epigram celebrating the Hellenistic poet Machon as a writer of comedies in the style of the *Archaia* (7.708 = 24 G-P).[21] This tightly interwoven sequence reflects, as Kathryn Gutzwiller put it, 'a contemporary appreciation of pre-classical drama and its archaizing revival in the third century'.[22] Significantly, it is concluded by Machon's proud proclamation to Athens that 'among the Muses the sharp thyme [i.e. the wit of Attic comedy] from time to time also grows by the Nile' (Κέκροπος πόλι, καὶ παρὰ Νείλῳ/ἔστιν ὅτ᾽ ἐν Μούσαις δριμὺ πέφυκε θύμον, lines 5–6). The final epigram thus reflects the transfer of the dramatic tradition from its classical homeland to Egypt with its cultural capital, Alexandria, which was in all likelihood also the centre of Dioscurides' literary activity.[23]

Considering their manifold verbal and thematic links, it is very likely that these epigrams, assembled in chronological sequence, constituted a kind of 'Poets' Corner' within Dioscurides' book of epigrams offering a brief history of drama in the form of tombstone inscriptions.[24] Epitaphs on other poets (such as the ones on Sappho, *AP* 7.407 = 18 G-P, and Anacreon, *AP* 7.31 = 19 G-P) may have stood nearby, forming a literary necropolis of sorts, where the reader, in his role as metaphorical passer-by, was invited to stroll from one tomb to

---

[19] On companion pieces in epigram, cf. Kirstein (2002).

[20] Cf. Gabathuler (1937), 80–90 and Fantuzzi (2007), 487–95.

[21] According to Athenaeus 6.241F, this poem was inscribed on Machon's tomb in Alexandria. Gow and Page (1965), vol. 2, 257 argue that Athenaeus may have made up the connection with a genuine monument, though they also consider it possible that he saw the epigram inscribed.

[22] Gutzwiller (1998), 260.

[23] For Dioscurides' connection with Egypt, cf. Galán Vioque (2001), 16.

[24] Even if the poems on Thespis and Aeschylus are not explicitly sepulchral— Θέσπις ὅδε (20.1 G-P) might simply refer to a statue—the context appears to be epitaphic; cf. Gabathuler (1937), 83.

another.[25] One might object that these considerations are rather
speculative, since the epigrams are not actually transmitted as a
group. However, not only are the cross references strongly suggestive
of the poems' juxtaposition, but there is also good evidence that
Meleager, who included these epigrams in his *Garland*, likewise
presented them as an ensemble within a 'Poets' Corner' of his own.


POETS' TOMBS IN THE *GARLAND* OF MELEAGER

Even though we do not have direct access to Meleager's *Stephanos*,
which was published *c.*100 BCE,[26] the *AP* preserves several large blocks
taken more or less unaltered from his anthology that still grant us a
sense of its original arrangement. As Alan Cameron has shown,
Meleager's collection was divided into four books, containing *erotika,
anathematika, epitymbia*, and *epideiktika* respectively.[27] Building
upon his observations, Kathryn Gutzwiller has brilliantly analysed
the *Garland*'s structure, demonstrating that each book was a carefully
designed unit, divided into thematic subgroups, which contained
numerous sequences of epigrammatic variations with copies typically
placed next to their respective models.[28] According to her, the sepul-
chral book consisted of four major sections comprising epitaphs for
1) famous persons, followed by enigmatic tombstone reliefs, 2) noble
men (especially war dead), 3) commonplace individuals, and 4)
people who died at sea.[29] Of greatest interest in our context is the
fact that the first section features almost exclusively epitaphs on poets.
    Unfortunately, it is impossible to recreate the precise structure of
this opening, since Cephalas removed multiple poems to the begin-
ning of *AP* 7, in which he combined epigrams from several sources in
a self-designed, thematically organized unit, starting with a long

---

[25] For the transformation of the passer-by addressed in epigraphic poetry into a
metaphorical wayfarer journeying through epigram books, cf. Höschele (2007) and
(2010), 100–46.
[26] On the date, cf. Cameron (1993), 49–56.
[27] Cf. Cameron (1993), 19–33. For an overview of the scholarly history regarding
the *Garland*'s arrangement, cf. Gutzwiller (1998), 277–9 and Höschele (2010), 72–6.
[28] Cf. Gutzwiller (1998), 276–322.
[29] Cf. Gutzwiller (1998), 307–15 with table V.

series of epitaphs on poets from Homer onwards (7.1–78).[30] Things are further complicated by the fact that Book 7 contains not one Meleagrean sequence, but three (I: 7.406–507a, II: 7.646–56, III: 7.707–40), which exhibit, as Weisshäupl (1896) recognized, a parallel thematic patterning (one may conclude that the three sections offer different selections from a single source, presenting the epigrams in the same order as in Meleager's *Garland*). Epitaphs of poets are prominently placed at the beginning of the first (7.406–29) and third series (7.707–19).[31] Epitaphs on non-poets are marked with an * in the table below:

| Poem | Dead Poet | Author | Poem | Dead Poet | Author |
|------|-----------|--------|------|-----------|--------|
| 406 | Euphorion | Theodoridas | 707 | Sositheus | Dioscurides |
| 407 | Sappho | Dioscurides | 708 | Machon | Dioscurides |
| 408 | Hipponax | Leonidas | 709 | Alcman | Alexander |
| 409 | Antimachus | Antipater | 710 | Baucis* | Erinna |
| 410 | Thespis | Dioscurides | 711 | Cleinarete* | Antipater |
| 411 | Aeschylus | Dioscurides | 712 | Baucis* | Erinna |
| 412 | Pylades | Alcaeus | 713 | Erinna | Antipater |
| 413 | Hipparchia* | Antipater | 714 | Ibycus | Anonymous |
| 414 | Rhinthon | Nossis | 715 | Leonidas | Leonidas |
| 415 | Callimachus | Callimachus | 716 | Phaenocritus | Dionysius Rhod. |
| 416 | Meleager | anonymous | 717 | Leucippus* | Anonymous |
| 417 | Meleager | Meleager | 718 | Nossis | Nossis |
| 418 | Meleager | Meleager | 719 | Tellen | Leonidas |
| 419 | Meleager | Meleager | | | |
| 420 | Lesbon, a flutist | Diotimus | | | |
| 421 | Meleager (enigmatic) | Meleager | | | |
| 422–9 | Enigmatic (428: Antipater) | Leonidas, Antipater (5x), Meleager, Alcaeus | | | |

Somehow combined with these poems were in all likelihood the following epigrams by Meleagrean authors, which now appear at the

---

[30] On the structure of Book 7, cf. Lenzinger (1965), 11–15. The opening sequence is followed by a section on philosophers (7.79–135), which contains a long series of epigrams plucked from Diogenes Laertius (7.83–133), cf. Weisshäupl (1889), 34–8.

[31] The second series sets in with common individuals (7.646–9), followed by deaths at sea (7.650–54); 7.655 and 656 concern humble tombstones and probably belonged to a brief concluding sequence identified by Gutzwiller (1998), 314–15.

beginning of Book 7 (as noted above, their arrangement goes back to
Cephalas and does not reflect Meleager's design):[32]

| Poems | Dead Poet | Author(s) |
| --- | --- | --- |
| 1–2, 5–6 | Homer | Alcaeus, Antipater, Alcaeus/anonymous, Antipater |
| 8–9 | Orpheus | Antipater, Damagetus |
| 11, 12?, 13 | Erinna | Asclepiades, anonymous, Leonidas/Meleager |
| 14–15 | Sappho | Antipater |
| 19 | Alcman | Leonidas |
| 20–2 | Sophocles | (anon.?), Simias (2x) |
| 23–31 | Anacreon | Antipater, Simonides (2x), Antipater (4x), (anon.?), Dioscurides |
| 34–5 | Pindar | Antipater, Leonidas |
| 37 | Sophocles | Dioscurides |
| 43, 50 | Euripides | Ion, Archimelus |
| 52, 54, 55 | Hesiod | Demiurgus, Mnasalces, Alcaeus |
| 60 | Plato | Simias |
| 75 | Stesichorus | Antipater |
| 78 | Eratosthenes | Dionysius |
| 80 | Heraclitus[33] | Callimachus |

Meleager's *epitymbia*, at least 282 in number,[34] thus included
a minimum of sixty epitaphs on literary figures, whose assembly
turned the book's beginning into a literary graveyard, a Poets' Corner.
While it is impossible to reconstruct the sequence in its entirety, we
can still determine (or reasonably speculate about) several clusters
of poems whose juxtaposition seems hardly coincidental. Returning
to Dioscurides' poems, we may observe that the first Meleagrean
series presents the epitaph for Aeschylus (7.411) right after the one
on Thespis (7.410), while the epitaphs on Sositheus (7.707) and
Machon (7.708) are paired together in the third series. Based on

[32] Antipater 7.745, transmitted out of sequence, on the death of Ibycus, may have
been juxtaposed with 7.714 on the same poet. According to Gutzwiller (1998), 308,
'[i]t is quite likely that many if not all of the Meleagrian poems on literary figures in
*AP* 9, though not formally epitaphic, were originally part of the funereal book.' The
poems in question are: Antipater, 9.66 (Sappho), *APl* 296 (Homer), Asclepiades 9.63
(Antimachus' *Lyde*), 9.64 (Hesiod), Callimachus 9.507 (Aratus), Leonidas 9.24
(Homer), 9.25 (Aratus' *Phaenomena*), *APl* 306–7 (Anacreon).
[33] Cephalas seems to have mistaken the poet for the Presocratic, since he placed
Callimachus' epigram in the section of philosophers (7.79–135), following an epigram
on his namesake (7.78).
[34] Cf. Cameron (1993), 26 and Gutzwiller (1998), 278.

Weisshäupl's findings, it is all but certain that the second group
(Sositheus/Machon) followed the first (Thespis/Aeschylus) in Melea-
ger's *Garland*, with the epigram on Sophocles (7.37), now at the
beginning of Book 7, standing between the two pairs (it is most unlikely
that Meleager would have separated the Sophoclean epitaph from its
companion piece).

Another ensemble worthy of note is the gathering of poems on
three females, Baucis, Cleinarete, and Erinna in series III (7.710–13).
At first sight, Antipater's epitaph for Cleinarete (7.711) seems to be an
intruder, since the deceased is not a poetess, but a young woman who
perished on the eve of her wedding day. Significantly, however, she
shares her fate, a *mors immatura*, with the other two (note, in
particular, how both Cleinarete and Baucis, who passed away soon
after her wedding, are characterized as νύμφαι at 7.711.1 and 7.712.1).
The dead bride, mourned by her συνάλικες ('playmates of equal age',
7.711.7), has thus come to rest next to a pair of age-mates, who, like
her, suffered a premature death. Baucis, as well, was not a poet, but
the childhood friend of Erinna, who lamented the girl's death in her
*Distaff*, a 300-line poem much admired by Hellenistic writers for its
stylistic finesse, and featuring more than once in this volume, too.[35]
Whether or not the two epitaphs for Baucis were penned by Erinna
herself or by someone else impersonating her,[36] their placement next
to an *epitymbion* (or rather a whole series of *epitymbia*) for Erinna
creates a striking image: author and literary character interred side by
side.[37] Erinna's portrayal as Baucis' συνεταιρίς in the *sphragis* to 7.710,
where the dead friend reveals her as the author of the words chiselled
onto her tombstone (ἁ συνεταιρὶς/Ἤρινν' ἐν τύμβῳ γράμμ' ἐχάραξε
τόδε, lines 7–8), thus retrospectively takes on an additional layer of
meaning: the two are comrades (συνεταιρίδες!) closely joined not just
in life but also in death.

---

[35] See pp. 26–9, 165–70. On ancient admiration for Erinna's *Distaff*, cf. Sens (2003).
Gutzwiller (1997a), 210 argues that Erinna composed this lament while gazing at her
distaff 'in place of performing an oral *goos* at Baucis' funeral. Her poetic achievement
was thus a direct response to her limited opportunity to speak in a public setting.' See
also Stehle (2001) on authentic female voice in the *Distaff* and fourth-century epitaphs.
On gendered voice in Erinna's Baucis poems, cf. also Murray and Rowland (2007),
217–26.

[36] On the question of authenticity, with an overview of previous scholarship, cf.
Neri (2003), 85–8, who includes the epigrams among the *dubia*.

[37] On tombs of literary characters, see the second section of this volume.

Antipater's epigram on Erinna (7.713), which follows the second Baucis poem, is not the only text honouring the dead poetess. The Cephalean section contains another three that most likely formed part of the same series: an epigram by Asclepiades (7.11) posing as a book tag but also referring to the early death of the nineteen-year-old singer, which served as model for subsequent variations on the theme; an anonymous epitaph lamenting how Moira, mistress of the distaff (δεσπότις ἠλακάτης, 7.12.4), led the *Distaff*'s author into Hades;[38] and an epigram ascribed to Leonidas or Meleager (7.13), which evokes Hades' kidnapping of the young poetess, a typical motif in epitaphs for unmarried girls.[39] What makes this version stand out is its concluding observation that 'indeed, the girl spoke truly while still alive: "You, Hades, are malicious"' (ἦ ῥα τόδ' ἔμφρων/εἶπ' ἐτύμως ἁ παῖς· Βάσκανός ἐσσ', Ἀίδα, lines 3–4). For here the author quotes the very words that Erinna had inscribed on her girlfriend's tomb (7.712.3), the words which Baucis asks the passer-by to address to Hades upon seeing the σάματα on her grave. We may assume that Meleager, by putting the two epitaphs in close proximity, made the intertextual relationship visible on the written page[40] and created a mini-narrative of sorts.[41] For could there be better proof of Hades' implacability, his βασκανία, than the short interval between the deaths of Baucis and Erinna, the latter's transformation from a friend bereaved to the object of mourning?

As these examples demonstrate, tombs were not randomly distrib-uted in Meleager's Poets' Corner: through the incorporation of pre-existing groups, as in the case of Dioscurides' playwright series, and the fashioning of new ones, the poet-editor turned the beginning of

---

[38] Note how καλὸς πόνος (7.12.5) picks up γλυκὺς πόνος from 7.11.1. Another anonymous epigram, 9.190, serving as a book tag to Erinna's work, replicates Asclepiades' παρθενικᾶς ἐννεακαιδεκέτευς in the same *sedes* (7.11.2 ~ 9.190.4), and is connected with 7.12 through the equation of Erinna's songs with honeycombs (μελισσοτόκων, 7.12.1 ~ κηρίον/μέλιτι, 9.190.1–2).

[39] Cf. Höschele (2010), 227–8.

[40] Cf. Gutzwiller (1998), 227: 'In turning to the topic of epigram variation, we explore a phenomenon by which the epigrams themselves, through overt intertext-uality, reveal or incorporate the literary context in which they are to be read, a context that was perhaps originally meant to be physically absent but in the case of antholo-gies became physically present.'

[41] Gutzwiller (1998), 309 considers the possibility that a later editor moved the epitaphs for Baucis and Cleinarete to the section on poets, but it strikes me as more likely that the arrangement is Meleager's.

his sepulchral book not just into a space for commemoration of individual poets, but also, and on a larger scale, invited his readers to reflect on the literary history of Hellas. What is more, he prominently inscribed himself into this history by concluding the book's first section with a cluster of four, possibly five, self-epitaphs (7.417–19, 421; the anonymous 7.416 may or may not be by himself). This sequence is immediately preceded by an epitaph that another poet, Callimachus, composed for himself (7.415), and it is not unreasonable to suppose that the self-epitaphs of Leonidas (7.715) and Nossis (7.718) stood nearby, their self-memorialization leading up to Meleager's very own *grand finale*. By describing a grave whose riddling symbols signify Meleager and his oeuvre, the last poem of this cluster (7.421), in turn, inaugurated the series of enigmatic tombstone reliefs.[42]

Already Reitzenstein and Wilamowitz suggested that the self-epitaphs of Nossis, Leonidas, and Callimachus originally served to conclude epigram books of these authors.[43] Given the poems' *sphragis*-like character and the sense of an ending inherent in the notion of death,[44] this is, indeed, a most attractive hypothesis. However, in proposing that Meleager's self-epitaphs each marked the conclusion of a different book within his anthology, Reitzenstein failed to recognize the epigrams' strategic placement among the tombs of famous poets that opened the *Garland*'s sepulchral book.[45] As Gutzwiller notes, '[t]his multiplicity of self-identifications not only plays up Meleager's editorial awareness of the earlier convention of self-epitaph in epigram collections but also looks back, humorously, to the multiple poems on single authors that must once have existed in

---

[42] This series includes several epitaphs by Antipater of Sidon (7.47), who seems to have been Meleager's most important model for the art of variation. As Gutzwiller (1998), 265–76 argues, Meleager may have taken the series of riddling tombstones directly from a book of Antipater's epigrams, paying due homage to his predecessor by composing an enigmatic epitaph in his honour (7.428), which he positioned directly after the cluster of poems from Antipater.

[43] Cf. Reitzenstein (1893), 139–40; Wilamowitz-Moellendorff (1913), 298–9 and (1924) I, 135, 140; followed by Gabathuler (1937), 48–9, 56, 67–8 and Gutzwiller (1998), 85–6, 108, 212. Though no *epitymbion* proper, Nossis' poem bears epitaph-like features. Callimachus' epigram, 7.415, was probably coupled with its companion piece, an epitaph for his father, evoking the image of a family plot, cf. Bing (1995), 126–8, Kirstein (2002), 117–21, and Höschele (2010), 133–5 with further references.

[44] On 'sense of an ending', cf. Kermode (2000). For the motif of death at the end of poetry books, cf. Höschele (2010), 298 n. 102.

[45] Reitzenstein (1893), 139–40 n. 2.

this section. If other poets had yet to write epigrams on Meleager himself [ . . . ], then Meleager chose to compose a series of them for his own anthology.'[46] Indeed, his self-epitaphs form a tightly knit ensemble, evoking the idea of a memorial inscribed with multiple interrelated poems, a common phenomenon in antiquity.[47] As I have shown elsewhere, the epigrams, which mutually supplement each other, provide the reader not simply with biographical information but stage the poet's life as a gradual movement away from the cultural periphery of the Hellenic world towards its centre (from his birth-place in Syria via Phoenician Tyre to Cos), while giving expression to the poetic programme of his anthology through the use of multi-layered metapoetic imagery.[48] By erecting this remarkable textual memorial to himself, Meleager emphatically stakes his claim to be counted among the members of Hellas' Dead Poets Society.

## POETS' TOMBS IN THE *GARLAND* OF PHILIP

The remnants of Meleager's *Garland*, then, still grant us a fairly good picture of how poets' tombs were placed in relation to each other within his collection. The *Garland* that Philip of Thessalonike plaited in rivalry with the Meleagrean *stephanos* (ἀντανέπλεξα/τοῖς Μελεαγρείοις ὡς ἴκελον στεφάνοις, AP 4.2.3–4) around the mid first century CE presents a more complicated case.[49] Nonetheless, I do believe that here, too, poets' tombs had a programmatic function and that, despite the fragmentary nature of the evidence, we can still draw some reasonable inferences about their location. The fact that Philip arranged poems in alphabetical order by their initial letter[50] not only makes it harder for us to get a sense of the anthology's original design, but also generally led to a dismissal of his procedure as purely mechanical.[51] As in the case of Meleager's *Garland*, Cephalas excerpted

---

[46]  Gutzwiller (1998), 308.
[47]  Cf. Fantuzzi (2008) and (2010) on variations in inscriptional poetry; Bing (2014) on the Daochos monument in Delphi; Höschele (2014) on a monument to the Muses of Thespiae inscribed with epigrams by Honestus.
[48]  Cf. Höschele (2013); see also Männlein-Robert (2007c).
[49]  Cameron (1980 = 1993, 56–65) convincingly argues for a date in the Neronian age.
[50]  Cf. Cameron (1993), 33–40.
[51]  For an overview of negative opinions regarding Philip, cf. Höschele (forthcoming).

epigrams from Philip in a linear manner, i.e. without rearranging them (hence the alphabetical sequences still visible in the *AP*), but—and this is a crucial difference—Cephalas had to distribute the texts among his books according to their subject matter. This, unfortunately, means that no Philippan sequence entirely preserves its original state: an epigram starting with *alpha* that today appears in *AP* 5 may thus have stood next to an *alpha*-epigram now in Book 6, 7, or 9 and so on.

In the 1960s, two scholars, Eduard Hirsch (1966) and Alan Cameron (1968), recognized independently from each other that what might strike us as a sterile, technical mode of arrangement was, in fact, anything but. By opting for an alphabetical organization, Philip imposed, one might say, an even greater challenge on himself than Meleager, as he could only group together poems with the same (or, possibly, subsequent) initial letters. Though Cameron and Hirsch have rightly identified his general modus operandi, a comprehensive analysis of the *Garland*'s structure remains a desideratum, a gap I am currently trying to fill within a larger study on Philip's anthology.[52] In what follows I would like to consider his positioning of poets' tombs, which, to my mind, suggests a direct response to the assembly of such epitaphs at the beginning of Meleager's sepulchral book.

Altogether, we do not have remotely as many poets' epitaphs from Philip's *Garland* as we do from Meleager's. Various reasons might account for this: it could be that the subgenre had, in general, become less popular, that Philip showed less interest in including poems of this type, or that Cephalas excerpted fewer examples from Philip. Whatever the case (and it could well be a combination of factors), their number is nonetheless hardly negligible. And if we look at their distribution, one striking fact immediately leaps out: almost half of the epitaphs that can be securely attributed to Philippan authors start with the letter *alpha*, and therefore must have formed part of the initial sequence in his anthology. The same is true of several poems that, though not properly sepulchral, praise a poet's oeuvre; in addition, some anonymous epitaphs for poets, which also start with *alpha*, may have formed part of this group. Hirsch noted in passing that these poems 'presumably all stood more or less together'.[53]

---

[52] For Philip's poetics of editing, cf. Höschele (forthcoming) and, with a special focus on the novelty of his undertaking vis-à-vis Meleager, Höschele (2017).

[53] Hirsch (1966), 411 (my translation).

Brief as his remark may be, it is of great significance and deserves further consideration.

Here is a list of the epigrams concerned with poets' tombs and/or their works, in alphabetical order (non-epitaphic poems are marked with an *, and adespota, whose inclusion in Philip's *Garland* is not guaranteed,[54] are underlined):

| Poem | Dead Poet | Author | Incipit |
|------|-----------|--------|---------|
| 7.17 | Sappho | Tullius Laureas | Αἰολικόν |
| 7.18 | Alcman | Antipater of Thessalonike | ἀνέρα |
| 7.36 | Sophocles | Erycus | αἰεί |
| 7.40 | Aeschylus | Diodorus | Αἰσχύλον |
| 7.41? | Callimachus | anonymous | ἆ |
| 7.42? | Callimachus | anonymous | ἆ |
| 7.47? | Euripides | anonymous | ἅπασ' |
| 7.48? | Euripides | anonymous | αἰθαλέοιο |
| 7.49 | Euripides | Bianor | ά |
| *9.97 | Homer | Alpheius of Mytilene | Ἀνδρομάχης |
| *9.192 | Homer | Antiphilus of Byzantium | αἱ |
| *9.185 | Archilochus | anonymous | Ἀρχιλόχου |
| 9.187 | Menander | anonymous | αὐταί |
| 7.370 | Menander | Diodorus | Βάκχῳ |
| *9.186 | Aristophanes | Antipater of Thessalonike | βίβλοι |
| *9.239 | Anacreon | Crinagoras | βύβλων |
| 7.38 | Aristophanes | Diodorus | θεῖος |
| 7.39 | Aeschylus | Antipater of Thessalonike | ὁ |
| 7.51 | Euripides | Adaeus | οὔ |
| 7.16 | Sappho | Pinytus | ὀστέα |
| 7.405 | Hipponax | Philip | ὦ |

The concentration of epigrams on poets in the *Garland's* initial section as opposed to later parts is remarkable. Even if we count only the securely Philippan poems, the ratio is 7:15, i.e. 46 per cent. Most of the poems are transmitted in the Cephalean sequence at the beginning of Book 7, which does not tell us anything about their original position in relation to each other, let alone to the rest of the *alpha*-poems. It is, however, a fair guess that they formed a thematic subgroup, if not as close-knit and prominently placed a unit as the epitaphs belonging to Meleager's Poets' Corner. In fact, it strikes me as very probable that Philip deliberately chose a

---

[54] Hirsch (1966), 411 speculates about the inclusion of these epigrams as well as the anonymous *AP* 9.188 on Plato in Philip's *Garland*.

significant number of epitaphs that started with the first letter of the alphabet so as to be able to place them somewhere towards the beginning of his anthology. The nature of the initial letter obviously played no role in their composition; it was Philip who selected poems according to alphabetical criteria. That the high frequency of *alpha*-epitaphs in Philip's *Garland* is not coincidental may be corroborated by the much lower ratio of such epigrams in Meleager's sepulchral book, where—unsurprisingly—only five out of sixty epitaphs for poets, i.e. 12 per cent, happen to start with this letter.[55]

Among the transmitted poems we can still make out possible subgroups such as the triad of tragedians (7.40 on Aeschylus, 7.36 on Sophocles, 7.49 on Euripides) or epigrams on the two main representatives of Old and New Comedy, Menander and Aristophanes, whose grouping may, in fact, have formed a bridge from the *alpha*- to the *beta*-section. As Hirsch suggested, the anonymous 9.187, which praises Menander's oeuvre in the *alpha*-sequence, could have preceded Diodorus, 7.370 on Menander's tomb as the initial poem of the *beta*-sequence, which in turn might have been coupled with Antipater of Thessalonike, 9.186, another *beta*-poem, on the books of Aristophanes.[56] Significantly, the latter two epigrams closely associate both Menander and Aristophanes with Dionysus (7.370 even starts with Βάκχῳ): is this pure coincidence, or could it substantiate the idea that they were once juxtaposed?

There is, of course, no definite answer to the question, and we should not let ourselves be carried away by further speculation. What I would like to point out, however, is that the *alpha*-section also contained a conspicuous number of poems on wine, song, the Muses, bees, and cicadas, all of which have metapoetic potential.[57] Indeed, Meleager exploited, as Gutzwiller has shown, the programmatic value of these motifs by opening his book of erotic epigrams with a sequence of poems on 'wine' (5.134–7), 'song' (5.138–41), and 'garlands' (5.142–9).[58] It is my contention that Philip picked up on the programmatic function of those epigrams as well as the poets' epitaphs in Meleager, and made a point of weaving such texts into

---

[55] Cf. *AP* 7.35, 54, 408, 419, 428.
[56] A similar transition from one letter section to another might have been created by a pairing of Antiphilus, 7.141 on Protesilaos' tomb, starting with *theta*, and Philip's variation on the topic (7.385), starting with *eta*, as observed by Hirsch (1966), 402 and Cameron (1993), 42; cf. Höschele (forthcoming).
[57] Cf. Höschele (2017), 21.    [58] Cf. Gutzwiller (1997b) and (1998), 284–6.

the introductory section of his own anthology. The *alpha*-sequence seems to have been one of the longest in his *Garland* (with over one hundred epigrams still extant),[59] and it is unfortunate that the state of transmission does not permit us to determine exactly how Philip positioned the tombs of poets. It is a fair guess, though far from certain, that they were assembled towards its end, leading up to the next sequence whose beginning may have been marked by the tomb of Menander.

In concluding this chapter, I would like to turn to Philip's use of another poet's epitaph—one he himself composed[60]—in the final sequence of his anthology. Starting with the words ὦ ξεῖνε, φεῦγε (and hence clearly belonging to the last section), poem 7.405 (= 34 G-P) warns the passer-by to stay away from the tomb of Hipponax lest he awaken the 'sleeping wasp' (σφῆκα τὸν κοιμώμενον, line 4) and cause the iambographer to launch a verbal attack.[61] Could there be any special significance attached to the placement of so uninviting and aggressive a tomb towards the end of Philip's *Garland*? Remarkably, it is not the only *omega*-epigram to exhibit such rhetoric. Among the sixteen poems starting with the last letter of the alphabet,[62] we find a text addressed to a patricide, who will not escape death no matter where he flees (Antiphanes, 11.348), an epigram on a man exiled from the Egyptian court (Crinagoras, 7.645), a warning to refrain from cutting down an oak tree (Diodorus Zonas, 9.312), and, most importantly, a group of three epigrams (*APl* 240–2) featuring the ithyphallic garden god Priapus, whose job it is to keep people away from the fruit he is guarding. In the first two, composed by Philip and Marcus Argentarius, Priapus declares that he is keeping close watch on the ripe figs (ὡραίας . . . τὰς ἰσχάδας, *APl* 240.1; ὥριμος, *APl* 241.1), threatening the passer-by with anal penetration should he touch the fruit.

The warning to stay away issued from Hipponax' tomb is thus paralleled by several messages similarly apotropaic in tone. On a figurative level, these epigrams may, I submit, be understood as chasing

---

[59] The sections greatly vary in length: *alpha*-, *epsilon*- and *eta*-epigrams together account for over a third of the transmitted material, while other sections contain only a handful of poems; cf. Höschele (forthcoming).

[60] As Gow and Page (1968) ad loc. remark, the alternative ascription to Mimnermus is 'inexplicable'.

[61] On this and other epitaphs for Hipponax, cf. Rosen (2007), 466–72.

[62] Cf. 5.132, 133; 6.198; 7.405, 645; 9.178, 311, 312; 11.23, 24, 348; *APl* 93, 216, 240, 241, 242.

the reader away and thus herald the end of the collection. Could the reference to the ripeness of the figs in the Priapean epigrams not suggest that the *Garland* itself, with its underlying vegetative imagery, is 'ripe', i.e. about to be completed, and Priapus' threats be taken as a metaphorical warning not to meddle with any of its poems?[63] It is, at any rate, very tempting to imagine a statue of Priapus standing close by the tomb of Hipponax, himself a Priapic figure, the two of them shooing the reader away towards the book's exit.[64] Despite the self-imposed constraint of an alphabetical arrangement, Philip evidently managed meaningfully to interweave poems by his predecessors with texts of his own. His collection, too, had its Poets' Corner.

---

[63] On the close connection between fruit and poetry in the *Carmina Priapea,* cf. Höschele (2010), 279–82. A fascinating example for an apotropaic gesture at the conclusion of a book is provided by an *Iliad* papyrus of the first century CE (P. Lit. Lond. 11), which ends with a poem spoken in the voice of the *coronis*: characterizing itself as a guardian of letters (γραμμάτων φύλαξ), it warns readers from maltreating the book and threatens to slander any culprits to Euripides, its final word being ἄπεχε; cf. Bing (1988a), 35.

[64] Not only did Philip position a poet's tomb in his final sequence, but he also picked up the motif of wine-drinking by including two epigrams of Antipater of Thessalonike (11.23 and 24), which, I argue, took on a new metapoetic meaning through their placement at the *Garland*'s end: Höschele (2017), 21–8.

# 10

## Impermanent Stones, Permanent Plants

### The Tombs of Poets as Material Objects in the *Palatine Anthology*

*Silvia Montiglio*

## IMMATERIAL TOMBS

In a splendidly illustrated volume, *Tumbas*, Cees Nooteboom narrates his intellectual and emotional experiences visiting graves of poets and philosophers all over the world. Nooteboom lets his meditations wander freely: from the shape of the tomb and the landscape surrounding it to the life and words of the buried dead, and back again to the grave itself, whose physical presence triggers more reminiscences. It is to hear the poets again that we visit their tombs: 'pour entendre malgré tout ces mots, dans le silence de la mort'.[1] Personal contact with the site of burial revives the writer's acquaintance with the poets of the past and inspires his writing about them and their tombs.

The epitaphs for poets collected in the *Palatine Anthology* stand in opposition to Nooteboom's project, filled as it is with on-site inspiration. The authors of those epitaphs were not inspired by the physical presence of real-life tombs. Instead, they sprinkled their books with fictional tombs, producing a literary graveyard of the imagination through which readers could stroll with their mind.[2] The epitaphs' lack of a material support, however, does not prevent the tombs on which they are purportedly inscribed from being 'there'. Commenting

---

[1] Nooteboom (2009), 9.
[2] See Höschele (2007) and in this volume, Chapter 9.

on the epitaphs for Homer, Sarah Bolmarcich speaks of 'a very strong sensation of the presence of a tomb'.[3] This observation could be extended to several epitaphs for other poets. But how visible and tangible are those tombs? Does their materiality matter, since poets are credited with earning immortality from their poetry alone?[4] How can a tomb made of perishable stone enhance a poet's undying fame?

To begin with a simple observation: tombs of poets in the *Palatine Anthology* are barely described. This is notable because literary epitaphs tend to give more detail than inscribed ones. As Anja Bettenworth puts it, 'while epigrams intended for a real object can function with a minimum of details, since the context against which they must be read is provided by the monument, a literary epigram that lacks such a context often includes information about the situation in which it is to be imagined.'[5] In the case of epitaphs, such information can, and often does, include descriptions of the non-existent tombs that poets would like their readers to imagine.

We might expect tombs of poets to prompt more detailed descriptions than those of ordinary citizens. Poets are generally well known, so the epigrammatist could, in theory, spend more time dwelling on the monument than on the individual it contains. Yet the opposite is in fact the case. A significant number of tombs of ordinary citizens in the *Anthology* are given concrete shapes and decorations. By contrast, epitaphs for poets, although they sometimes locate the tomb geographically (engaging in ongoing polemics about geographical allegiances found in the biographical tradition) or in the natural landscape (under a rock on the shore for Homer; near the sea for Archilochus; under a plane tree for Ibycus),[6] they rarely give particulars. This reticence accords with the manner in which tombs are seen to support a poet's fame: not through their own monumentality but by effacing themselves, as it were, and becoming a trigger for the celebration of the poet's art.[7]

---

[3] Bolmarcich (2002), 79.

[4] See Männlein-Robert (2007a), 200: 'Das Medium der Dichtung allein kann ... Unsterblichkeit bewirken' ('the medium of poetry by itself can ... afford immortality').

[5] Bettenworth (2007), 73.

[6] *AP* 7. 1 = Alcaeus 11 G-P; 7. 71, 7. 714 = anon. 52 G-P respectively.

[7] Kimmel-Clauzet (2013), 133, noting the total absence of information on the shape of Homer's tomb, argues that authors are not interested in the monument per se but in the polemics in which it can be inscribed and in 'la représentation du statut exceptionnel du poète'. The latter point can be extended to every poet.

Time and again epigrams stress the material insignificance of a poet's tomb as a space too small for the deceased.[8] This leitmotif, which applies to other famous men as well, inspires playful conceits. Two epitaphs for Pompey and his sons attributed to Pseudo-Seneca (8–8a)[9] turn the motif upside down by contending ironically that the family burial, which covers Italy, Spain, and Africa, aptly matches the greatness of the dead. The gist of the first poem is 'your greatness is mirrored in the worldwide dispersion of your ashes' (*quam late uestros duxit Fortuna triumphos,* | *tam late sparsit funera, Magne, tua*). The second reads: 'the whole world has a share in your fall, for it was so great that it could not lie in one land' (*uno non potuit tanta iacere solo*).[10] The worldwide demise of the Pompeians is fittingly reflected in a worldwide burial.

An epitaph for another statesman, Themistocles, by Geminus (first century BCE), contemplates replacing the inadequately small tomb with an adequately large one, challenging the topos of small tomb/ great dead:

Ἀντὶ τάφου λιτοῖο θὲς Ἑλλάδα, θὲς δ' ἐπὶ ταύταν
  δούρατα βαρβαρικᾶς σύμβολα ναυφθορίας
καὶ τύμβῳ κρηπῖδα περίγραφε Περσικὸν Ἄρη
  καὶ Ξέρξην· τούτοις θάπτε Θεμιστοκλέα.
στάλα δ' ἁ Σαλαμὶς ἐπικείσεται ἔργα λέγουσα
  τἀμά. τί με σμικροῖς τὸν μέγαν ἐντίθετε;

Instead of a bare tomb put Hellas, and on it put
  ships, symbols of the barbarians' naval defeat,
and draw around the tomb as its basement the Persian War
  and Xerxes: there you bury Themistocles.
Salamis will be the tombstone on top and will speak
  of my deeds. Why do you lay me, so great a man, in a small space?
(7.73)

Geminus engages with the topos here by quoting it in its standard formulation: τάφος λιτός. The word λιτός is usually translated as 'simple', but more specifically it might point to the absence of engravings

---

[8] See Acosta-Hughes and Barbantani (2007), 432. Though the topos is often noted (see also, e.g., Skiadas (1965), 56; Clay (2004), 80), its implications for the materiality of the poets' tombs in epigrammatic poetry have not been sufficiently teased out.
[9] Texts and commentary in Breitenbach (2009), 71–88.
[10] A third one stays closer to the topos: 'the greatest defeat of the civil war is buried in such a small lot—the whole world!' (8b).

or drawings.[11] The poet sets out to replace the putative bare tomb with an elaborate one. This illustrated monument has a tangible and visible materiality, suggested by such verbs as 'put' and 'draw'. Salamis now provides the tombstone and the Persian War the tomb's support. Thus rebuilt, the monument befits the greatness of the dead Themistocles.

In another epitaph, Themistocles gives the poet directions for the manufacture of a tomb with which he will be satisfied. Once again, it is a concrete monument, engraved with earth and sky:

Οὔρεά μευ καὶ πόντον ὑπὲρ τύμβοιο χάρασσε,
    καὶ μέσον ἀμφοτέρων μάρτυρα Λητοΐδην,
ἀενάων τε βαθὺν ποταμῶν ῥόον, οἵ ποτε ῥείθροις
    Ξέρξου μυριόναυν οὐχ ὑπέμειναν Ἄρην·
ἔγγραφε καὶ Σαλαμῖνα...

Carve on my tomb the mountains and the sea,
    and in between them the Sun as witness,
and the deep current of everlasting rivers, whose streams once
    did not submit to Xerxes' host of thousands of ships.
Draw on it also Salamis...
                        (Alpheius of Mytilene, 7.237.1–5)

No such poetic fantasies are deployed for the tombs of poets. Superficially, two epitaphs for Euripides might suggest otherwise. Here is the first:

Μνᾶμα μὲν Ἑλλὰς ἅπασ' Εὐριπίδου, ὀστέα δ' ἴσχει
    γῆ Μακεδών, ἧπερ δέξατο τέρμα βίου.
πατρὶς δ' Ἑλλάδος Ἑλλάς, Ἀθῆναι.

The monument of Euripides is all of Hellas, but the Macedonian land
    holds his bones, for it hosted the end of his life.
His native land was the Hellas of Hellas, Athens.
                        (7.45.1–3, attributed to Thucydides)

Greece, which appropriates the memorial function of the place of burial, would be the adequate tomb for Euripides.[12] But 'all of Hellas'

---

[11] Bruss (2005), 67 thinks that λιτός denotes not 'bare' but 'losing its engraved images'. This meaning fits *AP* 7.478.4 = Leonidas 73 G-P (on which he focuses) but not Themistocles' tomb or the tombs of poets: the contrast between the insignificance of the monument and the greatness of the dead would lose force if the stone had originally been engraved.
[12] See also 7.47.

is not fashioned into a monument, as in the earlier epigram for
Themistocles: we do not see a painter or an engraver at work. Further-
more, the main point of the poem is not to stress that Euripides is too
great for his grave, but that he belongs to Athens, 'the school of
Hellas', rather than Macedon, where he died. The epitaph—which
quite likely dates to the fourth century and was inscribed on Euripi-
des' cenotaph in Athens—contrasts not the tomb as material object,
but the *place* of burial with the poet's fame, better represented by
his place of birth: the 'Hellas of Hellas'. As Flore Kimmel-Clauzet
observes,[13] Euripides' fame does not extend to the 'whole earth' or
'world'; it stays within Hellas, a restriction that betrays the poem's
pro-Athenian agenda. The second epitaph likewise denies Euripides'
place of burial its function, transferring it to the theatre as the site for
the perpetuation of his poetry (7.51.4–5): σὸν δ' οὐ τοῦτον ἐγὼ τίθεμαι
τάφον, ἀλλὰ τὰ Βάκχου / βήματα ('I do not account this [Macedon]
your tomb, but the altars of Bacchus'). Admittedly, the theatre here
becomes a τάφος, but like Greece in the previous epitaph it is not built
to be one: there is no placing, carving, or drawing of figures on this
metaphorical grave.[14]

Poets seem to benefit not from the substitution of a too-small tomb
with a monumental one, but from the very insignificance of the stone.
Alcman will not be judged by it: 'bare is the tomb to see, but it holds
the bones of a great man' (7.18.1–2). The size and decor of a poet's
grave do not matter when the grave is actually a cenotaph, as in this
epitaph for Sappho: 'The bones and the empty name of Sappho does
the tomb hold, but her skilled words are immortal' (7.16). Literary
cenotaphs typically elaborate upon the emptiness of the grave and the
dispersal of the bones.[15] Here, Sappho's bones are in her grave, yet
they belong together with her 'empty name': they are the equivalent of
the nothingness that a cenotaph holds. By contrast, her words—her
substance—are the equivalent of scattered bones, except that, in being
dispersed, they are not lost but immortal.

The tomb can function as an enhancer of immortality by being not
merely simple and small,[16] but also made of thin matter, contrasting

---

[13] Kimmel-Clauzet (2013), 173.
[14] In an epitaph for Hector (7.137), 'the *Iliad*, Homer, Hellas, and the Achaeans in
flight' fashion a much more concrete grave: it was with them that 'my mound was
raised' (ἐχωννύμεθα).
[15] See Bruss (2005), chapters 6, 7, and 8.     [16] See also 7.21 = Simias 4 G-P.

with the poet inside, who shapes metal into song. An epitaph for
Pindar by Antipater of Sidon (7.34 = Antipater 18 G-P) opposes the
insubstantial dust, κόνις—less neutral a term than 'earth', and per-
haps evocative of the dissolution and corruption of death[17]—to the
trumpeting vocal metallurgy of the poet, a 'heavily smiting smith of
far-seen hymns' (τὸν εὐαγέων βαρὺν ὕμνων/χαλκευτάν).[18] Even the
swarm of bees that produces Pindar's poetry appropriates preroga-
tives of the material artists by 'moulding' (ἀνεπλάσατο) it within his
dwelling of dust.[19]

The opposition between the insignificance of the grave and the
greatness of the dead does not stop at devaluing the stone. One
implication of the topos is that tombs are easily destroyed, but that
the poet's fame is in fact enhanced by their destruction: a point
expressed with special force in Callimachus' 'Tomb of Simonides'.[20]
An essential function of sepulchres is, of course, to keep the memory
of the dead alive, as in this arresting epitaph by Leonidas of Tarentum,
which graphically ties together the disappearance of the monument
and the disappearance of the dead:

Τίς ποτ' ἄρ' εἶ; τίνος ἆρα παρὰ τρίβον ὀστέα ταῦτα
 τλῆμον' ἐν ἡμιφαεῖ λάρνακι γυμνὰ μένει;
μνῆμα δὲ καὶ τάφος αἰὲν ἁμαξεύοντος ὁδίτεω
 ἄξονι καὶ τροχιῇ λιτὰ παραξέεται.
ἤδη σευ καὶ πλευρὰ παρατρίψουσιν ἄμαξαι,
 σχέτλιε, σοὶ δ' οὐδεὶς οὐδ' ἐπὶ δάκρυ βαλεῖ.

Who are you? Whose poor bones are these, which remain
 exposed by the roadside, bare in a coffin half-open to the light?
The monument and the tomb is ever scraped smooth
 by the axle and the wheel of the traveller's wagon.
Soon the wagons will crush your sides,
 wretched one, and no one will shed a tear for you.
                              (7.478 = Leonidas 73 G-P)

[17] So Bruss (2005), 35.
[18] Acosta-Hughes and Barbantani (2007), 437 rephrase thus: an 'unweakening
artisan, forging long-lasting poems'. On the characterization of Pindar as a voice,
see Männlein-Robert (2007a), 195.
[19] At 7.6 (= Antipater 9 G-P), dust performs the impossible task of covering 'the
un-ageing mouth of the whole world' (Homer), though the emphatic position of κόνις
as the last word of the poem might indicate the willingness of the author to 'kill'
Homer: see Bolmarcich (2002).
[20] See Rawles' discussion in Chapter 2 of this volume.

The deceased cannot answer the passer-by's canonical question, 'Who are you?', because the inscription is no longer visible. Causing his name to disappear, the erosion of the physical monument also effaces his memory, which relies on the permanence of a tombstone that preserves both the deceased's name and his remains.[21] The crucial role of the artefact for post-mortem survival comes to the fore in the emphatic duplication 'the monument and the tomb', which fore-grounds the essential memorial function of the physical grave.

The opposite is the case for poets. The destructibility of the material tomb, in fact, brings into relief the indestructibility of poetry. Sappho is not dead, but her grave will be: 'it was built by human hands, and such works of mortals precipitate into swift oblivion' (7.17.1–4). The sea has washed away a picture of Odysseus: 'What did it gain? In Homer's words his image is engraved in immortal pages' (16.125.3–4), and the rain has washed away Laertes' tomb, 'but the name of the hero is forever young, for time cannot, even if it will, blunt (ἀμβλύνειν) poetry' (7.225.5–6).

The impermanence of these monuments sets them in opposition to the tomb of Midas, which is guarded by a statue that will stand there forever to speak his name (7.153).[22] Here, the statue claims to be imperishable by pairing its existence with ever-flowing water and the ever-recurrent blossoming of trees.[23] It is the unbreakable per-manence of this sculpted messenger that guarantees eternal renown to the buried dead. The monument's perpetual broadcast of Midas' name recalls the likewise unceasing messaging promised by a fifth-century tombstone: an 'untiring stele' (στήλην ἀκάματον), which will insistently tell passers-by every day: 'Timarete has erected me <on the grave> of her dead beloved son' (*CEG* 108.6–7).[24] In both epitaphs, the perpetuation of the dead person's memory (and in the second example of the dedicator's memory, too) is assured by the fanciful conceit of an undying and indestructible activity emanating from a tombstone or statue.

---

[21] See also Bruss (2005), 67.

[22] The text is quoted at pp. 60–1 of this volume.

[23] The natural elements are a topos: see Bing (1995); they do not point to the tomb's location. Differently, Bruss (2005), 58, 60.

[24] See Höschele (2007), 345 (her translation).

Simonides reportedly attacked Midas' epitaph because it claimed permanence for a monument: only a fool could have written that.[25] Rather than being as everlasting as the waves, tombs can be destroyed by waves, as by human hands; rather than recurring like spring flowers, tombs disappear under the wild growth of floral vegetation. For Simonides, an epitaph that celebrates a tomb's eternity is nonsensical, but we might be less intransigently commonsensical than Simonides and accept the poetic conceit for what it is. The epigram can be read as aptly celebrating the peculiar talent of the buried— turning everything he touched into gold—through the fantasy of an indestructible statue: Midas' special gift has allotted to his funeral monument an imperishable metal decoration that speaks of his gift by its very imperishability.

While most of the poets' epitaphs in the *Palatine Anthology* contain little descriptive detail about how we are to imagine the material monument, there are four instances of epitaphs that do describe the monuments on which they are inscribed: those of Sophocles, the Hellenistic tragedian Sositheus in two poems by Dioscorides (7.37 = Dioscorides 22 G-P and 707 = Dioscorides 23 G-P), and the tombs of Meleager and Antipater of Sidon in two epitaphs by Meleager (7.421 = Meleager 5 G-P and 428 = Meleager 122 G-P). The interesting point here is that the descriptions stress not the durability of the monument (in fact, only one mentions the material, gold, out of which it is fashioned) but the symbolic function of the figurations engraved or sculpted on its surface. The two epitaphs for Meleager and Antipater are puzzles. The author draws elaborately decorated tombs to compete with the visual artists by setting himself up as not only the tomb's creator but also its interpreter. The poet makes sense of the monument he fabricates, leaving no room for the hermeneutic activity of the imagined viewer.[26] The tombs of Sophocles and Sositheus are decorated with two kindred satyrs. Their function is to provide a

---

[25]  Fr.581 *PMG* (Diogenes Laertius 1.89–90 has both poems), for further discussion see Rawles, pp. 62–4 in this volume.

[26]  In this respect, the puzzle-epitaphs widely differ from inscribed epitaphs, which cannot control viewing but can only frame it: see Day (2007), 32. On the symbolism of the tomb at 7.421, see Höschele (2013), 26–7; on the epigrammatist's interest in guiding the reader, see Meyer (2007), 193, and, specifically on ekphrastic epigrams, Männlein-Robert (2007a), ch. 3 and (2007b). See also Goldhill (1994), 205; Gutzwiller (1998), 265–6; Gutzwiller (2002).

precis of dramatic history,[27] not to broadcast the poet's name unceasingly, like the bronze maiden on Midas' tomb. Contrary to Midas' talent, a poet's would be undermined by the fantasy of an ever-memorializing statue guarding an everlasting grave. The epitaph for Sappho, the one for Laertes, and the epigram for Odysseus' statue turn the stark fact that monuments are weathered into a compliment to the poets. In the epitaph for Laertes, the verb ἀμβλύνειν (7.225.6) casts poetry, and not the tomb, as hard matter: time cannot take the edge off it in the way that it can deface a physical monument.

Because poetry lasts longer than stone or metal, it can turn the poet into 'the monument of his monument', as happens to Euripides in one epitaph (7.46). This idea drives yet another modulation of the topos 'small tomb/great dead', according to which the humble place of burial prides itself on the great poet it holds, who in turn makes the place famous. The trophy-poet is almost always Homer.[28] This privilege might stem from the age-old dispute over Homer's place of burial, perhaps from his divinization, and certainly from his position in the canon.[29]

In order to be the monuments of their tombs, however, dead poets need their praising epitaphs, which thereby become the poets' true monuments. An extreme rendition of this idea is found in an epigram by Antipater of Sidon, composed in honour of the mid-fourth-century poetess Erinna—a poem which complements and crowns those discussed by Verity Platt and Peter Bing at pp. 26–9 and 165–70 in this volume:

> Παυροεπὴς Ἤριννα καὶ οὐ πολύμυθος ἀοιδαῖς,
> ἀλλ' ἔλαχεν Μούσας τοῦτο τὸ βαιὸν ἔπος.
> τοιγάρτοι μνήμης οὐκ ἤμβροτεν οὐδὲ μελαίνης
> νυκτὸς ὑπὸ σκιερῇ κωλύεται πτέρυγι,
> αἱ δ' ἀναρίθμητοι νεαρῶν σωρηδὸν ἀοιδῶν
> μυριάδες λήθῃ, ξεῖνε, μαραινόμεθα.

---

[27] See Fantuzzi (2007); Höschele (2007), 356–7; Kimmel-Clauzet (2013), 151–3; Bing (2014), 16. The tombs in these poems might also have served as structural literary landmarks: Höschele (2007), 357 and her chapter in this volume, pp. 197–215.

[28] 7.1.7–8 = Alcaeus 11 G-P; 7.2.9–10 = Antipater 8 G-P; 7.2b; 7.4, with Skiadas (1965), 57, 59–61. But see 7.39.4 (Aeschylus' tomb makes Gela famous) and 7.19.3 = Leonidas 57 G-P (Alcman's tomb graces Sparta).

[29] See especially 7.2b, with Kimmel-Clauzet (2013), 178. Graziosi, however, argues that there is no evidence that Homer's tomb, unlike those of heroes, was ever worshipped: Graziosi (2002), 152–4.

Few are Erinna's verses. She does not speak many words in her songs.
  But her little work has a share of the Muse.
Thus she does not fail to be remembered, nor will she be hidden
  under the dark wing of black night.
But we, countless myriads of later singers, lie in heaps,
  stranger, and wither from oblivion.

                              (7.713.1–6 = Antipater 58 G-P)

The speaking voice of this epigram belongs to the dead poets of
younger generations ('we, countless myriads of later singers'), in
whose judgement Erinna's inspired work is not forgotten or covered
'under the dark wing of black night'. By contrast, their destiny—to lie
on top of each other in an imagined communal grave—causes them
to fall into oblivion. As has been noted,[30] the situation is paradoxical:
the dead poets who supposedly address the passer-by do not speak
from individual tombs and do not ask to be called by name and be
remembered, as is typically the case in epitaphs, whereas Erinna, who
is not the speaking dead and has no tomb, nonetheless obtains μνήμη,
independent of a monument. Antipater's poem, which celebrates her
poetry, is in fact her memorial.


## FOREVER GREEN, FOREVER SINGING

In the epitaphs reviewed so far, tombs play a role in the immortal-
ization of poets only inasmuch as they give the living author of the
epitaph a starting point to sing about the greatness of the dead, which
is contrasted with the monument's insignificance and outlives its
fragility. Yet epigrammatists do create tombs that provide for a
poet's immortalization: not through everlasting stone, but through
ever-growing plants. Let me start with one epitaph in which the dead
poet, rather than the grave, produces the plants. Hipponax 'even dead
does not cause cultivated vine to grow (ἐπιτέτροφε) on his tomb, but
brambles' and acerbic fruits (7.536 = Alcaeus 13 G-P). The conceit of
the poet landscaping, or rather 'feeding' (ἐπιτέτροφε) his own tomb
underlines the monument's subordinate position in relation to the
author memorialized. The vegetation is the outgrowth, willed by

---

[30] See Sens (2007), 380.

Hipponax, of his poetic persona as perceived by the epitaph's writer and his contemporaries: a perpetually bad-tempered character indiscriminately spits out vituperation.[31] Brambles, which caused real tombs to disappear,[32] here draw attention to the monument, becoming the symbol, controlled by the dead poet, of his everlasting vocal presence.

The relationship, however, can be turned around. The author of an epitaph for Sophocles exhorts ivy, roses, and grapevine to creep softly on the tomb for the sake of the 'honey-sweet' poet (7.22). In this example, the poet himself does not cause growth, as in the epitaph for Hipponax, but is honoured by luxuriant vegetation. So, too, is the comic playwright Machon, in an epitaph by Dioscorides, which may have been inscribed on the poet's actual tomb (7.708 = Dioscorides 24 G-P).[33] The author addresses this request to the 'light dust': 'Bring living ivy that loves the stage on the tomb of Machon, the writer of comedy' (lines 1–2). 'Living' is the keyword: it points up the unending renewal of the vegetation, which will permanently celebrate Machon's poetry. Dioscorides asks the dust to produce ivy in order to reward the quality of the dead poet's art (lines 3–4), suggesting that the plant will perpetuate his memory by allowing his poetry to be crowned over and over with victories. Vegetable growth will do even more: it will vivify the poet himself, causing him to speak from underneath: 'this the old man *will say* (ἐρεῖ)' (line 5), when the plant sprouts.

A lively growth will likewise furbish Anacreon's tomb, nourishing the poet and his poetry. So reads an epitaph for him attributed to Simonides:

Ἥμερὶ πανθέλκτειρα, μεθυτρόφε, μῆτερ ὀπώρας,
    οὔλης ἢ σκολιὸν πλέγμα φύεις ἕλικος,
Τηίου ἡβήσειας Ἀνακρείοντος ἐπ᾽ ἄκρῃ
    στήλῃ καὶ λεπτῷ χώματι τοῦδε τάφου,
ὡς ὁ φιλάκρητός τε καὶ οἰνοβαρὴς φιλόκωμος[34]
    παννύχιος κρούων τὴν φιλόπαιδα χέλυν

---

[31] See Rosen (2007). This epitaph is often read together with one for the misanthrope Timon, who exhorts the 'dry dust' to grow brambles and thorns on his grave so that it will become unapproachable (7.315 = Zenodotus 3 G-P). A difference, though, is that Hipponax does not want to be left alone and rest, like Timon (7.315.3–4), but to hurt the passer-by with the thorns of his tomb as with his tongue, should he awaken.

[32] A famous instance is the tomb of Archimedes, discovered by Cicero: it was *saeptum undique et vestitum vepribus et dumetis* (*Tusc.* 5.64).

[33] See Gow and Page (1965) ad loc.    [34] φιλόκωμος follows Gow and Page.

κἢν χθονὶ πεπτηώς, κεφαλῆς ἐφύπερθε φέροιτο
   ἀγλαὸν ὡραίων βότρυν ἀπ' ἀκρεμόνων,
καί μιν ἀεὶ τέγγοι νοτερὴ δρόσος, ἧς ὁ γεραιὸς
   λαρότερον μαλακῶν ἔπνεεν ἐκ στομάτων.

Cultivated vine, you that charm all, nurse of wine, mother of the harvest,
   you that grow a twisted web of curling tendrils,
flourish green on top of the tombstone of Teian Anacreon,
   and on the thin soil of his tomb,
so that the lover of pure wine, the reveller heavy with wine,
   playing his lad-loving lyre in night-long revels, may,
though dead and buried,[35] wear on his head the shining cluster
   of the grape, hanging from ripe branches,
and ever be moistened by wet dew, which scented the old man's
   breath from his tender mouth much sweetly.

(7.24 = 'Simonides' 3 G-P)

The plant's vivifying power is again front and centre. The vine, as nurturing as a mother or a nurse, will grow 'green' or 'young' on the tomb to support the poet's playing and revelling. The plant will provide both the leaves for his crowns and the 'dew' (wine), a nourishment that will last forever and forever keep Anacreon from drying out or 'going dry'.

Three more epitaphs for Anacreon, all by Antipater of Sidon, also play up the nourishing power of plants and wine. One pairs Anacreon's post-mortem singing with the presence of fragrant ivy on his tomb: 'He still sings to the lyre a song of longing for Bathyllus, and the white stone is scented with ivy' (7.30.3–4 = Antipater 17 G-P). Anacreon's grave does not host a dead man but a 'sleeping swan' (lines 1–2), or rather a non-sleeping love poet still at work: the plant that perfumes the monument is the visible sign of his invisible vitality.[36]

In the second poem, as Kathryn Gutzwiller has pointed out, Anacreon's tomb is imagined to be the site of a Dionysiac miracle, recalling Euripides' *Bacchae*:[37] 'Let the four-clustered ivy bloom around you, Anacreon, and the soft flowers of purple meadows. Let springs

---

[35] As translated by Gow and Page (1965).
[36] On the continuing activity of the dead poet, which contradicts the finality of the initial statement 'This is the tomb', see Gutzwiller (1998), 264. Another bird associated with post-mortem poetic vitality is the nightingale: see Graziosi, in this volume, pp. 188, 190–4, and Garulli, in this volume, 89, 91, 97–8.
[37] Gutzwiller (1998), 263.

of white milk bubble up and let fragrant wine gush from the earth, so that your ashes and bones may rejoice, if any merriment touches the dead' (7.23 = Antipater 13 G-P). In the third (7.26 = Antipater 14 G-P), the 'bare tomb' (τάφον . . . λιτόν) becomes a site for libations of wine from a passer-by, 'who loved my books' (in other words, a reader of lyric),[38] to keep Anacreon's bones 'moist' (νοτιζόμενα) as the wine turned to dew does in Simonides' poem. These epitaphs, to be sure, do not place so much emphasis on the perpetuation of Anacreon's poetry as on the assurance that his imbibing and revelling will never stop. Anacreon, in epigrammatic poetry, is a character rather than a more abstract author;[39] he is presented as a drunken old man singing love songs.[40] But the reader who loves his books and makes a libation of wine on his tomb knows that wine is a theme of his poetry, that those books are drenched in Dionysus' liquor. As another epigram puts it (9.239), he 'wrote by wine or with the Loves' (ἔγραψεν ἢ παρ'οἶνον ἢ σὺν Ἰμέροις),[41] and as yet another says, he was himself a libation poured to Dionysus as well as to Eros and the Muses.[42] To keep Anacreon's bones 'moist' is to keep his poetry alive.[43]

The power of plants to eternalize the poetry of the deceased becomes explicit in the epitaph for Sophocles (Erycias, 7.36), quoted and discussed by Platt in the first chapter of this volume.[44] In a chiastic movement, the poem ties the vivifying activity of ivy and bees together: at each end, the perennial growth of ivy—identified with Sophocles' art by means of the epithet 'of the stage' and by the epigrammatist's desire that the plant should dance on the poet's tomb—ensures that Sophocles' plays will always be crowned with victory, while in the middle the likewise perennial population of bees ensures that the playwright will always have material for his writing. This fantasy, which seems to reflect the keenness felt in this period for textual transmission through editions and copies, encodes the reproduction of Sophocles' poetry as the act of the poet himself,

---

[38] See Bing (1988a), 63; Gutzwiller (1998), 264.
[39] See Acosta-Hughes and Barbantani (2007), 442.
[40] See Rosenmeyer (1992), ch. 1.     [41] The text follows Beckby (1965-8).
[42] 7.27.9-10 = Antipater 15 G-P, with Rosenmeyer (1992), 38.
[43] This is clear at 7.24.10 = 'Simonides' 3 G-P, where the dew of the wine is called less sweet than the 'mouth' of Anacreon. 'Mouth' is of course a metonymy for the poet: see Männlein-Robert (2007a), 196, n. 39.
[44] See pp. 46-7.

ever writing, even in his tomb. The unending transmission of his works is cast as a creative process comparable to, or even identical with, poetic composition in its inception, when the poet writes sketches on waxed tablets, before committing the final version to papyrus.[45]

Meanwhile, we may ask what has happened to the tomb. As the site for the perennial activity of vegetation and bees, it guarantees the perpetuation of Sophocles' poetry. This verse-nourishing monument, clustered with ivy, stands in sharp contrast to the insignificant grave of Sophocles in another poem (7.21 = Simias 4 G-P), where it is set off both against the ivy that crowned the poet in life and against the immortality of his pages after death.[46] We might, at this point, ask why the immortalizing agent for Sophocles is the written page, whereas for Euripides it is the theatre (see 7.51). Could this difference point to an Aristotelean appreciation of Sophocles' plays as the greatest μῦθοι, regardless of their staging, and vice versa, to the popularity of Euripides on the stage? In this epitaph, at any rate, it is the tomb that grows the ivy tendrils and provides the writing tablets. Its key role in the (re)production of Sophocles' poetry makes it indispensable and (ideally) everlasting.

The permanent tomb must be well maintained, as implied by λιπαρός, 'polished', 'shiny'. But the adjective also connotes an aspect of Sophocles' poetry, for λιπαραί is one of the favourite epithets for Athens.[47] Together with the 'Attic tablet' and the 'honey from Hymettus', λιπαρός underscores the strong connection of Sophocles' life and poetry with his native city. The stone's shiny smoothness, therefore, works on a metapoetic level to reflect Sophocles' status as an Athenian. Even the adjective that describes the tomb draws the reader's attention as much to the poet's art as to the appearance of the monument. Moreover, the monument's durability is not spelled out. The epigram asks the ivy and the bees, not the stone, to be there forever. The assumption that their material support must endure remains implicit. The plant-growing stone is even more evanescent in other epitaphs, for Machon's tomb is 'dust', and Anacreon's, in one poem, is called λεπτός 'thin' (i.e. insignificant),[48] and λιτός, 'simple' or

---

[45] On this function of the δέλτος, see Höschele (2013), 25.
[46] See Kimmel-Clauzet (2013), 177.     [47] See LSJ s.v. λιπαρός, V.
[48] See Gow and Page (1965) ad loc.

'bare' in another.[49] The tomb, in these epitaphs, is there not to be noticed as a monument in itself, but as a means for supporting vegetable growth. It is the plants, not the stone, that will be noticed.[50]

The role of plants in undermining the tomb's materiality can be pressed further: what will plants and flowers suggest to a reader of epigrams if not, in the first place, the flowers of verse, and in particular those 'gathered' in *antho*-logies to form, as in Meleager's collection, a 'garland'?[51] The vegetation growth that vitalizes the tombs of poets is a metapoetic imagery, pointing not at a concrete thing but at poetry itself. Furthermore, the luxuriant vegetable growth is a cue that the tomb is fictional, not because plants did not surround real tombs, of course,[52] but because impermanent elements like plants normally belong in literary ἔκφρασις, not inscribed verse.[53] This additional metapoetic role of vegetation as an indicator of the tomb's fictionality comes to the fore in an epitaph for Protesilaus, whose sepulchre is encircled by trees that sympathize with the hero by withering if they see Troy (7.141; see also 7.385). These plants embody a poetic conceit, pathetic fallacy, and, by their empathetic behaviour, they remind the reader that the monument they surround is, like them, a poetic creation.

The presence of reviving, or even inspiring vegetation, thus aligns the tomb with the poetic text itself. This is also suggested by a parallel between the treatment of tombs with sprouting plants that aliment the dead poet's song and the treatment of a book, the oeuvre of Aristophanes, which attracts the same vegetable population as those tombs (9.186, by Antipater of Thessalonica): on his βίβλοι, 'the ivy of Acharnae shook its green locks in abundance. And see how the page is full of Dionysus' (lines 1–3). Ivy and wine are visible in the book roll as the matter of Aristophanes' poetry, its original nourishment and its enduring substance. On Anacreon's tomb, ivy and wine will continue to nourish poetry, and, on Sophocles', bees will perpetuate the transmission of his tragedies and ivy their crowning.[54]

[49] See 7.708.1 = Dioscorides 24 G-P, 24.4 = 'Simonides' 3 G-P, and 26.1 = Antipater 14 G-P respectively.

[50] Another example is 7.714 = anon. 52 G-P, for Ibycus, where the city is thanked for shedding much ivy on his tomb and planting white reeds. Perhaps here also the vegetation will keep Ibycus' poetry everlasting. Why 'reeds', though, is unclear because Ibycus played a string instrument: see Gow and Page (1965) ad loc.

[51] On flowers as metaphors for verse, see, in this volume, Platt p. 27, discussing 7.13.

[52] See below.  [53] See Meyer (2007), 206.

[54] See 7.24 = 'Simonides' 3 G-P and 7.36, above.

The fantasy of a tomb luxuriating with ever-growing ivy or vine must have resonated with contemporary readers, for decorating tombs with plants was in fashion. A Latin metrical inscription (from the province of Numidia) matches the spirit of the Greek epitaphs on poets' tombs, lush with vegetable growth and flowing with honey:

> [Dequ]e meis tumulis avis Attica parvula venit
> et satiata thymo stillantia mella relinquit,
> mi volucres hic dulce [c]anent viridantibus antris.
> hic viridat tumulis laurus prope Delia nostris
> et auro similes pend[e]nt in vitibus [uva]e.

> Down on my tumulus the small Attic bird comes
> and, sated with thyme, leaves dripping honey.
> Here birds shall sing sweetly to me in verdant grottoes.
> There on my tumulus buds the Delian laurel nearby,
> and gold-like bunches of grapes hang on the vines.[55]

> (*CIL* VIII 7854)

A major driving force behind the fashion for cultivating trees and flowers around tombs was the feeling of continuing life that some plants could give,[56] a feeling that is shared today.[57] It was believed that the vegetation could grow enough produce to sustain the shade of the dead year after year.[58] Vineyards were planted to provide wine for libations (*CIL* XII 1657); gardens were maintained so that roses could be presented to the dead as a birthday gift, generation after generation, as in this deceased's hope that his survivors and descendants 'from this garden may offer roses to me on my birthday in perpetuity' (*ex horum hortorum reditu natale meo [fer(ant)] rosam in perpetuo*, *CIL* V 7454):[59] in perpetuity, just as the ivy will provide crowns, and the beeswax a writing board for Sophocles in perpetuity, and the grapevine wine for Anacreon's sustenance, forever and ever.

Though highly appreciated by all in real life, in the *Anthology*, tombs decorated with plants honour poets almost exclusively. There are only four specimens belonging to other categories of deceased,

---

[55] The inscription is also in Jashemski (1970–1), 101 and Campbell (2008), 35.

[56] See Campbell (2008), 35–6.

[57] Of evergreens, arborist Larry Caplan of Purdue University says: '[they] are frequently used in cemeteries because they remain green and living all year around. Visitors want to feel the concept of "rebirth" and "eternal life" that evergreens represent' <agraveinterest.blogspot.co.uk>.

[58] Toynbee (1971), 94–8; Campbell (2008), 35.

[59] *fer(ant)* is a tentative reconstruction offered in the *CIL* for the transmitted *per*.

and in none of these do the plants offer their vivifying services. The misanthropist Timon wishes thorns to grow on his grave in order to make it inaccessible (7.315 = Zenodotus 3 G-P); the trees that encircle Protesilaus' tomb, as we have seen, have the poetic function of sympathizing with him (7.141; 7.385); and the plane tree that stands near the tomb of a fowler, far from reviving the dead, is a reminder that he is dead, for it lets the birds, safe at last, sit on its branches (7.171 = Mnasalces 8 G-P). In epigram, the feeling of continuing life that plants could give is turned into an actual perpetuation of post-mortem life, but is reserved only for a small number of celebrated poets. These dead are a select few, fewer even than the deceased who are honoured with a tomb too small or too frail for their greatness.

Why are there so few? Why is it that vivifying plants will creep over the tombs of Anacreon, Sophocles, and Machon, but not over those of other, even more renowned, poets? Why are Sappho, Pindar, Alcman, Hesiod, or even the godlike Homer or Orpheus not blessed with such energizing growths in the *Palatine Anthology*?[60] I suspect that an answer might lie in the privileged connection of the poets who obtain planted tombs with Dionysus. The vitalizing plants are mostly ivy and grapevines, which have nourished those poets' songs in life. Sophocles is said to have 'fed on (ἐρεπτόμενος) the dark clusters of Bacchus' (7.20). The Dionysiac growth[61] thus provides the epigrammatists with a ready image to suggest the possibility that the Dionysiac poet inside the tomb will keep on singing forever.[62]

---

[60] The only other poet whose tomb has plants is Ibycus (7.714 = anon. 52 G-P).

[61] See also 7.22 = Simias 5 G-P for Sophocles.

[62] My hearty thanks to Nora Goldschmidt and Barbara Graziosi for inviting me to the conference where I presented a draft of this paper and for their painstaking editorial work, to both of them and to Erika Taretto for their generous hospitality, to Peter Bing and Regina Höschele for providing precious bibliographical guidance, and to the anonymous readers.

# 11

## Pausanias' Dead Poets Society

### *Johanna Hanink*

Every year on 7 October, the Dead Poets Society of America encourages the celebration of 'Dead Poets Remembrance Day', an unofficial national holiday whose origins stretch back to the murky antiquity of 2010. The society enjoins us to celebrate the day 'by gathering with friends at a poet's grave'.[1] The Dead Poets Society of America is an organization that bills itself as 'a community of like-minded people who are enthusiastic about the life, works, and gravesites of American poets'. Their website includes a Google Maps-based atlas of poets' tomb sites, with pinned photographs of hundreds of graves and memorials. These resources are part of the society's project of developing what it calls 'a community of sharing: of insights, pictures, videos, and original research on death and the American poet'. Their statement explains: 'We seek to weave a digital and corporeal tapestry to honor and learn about the lives, times, and deaths of our past poets.' Those who celebrate Dead Poets Remembrance Day are urged to do so not only by meeting at poets' gravesites, but by adorning those graves with art inspired by the poets' works and—naturally—by reading or reciting the deceased's verses aloud: 'Be creative!' the society directs. 'Our dead poets were, and they appreciate your concern.'

The Dead Poets Society of America thus formulates its objectives by placing an emphasis upon the building of networks. One network joins the living, who share in the Society's particular, and some might say morbid, passion; another network connects the dead poets—more than five hundred of them—to each other in what the Society calls 'a digital and corporeal tapestry'. The image is at once unsettling and strangely beautiful.

---

[1]  <http://deadpoets.typepad.com/>.

## ANCIENT PINS ON A POETS' MAP

Perhaps the earliest precedent for the Dead Poets Society's attempt at constructing a corporeal, or at least sepulchral, network of dead poets is Pausanias' *Description of Greece* (mid to late second century CE). This lengthy text, an immensely valuable ancient guidebook (and so much more),[2] is saturated with references to tombs of mythical, historical, and more strictly literary figures: the word 'tomb' or 'grave' (*taphos*) occurs some one hundred and fifty times over the ten books of the *Description*, and the word for 'tomb' or 'monument' (*mnēma*) appears more often still. A number of poets are among the recorded dead, and these poets belong almost exclusively to what, even for Pausanias, were distant eras (archaic and classical, in modern terms) of the Greek past—Pausanias' entire work is characterized by a sense of 'displacement from the present'.[3] His network of poets reflects a purist and pre-Hellenistic vision, where the literary history of Greece is both rooted in and coterminus with the native Greek land.

Within Pausanias' topographical vision, these poets become part of the mythical history that, for him, is embodied—and entombed—in the Greek landscape, a landscape mapped and defined by its numinous places and monuments. The Greece of the *Description* is, as recent scholarship has underscored, a landscape filled with the temples, haunts, and monuments of gods and illustrious Greek ancestors. It is also, to borrow Alcock's memorable formulation, a 'landscape of memory',[4] where stones, statues, and man-made structures mark permanent material interventions, as rooted in the local soil as any plant or tree. Those interventions, in turn, serve as prompts for historical 'digressions', and a wider scope for remembering and memorializing. It is precisely by way of those digressions that this ostensibly geographical work simultaneously becomes 'un'antologia, una grandiosa epitome, . . . un'enciclopedia *sub specie spatii*'.[5]

---

[2] The bibliography on Pausanias has grown immensely in recent decades; for overviews, see esp. Habicht (1998) and Pretzler (2007), both of which focus on Pausanias' role as travel writer and guide.

[3] Porter (2001), 64, who uses the phrase to describe a commonality between Pausanias and Longinus; cf. Habicht (1998), 132–3.

[4] From the title of Alcock (1993b). On Pausanias' landscape as a 'sacred landscape', see esp. the foundational Alcock (1993a), 172–214.

[5] Musti (1984), 10.

When the monuments are graves of poets, Pausanias tends to embroider his remarks with information about the lives, works, and reputations of the tombs' occupants. Such additional details might explain the significance of a specific poet in the ancient literary tradition, as in the case of the Boeotian lyric poet Corinna (the sole female poet whose grave earns Pausanias' mention):[6]

Κορίννης δέ, ἣ μόνη δὴ ἐν Τανάγρᾳ ᾄσματα ἐποίησε, ταύτης ἔστι μὲν μνῆμα ἐν περιφανεῖ τῆς πόλεως, ἔστι δὲ ἐν τῷ γυμνασίῳ γραφή, ταινίᾳ τὴν κεφαλὴν ἡ Κόριννα ἀναδουμένη τῆς νίκης ἕνεκα ἣν Πίνδαρον ᾄσματι ἐνίκησεν ἐν Θήβαις.

There is a memorial of Corinna, the only lyric composer from Tanagra, in a highly visible part of the city, and in the gymnasium there is a painting which depicts Corinna binding her head with a ribbon after the victory in which she defeated Pindar in a contest of lyric song in Thebes.
(9.22.3)

In the same passage, Pausanias goes on to explain that Corinna's victory was most likely owed to the Aeolian dialect in which she composed but also, judging by the painting in the gymnasium, to her exceptional beauty. The sighting of Corinna's tomb in her native Tanagra thus prompts Pausanias to tell a Greek literary-biographical anecdote par excellence. The anecdote contains two tropes in the fictional ancient traditions about the lives of Greek poets: notice of a *poetic competition* with a formidable rival (Pindar) and so an implied *synchronization* of the two famous poets' careers.[7]

Pausanias, who shows a general interest in inscriptions throughout his *Description*,[8] also occasionally pauses to record epitaphs. He transcribes Hesiod's epitaph as the capstone to the story of how the people of Orchomenus recovered the poet's bones from Naupactus:

Ἄσκρη μὲν πατρὶς πολυλήϊος, ἀλλὰ θανόντος
ὀστέα πληξίππων γῆ Μινυῶν κατέχει
Ἡσιόδου, τοῦ πλεῖστον ἐν Ἑλλάδι κῦδος ὀρεῖται
ἀνδρῶν κρινομένων ἐν βασάνῳ σοφίης.

---

[6] On Corinna's victory in the context of Pindar's biographical tradition, see Lefkowitz (2012), 69.
[7] See the index of Lefkowitz (2012), s.v. 'contests'. Kivilo (2010), 227 files synchronization as 'links with other figures' in her table of formulaic themes in the traditions about poets.
[8] The topic has attracted much attention; see e.g. Whittaker (1991).

Ascra of the many cornfields was his native home, but now that he is dead
    The land of the horse-driving Minyans [i.e. Orchomenus] holds the bones of
Hesiod, whose fame will emerge as the greatest in Greece
    When men come to be judged on the touchstone of wisdom.

                                             (9.38.4)

The treatment of Hesiod in the *Description* is extraordinary not least
because Pausanias 'devotes twice as much space to Hesiod's death as
to his life and works';[9] I revisit the story about this poet's bones
below. For now, I note that the presence of tombs in the Greek
landscape gives Pausanias fodder for a range of narratives, not all of
them strictly morbid.[10]

In the case of Euripides, the poet's (empty) tomb leads Pausanias into a
wide-ranging digression on literary history. His sighting of Euripides'
cenotaph provides an opportunity to catalogue other illustrious ancient
Greek poets—Anacreon, Aeschylus, Simonides, Philoxenus, Antagoras
of Rhodes, and Aratus of Soli—who, like Euripides with King Archelaus
of Macedon, served in the courts of tyrants and kings.[11] Thus, even
though many quotations of verse (mostly epic and lyric) pepper the
*Description*,[12] dedicated information about the poets themselves tends
to be prompted by Pausanias' encounters with memorials in their
honour. Like the dropped pins on maps curated by the Dead Poets
Society, poets' graves in this work act as aggregators for whole clusters
of information—not for photos of tombs and hyperlinks to cemeteries,
but for biographical anecdotes, historical observations, and even (as in
the case of Corinna) minor critical appraisals.

---

[9] Lefkowitz (2012), 12.

[10] I cannot resist mentioning as a parallel Nathaniel Philbrick's (2006), 105
account of the 'memory holes' created and tended by Native Americans in seventh-
century New England:

> ...the Englishmen learned that to walk across the land in southern New
> England was to travel in time. All along this narrow, hard-packed trail were
> circular foot-deep holes in the ground that had been dug where 'any remarkable
> act' had occurred. It was each person's responsibility to maintain the holes and
> to inform fellow travellers of what had once happened at that particular place so
> that 'many things of great antiquity are fresh in memory'.

In a sense, tombs, too, can be 'memory holes'.

[11] Paus. 1.2.3; for a similar passage Lucian, *Parasite* 31. Aeschylus and Simonides
were said to have served at the court of King Hieron in Sicily (early fifth century BCE);
Philoxenus at the court of Sicily's Dionysus II (early fourth century BCE), and Antagoras
and Aratus at the court of Antigonus Gonatas in Macedon (early third century BCE).

[12] Cf. Habicht (1998), 132–3.

Statues of poets, like their tombs, also teem with narrative potential, for the course of Pausanias' winding *Description* is determined largely by the path of his journey past material interventions in the landscape. A passage in Book 1 illustrates the affinities between the two types of memorials. After Pausanias mentions seeing the portrait statue of Sophocles in Athens' Theatre of Dionysus he goes on to relate a story about the tragedian's death. He never records the location of Sophocles' actual tomb (situated, according to other sources, eleven stades outside Athens' city wall and adorned, according to some accounts, with a sculptural Siren),[13] though he does tell of certain exceptional rights that the poet supposedly received at it:

λέγεται δὲ Σοφοκλέους τελευτήσαντος ἐσβαλεῖν ἐς τὴν Ἀττικὴν
Λακεδαιμονίους, καὶ σφῶν τὸν ἡγούμενον ἰδεῖν ἐπιστάντα οἱ Διόνυσον
κελεύειν τιμαῖς, ὅσαι καθεστήκασιν ἐπὶ τοῖς τεθνεῶσι, τὴν Σειρῆνα τὴν
νέαν τιμᾶν· καί οἱ τὸ ὄναρ ἐς Σοφοκλέα καὶ τὴν Σοφοκλέους ποίησιν
ἐφαίνετο ἔχειν, εἰώθασι δὲ καὶ νῦν ἔτι ποιημάτων καὶ λόγων τὸ ἐπαγωγὸν
Σειρῆνι εἰκάζειν.

It is said that when Sophocles died the Lacedaemonians invaded Attica, and that Dionysus appeared to their general in a dream and bade him to honour, with all the customary honours of the dead, the new Siren. And he [i.e. Lysander, the Spartan general] interpreted the dream as meaning Sophocles and his poetry, and to this very day people still compare pleasing poetry and prose to a 'Siren'.

(1.21.1)[14]

Here Sophocles' statue prompts Pausanias to recall a tale about his grave, another form of monument to the tragedian. The tale of the general's dream also helps to illustrate one quality that causes the tombs of poets to stand out within Pausanias' sprawling sepulchral master-network. In the textual world of the *Description*, graves serve to activate narrative, but in the material world tombs act as sites for continued audience reception of the poets' work: Dionysus' order that Lysander perform 'all the customary honours of the dead' ('at the gravesite' is implied) is meant to secure Sophocles' reputation as the new Siren for many generations to come. But poets' graves can also mark sites themselves imbued with song and verse, where poetry

---

[13] *TrGF* 4, Test. 1.15.
[14] In the next passage, a painting of Aeschylus prompts Pausanias to tell how Dionysus appeared to a young Aeschylus, who was napping in a vineyard: 1.21.1. On dreams in Pausanias, see Platt (2011), 266–77.

continues to live a life of its own. The commonplace finds its strongest articulation in Book 9 of the *Description*, where Pausanias recounts a mystical tale of a shepherd who fell asleep at the tomb of Orpheus—an urn standing atop a pillar: the episode is discussed in detail by Graziosi on pp. 187–90 of this volume. As the shepherd slept, he suddenly began to sing Orpheus' poetry. So many people crowded around to hear the shepherd sleep-sing that the jostling of their limbs knocked over Orpheus' urn and exposed his remains to the bleaching sun.[15]

On the basis of the *Description* alone, one would never know the difference between an Orpheus and a Sophocles (the one we now regard as mythical, the other as historical). Any sense of distinct and detailed chronology is collapsed and effaced in the interest of a geographically oriented narrative.[16] Pausanias even explicitly distances himself from chronological matters just after mentioning a statue of Hesiod on Mount Helicon: 'I would not enjoy writing about the Age of Homer and Hesiod, though I have made a detailed study of it, as it is the subject of great controversy, not least among those who today busy themselves with epic poetry.'[17] This recusal serves as a reminder that forays into literary history had traditionally been intertwined not with geography but with chronography: writing on the order and dating of past events.[18] The most famous testament to this other method is the inscribed Parian Chronicle or *Marmor Parium* (third century BCE), a monument that takes a poet-heavy approach to constructing the history of Greece. Though dense with geographical references,[19] the Parian Chronicle relies on chronology for its own mapping of history, placing a disproportionate emphasis on the births, debuts, victories,

---

[15]  Paus. 9.30.10.

[16]  Athens, in Pausanias' narrative, is particularly dense with tombs: there 'each tomb provides for Pausanias an opportunity to mention Athens' history, and there are tombs from just about every historical period. In this way, monument by monument, Pausanias manages to sketch a fair picture of the most crucial events of Athens' history, but the various parts of that picture are scattered throughout the text like pieces of a jigsaw puzzle': Hutton (2005), 296.

[17]  Paus. 9.30.3.

[18]  Kivilo (2010) demonstrates the close link between early Greek chronographical inquiries and research into archaic poets' lives.

[19]  See the splendid digital edition of the marble, with resources including a map and visualized timeline, at <http://opengreekandlatin.github.io/DigitalMarmorParium/>. The overlooked geography of the Chronicle is truly impressive: altogether its chronologically organized entries contain some two hundred and fify references to eighty-six different places.

and deaths of poets over other illustrious historical figures.[20] Pausanias essentially inverts the Parian Chronicle's conceptual axis by using location as his own organizing principle: his treatment of poets' tombs not only sees graves as sites for connecting and communing with dead poets, but connects Greece's literary patrimony in a lithic geographical network that, like the Google Map of the Dead Poets Society, narrates history in terms of space rather than time.

## HEROES AND BONEHUNTERS

Bones, too, take root in the ground, and Vermeule is surely right in observing that tombs will have been 'visible reminders to the Greeks that the past was longer than their knowledge of it, and that the bones of older generations literally supported all their undertakings'.[21] An early glimpse at this kind of thinking seems to be present in the orator Dinarchus' fourth-century-BCE speech *Against Demosthenes*. There Dinarchus argued that part of the power of the Areopagus derived from its status as guardian of 'the ineffable deposits'—perhaps oracles, perhaps secret tombs—'wherein lies the safety of the state'.[22] Pausanias himself claims that Oedipus' tomb was located on the hill of the Areopagus in a sanctuary of the *Semnai Theai* (Aeschylus' Erinyes).[23] The bones of this hero may well have constituted one of the 'ineffable deposits' which Dinarchus had in mind as a source of Athens' strength and 'salvation' (*sōtēria*), a source of support for the city's endeavours.[24]

Though poets' tombs prove to be especially 'communicative' sites in Pausanias' landscape, the line distinguishing the network of poets' graves from the larger network linking tombs of all dead heroes is blurry. This is in part because Pausanias' stories about the talismanic power of poets' bones rely on the same narrative structure that

---

[20] Rotstein (2015) is the first full-length study of the Parian Chronicle's treatment of literary history.

[21] Vermeule (1979), 207.

[22] Dinarchus 1.9. The Areopoagus φυλάττει τὰς <u>ἀπορρήτους διαθήκας</u> ἐν αἷς τὰ τῆς πόλεως σωτήρια κεῖται.

[23] Paus. 1.2.8.5–7.

[24] See Marx (2012), 24–5 on the significance of Oedipus' tomb in Athens.

governs many narratives about the remains of heroes.[25] And it is no
wonder that this is the case: with the exception of the Mnesiepes
inscription, a detailed attestation of the cult of Archilochus on
Paros (see Platt, pp. 42–3 and Bing, pp. 164–5 in this volume), no
other text provides so many windows onto the *hero* cults of ancient
Greek poets.[26] In the *Description*, Pausanias simply respins familiar
stories about the remains of mythical heroes from the fibres of
more poetic bones.

On his travels through Larissa, Pausanias supposedly heard of
how the Macedonians carried off the bones of Orpheus from Libethra
and buried them in their own land, where our singing shepherd
later dozed. This anecdote has parallels in stories that he tells else-
where about the bones of other bards: for example, a dream sup-
posedly instructed King Philip of Macedon to retrieve the bones of
the mythical poet Linus (later apparitions instructed Philip to return
the bones to Thebes).[27] As noted earlier, a surprising amount of space
in the *Description* is also devoted to the transfer of Hesiod's bones to
Orchomenus, an event which is also mentioned in the *Contest of
Homer and Hesiod*.[28] Pausanias records the story as follows:

καταδέξασθαι δέ φασιν οὕτω τοῦ Ἡσιόδου τὰ ὀστᾶ. νόσου καταλαμβανούσης
λοιμώδους καὶ ἀνθρώπους καὶ τὰ βοσκήματα ἀποστέλλουσι θεωροὺς παρὰ
τὸν θεόν· τούτοις δὲ ἀποκρίνασθαι λέγουσι τὴν Πυθίαν, Ἡσιόδου τὰ ὀστᾶ ἐκ
τῆς Ναυπακτίας ἀγαγοῦσιν ἐς τὴν Ὀρχομενίαν, ἄλλο δὲ εἶναί σφισιν οὐδὲν
ἴαμα. τότε δὲ ἐπερέσθαι δεύτερα, ὅπου τῆς Ναυπακτίας αὐτὰ ἐξευρήσουσι·
καὶ αὖθις τὴν Πυθίαν εἰπεῖν ὡς μηνύσοι κορώνη σφίσιν. οὕτω τοῖς
θεοπρόποις ἀποβᾶσιν ἐς τὴν γῆν πέτραν τε οὐ πόρρω τῆς ὁδοῦ καὶ τὴν ὄρνιθα
ἐπὶ τῇ πέτρᾳ φασὶν ὀφθῆναι· καὶ τοῦ Ἡσιόδου δὲ τὰ ὀστᾶ εὗρον ἐν χηραμῷ
τῆς πέτρας.

They say that this is how they recovered the bones of Hesiod: when a
plague fell upon their people and farm animals, they sent envoys to the
god. They say that the Pythia responded that they must recover the

[25] See esp. Ekroth (1999) on Pausanias and hero cult: in the *Description*, 'there are
more than a hundred heroes who had some kind of physical monument or remains
that Pausanias saw or was told about.'
[26] See Clay (2004), 9–39 on the cult of Archilochus on Paros (with pp. 10–24 on
the Mnesiepes inscription) and Rotstein (2014) on the affinities of the Mnesiepes
inscription with the *Marmor Parium*.
[27] Paus. 9.29.8–9.
[28] *Certamen* 247–54. On the *Certamen* and its relationship to the hero cult of
Hesiod, see Clay (2004), 75–6; on Hesiod's 'heroic status' in antiquity more generally,
see Lefkowitz (2012), 10–11.

bones of Hesiod from Naupactus—there was no other remedy. They asked the follow-up question of where in Naupactus they would find them. And the Pythia responded in turn that a crow would show them. So they say that when the envoys disembarked in that land, they saw a rock no further than the side of the road, and the bird was atop the rock. And they found the bones of Hesiod in a hollow of the rock.

(9.38.3–4)

Pausanias then goes on to transcribe the epitaph for Hesiod that we encountered earlier.

Such tales of poets' talismanic bones evoke other familiar stories about the bones of ancient heroes.[29] These include Herodotus' account of the relocation of Orestes' bones from Tegea to Sparta,[30] and Plutarch's description of Cimon's triumphant return of Theseus' bones to Athens.[31] Pausanias, too, records other divinely ordered exhumations. Just after transcribing Hesiod's epitaph, he notes how the Pythia told the Orchomenians that, if they wanted to stop the ghost that was destroying their land, they must recover and bury the bones of Actaeon.[32] A similar oracle had ordered that Hippodameia's bones be retrieved from Argive Medeia and reburied in her native Olympia.[33] In his description of Olympia, Pausanias recounts a story about a single bone of Pelops. When the Eretrian fisherman Damarmenus caught the bone (Pelops' shoulder blade) in his haul, he went to Delphi to inquire of the oracle what he should do with it. At that time, an embassy from Elis happened to be at Delphi with the purpose of asking the Pythia how they might ward off a local pestilence. She seized upon the coincidence and ordered the Eleans to recover the bone of Pelops from the fisherman and bring it back home.[34]

Each of these passages cites oracular intervention as the impetus for bone gathering: the location of heroes, and of poet-heroes' tombs, was thus often a matter ordained by the god. Further similarities between Pausanias' Hesiod passage and Plutarch's account of Theseus' bones are striking:

[29] See esp. Boedeker (1993) on the story pattern (with a number of further examples in notes to p. 171), and Ruiz Pérez (1995), 1–12 on oracles commanding the retrieval of heroes' bones.
[30] Hdt. 1.66–8; for analysis and interpretation of the much-discussed passage, see Boedeker (1993).
[31] Plut. *Thes.* 36.1–2.    [32] Paus. 9.38.5.    [33] Paus. 6.20.7.
[34] Paus. 5.13.1–6.

καὶ γὰρ ἦν χρησμὸς Ἀθηναίοις, τὰ Θησέως λείψανα κελεύων ἀνακομίζειν
εἰς ἄστυ καὶ τιμᾶν ὡς ἥρωα πρεπόντως, ἀλλ᾽ ἠγνόουν ὅπου κεῖται,
Σκυρίων οὐχ ὁμολογούντων οὐδ᾽ ἐώντων ἀναζητεῖν. τότε δὴ πολλῇ
φιλοτιμίᾳ τοῦ σηκοῦ μόγις ἐξευρεθέντος, ἐνθέμενος ὁ Κίμων εἰς τὴν
αὑτοῦ τριήρη τὰ ὀστᾶ καὶ τἆλλα κοσμήσας μεγαλοπρεπῶς, κατήγαγεν
εἰς τὸ ἄστυ δι᾽ ἐτῶν σχεδὸν τετρακοσίων. ἐφ᾽ ᾧ καὶ μάλιστα πρὸς αὐτὸν
ἡδέως ὁ δῆμος ἔσχεν.

The Athenians had once been given an oracle commanding them to
bring back the bones of Theseus to Athens and pay them the honours
due to a hero; but they did not know where he was buried, since the
people of Scyros would neither admit that the story was true nor allow
any search to be made. Cimon, however, attacked the task with great
enthusiasm and after some difficulty discovered the sacred spot. He
had the bones placed on board his trireme and brought them back
with great pomp and ceremony to the hero's native land, almost four
hundred years after he left it. The people were of course delighted by this.

(Plutarch, *Life of Cimon* 8.6–7, trans. Scott-Kilvert, modified)

A common template lies behind such stories of oracle-ordered relo-
cations of heroes' and poets' bones. That template—what Boedeker
has called the 'hero-translation plot'—guides narratives told across
Greek literature about some dozen ancient heroes.[35] Each author who
tells these kinds of stories nevertheless uses and adapts the template
in the service of his own narrative agenda: Herodotus uses the bones
of Orestes to establish a contrast between Athens and Sparta;[36]
Plutarch employs the story of Theseus' remains to show how
Cimon earned the love of his fellow Athenians. In the case of the
*Description*, the commonalities that the stories about the bones of
Orpheus, Linus, and Hesiod share with the 'translation' narratives
about other dead heroes dissipate any clear distinction between the
poets who composed about heroes and heroes themselves. In other
words, the juxtaposition of all of these stories serves to write the dead
poets into the very mythical world of the heroes—the world of
Orestes, Theseus, and Actaeon—which those poets were remembered
for having created and sung of in life.[37] In Pausanias' Greece the

[35] Boedeker (1993), 171.    [36] So Boedeker (1993), 172–3.
[37] One thinks of Virgil's presence in 'his own' underworld in Dante's *Inferno*, or of
the way that the ancient author of the *Epitaph for Bion* writes the poet Bion into his
own bucolic settings (see esp. Troia (2016)); see also Laird (2016). For ancient tombs

worldly remains of poets receive the same veneration, and display the
same supernatural properties, as the relics of other, perhaps more
paradigmatically heroic, ancient Greek heroes.[38]


### TRAGEDY AT THE TOMB


To gain a better appreciation of Pausanias' approach to dead poets'
graves we might look to the stories that attend the bones of three
poets in particular, the three great poets of Athens' classical tragic
tradition. At least in later antiquity, the bones and tombs of Aeschylus,
Sophocles, and Euripides were each seen as relics imbued with super-
natural powers. Each poet's tomb was said to have been attended by its
own set of curious circumstances and phenomena. All of the inter-
twining and fanciful traditions about the tombs of the tragedians, the
crowds that they drew, and the activity that took place at the gravesites,
gesture to the hero cults of ancient poets that, like all hero cults, were
centred on their tombs.[39]

Like Euripides, Aeschylus died far from his native Athens. His
tomb site in Gela, Sicily, attracted later performers to make pilgrim-
ages there to do exactly what the Dead Poets Society of America urges
of its own cemetery-going public: recite the poet's works at his
graveside.[40] In the case of Euripides himself, Pausanias' Roman con-
temporary Aulus Gellius presents an account of a *failed* example of
the 'hero-translation plot'. In Athens, Pausanias saw only a cenotaph
for Euripides because the poet had supposedly died while in the


and epitaphs dedicated to the 'literary' characters that poets created, see Bing,
Chapter 7 in this volume.

[38]  On Pausanias as 'religious tourist'—even more so than as antiquarian—see esp.
Elsner (1995), ch. 4.

[39]  See esp. Clay (2004) and Kimmel-Clauzet (2013). On the relationship between
poetry and hero cult, see also Bing, pp. 151–3 in this volume.

[40]  *TrGF* 3 Test. 1.11 = *Life of Aeschylus* 10–11. Clay (2004) observes, with respect to
Aeschylus' tomb in Gela, that this 'must have been an essential and distinguishing
feature of the cult of poets—the performance of poetry' (p. 81). See also Wilson
(2007), 356–7 on this notice and the evidence for choral competitions in Sicily as part
of the rites of an Aeschylean hero cult. For a detailed discussion of Aeschylus' tomb
and an argument in favour of positing an early cult of Aeschylus at Gela, see Bakola,
Chapter 6 in this volume.

service of King Archelaus of Macedon (on Euripides' empty tomb in Athens, see also Platt, pp. 31–6 in this volume).[41] According to Gellius, the Macedonians firmly denied the request made by Athenian ambassadors to hand over Euripides' bones for burial in Athens. Plutarch, in his *Life* of the Spartan lawgiver Lycurgus, also related that the poet's true tomb lay at the spring of Arethusa and was once struck by lightning (the same had happened to Lycurgus' tomb: a sign of the men's eminence).[42] In *De architectura*, Vitruvius provides the further information that the tomb was actually located at the confluence of two streams—one with good water, the other deadly. The salubrious stream, Vitruvius notes, was a popular site for picnics.[43]

Sophocles' death, as we already know from Pausanias, inspired the mystical dream-appearance of Dionysus to the Spartan general Lysander.[44] By the second century CE, Sophocles had an impressively far-reaching reputation for his associations with divinity: in the *Life of Numa*, Plutarch writes that Sophocles received the god Asclepius in his own home during his lifetime,[45] and that when he died 'another god, the story goes, provided for his burial' (*taphē*, i.e. 'burial' or 'burial site').[46] But the most elaborate version of this story appears in the ancient *Life of Sophocles* (transmitted, like the *Life of Aeschylus*, in manuscripts containing his plays). From the *Life*, we hear that Lysander ignored the first dream that Dionysus sent to him, but that when the god appeared to him for a second time, he declared a temporary truce between the Athenians and Peloponnesians so as to allow Sophocles' body to be buried.[47] It is difficult to imagine that Sophocles' own *Antigone* does not underpin this last narrative flourish, just as Pentheus' fate in Euripides' *Bacchae* surely informs ancient

[41]  On the tradition, see esp. Hanink (2008).

[42]  Plut. *Lyc.* 31.5, also *AP* 7.51 on the spring of Arethusa as the site of Euripides' tomb.

[43]  Vitr. 3.16.

[44]  Pausanias thus synchronizes Sophocles' death with the fall of Athens at the end of the Peloponnesian War in 404 BCE, though other sources place it a year earlier, in 406/5 (Diodorus Siculus 13.103.4 = *TrGF* 4 Test. 85; *Marmor Parium* entry 64).

[45]  On the tradition, see esp. Connolly (1998). Heracles is also said to have appeared to him in a dream: *TrGF* 4 Test. 1.12.

[46]  Plut. *Num.* 4.6. The story also appears in Plin. *HN* 7.109 (*TrGF* 4 Test. 92).

[47]  *TrGF* 4, Test. 1.15; cf. Lefkowitz (2012), 84–5 on the Sophoclean *Life* and its attestations of the tragedian's hero cult.

references to Euripides' own dismemberment either by a pack of dogs or a mob of angry women.[48]

The three great tragedians make for rich case studies in poets, bones, and tombs because a variety of testimonia about their deaths and resting places attends their biographical traditions. But the examples they provide are also instructive since their own poetry was so explicitly concerned with the graves and burial rites of heroes. As Clay and others have demonstrated, at the core of the cults of poets are hero cults born of poetic verses. Greek poetry, tragedy in particular, displayed a fascination with the gravesite and located a number of events around the tombs of heroes.[49] The ghost of Darius is raised from his tomb in Aeschylus' *Persians*; Aeschylus' *Libation Bearers* and Sophocles' *Electra* stage the first encounters between Electra and Orestes at the tomb of Agamemnon; the question of the tomb lies at the heart of Sophocles' *Antigone* and the latter part of his *Ajax*—Antigone even apostrophizes her own tomb in her last monologue.[50] Above we briefly noted that the bones of Oedipus promise protection for Athens in Sophocles' *Oedipus at Colonus*, and Eurystheus enigmatically offers up his own bones as talismans for the city towards the close of Euripides' *Children of Heracles*. Cenotaphs, too, are fittingly present in the plays of Euripides, whose only memorial in Athens was to be a cenotaph just outside the city. When, in *Iphigenia in Tauris*, Orestes believes that he is about to be sacrificed, he instructs Pylades to set up a cenotaph for him in Argos.[51] At the end of Euripides' lost *Erechtheus*, Athena enjoins the king's grieving widow to build a shrine to her husband on the Acropolis—a cenotaph of sorts, for Erechtheus had been swallowed up by a chasm in the earth, cleft by a blow from Poseidon's trident.[52]

---

[48] In some versions *Antigone* was actually responsible for the poet's death—he suffocated to death after reciting a long passage without taking a breath (*TrGF* 4 Test. 1.14). On Euripides' death and its various versions and sources, see Lefkowitz (2012), 98–9.

[49] In addition to Clay (2004), see especially Henrichs (1993), a full exploration of how two of Sophocles' plays (*Ajax* and *Oedipus at Colonus*) dramatize the incipient stages of hero cult as formed around the heroes' tombs; cf. also Festugière (1973). On Oedipus and hero cult, see also Edmunds (1981). Kowalzig (2007) discusses how, in an imperialistic spirit, tragedy 'Athenianised' hero cults of mythical figures from across Greece. For an overview of hero cult generally, see Antonaccio (1995) and the more succinct Ekroth (2007).

[50] Sophocles, *Antigone* 891–2.    [51] Euripides, *Iphigenia in Tauris* 702–5.
[52] *TrGF* 5.1 Fr.370.90–4.

Tragedy thus provides an especially fertile ground for examining
the relationship between the content of the plays (its infatuation with
tombs of heroes) and the biographical traditions about the deaths of
the genre's great practitioners. Yet these connections are by no means
limited to tragedy—to argue, for example, for the importance of
graves to the *Iliad* would be to reinvent the wheel.[53] Pindar's verses
on the tombs of heroes such as the Argives who fell at Thebes, or
Pelops (who 'now shares in splendid funeral sacrifices, on the strait of
the Alpheus where he lies buried in a tomb busy with visitors, beside a
much-frequented altar', *Olympian* 1.90–3)—also point to an entire
poetic mythscape of heroes' tombs.

In Pausanias, the poets whom we think of as belonging more
properly to the world of myth—Musaeus, Orpheus, and Linus—are
in no way distinguished from the poets that we can authenticate as
'real' historical figures, such as Pindar and the Athenian playwrights.
And the uncanny circumstances surrounding the deaths and bones
of both the real and mythical poets share the same essential qualities:
what difference of spirit divides the account of the shepherd singing
at Orpheus' tomb from the story that Pausanias elsewhere tells about
how Pindar's shade sung a new hymn to Persephone to an old woman,
just days after his death?[54]

In the early seventeenth century, the Cambridge scholar Samuel
Purchas published a collection of travel narratives in which he
claimed that 'Chronology and Geography are the two Eyes of History.'[55]
The combination of Pausanias' choice to give almost exclusive notice
of archaic and classical—that is, already 'ancient'—poets' tombs and
also to view history with the 'eye' of geography is precisely what
allows him to draw the poets and their graves into the poets' own
mythical, heroic world. That same world, within the framework of the
*Description* itself, housed the tombs of Oedipus and Agamemnon.[56]

---

[53] On hero cult in Homer, see recently Nagy (2012) with bibliography and
overview of some debated points.

[54] Paus. 9.23.3–4.      [55] Quoted at Merrills (2005), 1.

[56] Pausanias notes the presence of the tombs of Atreus, Agamemnon, Electra,
Clytemnestra, and Aegisthus in Mycenae at 2.16.6–7. Pausanias' *Description* was in
fact critical to Heinrich Schliemann's location of the ancient site of Mycenae: his name
appears throughout the account of his work there in Schliemann (1878).

BONES AND ANTIQUITIES

Just over a century ago, in 1910, William Ridgeway published his anthropological study *The Origin of Tragedy: With Special Reference to the Greek Tragedians*. This was the first monograph in which Ridgeway fully mapped out his theory that 'Tragedy originated in the worship of the dead.'[57] Herodotus' enigmatic reference to the 'tragic choruses' who commemorated the sufferings of Adrastus—choruses who danced at the hero's gravesite in Sicyon—constituted a critical file in his dossier of evidence.[58] Ridgeway argued that 'when the tragic chorus was taken from [Adrastus], the tomb round which the chorus danced now became the altar of Dionysus': the altar on the orchestral floor in the theatre.[59] The concluding chapter, on 'Survivals of the Primitive Type in Extant Greek Tragedies', offers a far more ample catalogue than the one I have provided above of 'tombs in Greek tragedies', as well as an account of the funeral rites that are performed in the various plays. One does not need to subscribe to Ridgeway's theory about the origins of tragedy to see his work as a sign of just how easy it is to draw a line between the stories that poets told about bones of heroes and the stories that later prose authors told about the graves and bones of poets.

In the world of more contemporary scholarly debate, bones are a common metaphor in the academic field of Performance Studies. In the wake of work by Diana Taylor, scholars often distinguish (and problematize) a difference between the 'archive' and the 'repertoire' as means of transmitting knowledge and memory of performance. Taylor has defined the 'archive' as the *corpus* (a fitting term in this context) of 'supposedly enduring materials' which she glosses as 'texts, documents, buildings, bones'. The repertoire, on the other hand, is more evanescent, residing in embodied practice and knowledge.[60] As such, it seems more susceptible to decay and disappearance over time. Pausanias, perhaps more than any other ancient author, explores the permanence of bones as pieces in his own archive, an archive of the whole of 'ancient' Greek culture: for him the bones of poets and heroes reside in an archive housed in the

[57] Ridgeway (1910), vii.
[58] Hdt. 5.67; for a fresh interpretation of the passage, see Wellenbach (2016).
[59] Ridgeway (1910), 39.　　[60] Taylor (2003), 19.

Greek soil and landscape. Archaeologist Yannis Hamilakis makes a lyrical observation about an assumption underlying discourses of Greek national modernity: 'Antiquities come from the earth, the earth that contains the bones of the ancestors; antiquities are bones, they are the marble bones of the body of the nation.'[61] In the case of Pausanias' *Description of Greece* we would do well to observe that even in *antiquity* bones, too, could be *antiquities*, underpinning the land (if not yet the nation) of Hellas.[62]

In the end, Pausanias' approach to poets' tombs differs little from the Dead Poets Society of America. In both traditions, tombs inspire ever-renewed performances of, and encounters with, the dead poets' work. Both also use notice of tombs to aggregate clusters of other information about the dead poets—about their tombs and the strange circumstances that surrounded their deaths, but also about their careers and lives. Yet Pausanias' is the more wide-ranging project, and his choices to privilege space over time and to discuss poets exclusively of the pre-Hellenistic past, ultimately enfold the poets' tombs he discusses into the work's broader concern with heroes and their gravesite cults. In the *Description*, the bones of heroes and poets thus belong to the same network, the same vibrant 'corporeal tapestry'—or really rather root system—that in Pausanias' imagination nourishes the sacred Greek landscape, ensuring that the memories it holds always stay lush with life.[63] If there is any truth to the premises in the manifesto of the Dead Poets Society of America, Greece's own dead poets must surely have appreciated Pausanias' concern.

---

[61] Hamilakis (2007), 121.

[62] See Pretzler (2007) ch. 10, 'Discovering Greece with Pausanias', for an overview of the way that Pausanias' *Description* shaped early modern travellers' expectations and views of Greece and so affected the modern Greek landscape itself—from toponyms to national archaeological priorities. Pausanias' influence, she writes, 'is most manifest in the memorial landscape of Greece today, which, through rediscovery as well as invention during the last four hundred years, has acquired numerous place names, sites and specific monuments which are directly related to the *Periegesis*' (130).

[63] See also Montiglio in this volume, pp. 226–33.

# IV

# The Tomb of Virgil

# 12

## Dead Letters and Buried Meaning

### Approaching the Tomb of Virgil

*Andrew Laird*

A notice recently displayed in the Classics Reading Room of the Bodleian Library (to draw attention to the Loeb online collection) ends as follows:

Physical copies are available, shelved under the author.

The sense of that is clear enough for practical purposes. But there is also a poetic innuendo in those words suggesting that the authors might occupy a physical space in the library—beneath which the copies of their works are located or buried. From antiquity through the Renaissance until the present time, imaginings of the remains and tombs possessed by classical poets, like the localities they inhabited when they lived, have played an important part in the reception of their compositions, whenever the biography of an author has been involved in literary interpretation.[1] For example, the exiled Ovid's description of the bookcases he left behind in Rome, in which his own titles occupied a significant position, is also a reflection on the future standing of his oeuvre, in the manner of a posthumous inscription.[2]

---

[1] Highet (1957) and Jenkyns (1998). In the Renaissance, Petrarch, *Familiares* 24.11 and Vida, *De arte poetica* hint that successful interpretation and emulation of Virgil are connected to knowledge of the region he inhabited.

[2] Ovid, *Tristia* 1.1.105–18; Jansen (2014), 271–80. Peirano Garrison, Chapter 13 and Smiles, Chapter 15 in this volume consider Silius' veneration of Virgil's tomb in Pliny, *Epistles* 3.7 and its literary legacy.

Discourses about tombs in particular, not least epitaphs supposedly or actually carved on tombs, cut right into questions about how we interpret the relation between a poet, his work, and his audience, and about how we interpret the written word itself. This discussion will consider these questions in a set of case studies of passages from Virgil, each of which serves to contextualize Virgil's supposed epitaph, and each of which raises issues concerning closure: the absence of the author that is enhanced and even effected by reading his text, the metatextual function of 'retelling' in a narrative, and the parallel fluctuation between the first and third person in epigraphic and poetic discourse. The overall objective is to explore the realm between literary reception and material culture, in which epitaphs have a central place.

## CLOSURE, INDETERMINACY, AND VIRGIL

Rather like the problem of reliability or unreliability of the ancient lives of poets, questions about how Greek and Latin texts ended had long been deemed a matter for historians, or those concerned with empirical matters of transmission: do we have the original, authentic end of the *Iliad*, the *Aeneid*, and of a whole host of other classical texts, or have they been tampered with? But then came the realization—and it was Don Fowler who best expressed it—that these apparently empirical questions could be, and indeed could *only* be, contextualized in terms of the reader: perceptions that a text signalled or did not signal its own end, could be determined by his or her cultural, psychological, aesthetic, poetic, or political horizons of expectation.[3] Moreover the clash between semantic determinacy (in a closed decisive reading of a text) and semantic indeterminacy (an 'open' reading which foregrounds and thematizes ambiguity) is not something that happens within the text, as was first thought. That clash is *triggered* by the text: this is what Don Fowler made clear in his essay 'Second Thoughts on Closure', and it is worthwhile to consider both lives of the poets and their epitaphs in the light of that important discussion.[4]

---

[3] Fowler (1989), (1994), (2000). Asper (2013), 63–82 and Lowrie (2013), 83–102 are also pertinent.

[4] Such questions were not addressed directly by Fowler or by the discussions in Grewing, Acosta-Hughes, and Kirichenko (2013).

The clash between determinacy and indeterminacy is an inevitable feature of the funerary text that inscribed, adorned, or even constituted a tomb—or of what was called in Greek a *sēma*, a sign.[5] Indeed that clash between determinacy and indeterminacy is more exposed and acute in the apprehension of epitaphic texts than it is in many other contexts for reading. The Graeco-Roman tomb inscription often speaks for the one who is dead, presenting the words of someone who is not present, exacerbating his or her absence, and thereby highlighting the paradoxes of representation.

The epitaph for Virgil presented in the *Life* of Suetonius-Donatus (*VSD*) nicely illustrates this issue of an inscription presenting the words of someone who is not present, irrespective of whether we were ever meant to imagine that Virgil wrote it:

Mantua me genuit, Calabri rapuere, tenet nunc
  Parthenope. cecini pascua rura duces.

Mantua brought me to life, Calabria snatched me away,
  Now Parthenope holds me: I sang of pastures, farms, leaders.

(*VSD* 36)

All forms of written discourse have that representative function and bring about a situation in which the written word which begins as a substitute for the mortal speaker ends up outliving and eventually occluding or 'covering over' that speaker. That is just as true of the opening verses of the *Aeneid*:

arma virumque cano, Troiae qui primus ab oris
Italiam fato profugus Laviniaque venit
litora, multum ille et terris iactatus et alto
vi superum, saevae memorem Iunonis ob iram.

I sing of arms and the man who first came from the coast of Troy, a fugitive by fate, to Italy and the Lavinian shores, buffeted about endlessly by land and sea, by the will of the gods, by cruel Juno's unforgetting anger.

(*Aeneid* 1.1–4)

We think of those verses as being in the poet's voice—the voice of one who speaks even though he is no longer there, even though the

---

[5] Nagy (1983), reformulated in Nagy (1990b), 202–22, on the 'decoding' of heroes' tombs in Homer and Hesiod. Svenbro (1993), 8–25 gives attention to these questions and considers the speech act in early Greek inscriptions at 26–43. On the tomb as *sēma*, see also Platt, pp. 24–6 in this volume.

'first-person' discourse with which the *Aeneid* begins here is not sus-
tained.[6] But, again, that function of a text or written discourse conveying
the poet's voice, when it covers over and takes the place of a live speaker,
is more exposed and acute in the convention of the epitaph.[7]

The preoccupation with Virgil's tomb and his epitaph point to the
paradoxes of absence and representation that are part of reading, and
of reading Virgil in particular. These paradoxes loom large in many
readings of Virgil, and though they have been interpreted in different
ways, they could well account for that long-standing preoccupation.
They are evident, in interconnected ways, in the series of exemplary
passages considered below.


## RECURRENT EPITAPHIC FORMULAE

Such formulae are applied in the *Aeneid* to dead warriors in their
*aristeiae*, to characters in their last words about themselves, and in
narratorial comment in other contexts. The most celebrated 'auto-
epitaph' is Dido's final speech with its lapidary style, long ago observed
by Eduard Fraenkel:[8]

> vixi et, quem dederat cursum Fortuna, peregi,
> et nunc magna mei sub terras ibit imago.
> urbem praeclaram statui, mea moenia vidi
> ulta virum poenas inimico a fratre recepi.

I lived, and followed the course Fortune gave, and now my great shade will go
under the earth. I established a famous city, my own walls I saw, avenging my
husband, I extracted punishment from my brother and enemy.

(*Aeneid* 4.653–6)

---

[6] Genette (1983), 244: 'The presence of first-person verbs in a narrative text can
therefore refer to two very different situations which grammar renders identical but
which narrative must distinguish: the narrator's own designation of himself as such, as
when Virgil writes "*I* sing of arms and the man . . .", or else the identity between the
narrator and one of the characters in the story, as when Crusoe writes "*I* was born in
the year 1632, in the city of York . . .". The term "first-person narrative" refers, quite
obviously, only to the second of these situations.' The move between the first and the
third person in epitaphic discourse can be connected to literary fiction and poetry:
compare the end of the section of this chapter on Fernando del Paso and Laird (2001a).

[7] Mac Góráin (forthcoming) is a full discussion of the paratextual resonance of
*arma virumque* throughout the *Aeneid*: see below, n. 12.

[8] Fraenkel (1954).

In a thorough study of the cameo obituaries of minor heroes in the *Aeneid*, Martin Dinter demonstrated that such verses show the hallmarks of Hellenistic funerary epigram and that this was a significant incorporation in Latin epic, as part and parcel of a broader programme of generic mixing.[9] This was facilitated by Virgil's practice of 'following a Hellenistic tradition of encoding literary statements into obituaries'.[10] The epilogue of Dinter's article goes further in giving explicit consideration to the relevance of the prior observations for Virgil's poetic career, and there are also implications for the question of closure. The embedded epigrams, when seen in relation to Virgil's own *Mantua me genuit* epitaph and the incipit to the *Aeneid* (*ille ego qui quondam*, discussed below), enhance 'the *Aeneid*'s epitaphic gesture . . . as the poet's legacy, his everlasting monument'.[11]

There are some addenda to those important observations about such cameos in the *Aeneid*. The epitaphs quoted below, of Misenus and of Caieta—the names of each became toponyms in southern Italy—indicate the sites in which each personage perished and which, eventually in both cases, came to be the locations of their tombs:

> indigna morte peremptum,
> Misenum Aeoliden, quo non praestantior alter
> aere ciere viros Martemque accendere cantu.
> [ . . . ]
> sed tum, forte cava dum personat aequora concha,
> demens, et cantu vocat in certamina divos,
> aemulus exceptum Triton, si credere dignum est,
> inter saxa virum spumosa immerserat unda.

Cut off by an undeserved death, Misenus, son of Aeolus, surpassed by none in rousing men with his trumpet and inciting war with his chorus . . . but once while he happened to sound out over the sea with his hollow conch, and madly called the gods to contest with his fanfare, jealous Triton, if it is worthy of belief, caught and plunged him in the waves amidst the rocks.

(*Aeneid* 6.163–5; 171–4)

> Tu quoque litoribus nostris, Aeneia nutrix,
> aeternam moriens famam, Caieta, dedisti

You too, Caieta, the nurse of Aeneas, in your death have given eternal fame to our shores . . .

(*Aeneid* 7.1–2)

---

[9] Ramsby (2007) is a discussion of the comparable incorporation of Hellenistic funerary in Roman elegy.

[10] Dinter (2005).     [11] Dinter (2005), 169.

These two sets of verses have a structural function.[12] They directly enclose the *katabasis* narrative of Book 6—accounting for a marked escalation from the first lapidary passage to the second: the Sibyl had had to instruct Aeneas and Achates to bury Misenus before his identity was revealed as they came upon his body; Caieta is interred in the verse immediately following the notice of her death. And the escalation is also indicated by the poet's direct apostrophe to Caieta: the significance of this first death to follow the vision of the underworld is, as a result, all the more salient to characters and readers alike. The changes rung by Virgil on the literary epitaph and the remarkable innovation of his *katabasis* mutually lend weight and impact to each other.

It has long been observed that the figure of Cretheus, the poet cut down in battle in *Aeneid* 9.774–7, whose reported singing recalls the very opening of the *Aeneid* (*arma virumque cano*) could be a cameo for Virgil himself:[13]

> amicum Crethea Musis,
> Crethea Musarum comitem, cui carmina semper
> et citharae cordi numerosque intendere nervis,
> semper equos atque **arma virum** pugnasque **canebat**.

Cretheus friend of the Muses, companion of the Muses, for whom songs and the lyre were always dear and who set verses to music, and who was always **singing** of horses and **of the arms of men** and battles.

*(Aeneid 9.774–7)*

But the instance of Cretheus suggests that other such obituaries might have a metatextual force, acting on or characterizing the poet himself in other ways. Such a possibility further underscores the association between the Virgilian text and the Virgilian tomb. To take the examples just discussed, in *Aeneid* 7.1–2, Caieta is addressed by the poet, and the phrase *litoribus nostris* is the only spatial indexical in the text to reveal the provenance of the speaking poet—who would have to be an Italian.

---

[12] Horsfall (2000), 46 on *tu quoque*. Barchiesi (1979) treats another important relation—between Caieta and Palinurus. Mac Góráin (forthcoming) suggests the recollection of the incipit in the narration of Misenus' funeral at 6.233 (*imponit suaque arma viro*, 'Aeneas places on the hero his arms') points to the 'commemorative function of epic'.

[13] Bloch (1970); Della Corte (1984); Hardie (1986), 59: 'it is difficult in this instance not to see a reference to Virgil's own subject [of arms and the man].' Hardie here cites Desport (1952) on Virgil's representation of fictional poets.

The tradition sustained by Virgil's epitaph and ancient biographies that his tomb was in Naples harmonizes with the poet referring to the shores of *south* Italy as his 'own': perception of a deeper meaning of *nostris* is thus generated by (or may have been partly responsible for) the legendary locations of the poet's death and burial. In *Aeneid* 6.163–5, Misenus could also be seen as a cypher for a martial poet or *the* poet: this episode includes one of Virgil's densest emulations of Ennius—and Virgil goes on to describe how Misenus' own deranged attempt to compete with Triton by blowing his own trumpet led to his demise.[14] Finally, Dido's auto-epitaph has a metatextual dimension linking it to the poet of the *Aeneid*, as she rehearses what we have already been told in Book 1, recapping the narrative of the epic itself.[15]

## THE PALINURUS EPISODE

The story of Palinurus in the *Aeneid* involves a complex cluster of events. The steersman victimized by Neptune has his first epitaph pronounced by Aeneas at the end of Book 5:

> o nimium caelo et pelago confise sereno,
> nudus in ignota, Palinure, iacebis harena.

> Ah, having trusted too much in the calm sky and sea,
> naked will you lie, Palinurus, on unknown sands.
>
> *(Aeneid 5.870–1)*

That anticipates the demand Palinurus' shade later expresses for a tomb, after he explains he did not actually drown: his shade recounts how he fell into the water, and reached Italy after being borne for three days—but just as he made it to the shore, native savages rushed at him and attacked him. He was thus killed by a sword, but his auto-epitaph still seems to be that of a man lost at sea:

---

[14] Ennius, *Annales* 175–9 (Skutsch) is evoked in the *antiquam silvam* at 6.179–82 (Hinds (1998), 10–14), as Book 6 of the *Annales* as a whole is recalled in the sixth book of the *Aeneid*: Fantham (2006). *Aeneid* 6.171–4 refers to Misenus' contest with Triton.

[15] The Dido episode is distinguished in the *Aeneid* by the extent to which its narrative is sustained simply by *retellings* or reapprehension of exactly the same essential story—first by Venus, then by the poet, then by *Fama*, by Iarbas, then by Jupiter, Mercury, and Dido herself; Laird (1999), 274.

nunc me fluctus habet versantque in litore venti.

Now the wave holds me and winds turn me about on the shore.

(Aeneid 6.362)

He begs either for earth to be thrown on his corpse or for Aeneas to
take him across the river Cocytus, but he is reassured by the Sibyl that
he will be buried in a place that will be called after him:

> 'sed cape dicta memor, duri solacia casus.
> nam tua finitimi, longe lateque per urbes
> prodigiis acti caelestibus, ossa piabunt
> et statuent tumulum et tumulo sollemnia mittent,
> aeternumque locus Palinuri nomen habebit.'
> his dictis curae emotae, pulsusque parumper
> corde dolor tristi; gaudet cognomine terra.

'But hear and remember my words as a comfort for your hard fortune:
neighbouring people throughout cities all over the region will be impelled
by heavenly portents to honour your remains and set up a tomb and perform
rites at the tomb, and the place will for ever hold the name of Palinurus.'
These words drove away his cares and for a while pain was dispelled from his
sad heart; and the land takes joy in his name.

(Aeneid 6.377–83)

No explanation is provided for how his name, whether *nomen* or
*cognomen*, was known so that it could to be attached to the tomb.
This prompts reflection on the place of names in epitaphs more
generally, including Virgil's own. The poet's name was not, after all,
included in his supposed tomb inscription, and a further parallel
between Palinurus and the poet is suggested by the phrasing of
Palinurus' auto-epitaph—*nunc me fluctus habet*—which is delicately
echoed in Virgil's own: *me . . . tenet nunc Parthenope*.

Palinurus' enormous literary reception adds some support to this
association between character and poet: beyond the references in Ovid
and Lucan, in More's *Utopia* he is a reckless traveller.[16] That is
something he has in common with the figure of Virgil in the *VSD*:
the poet's decision to continue his journey to Brundisium, in spite of
contracting a fever, was what led to his death.[17] Palinurus has endured

---

[16] Ovid, *Remedia amoris* 577–8; *Metamorphoses* 14.88; Lucan's apostrophe to
Palinurus in *De bello civili* 9.42 considered in Fratantuono (2012), 97; More (1989), 10.
[17] *VSD* 35, quoted at the very beginning of this volume, pp. 1–2.

in post-classical literature as a stock tragic figure, as a loyal servant or a victim in need of burial.[18] The evocation of Palinurus in Cyril Connolly's *The Unquiet Grave* (1944) was recalled exactly thirty years later in Fernando del Paso's *Palinuro de México* (1974), a novel offering a complex homage to Virgil.[19] The interior monologue of the principal narrator oscillates, in epitaphic mode, between the third and the first person, as Palinuro recounts his own life, and then appears to describe events following his own death through a kind of *katabasis*.


## VIRGIL'S AUTO-EPITAPHS

The third point of connection between Virgil's works and his tomb is provided by the epitaphic quality of the poet's own discourse, which has the effect of 'covering over', supplanting, and forever replacing the voice of the mortal, historical Virgil. The incipit or *pre-proemium* to the *Aeneid* not only endows the narrator of *arma virumque* with the authorial identity of the poet of the *Eclogues* and *Georgics*: it can also be seen as providing a sepulchral frame for the whole epic to follow, with the first two words signalling the kind of *Lapidarstil* attributed to Dido's auto-epitaph for what follows:[20]

> ille ego qui quondam gracili modulatus avena
> carmina et egressus silvis vicina coegi,
> ut quamvis avido parerent arva colono,
> gratum opus agricolis, at nunc horrentia Martis
> arma virumque cano

I am the one who once in a pastoral strain, composed poetry and coming from the woods compelled neighbouring fields to be their owner, however demanding. A work pleasant for farmers, but now I sing of Mars's bristling arms and the man . . .

(Pseudo-Virgilian incipit and Aeneid 1.1)

---

[18] Usher (2013), 56–8 treats Palinurus in early modern French drama and in the poetry of Joachim Du Bellay.

[19] Schiesaro (2001) treats the reception of Palinurus in Cyril Connolly whose tombstone was inscribed with a line from the *Aeneid*.

[20] This is explored in Dinter (2005) and Laird (2016), 90–3.

The *sphragis* to the *Georgics* is especially interesting:

> haec super arvorum cultu pecorumque canebam
> et super arboribus, Caesar dum magnus ad altum
> fulminat Euphraten bello victorque volentis
> per populos dat iura viamque adfectat Olympo.
> illo Vergilium me tempore dulcis alebat
> Parthenope studiis florentem ignobilis oti,
> carmina qui lusi pastorum audaxque iuventa,
> Tityre, te patulae cecini sub tegmine fagi.

Thus of the care of fields, of cattle, and of trees I sang, while great Caesar thundered in war near the deep Euphrates and while he, as a conqueror giving laws to willing peoples, made his way to Olympus. At that time sweet Parthenope was nursing me, Virgil, flowering in the pursuits of unimpressive recreation; I played the songs of shepherds, and boldly in my youth sang of you, Tityrus, under the cover of a shady beech.

*(Georgics 4.559–66)*

The utterance of line 563, *illo Vergilium me tempore dulcis alebat* ('At that time it was me, Virgil, sweet Parthenope was nursing') represents a point at which the distinction between Virgil the poet and anyone else reciting these lines would become very pronounced. The sounding of Virgil's name makes Virgil's physical absence more conspicuous than it is at any other point in his work. The writers of both the apocryphal epitaph for Virgil (which mentions Parthenope) and the incipit to the *Aeneid* were excavating the epitaphic significance already lurking in those last lines of *Georgics* 4.

Finally, a similar significance may even be discerned in the first line of the *Eclogues*: *Tityre, tu patulae recubans sub tegmine fagi* ('You, Tityrus lie under the cover of a spreading beech', *Eclogue* 1.1). Trees provided a site for Roman tombs as well as a frequent decorative motif. The purpose of the 'garden tomb' was commemorative: '[a]s the primary motivation in constructing a tomb was remembrance, the key was to attract the attention of those passing by. Including lavish gardens, sweet smelling flowers, or providing simply *the shade of a single tree under which a weary traveller could rest* would have assured one's continued place amongst the living.'[21] Such a remark

---

[21] Campbell (2008), 43 (my emphasis). Montiglio in this volume (pp. 226–33) discusses lush vegetation in the context of epigrams on poets' tombs in the *Palatine Anthology*.

could have a suggestive implication for *Eclogue* 1: if the first line of the first poem of Virgil's first work were to have an epitaphic nuance, it would frame and haunt his entire oeuvre—and might even have helped to prompt the long-standing identification of Tityrus with the poet himself.[22]

## FURTHER REFLECTIONS

Other features of Virgil's poems could account for the emphasis and attention given to his own tomb and epitaph. The recurrence of *sepulcrum* (fifteen occasions) and *tumulus* (on twenty occasions) in the Virgilian text—and the contexts in which they occur may well bear on the prominence given to epitaphic discourse in the antique lives of Virgil, especially the *VSD* and Phocas, as well as in the *Culex*.[23]

The connections between the epigrammatic inclusions in the *Aeneid* and the *katabasis* in the poem have broader ramifications: Virgil can be viewed as a kind of *psychopompos*, a guide of souls to the place of the dead—after all, he presents the underworld in *Georgics* 4 as well as in the *Aeneid*. In both descents, the poet himself is occluded and at a mysterious remove, because the voices of *embedded speakers* (the Sibyl, Anchises, and other shades of the dead in the *Aeneid*, and Proteus in the *Georgics*) are what really convey the narrative.[24]

Servius implies in his introduction to *Aeneid* 6 that the book is a polysemous mystical text:

totus quidem Vergilius scientia plenus est, in qua hic liber possidet principatum . . . et dicuntur aliqua simpliciter, multa de historia, multa per altam scientiam philosophorum, theologorum, Aegyptiorum, adeo ut plerique de his singulis huius libri integras scripserint pragmatias.

---

[22] Servius' comment on Tityrus' words in *Eclogue* 6.5 suggests ancient identification of the speaker with Virgil: *sane . . . quidam volunt hoc significasse Vergilium, se quidem altiorem de bellis et regibus ante bucolicum carmen elegisse materiam, sed . . . mutasse consilium* ('Some think these words meant that Virgil had preferred the more elevated subject of wars and kings to bucolic poetry, but changed his mind'). The readings of Thomas (1999), 288–96 and Kania (2016), 97–110 are developed in the light of this legacy, which is treated in depth in Caviglia (1990), the article on Tityrus ('Titiro') in the *Enciclopedia Virgiliana*.

[23] Laird (2017).

[24] Both those descents are recalled, again, in the *Culex*: Laird (2001b).

Though all of Virgil is full of knowledge it is predominant in this book...
Some things are simply said, many from history, many from the deep
wisdom of philosophers, theologians, Egyptians; so that several have written
whole treatises about these individual aspects of this book.

(Servius, Introduction to *Aeneid* 6)

Such opinions must have some part in explaining later biographical
configurations of Virgil as a sage and magus. The very expression of
those opinions is an invitation to open up our readings of the poet, and
even of the early biographies of Virgil: the latter have the capacity to
generate new meanings for the poet and his work. Discussions of Virgil
in other texts from later in antiquity, like Fulgentius' *Continentia*
or Macrobius' *Saturnalia* or the medieval commentary of Bernard
Silvestris, might help us to see the potential of the *Lives* in themselves
as mystery or wisdom literature. This is where those who are still
inclined to attempt literal interpretations of the *VSD* as veridical
documentary are missing out, and, worse, closing off the different
ways we can read Virgil.

Contemporary works like Alice Oswald's *Memorial*, a poetic rewrit-
ing or 'cover' version of the *Iliad*, or Zachary Mason's *The Lost Books of
the Odyssey*, excavate these preoccupations in the Homeric texts they
refashion. They are an important reminder that the resistance to
closure in the epitaphic complex is by no means specific to Virgil or
even to Roman poetry. The important thing to emerge is a general
realization about language—or at least about poetry as written lan-
guage: in antiquity, Latin and Greek always had a central epitaphic role.
Writing in most of its manifestations was to commemorate, to provide
monuments, and this function naturally passed into poetry, historiog-
raphy, and other forms of literature.

# 13

## The Tomb of Virgil between Text, Memory, and Site

*Irene Peirano Garrison*

According to the *Life of Virgil* of Suetonius-Donatus, the end of Virgil's life was a peripatetic affair. Having resolved to go away to Greece and Asia to put the finishing touches on the *Aeneid*, he met with the emperor Augustus in Athens and resolved to come back to Italy with him. The poet, however, caught sunstroke on a visit to the nearby town of Megara, fell gravely ill on the journey back home, and finally died at Brindisium. His bones were taken to Naples presumably because, as mentioned earlier in the *Life*, 'he had a house in Rome on the Esquiline near the gardens of Maecenas, although he mostly took advantage of secluded living in Campania and Sicily'.[1] The *Life of Virgil* gives a specific location for Virgil's burial ground in Naples: 'on the Via Puteolana, less than two miles from the city'.[2]

The Neapolitan burial has long thought to be corroborated by a story, found in several imperial sources, according to which the poet Silius Italicus, having retired from life in the city, bought one of Cicero's Campanian properties as well as Virgil's tomb (Martial, *Epigrams* 11.48–9), which he restored to its former glory and honoured as a temple (Pliny, *Epistles* 3.7; Statius, *Silvae* 4.4.51–5). The tomb is last mentioned by Sidonius Apollinaris in the fifth century (*Carmina* 9.217–20) but

---

[1] *VSD* 13: *habuitque domum Romae Esquiliis iuxta hortos Maecenatianos, quamquam secessu Campaniae Siciliaeque plurimum uteretur*. For Virgil's connection to Campania, see also *G.* 4.563–4 and *Catal.* 5. Other villa owners in the area included Cicero (Pliny, *HN* 31.7) and Sulla (Plut. *Sull.* 37.3). See McKay (1971), 211–12.

[2] *VSD* 36, quoted at the beginning of this volume, pp. 1–2. According to Horsfall (1995), 21, 'date and site of the tomb are unassailable'.

has been identified since the thirteenth century with a columbarium-type grave at Piedigrotta near the entrance to the tunnel that cut through the promontory of Posillipo between Naples and Puteoli.[3] This burial site is known as the 'Grotta di Virgilio' and has its own history in visual and literary sources from the Middle Ages to Romanticism and beyond.[4]

This chapter investigates Virgil's tomb as a literary, biographical, and spatial construct in the context of the ancient reception of Virgil's works. The locale of the tomb in *VSD* should be read as more than a generic reference to Virgil's Neapolitan retreat. The reference to the Via Puteolana activates a memory both of the locale of Aeneas' *katabasis* in subterranean Avernus and of the epitaphic gestures performed in its vicinity by Aeneas and retrospectively read as prefiguring the poet's final resting place.[5] Moreover, on the road to Puteoli, the physical remains of the poet are situated on a busy artery built by Augustus and connecting the site of Aeneas' landfall with the Campanian capital. In the second part of the chapter, I analyse the ways in which Martial and Pliny the Younger construct the tomb as a Virgilian pastiche and exploit it in the context of Silius' own claim to be the heir to the Mantuan poet. The rediscovery of the tomb is fruitfully compared to similar narratives of rediscovery of neglected sepulchral sites, above all Cicero's account of his discovery of Archimedes' tomb in the *Tusculan Disputations* (5.64–6) as reinterpreted by Silius Italicus in *Punica* 14. Here the neglect of the tomb highlights the immortality of the deceased's work, which transcends the confines of the physical body, and thus emphasizes an ensuing tension between literary and material monumentality. The care of the tomb, in these narratives, is a figure for the reader's attempt to cultivate and imitate an author. Finally, with Statius' representation of his Neapolitan *otium* at the site of Virgil's shrine in *Silvae* 4.4, the tomb as a site on a travelled road comments on the place of the monument—and implicitly the poet's work—within imperial Rome.

---

[3] Trapp (1984), 7.
[4] Capasso (1983); Trapp (1984); Trapp (1986); see also the last two chapters in this volume and Goldschmidt's contribution, Chapter 5, on Ovid's tombs.
[5] For the ways in which the landscape of Aeneas' landfall in Books 5–7 of the *Aeneid* is reimagined as a burial site for the poem's author and the epitaphic gestures therein retrospectively read as anticipating the poet's burial, see Laird, Chapter 12 of this volume.

## ON THE ROAD TO PUTEOLI: THE TOMB IN *VSD*

While the reception of the tomb in the post-classical period has been well investigated, surprisingly little work has been done on the significance of the *via Puteolana*, the location mentioned in *VSD*.[6] Puteoli forms the southern border of the region known as the Phlegraean Fields. Pliny the Elder writes that, 'as the Campanian plain surpasses all the lands of the world, so by the same degree Campania itself is surpassed by the part of it called Leboriae, and by the Greeks the Phlegraean Plain. This district is bound on either side by consular roads that run from Puteoli and from Cumae to Capua' (*Natural History* 18.111). Within the region delimited by these highways, the Via Puteolana was the road that led from Naples to Puteoli, although the name is not found outside *VSD* and is thought to be a local name rather than the official one.[7] While the old road known as the Via Antiniana connected Naples and Puteoli through the hills of Vomero, during the war with Sextus Pompey in 37–36 BCE, a tunnel was dug by the architect Lucius Cocceius Auctus at the request of Agrippa which connected the two towns and significantly shortened the journey between them.[8] Known as the 'crypta Neapolitana', this new road was part of a series of tunnels dug in the area by Agrippa, one of which connected Lake Avernus to Cumae, the other Lake Avernus to Lake Lucrinus.[9] In the Middle Ages, a legend developed that Virgil himself had dug out the tunnel using his magical powers.[10]

The engineering project, and specifically the creation of the harbour of Portus Iulius north of Puteoli, is praised by Virgil at *Georgics* 2.161–4 in his *Laudes Italiae*. The Servian commentary remarks on the

---

[6] Rostagni (1961), 175 n. 19; Benario (1959).

[7] Johannowsky (1952), 86–7, which is still the definitive study, points out that the miles on the *via* are numbered from Puteoli to Naples, making it unlikely that Via Puteolana was the official name.

[8] Strabo 5.4.5; Dio 48.50–1; *CIL* x.1614. See Rädke (1981), 156; Beloch (1879), 83–5 and 142.

[9] Frederiksen (1984), 333–4; D'Arms (1970), 134–5; Huilsen, s.v. 'Crypta Neapolitana' in *RE*, IV (1901), 1733. Nero started but never brought to completion an ambitious engineering project which would have connected Lake Avernus to Ostia, thus securing not only Rome's food supply but also a passage to Baiae: Champlin (2003), 158–9.

[10] D'Ovidio (2014), 10–14.

encomiastic value of this reference, stating that 'the glory of this deed went to Augustus'.[11] In another passage, commenting on the etymology of Avernus from Greek *aornos* ('birdless'), Servius highlights Augustus' understanding that the swampy terrain was a cause of death for the birds and 'undertook to cut down the woods and turn the place from one ridden with pestilence to beautiful'.[12] In the early imperial period, the crypta is mentioned by Seneca the Younger (*Epistles* 57) as an unattractive, dark, and smelly alternative to a boat ride between Puteoli and Naples.[13] Puteoli remained Rome's largest maritime port into the second century and was the sight of the last *salutatio* (the morning call traditionally made by clients to their partons) received by Augustus, according to Suetonius (*Life of Augustus* 98). Although *VSD* does not mention the crypta, the generic 'Via Puteolana' would have evoked this tunnel. For this reason, the reference activates not just a broad Virgilian connection with Campania but an engineering project spearheaded by Augustus and celebrated by Virgil himself in the *Georgics*.

Strabo, a contemporary of Virgil, remarks on the geographical significance of this underground passage when he connects Cocceius' choice to dig a tunnel to the history of the region in Homeric times. According to Strabo, Lake Avernus was the entrance to the underworld and the historian Ephorus mentioned that the Kimmerians lived in the area on the basis of *Odyssey* 11.15–16—'nor does the shining sun ever set eyes on them'. This was taken as evidence that the Kimmerians lived in underground tunnels.[14] Thus, Strabo writes, 'Cocceius, who made this tunnel as well as the one that from Dicearchia [Greek name for Puteoli] goes to Naples, wished to follow the practice of the Kimmerians we have already described, or fancied that it was natural to this place that its roads should be made underground' (Strabo 5.4.5). The Via Puteolana can thus be read as a gateway to the Avernus region, not only regarded as the site of the

---

[11] Serv. *Dan.* ad *G.* 2.161: *Agrippa in secundo vitae suae dicit, excogitasse se, ut ex Lucrino lacu portum faceret. verum huius <operis> gloria Augusto cessit.* The note also mentions the appearance of sweat on a statue at Avernus (cf. Dio above, and see Thomas (1988), vol. I, 186–7), which was interpreted as a signal of nature's resentment against the barricades.

[12] Servius ad *Aen.* 3.442.

[13] Cf. Petronius fr.16 Müller: *satis constaret eos nisi inclinatos non solere transire cryptam Neapolitanam.*

[14] Cf. Diod. Sic. 4.22.1–2; Lycoph. 695–702 with Sbordone (1984).

entrance to the Homeric underworld since the fourth century BCE, when Ephorus was active, but also more specifically as the site of Aeneas' own *katabasis* in *Aeneid* Book 6.[15] Although the connection is not made explicit in antiquity, some have suggested that Virgil's description of the entrance to Avernus as a *spelunca* (a 'cave' or 'cavern', *Aen.* 6.237) is inspired by his experience travelling in the Cocceian tunnels. According to McKay, 'the account of the hero's descent in all probability owes much of its character to Virgil's experience with the tunnels, old and new, in the environs of Portus Julius'.[16] When Seneca describes his experience through the 'crypta Neapolitana' (*Epistles* 57), he does so to expound on man's irrational fear of death, equating the journey through the darkness of the tunnel to a near-death experience. Thus the Via Puteolana can be seen as a site already connected with death itself and possibly with Aeneas' descent into the underworld.

## THE TOMB OF VIRGIL IN FLAVIAN LITERATURE

In the Flavian period, Martial and Pliny use Virgil's tomb, supposedly restored by the poet Silius Italicus, to highlight and contest the latter's epigonal relationship with his epic model. The *monumentum* is constructed as a site of poetic worship through creative reworking of Virgilian grave scenes as mediated by Silius Italicus' intertextual engagement with them. Here the tomb, ambiguously framed as both ephemeral matter and enduring memory, dramatizes the question of literary legacy: what does it mean to cultivate the memory of the great Maro?[17]

Martial is likely one of our earliest sources regarding Silius Italicus' cult of Virgil's tomb. According to him, Silius came to the rescue of

[15] See especially *Aen.* 5.731–3 (*Ditis tamen ante / infernas accede domos et Auerna per alta / congressus pete, nate, meos*) and 6.126 (*facilis descensus Averno*). For Virgil, Cumae is the home of the Sibyl and is to be distinguished from Avernus, the entrance to the underworld; contra Naevius fr.18 Morel, Strabo 5.4.5; and Pliny *HN* 3.61 (*Acherusia palus Cumis vicina*): see Horsfall (2013), 198 ad *Aen.* 6.201; Poccetti (2002); Clark (1991); Paratore (1977).

[16] McKay (1971), 216; and cf. Horsfall (2013), 215–16 ad *Aen.* 6.237.

[17] For Joseph Wright of Derby's visual reception of the issue, see Smiles' discussion at pp. 301–5.

the poet, whose monument had been neglected. One of the two epigrams which treat the subject, both from Book 11, insists on Silius' status as a continuator of Virgil, explaining his worship of the poet as that of one *vates* for another, but presenting the two as equals:[18]

> Iam prope desertos cineres et sancta Maronis
>    nomina qui coleret pauper et unus erat.
> Silius orbatae succurrere censuit umbrae,
>    et vates vatem non minor ipse colit.

There was only one man, a poor man, to honour Maro's almost forsaken ashes and sacred name. Silius decided to come to the rescue of his destitute shade, and honours the poet, no lesser poet he.

(Martial, *Epigrams* 11.50)

The other epigram comes back to the worshipping of Maro's tomb by the poet who is designated as an heir and owner of the tomb (Virgil's), but this time Silius is also linked with Cicero, whose property he is said to have acquired:

> Silius haec magni celebrat monumenta Maronis,
>    iugera facundi qui Ciceronis habet.
> heredem dominumque sui tumulive larisve
>    non alium mallet nec Maro nec Cicero.

Silius, who possesses the acres of eloquent Cicero, honours this monument of great Maro. No other heir and proprietor of his tomb or dwelling would either Maro or Cicero choose.

(Martial, *Epigrams* 11.48)

Here Silius' ownership of Virgil's tomb and Cicero's property is a function of his status as an imitator and devotee of both.[19] The opening of the poem plays on the semantic range of the word *monumentum* as referring both to literary and to physical structures.[20] At first, one might expect the *monumenta* of the great Maro (*haec magni celebrat monumenta Maronis*) celebrated by Silius to be his literary oeuvre,

---

[18]  This book is dated to the *Saturnalia* of 96 CE by Kay (1985), 1; see 11.4 on the fourth consulship of Nerva, which began in 97 CE. Text and translation of the epigrams are taken from Shackleton Bailey's Loeb edition.

[19]  For Silius as subsuming the qualities of both Cicero and Virgil, see Martial, 4.14; 7.63.5–6 (*sacra cothurnati non attigit ante Maronis / impleuit magni quam Ciceronis opus*); and 9.86. For the pairing of Cicero and Virgil in the *Punica*, see 8.404–11 (Cicero) and 592–4 (Virgil), with Ripoll (2000) and Vessey (1974).

[20]  See Kraus (1994).

like the *monumentum* 'more permanent than bronze' which Horace declares himself to have erected at the end of the third book of his *Odes* (3.30.1).[21] It is only when we get to the pentameter with the word *iugera* ('acres') prominently fronted that the reader might be expected to visualize the *monumentum* not as text but as physical site. The deictic *haec* does nothing to resolve the tension: is Martial's poem inscribed on an edition of Virgil's works or on his tomb?[22]

A similar tension between the tomb as a physical monument and the tomb as a meaningful figure for the reader's attempt to cultivate and keep alive the memory of the text is staged in Pliny the Younger's biography of Silius.[23] Here Pliny tells us that in his retirement in Naples, Silius Italicus surrounded himself with books, statues, and paintings, and also acquired and venerated the tomb of Virgil.[24]

multum ubique librorum, multum statuarum, multum imaginum, quas non habebat modo, verum etiam venerabatur, Vergili ante omnes, cuius natalem religiosius quam suum celebrabat, Neapoli maxime, ubi monimentum eius adire ut templum solebat.

He had everywhere many books, many statues, many paintings which he did not just possess but even venerated, above all that of Virgil, whose birthday he celebrated more strictly than his own, especially at Naples where he used to frequent his tomb as a temple.

(Pliny, *Epistles* 3.7.8)

Whereas, in Martial, Silius is praised as a peer to Virgil, in Pliny, the care invested in the upkeep of the physical structure is implicitly linked to Silius' propensity for polished writing: *scribebat carmina maiore cura quam ingenio*, 'he wrote poems with more polish than inspiration' (*Epistles* 3.7.5).[25] In this reading, the physical monument becomes a cypher for the material aspects of poetry, which are in opposition to its enduring intangible values. The zeal with which Silius

---

[21] Indeed, the monument is the vehicle through which one usually celebrates achievements rather than it being itself celebrated: see e.g. Livy, 7.21.1 and Cicero, *Rep.* 2.63.

[22] Cf. the use of the deictic in epigrams about books in the *Apophoreta*: e.g. 14.187; 191; 192; and *passim*.

[23] Since Martial Book 11 was published in December of 96 CE (see above, n. 18), it is possible that Pliny is familiar with Martial's poems. Though the dates of publication of the individual books are a matter of dispute, the general consensus is that Books 1–9 were published between the time of his consulship in 100 CE and his departure to Bythinia in 110 CE: Marchesi (2008), 12 n. 1; Sherwin-White (1969), xviii.

[24] For the discourse of art ownership in Pliny, see Myers (2005).

[25] See Hulls (2011).

attends to Virgil's material remains is a mark of his obsessive reliance on the model—in other words of his epigonality.

Silius' obsession with the past, however, is itself modelled on that of two Virgilian characters. For the presentation of the tomb as a temple is constructed in Martial and Pliny through a creative reworking of two Virgilian grave scenes in which a female character comes to a tomb to worship the deceased. Thus in Book 3, we find Andromache worshipping Hector at a cenotaph:

> . . . Andromache manisque vocabat
> Hectoreum ad tumulum, viridi quem caespite inanem
> et geminas, causam lacrimis, sacraverat aras.

. . . Andromache was calling upon the shades at the grave of Hector, which she had consecrated empty with green turf together with twin altars, a cause for tears.

*(Aeneid* 3.303–5)

By far the most important model, however, is the shrine Dido built for her deceased husband:

> praeterea fuit in tectis de marmore templum
> coniugis antiqui, miro quod honore colebat,
> velleribus niveis et festa fronde revinctum.

Besides there was inside the house a temple made of marble to her former spouse which she revered with exceeding honour, all surrounded with white fleeces and festive turf.

*(Aeneid* 4.457–8)

Pliny's description of Silius attending Virgil's tomb (*monumentum*) as a temple (*ut templum*) recuperates Dido's extraordinary and obsessive worship of her dead husband.[26] In Virgil, the tomb, too, is described as a *templum* and is adorned with white fleeces and festive turf, which Servius interprets as a sign of the deification of the dead Sychaeus.[27]

Silius' worship at the tomb of Virgil should be approached not only as a reading of Silius' Virgilian pedigree but also as a form of engagement with Silius' own reworking of these tomb scenes at the

---

[26] Cult of the dead was, of course, common in Rome but centred on specific occasions, e.g. the deceased's birthday, the *Parentalia* in February, and the *Lemuria* in May: Toynbee (1971), 61–4; Dolansky (2011); de Visscher (1963), 43–63.

[27] See Servius ad *Aen.* 4.459 (*FESTA FRONDE: divina, tamquam numen coleret*). For *vittae* and *frons* as adornments for temples, see Propertius 4.9.29–30 and Tacitus, *Hist.* 4.53.

beginning of the *Punica*. As scholars have pointed out, the immediate dramatic engine and *casus belli* is the oath sworn by Hannibal at the start of the poem; yet by making Hannibal swear allegiance to Dido herself (*Punica* 1.118–19: *hanc mentem iuro nostri per numina Martis, / per manes, regina, tuos*) rather than to the traditional gods (cf. Livy 35.19.6; Nepos, *Hannibal* 2.3; Polybius 3.11.5), Silius invites us to read Hannibal's oath as a figure for his poetic and intertextual allegiance to Virgil.[28] Silius introduces the oath with an elaborate ekphrasis which describes the temple of Dido where Hamilcar has summoned Hannibal:

> urbe fuit media sacrum genetricis Elissae
> manibus et patria Tyriis formidine cultum,
> quod taxi circum et piceae squalentibus umbris
> abdiderant caelique arcebant lumine, templum.
> hoc sese, ut perhibent, curis mortalibus olim
> exuerat regina loco.

There was a temple in the middle of the city sacred to the shades of the ancestress Elissa and tended to with native awe by the Carthaginians, which yew trees all around and pitch pines had hidden untilled with shade and which kept away the light of the sky. It was here in this place, they say, that the queen had laid aside her mortal cares.

*(Punica* 1.81–6)

The phrase *urbe fuit media* (84) recalls Virgil's description of the city of Carthage at *Aeneid* 1.12 (*urbs antiqua fuit*) and of Juno's temple in Carthage at *Aeneid* 1.441 (*lucus in urbe fuit media, laetissimus umbra*).[29] In Silius, the word *templum*, emphatically delayed to the very end of the line and of the passage, connects the reader to the marble *templum* of Sychaeus at *Aeneid* 4.457.[30] In Silius' appropriation, the tomb scene in *Aeneid* 4 becomes magnified in its religious significance—Dido and her husband being joined by a hundred altars to the gods of light and Erebus—and interpreted as the site of the ancestor worship ultimately responsible for the Punic wars. Thus Silius' worshipping of Virgil's tomb as a temple can be

---

[28] Hardie (1993), 64–5; on the oath in general, see Ganiban (2010), 80–3; Feeney (1982), 71.
[29] Note the contrast between *laetissimus umbra* at *Aen.* 1.441 and *squalentibus umbris* at *Pun.* 1.83.
[30] Feeney (1982), 66–7 comments on the anomaly of this delay in light of the standard practice of fronting the head noun in ekphrasis.

seen to leverage Virgil's depiction of Sychaeus' tomb as mediated through Silius' own appropriation of the scene at the start of the *Punica*.

The anecdotes in Martial and Pliny surrounding the rediscovery of the Virgilian tomb on the part of Silius Italicus form a striking contrast with other narratives of poets' funerary monuments which either construct the work as a superior substitute for the lost monument (Cicero, *Pro Archia* 22) or present the patron's monument as subsuming or even incorporating the poet's (such as the statue of Ennius in the tomb of the Scipiones, as discussed by Martelli in this volume, or Horace's burial next to Maecenas' tomb: *iuxta Maecenatis tumulum*).[31] By contrast, this story surrounding the tomb of Virgil must be read in the context of other stories involving ancient tourism around funeral monuments, including rediscovery of neglected ones.[32] Troy was an important site for tomb tourism notably around the shrines of Achilles at Sigeum and Ajax at Rhoeteum.[33] Julius Caesar visits them both in Lucan (*Bellum civile* 9.961–5). Alexander before him ran a race past Achilles' tomb when he visited Troy (Plutarch, *Life of Alexander* 15.8): according to Arrian, Alexander's companion visited Patroclus' tomb (*Anabasis* 1.12.1). In turn, Alexander's tomb located in Alexandria (not in Babylon where he died) is visited by Augustus after his victory at Actium in 31 BCE (Suetonius, *Life of Augustus* 18; Cassius Dio 51.16.5) and by Caesar before him (Lucan, *Bellum civile* 10.14–19).[34] The visit to the tomb as represented in these narratives is a meaningful figure for the tourist's attempt to cultivate and keep alive the memory of the buried hero.[35]

It is above all useful to compare the narrative of Silius' rediscovery of the neglected site of Virgil's tomb to other narratives of rediscovered sepulchral sites.[36] Strabo tells us that Augustus returned Ajax' statue to his tomb at Rhoeteum after it had been taken by Antony to Alexandria

---

[31]  Suetonius, *Life of Horace* 40.69 Reifferscheid.

[32]  For modern tourism, especially to the tomb of Virgil, see Chapter 14 in this collection.

[33]  Pliny, *HN* 5.124–2; Paus. 1.35.3–5; and see further Minchin (2012).

[34]  On Alexander's tomb, see Erskine (2002); Malamud (1995), 12–14.

[35]  For the ways in which Alexander cultivated an image of himself as a second Achilles, see Stewart (1993), 78–86.

[36]  There is also a useful contrast with mythical figures whose tombs are never found, as is the case for Moses' tomb at Deuteronomy 34.5–6. Here the absence of the tomb highlights the immortality of the deceased's work, which transcends the confines of the physical body.

as a gift to Cleopatra.[37] Hadrian later visited the tomb of Ajax and had
it restored.[38] Especially important to our understanding of the Flavian
anecdotes is Cicero's account of his discovery of Archimedes' tomb in
the fifth book of the *Tusculan Disputations*. Cicero here focuses on his
search for the lost monument when he was quaestor in Sicily, omitting
altogether any mention of the controversial death of Archimedes
during the capture of Syracuse by the Roman general Marcellus in
211 BCE:[39]

> ex eadem urbe humilem homunculum a pulvere et radio excitabo, qui
> multis annis post fuit, Archimedem. Cuius ego quaestor ignoratum ab
> Syracusanis, cum esse omnino negarent, saeptum undique et vestitum
> vepribus et dumetis indagavi sepulcrum. tenebam enim quosdam senar-
> iolos, quos in eius monumento esse inscriptos acceperam, qui declar-
> abant in summo sepulcro sphaeram esse positam cum cylindro.
>
> [65] ego autem cum omnia conlustrarem oculis—est enim ad portas
> Agragantinas magna frequentia sepulcrorum—, animum adverti colu-
> mellam non multum e dumis eminentem, in qua inerat sphaerae figura
> et cylindri. atque ego statim Syracusanis—erant autem principes
> mecum—dixi me illud ipsum arbitrari esse, quod quaererem. Inmissi
> cum falcibus multi purgarunt et aperuerunt locum.
>
> [66] quo cum patefactus esset aditus, ad adversam basim accessimus.
> apparebat epigramma exesis posterioribus partibus versiculorum dimi-
> diatum fere. ita nobilissima Graeciae civitas, quondam vero etiam
> doctissima, sui civis unius acutissimi monumentum ignorasset, nisi ab
> homine Arpinate didicisset.

> But from Dionysius's own city of Syracuse I will summon up from the
> dust—where his measuring rod once traced its lines—an obscure little man
> who lived many years later, Archimedes. When I was quaestor in Sicily
> I managed to track down his grave. The Syracusans knew nothing about it,
> and indeed denied that any such thing existed. But there it was, completely
> surrounded and hidden by bushes of brambles and thorns. I remembered
> having heard of some simple lines of verse which had been inscribed on his
> tomb, referring to a sphere and cylinder modelled in stone on top of the
> grave. And so I took a good look round all the numerous tombs that stand
> beside the Agrigentine Gate. Finally I noted a little column just visible above
> the scrub: it was surmounted by a sphere and a cylinder. I immediately said
> to the Syracusans, some of whose leading citizens were with me at the time,

[37] Strabo 13.1.30 and Bleisch (1999), 194–7.   [38] Philostr. *Her.* 8.1–2.
[39] On which, see *Verr.* 2.4.131; Livy 25.31.10; Plut. *Marc.* 19; Val. Max. 8.7.ext.7.

that I believed this was the very object I had been looking for. Men were sent in with sickles to clear the site, and when a path to the monument had been opened we walked right up to it. And the verses were still visible, though approximately the second half of each line had been worn away. So one of the most famous cities in the Greek world, and in former days a great centre of learning as well, would have remained in total ignorance of the tomb of the most brilliant citizen it had ever produced, had a man from Arpinum not come and pointed it out!

(Cicero, *Tusculan Disputations* 5.64–6, trans. Grant (1971))

As Mary Jaeger has argued, the rediscovery of the monument, all but forgotten by the Syracusans, is meant to highlight Cicero's ability to lead the Greek life of inquiry and knowledge.[40] Tellingly, the theoretical skills of Archimedes, the famous Greek inventor, are transferred to Cicero himself, as the verbs used to describe his search for the monument—*indagavi*; *conlustrarem oculis*; *adverti*—are all drawn from the semantic sphere of scientific inquiry. To quote Jaeger, 'the rediscovery of the monument emerges as a symbolic point of intersection for the Greek and the Roman'.[41]

In Martial and Pliny, the act of rediscovering the neglected monument similarly highlights a connection between the dead and the living figure who restores the tomb, casting Silius as Virgil's material and intellectual heir (*heredem*, Martial 11.48.3). What is more, the death of Archimedes also features prominently in Silius Italicus' narrative of the fall of Syracuse in *Punica* 14.[42] Silius makes a smooth transition from Marcellus' victory to a pathetic apostrophe to Archimedes, who was killed while drawing shapes in the sand, unperturbed by the fall of the city:

> tu quoque ductoris lacrimas, memorande, tulisti,
> defensor patriae, meditantem in puluere formas
> nec turbatum animi tanta feriente ruina.
> ast relicum uulgus resoluta in gaudia mente
> certarunt uicti uictoribus. aemulus ipse
> ingenii superum seruando condidit urbem.
> ergo extat saeclis stabitque insigne tropaeum
> et dabit antiquos ductorum noscere mores.

You too, memorable one, defender of the fatherland, won the tears of the general; such great ruin struck you while you were drawing shapes in the sand and not at all troubled at heart. But the rest of the people gave themselves to joy, the vanquished competing with the conquerors. He

---

[40] Jaeger (2002).      [41] Jaeger (2002), 61.      [42] On which, see Scaffai (2004).

himself [i.e. Marcellus] rivalling the gods in temper, founded the city by preserving it. Therefore, it survives and it will remain standing for future generations as an eminent trophy and it will enable us to know about the character of our generals in old times.

(*Punica* 14.676–83)

Silius echoes Livy's description of the last moment of Archimedes' life (with *meditantem in puluere formas*; cf. Livy 25.31 *intentum formis quas in puluere descripserat*).[43] Yet Silius' main model in this passage is Cicero's description of Marcellus in the second Verrine oration, to which he owes the paradoxical hyperbole describing Marcellus in line 681 as the one who 'founded the city by preserving it' (*seruando condidit urbem*).[44]

But what about Archimedes' tomb? It is noteworthy that among our extant sources, Cicero is the only one who mentions it explicitly.[45] Although Silius does not actually name the tomb, he alludes indirectly to it and thus to the passage in the *Tusculan Disputations*. First, he does so by way of a Virgilian intertext, employing the epitaphic address to the dead *tu quoque* (676) which in the *Aeneid* marks the description of Caieta's tomb (*Aeneid* 7.1: *tu quoque litoribus nostris, Aeneia nutrix / aeternam moriens famam, Caieta, dedisti*). Furthermore, the notion of a physical structure is recalled in 682, where we are told that a 'trophy' (*tropaeum*) 'survives and will remain standing for future generations'. The indefinite nature of the subject of these two verbs—is the trophy the city or Marcellus' fine actions?—once again collapses physical and literary monument. The trophy is at once an object and the literary work which preserves its memory. Martin Dinter has argued that Silius' construction of Archimedes' 'literary' tomb is a response to Cicero's restoration of Archimedes' physical tomb.[46] I would add that, with this sophisticated reworking of the scene, Silius supplies the epitaph for Archimedes which is mentioned by Cicero in the *Tusculan Disputations* but not cited, and which, being half lost in Cicero, called for completion.[47] Moreover, in Silius, there is a noticeably unresolved tension between memory as a human achievement and memory as a physical structure. Though the verses present themselves stylistically

---

[43] Plutarch offers three versions of the story of the death of Archimedes, all different: *Marc.* 19.4–6.

[44] Scaffai (2004), 508; Burck (1984), 59–60; and see *Verr.* 4.115.

[45] Though Livy has a generic reference to 'care devoted to the grave' (25.31.10).

[46] Dinter (2013), 280.     [47] *Tusc.* 5.66.2, quoted above.

as inscribed words, the tomb itself is elusive. Instead, the epistemic function of the monument—here embodied by its ability to impart knowledge of the characters of the leaders of old (*dabit antiquos ductorum noscere mores*, 683)—is displaced from physical to literary structures, the historiographical work of Livy (cf. *memorande*, 676) and Cicero.

It is hard to say whether or not Martial had the story of the restoration of Archimedes' tomb in Cicero, and Silius' prequel to it, in mind in *Epigrams* 11.48 when pairing Cicero's estate and Virgil's tomb as the object of Silius' worship and upkeep. What seems striking, however, is the way in which the restored monument of the poet (Virgil) or the scientist (Archimedes) acts as a conduit not just for materializing the restorer's claim to subsume the virtues of the deceased, but also for staging the competing claims of different media and their memorializing powers. Our last case study, Statius *Silvae* 4.4, possibly our earliest reference to the tomb of Virgil, highlights once again the potential for the sepulchral site to be read as a metonymy for the work through creative engagement with Virgil's representation of his Neapolitan retreat and the generative slippage between material and literary monumentality that we have observed in the other sources.[48] Here, however, the privileged point of view is that of the tomb as a static monumental presence on a travelled road site. The tomb is viewed as a fixed and permanent structure within a network of people, goods, and objects in transit. As a site of pilgrimage and in its location away from Rome, the tomb of Virgil in Statius can be seen to anticipate the intersection of mobility and stasis in *VSD*'s portrayal of the monument.

Statius declines to lead a life of *negotium* in Rome and asserts that he is instead singing by the tomb of Virgil:

> en egomet somnum et geniale secutus
> litus ubi Ausonio se condidit hospita portu
> Parthenope, tenues ignavo pollice chordas
> pulso Maroneique sedens in margine templi
> sumo animum et magni tumulis adcanto magistri.

Here I am, pursuing sleep and the delightful shore where Parthenope as a guest hid herself in the Ausonian harbour; with my idle thumb I pluck the

---

[48] *Silvae* 4.1 is dedicated to Domitian on his consulship of 95 CE. The book, therefore, is almost contemporary with Martial Book 11: Coleman (1988), xx–xxii.

slender strings and, sitting at the edges of Maro's shrine, I take up my courage and sing by the tomb of the great master.

*(Silvae* 4.4.51–5)

Not only do we find here a similar reference to the tomb as a *templum*, which we found activated by Virgil's depiction of the tomb of Sychaeus (*Aeneid* 4.457); Statius also uses the physical monument in similar ways to Pliny, as a metonymy for the poet's work. Thus the poet's location on the margin of the *templum* (54) equivocates between literary and physical monument: the margin stands both for the edge of the page and the threshold of a building.[49] Statius' positioning beside, but not within, the tomb is a testimony to his complex relationship to his model. As has been well recognized, his very Neapolitan retreat is constructed in strikingly Virgilian terms, recalling the poet's formulation at the end of *Georgics* 4.[50] Moreover, *secutus* (51) reminds us of Statius' metaphor at the end of the *Thebaid*, where he instructs his epic to 'follow' in the footsteps of the *Aeneid* from a distance and in adoration (12.817).

Just as the tomb of Virgil in *VSD* is situated on the road to Puteoli, Statius' poem—supposedly written beside the very same monument—is also on a journey, but that journey takes a different road. The previous poem, 4.3, celebrated the emperor's newly inaugurated Via Domitiana connecting Puteoli with Sinuessa, which significantly shortened the journey between Naples and Rome by eliminating an inland detour to Capua. Poem 4.4 opens with an invitation to the poem to 'run over the Euboean plains without delay . . . starting your journey here, where the venerable Appian Way bulges sideways . . .'. For Statius, the tomb of Virgil is a site for literary *otium*—specifically the composition of the *Achilleid* (94–6)—but it is enabled by the new imperially sponsored public artery which is presented as the continuation of the old Via Appia. This newly built Via Domitiana facilitates the mobility necessary to bring the poet's request for patronage back to Rome. Here we are reminded of the pivotal connection between burial, private aristocratic display, and public roads. In a culture where, starting from the late fourth century BCE, sepulchral monuments of aristocratic

---

[49] Hulls (2011), 165.

[50] Cf. *G.* 4.564: *Parthenope studiis florentem ignobilis oti*, echoed by *Parthenope* and *ignavo pollice* in line 53, with Coleman (1988), 147–8 ad loc.; see further *Silvae* 4.4.78–9: *haec ego Chalcidicis ad te, Marcelle, sonabam,* / *litoribus*, with *G.* 4.559: *haec super arvorum cultu pecorumque canebam.*

families lined public thoroughfares (like the tomb of the Scipiones),[51] tombs played a crucial element in the construction of the *suburbium*— the urban periphery—impressing passers-by travelling to and from the city of Rome.[52] By positioning himself as singing from the tomb of Virgil, Statius not only claims his position as the poet's heir but also metaphorically constructs the tomb as a stop on the imperially sponsored journey from Campania to the city, which the poem itself is retracing.

As reimagined by these Flavian authors, the tomb of Virgil is a vehicle for exploring a series of pressing questions about the role of memory, the endurance of song, and what it means to write epic after Virgil. The tomb—as a material object in need of upkeep, as a site neglected and rediscovered, and as an object of worship—channels the poets' desire both to disrupt the Virgilian legacy and to continue it.

---

[51] See Martelli, Chapter 3 of this volume.    [52] See Purcell (1987).

# 14

## Virgil's Tomb in Scholarly and Popular Culture

### Harald Hendrix

In recent years, around Virgil's tomb at Piedigrotta near Naples, a particular cult has developed testifying to the monument's prolonged ability to appeal to audiences that cross over from the learned to the popular. As reported in one of Italy's most reputed national newspapers, *La Repubblica*, in the inner part of the *tumulo*, where a tripod lamp has been placed as part of the carefully created sepulchral scenery of the place, modern visitors come across notes written by schoolboys and girls asking Virgil for help in preparing for their final exams in Latin.[1] These 'students on a pilgrimage to the tombs of the great poets', as the title of the report has it, perform what we are now used to defining as profane pilgrimages, or perhaps more generally as heritage tourism.

Of course, the behaviour of these students may be part and parcel of what clearly are organized school trips to some of the highlights of antique culture studied in a classroom situation. But what is striking is the emotional tone of directness that we may gather from such notes. The report, for example, starts with some of the notes left by a group of youngsters coming from a renowned secondary school in Utrecht, who, on their traditional Rome excursion, include a visit to Naples. One of these students writes—in English, not in Dutch, Latin, or Italian: 'Dear Virgil, thank you for your most inspiring words. Now please help us to pass the final exam in Latin with the highest votes.' There are also notes of a more private nature, asking the poet's intervention in matters relating to health and love.

---

[1] Niola (2013).

What we witness here, in a setting that is in many ways comparable to other contemporary manifestations of fan culture, is the desire to connect spiritually—one might even say magically—to a celebrity considered (in earnest or in jest) able to offer some kind of useful advice, help, or inspiration.[2] To establish such contact, though, and thus to facilitate that kind of mediation, a material location is clearly a necessary prerequisite. It is the presence of the Virgil tomb itself that not only gives a focus to the school trip's programme, but also adds to the intensity of the contact between the poet's work and heritage, on the one hand, and its audience, on the other. The incorporeal nature of the legacy of a man of letters like Virgil here shifts into a dimension of materiality, a mechanism which reveals some of the most important limits of the immaterial art of language, but also some of its strongest potential. It shows that at least some parts of literature's audiences feel the need to add a material dimension to what is not otherwise a corporeal experience. But it also illustrates the capacity of the immaterial word to evoke realities so convincingly that this produces a desire to materialize them.

In this phenomenon of materializing literary memories, the case of the tomb of Virgil is one of the most illuminating, as Trapp for one demonstrated in a seminal study of 1984.[3] Taking his study as a rich point of departure, this chapter identifies key contexts responsible for the cult of the tomb of Virgil in Naples and beyond, and thereby assesses this cult also from a comparative perspective.

## A CLUSTER OF SEPULCHRAL MONUMENTS

Making comparisons, or rather connections, is a productive strategy when investigating the significance of Virgil's tomb, as illustrated, for example, in the newspaper report in *La Repubblica* just discussed. The students visited not only the tomb of Virgil, but the nearby Leopardi grave as well: a 'pilgrimage to the tombs of the great poets: lining up for Virgil and Leopardi'.[4] The closeness of the two monuments is by

---

[2] On present and past fan cultures, see Duffett (2013); Hellekson and Busse (2014); Inglis (2010); Jenkins (1992); Krieken (2011); Marshall (1997) and (2006); and Mole (2009).
[3] Trapp (1984); cf. also his parallel work on the tombs of Ovid and Petrarch, Trapp (1973) and Trapp (2006), with Chapter 5 by Goldschmidt, Chapter 13 by Peirano Garrison, and Chapter 15 by Smiles in this volume.
[4] Niola (2013).

no means accidental and reveals some of the key mechanisms governing the cult of the tomb of Virgil since the fourteenth century. This is a consciously created phenomenon, a constructed cult that sets the example for many others, attracting parallel but connected memorial cultures. One more recent and quite visible addition to this phenomenon of duplication or accumulation of memorial cults is the grave of Giacomo Leopardi.[5] This tomb was added as recently as 1939, over a century after the Romantic poet's death in 1837, when his original grave in the Fuorigrotta church of San Vitale, itself not far from Virgil's tomb, was demolished. Its relocation to the area immediately next to the grave of Virgil was part of the design of a landscape park dedicated to Virgilian memories, the Parco Virgiliano, one of the initiatives undertaken to celebrate the ancient poet's bimillennium in 1930.

Leopardi's grave in turn followed a pattern which had been established centuries before, by an illustrious predecessor. The sepulchral monument commemorating the Neapolitan court poet Iacopo Sannazaro, in the nearby church of Santa Maria del Parto, was built by Sannazaro himself as part of his suburban residence, and was deliberately situated near Virgil's tomb.[6] In fact, it was this link to Virgilian heritage that motivated Sannazaro to project the building of a private residence in combination with his tomb, as I argue in greater detail below. Such incrustations arising around the original nucleus of Virgil's tomb may be found all through its long history. One might think of a late nineteenth-century booklet called *Le ricreazioni letterarie sui colli di Paussillipo e Mergellina, ossia una visita alle tombe di Virgilio di Sannazaro e di Leopardi. Libro di lettura amena*, written by a certain Niccola Guida Da Morano, that documents how, by 1870, visiting the tombs of Virgil, Sannazaro, and Leopardi had become an integral part of Neapolitan leisure culture.[7] But one might just as well recall the curious tomb of a Sannazaro fan, Fabrizio Manlio, a young man from Barletta whose only passion was to read near the spot where his idol was buried, as the epitaph on his 1566 grave in Sannazaro's Santa Maria del Parto recalls.[8]

---

[5] Little scholarship is available on Leopardi's tomb, though there is some information in the Guide published by the Touring Club Italiano (2005), 298–99, as well as in Marcon (2012).

[6] Deramaix and Laschke (1992); Carrella (2000); Laschke (2002); Addesso (2005); and Divenuto (2009).

[7] Da Morano (1871).

[8] FABRITIO MANLIO NOBILI BAROLITANO / MAGNAE SPEI IUVENI / CAMILLUS PATER MUNUS LACRIMABILE // HIC ADEO MERGILLINAM

What we see here is the tendency of memorial cults to attract more cults, to expand within their own domain by multiplication, but also by moving between what we might call high and low culture, or, to be more precise, between the culture of scholarship and the culture of leisure, both governed by the pleasure of reading and reciting. And at the very origin of this dual mechanism is the memory of Virgil as projected on his Piedigrotta tomb, a memory which is both authoritative and flexible, since it relates, on the one hand, to a more or less precise knowledge of the poet's work and biography, but, on the other, easily slides into a more comprehensive dimension of nostalgia for a golden age situated in a long-gone but glorious past.


## INVENTING THE TOMB OF VIRGIL

It is useful to keep in mind the intersection of knowledge and pleasure, of scholarly work and free-time distractions, when tracking the origin of the cult of Virgil's grave. This then needs to be combined with a third element which had an all-pervasive power in the early modern context in which this cult arose: the aspiration to glory, be it on a personal, local, or political level.[9] It is this combination of humanistic erudition, rising leisure culture, and aspirations of glory rooted in identity constructions that constitutes the backdrop against which a cult like Virgil's develops in the early modern period. This goes for the two manifestations of that cult I would like to discuss in more detail in what follows: first, the Neapolitan humanistic or rather proto-humanistic context in which the cult was invented and constructed, and secondly its huge international success as documented in the imposing phenomenon of the Grand Tour, and, to be more precise, in its sixteenth-century early variant, the *peregrinatio academica*.[10]

---

ADAMAVIT / UT AD EAM INFIRMUS FERRI / IN EA MORI IN EA SEPELIRI VOLVERIT / A. M.D.L.XVI. OBIIT A. M.D.LXI.

[9] On the humanist cult of glory, see Braudy (1986); Clark (2006); Hardie (2012); Jardine (1995); and Potts (2009).

[10] On the *peregrinatio academica*, see Babel and Paravicini (2005); Berghoff et al. (2002); Berns (1988); Boyer (2005); Leibetseder (2004); Ridder-Symoens (1983); Rubiés (1996); Stagl (1983) and (1995); Stannek (2001); and Tervoort (2005).

The earliest development of the cult may be attributed to the Neapolitan court circles that Boccaccio frequented during his stay in Naples in the 1340s.[11] A key figure here is Giovanni Barilli, King Robert of Anjou's assistant, who apparently had done some research on the various antique references to a Neapolitan tomb of Virgil's and had tried to locate this building near the Piedigrotta tunnel mentioned in these references, since it had long been associated with the allegedly magical powers of Virgil. Barilli not only passed this knowledge on to Boccaccio, but also to Petrarch, while making arrangements for his 1341 coronation as poet laureate. During these preparations, Barilli took Petrarch on a tour of what was clearly already something of a standard trip in contemporary Neapolitan court culture. They saw several places associated with Virgilian memories: not only the so-called tomb, but also the nearby tunnel of Piedigrotta, as well as some of the locations near Baia mentioned in Virgil's works. Petrarch has given an account of these trips in a series of letters written only several years later, in the 1350s, which quickly became the foundation for the myth of Virgil in the Neapolitan landscape, within and beyond the local courtly community. Petrarch only mentions the locations related to Virgil's work in these letters, but we may be sure that he was shown the tomb as well, since he still vividly recalls it in a detailed report of the visit included in his *Itinerarium Syriacum,* written fifteen years later, in 1357.[12]

Petrarch was driven by his admiration for the Latin poet, whom he tried to imitate while forging a literary and intellectual profile of his own, particularly as he prepared for his 1341 coronation as poet laureate. Here we have a clear case of identity construction: indeed, we might conclude that, though not uncritical, Petrarch's attitude towards the ancient resonances of these Neapolitan *lieux de mémoire* combined admiration based on the authority of classical texts with a more critical stance linked to his personal, 'on the spot' explorations. He intimates that he could hardly suppress his emotions while viewing the sites celebrated by his classical forebear, and yet simultaneously displayed some scepticism and even sarcasm with regard to the alleged magical powers of the poet.

When it came to identifying the Latin poet's grave, Petrarch's eagerness to forge a personal connection with his admired predecessor

---

[11] Cf. Trapp (1984).     [12] Cachey (2002), 27, 49, n. 110, f. 10r.1.

seemed to overcome his probing disposition. His reservations about
the rather imprecise reports on this site, preserved in earlier texts
whose documentary accuracy he considered questionable, were bal-
anced by his own explorations during his 1343 trip and supplemented
by the testimonies of some local informants he consulted. This
enabled him to identify a Roman columbarium near the Piedigrotta
entrance to the Posillipo tunnel as Virgil's tomb, an identification
which has maintained its authority ever since, despite the fact that
its legendary status has long been demonstrated. 'Virgil's tomb' is in
fact a projection of literary memories and associations, inscribed
into physical remains of antiquity that were otherwise difficult to
document, and which therefore had little meaning independent
of its literary reception. This construction clearly originates in a
local context—the circle around Barilli—but develops only when it
becomes functional in communicating to outsiders a message config-
ured around ideas of identity.

   This invention of Virgil's tomb not only signals the dominance of a
literary perspective in the revival of Neapolitan antique heritage, but
indicates a desire to connect this heritage to contemporary needs and
ambitions. Petrarch considered Virgil his alter ego, and wanted to feel
close to him in a material as well as a literary sense: this involved
visiting the locations where Virgil's presence was most intensely felt,
whether this meant his body (in the legendary tomb), or the places
mentioned in his literary works (in the Baia locations described in the
*Aeneid*). Such material closeness to an ancient model had more than a
memorial function: it served to provide new literary inspiration,
urging the 'receiving' poet to compete with, and surpass, his model.
In a characteristically humanistic manner, the inspiring memory of
Virgil's literary accomplishments was projected onto a specific loca-
tion framed as being closely linked to the poet's biography and
enabling later generations to pay their respect. This act of what one
might call a memorial performance closely followed the example of
antique forebears, as Petrarch himself well knew. In his acceptance
speech for his coronation as poet laureate only two years earlier, in
1341, he took inspiration from Cicero's *De finibus* 5.1.2:[13]

---

[13] Wilkins (1955), 305 wrongly identifies the relevant passage as Cicero, *De legibus*,
2.2. The error has been reproduced in later Petrarchan scholarship.

Naturane nobis hoc, inquit, datum dicam an errore quodam, ut, cum ea loca videamus, in quibus memoria dignos viros acceperimus multum esse versatos, magis moveamur, quam si quando eorum ipsorum aut facta audiamus aut scriptum aliquod legamus? velut ego nunc moveor. venit enim mihi Platonis in mentem, quem accepimus primum hic disputare solitum . . .

Whether by a natural instinct or by some sort of illusion I cannot say, but we are more moved when we see the places where, by accepted memory, the great men of old spent their time than when we hear of something they did or read one of their works. This is how moved I am now. For Plato comes to my mind, the first man who, we are told, made it a habit of holding discussions in this place . . .

Still, the most outspoken example of this ambition to connect and compete with antique models, particularly Virgil, is not Petrarch but Sannazaro, for it was he who established a firmly material link to his venerated forebear. When, in 1499, his generous patron king Federico offered him the means to build a villa, Sannazaro selected a location on the seashore near Posillipo—Mergellina—that not only commanded associations with mythological nymphs but also evoked a direct and very material connection with the prestigious Virgilian heritage materialized in the nearby tomb at the entrance to the Piedigrotta tunnel.[14] Sannazaro did not hide his desire to mould his poetic persona on Virgil's, erecting his own sepulchral monument in a chapel on this estate in the immediate vicinity of the ancient poet's legendary grave. This merging of the identities of the modern and the classical poet was later eloquently expressed in the epitaph dictated by Pietro Bembo after the poet's death in 1530:

Da sacro cineri flores. Hic ille Maroni
Sincerus, musa proximus ut tumulo.

Bring flowers to the holy ashes: here lies Sincerus [Sannazaro], close to Maro [Virgil] in his grave as in his art.

The epitaph became a source of inspiration for many later examples all over Europe, including that inscribed on Edmund Spenser's grave in Westminster Abbey.[15]

---

[14]  On Sannazaro's villa and tomb in relation to Virgil, cf. n. 6 above.
[15]  See Höschele's discussion at pp. 197–200.

## VIRGIL'S TOMB AND NEAPOLITAN
## URBAN IDENTITY

Such appropriation of ancient literary memories through epitaphs typifies the identity construction we can observe in Naples around 1500, and especially in the humanistic circles of the Accademia Pontaniana, to which Sannazaro belonged. In this context, such epitaphs, or more generally labels, easily shifted from the personal to the civic sphere, focused on the construction of a distinguished urban identity. As a result, the memory of Virgil as projected onto his Piedigrotta tomb assumed even more general overtones, becoming a comprehensive marker of the glory of antique Naples used as a potent element of city branding.[16] That kind of reading of the city is indeed paramount in what can be seen as its first modern chorographical description, Ioan Berardino Fuscano's *Le stanze del Fuscano sovra la bellezza di Napoli*, published in 1531.[17] This poetic text explicitly aimed at praising the city through a description of what it called 'the most pleasant district of Naples', echoing a well-worn phrase from Sannazaro's recent *Arcadia*. In his two books of stanzas, Fuscano offered a highly literary view of Naples, which was closely related to, and indeed grounded in, ideas elaborated by Sannazaro and his circle. The text describes a one-day itinerary of two friends, Philologo and Alpitio, whose names denote the allegorical nature of their enterprise from the very start. They cross the city from east to west, heading for what turns out to be the ultimate goal of their journey—the Posillipo hill, which as a result of Sannazaro's endeavours is considered 'the temple of the sacred Mergellina'. In Book 2, the friends participate in a festive ritual on this hill, which is promoted by a group of nymphs and attended by a large number of contemporary Neapolitan poets close to the Accademia Pontaniana. This solemn feast is intended to celebrate poetry in a location that epitomizes artistic creation, and Virgil's grave close to the Piedigrotta tunnel is, significantly, the only spot which the poem describes with any geographical precision, albeit in a highly allegorical vocabulary appropriate for evoking the metaphysical processes of inspiration and creation undergone there.[18]

---

[16] What follows elaborates on my essays, Hendrix (2013) and (2015).
[17] Fuscano (1531) and (2007).
[18] Fuscano (2007), 72 (Book II, 76–7): 'Eran le ninfe giunte a un picciol piano, / ch'a due a due venian con lenti passi, / dov'era un spatio, più ch'uom trae con mano, / d'una valletta fra duo poggi bassi. / Ivi un vestigio, come d'alcun fano / che mostr'antiquità, solingo stassi, / d'arbori cinto et sempre esposto al sole, / pien tutto di ligustri et

While designating this specific location as an iconic place of Neapolitan urban identity, Fuscano was clearly voicing a sentiment that was shared more widely by his near contemporaries. Such a sentiment is testified, for instance, in the oldest known cartographic representation of Naples which gives a factual rather than a symbolic survey of the geographical situation—an image of the volcanic Monte Nuovo engraved shortly after its eruption in September 1538 (Figure 14.1).[19]

This remarkable 'true picture', *vero disegnio,* shows a panoramic map of the Gulf of Naples, naturally focused on the Pozzuoli section where an explosion created this new mountain while destroying the small village of Tripergola. But it also shows, alongside the obvious geographical indications—Baia, Solfatara, Bagni, Lake Agnano—the iconic places that the men of letters in and around the Accademia Pontaniana had successfully constructed as *lieux de mémoire* of Neapolitan urban identity: Virgil's grave, the Piedigrotta tunnel ('La Grotta'), and Sannazaro's villa at the Mergellina seaside.

**Figure 14.1.** G.A., 'Il vero disegnio in sul propio luogho ritratto [ ... ]' (Naples, 1540).

© Bibliothèque Nationale de France, Paris.

di vïole. // In mezzo v'era un'alta pino annosa, / la qual sorgea per dentr'un sasso rotto, / entrar là dentro alcun già mai non osa, / si non è spirto assai ben colto et dotto.'

[19] For this map by an artist known only by his monogrammatic name G.A., see Pane and Valerio (1987), 34–6.

This labelling of Naples as a place where ancient and modern cultures met and mingled, as summarized in the Posillipo Parnassus dominated by Virgil and Sannazaro, would indeed prove a lasting success, well beyond the circles of the Accademia Pontaniana where it had originated. It can be found in virtually all city descriptions of Naples up until the end of the seventeenth century, where it often served as an introduction to the virtual tour of the city itself.[20] It also figures prominently in the visual representations accompanying such texts as Joris Hoefnagel's attractive and much-copied image of his entry into the city of Naples, together with his friend and employer, the cartographer Abraham Ortelius, for whose 1578 version of the *Theatrum orbis terrarum* the engraving was produced (Figure 14.2).[21]

**Figure 14.2.** Joris Hoefnagel, 'Neapolis et Vesuvii montis prospectus', in Georg Braun and Franz Hogenberg, *Civitates orbis terrarum* (Cologne, 1578).
© Bibliothèque Nationale de France, Paris.

[20] For these references to the connected Virgil–Sannazaro memorials in Mergellina–Posillipo, see Hendrix (2013).
[21] Based on his 1578 trip with Ortelius to Naples, Hoefnagel produced five images, all focused on the city's district. On their trip, see Gerritsen (2003). On Hoefnagel's views of Naples and their long-lasting success, see Pane and Valerio (1987), 62–3, 69–70.

**Figure 14.3.** Sannazaro's villa and chapel Santa Maria del Parto, detail from the map of Naples by Baratta, *Fidelissimae urbis Neapolitanae cum omnibus viis accurata et nova delineatio* (Naples, 1629).
© Bibliothèque Nationale de France, Paris.

On their two-year journey through Italy, the two friends from Antwerp began their visit to Naples at the western entrance of the Posillipo tunnel, going directly from here to the Virgil tomb on the other side of the tunnel, and then on to the Sannazaro villa and chapel, a route that would become conventional in almost all city guides produced for foreign visitors to the city (Figure 14.3).

## VIRGIL'S TOMB IN EARLY MODERN
## TRAVEL CULTURE

What is apparent in these two last examples, the 1540 map and the 1578 Hoefnagel engraving, is that Virgil's tomb together with some strictly linked locations of literary memories, placed at what was the entrance to the city for those coming from the north in the mid sixteenth century, became a strong marker not only of Neapolitan urban identity but also of the city's topography. This is particularly relevant to the experience of non-local visitors, notably foreigners coming from the north like Hoefnagel and Ortelius, which brings us to a final and crucial cultural context of the tomb's reception, the incorporation of the cult of Virgil's grave in early modern travel culture. At this stage, the memory of Virgil as projected onto his Piedigrotta tomb loses much of its specificity. It comes to represent the globally accepted glory of literary culture attributed to Naples, and serves as a potent marker of civic pride as well as a curiosity-provoking artefact in the urban texture that enables visitors to direct their city explorations.

This perception of the tomb corresponds to a distinct new phase in the history of the monument, a phase that has a clear starting point in the decision, taken in 1554 by the owners of the Piedigrotta columbarium: the monks of Santa Maria di Piedigrotta explicitly labelled the building according to its by now secular interpretation as Virgil's tomb, and attached to it inscriptions explaining its nature and significance: *Siste viator quaeso pauca legito hic Maro situs est* ('Stop, traveller, I beg you, and read these few words: here lies Virgil', not documented before 1606), and *Qui cineres? Tumuli haec vestigia conditur olim / ille hoc qui cecinit pascua rura duces. / Can. Reg. MDLIIII.* (John Raymond provided a translation in his travel journal of 1648: 'What dust lies here: This heap protects his Hearse / Who whilome warbled Fields, Farms, Fights in Verse').[22]

The timing of the explicit labelling of the Piedigrotta columbarium as Virgil's tomb is not accidental: it corresponds to the first wave of foreign visitors coming to Naples in search of this famous monument commemorating the ancient literary past. They left their mark in the graffiti still visible near the monument today, such as, for instance, the signature of the Polish traveller Stanislaus Cencovius carved in 1589 on the plaque installed twenty-five years earlier (Figure 14.4).[23]

Interestingly, what this signature also highlights is the fact that the visitors who contributed to the diffusion of the cult of Virgil's tomb beyond its local context originated, in this period, mainly from the German Empire, notably present-day Poland, the Low Countries, and southern Germany. This should not surprise us, if we take into account the fact that, in the decades after 1550, a substantial group

---

[22] Trapp (1984), 12–13. For Turner's note of the inscription in his later sketch of the site, see Smiles in this volume, p. 313.

[23] Recorded also in Maçzak (1998), 370, and 440 n. 10.

**Figure 14.4.** Commemorative plaque (dating 1544) near the alleged grave of Virgil, Naples, with graffiti by Stanislaus Cencovius (1589) and other visitors. Photograph: Harald Hendrix.

of northern humanists interested in education began to promote travel as the perfect strategy for finishing the intellectual formation of young men who were expected to take on civic responsibilities.[24] In the numerous treatises produced by this group, Naples and its surroundings hold a privileged position, as the title of one of the best known among these writings makes clear, Hieronymus Turler's 1574 *De peregrinatione et agro neapolitano*, which has as its focal point the exact location where Virgil's tomb and Sannazaro's sepulchral monument together make up the new Temple of the Muses which Fuscano had described in his *Stanze*. It is indeed not difficult to draw a line between this essay and the students who, today, leave messages for Virgil at his tomb.

What happens in the second half of the sixteenth century goes somewhat beyond the cult of antiquity typically found in educational contexts. Parallel to the rapid rise of early modern travel culture, we again see a shift from the ancient to the modern, and from scholarly to popular culture. This may be first gathered from an important testimony on the reception of Virgil's tomb in this period, also from Poland, or to be more precise from Silesia, the book on sepulchral architecture published in 1574 at Breslau, *Monumenta sepulchrorum cum epigraphis ingenio et doctrina excellentium virorum aliorumque tam prisci quam nostri seculi memorabilium hominum*.[25] This highly attractive book is the result of an unusually long educational tour of

---

[24] Cf. references in n. 10 above, and Felici (2009).
[25] Fendt (1574); later editions were published in Frankfurt in 1584 and 1589. On this enterprise, see Michalski (1977) and Kubíková (2010).

Europe undertaken, between 1545 and 1554, by the young Seifried Rybisch (1530–84). The son of a prominent Silesian patrician family, Rybisch was particularly interested in sepulchral monuments as possible models for the design of his family's monumental tomb in Wroclaw, and consequently made meticulous drawings of more than a hundred and fifty such monuments commemorating famous men. Some twenty years later, when the local Breslau artist Tobias Fendt (*c.*1525–76) agreed to engrave these drawings, Rybisch's material found its way to the printing press, soon becoming a much sought-after model book for those interested in the design of sepulchral architecture.

Significantly, the book makes no distinction between ancient and modern heritage, putting the Antenore shrine in Padua next to the Erasmus epitaph in Basel, reporting on the monuments to Livy, Cicero, Ovid, and Euripides alongside those to Dante, Ficino, and Ulrich von Hutten. The Virgil tomb is immediately followed by the Sannazaro monument. Because of its high documentary value, this book made significant impact not only on sepulchral architecture in Europe, but also on the cult of Virgil's tomb. The image presented by Riebisch and Fendt quickly became the iconic representation of the tomb, and would remain so during much of the seventeenth century. We find it, for example, in the most popular of the many city guides dedicated to Naples and its surroundings, Pompeo Sarnelli's *Guida de' forestieri curiosi di vedere e d'intendere le cose più notabili della Regal Città di Napoli e del suo amenissimo distretto*, first published in 1685 but frequently reprinted and adapted up until the mid eighteenth century, invariably depicting Virgil's tomb in its representation by Riebisch and Fendt and always in combination with the Sannazaro monument (Figure 14.5).[26]

This was no longer presented as the product of scholarly culture but, rather, as a pocket-sized booklet produced in great quantities for the ever more popular visits by foreigners eager to experience Naples.

Fendt's attractive book on sepulchral monuments also produced an additional interest in epitaphs, both ancient and modern, inspiring a rich tradition of publications specifically dedicated to collecting such inscriptions, from the *Monumentorum Italiae libri quae hoc nostro saeculo & a Christianis posita sunt* published in 1592 by Lorenz

---

[26] Sarnelli (1685), 334 depicts the Sannazaro monument, also in its Riebisch–Fendt rendition.

**Figure 14.5.** Virgil's grave at the Piedigrotta entrance of the Posillipo tunnel, in Pompeo Sarnelli, *Guida de' forestieri curiosi di vedere e d'intendere le cose più notabili della Regal Città di Napoli e del suo amenissimo distretto* (Naples, 1692), *contra* p. 340.
Private collection, Harald Hendrix.

Schrader to the 1602 monumental *Inscriptiones antiquae totius orbis romani* by Ianus Gruterus. Significantly, this passion for collecting epitaphs was not limited to scholarly circles alone. It also found its way into the growing culture of early modern travel. One might even

argue that the two habits were intrinsically linked: collecting epitaphs
became one of the main activities of early modern travellers. Collec-
tions of epitaphs contained instructions for travellers copied from
relevant treatises, as in the instructions for epitaph-hunting travellers
in Nathan Chytraeus' 1594 *Variorum in Europa itinerum Deliciae*.[27]
More generally, travel literature of that period often included exten-
sive sections dedicated to epigraphy.[28]

One of many examples of this development—and an important
one in the history of Virgil's cult in Naples—is the case of Scipione
Mazzella, which enables us to understand how, by the late sixteenth
century, the memory of Virgil had developed into an instrument of
reflection and entertainment that combined elements of scholarly and
popular culture. In 1591, this Neapolitan polymath constructed a
completely different type of city guide compared to those available,
clearly intending to develop a new commercial product for the rapidly
growing market of foreigners coming to his native town. In the part
dedicated to the visit of Pozzuoli, in the *Sito ed antichità della città di
Pozzuolo e del suo amenissimo distretto*, Mazzella inserts an elaborate
discussion of the tomb of Virgil.[29] He not only presents an erudite
account of all the discussions of the tomb from antiquity to his own
day, including a long list of epitaphs allegedly written for the monu-
ment; he also gives an account of what actually happened at that
*lieu de mémoire*: a gathering of friends and the writing of poetry—
specifically epitaphs—at the site, combining scholarly competition
and leisure. Moreover, he recalls how visitors had the habit of taking
with them, as a souvenir, a few leaves of the laurel tree growing from
the columbarium's top. In the late nineteenth century, this habit was
to take a particular turn when people emigrating from Naples to the
Americas used to take these leaves with them as a potent marker of
their Neapolitan identity.[30]

The culture of literary leisure Mazzella describes as being per-
formed at the tomb of Virgil closely relates to some of the other
phenomena discussed in this chapter, from the gatherings of local
poets on the Mergellina hill, transformed into a new Parnassus by the
memory of Virgil, to today's schoolchildren leaving their messages at

[27] Chytraeus (1594).        [28] Cf. Hendrix (2018).
[29] Mazzella (1591). On this author and his guides to Naples and its surrounding
district, see Hendrix (2014).
[30] On the nineteenth-century phenomenon, see Cocchia (1889).

the tomb of Virgil. Establishing a connection with the intellectual heritage of Virgil—in the place where, according to tradition, he might have been buried—enables later generations to relate person-ally to what they all consider to be an authoritative and inspiring example. The urge to mark this connection by leaving graffiti or notes, by taking away laurel leaves, and by reciting and producing poetry, indicates that the idea of 'Virgil' here has developed into a comprehensive but general and unspecific notion, able to unite scholars, students, and erudite travellers with locals looking for leis-ure, or taking part in the Neapolitan diaspora.

# 15

## Ruins and Reputations

### The Tomb of the Poet in Visual Art

*Sam Smiles*

This chapter approaches the 'tomb of Virgil' through the eyes of artists working in the later eighteenth and early nineteenth centuries, when the vogue for travel and the growth of a market for topographical and antiquarian images produced the circumstances that gave new life to representations of the tombs of the Greek and Roman poets. Building on Joseph Trapp's survey of changing attitudes to the tomb, as witnessed by textual and visual descriptions of its presumed location outside Naples,[1] it focuses specifically on the work of two artists who visited the spot: Joseph Wright of Derby, who produced a number of variants of a highly poetical approach to the tomb, and J. M. W. Turner, whose motives were rather different. As a conclusion to this chapter, I also briefly consider Turner's later depiction of Ovid's tomb.

REPRESENTATIONS OF VIRGIL'S TOMB
IN THE EIGHTEENTH CENTURY

The middle of the eighteenth century marks the moment when a certain amount of accuracy was invested in depicting the supposed site of Virgil's resting place, notably in the comprehensive plan and description of the tomb given in Paolo Paoli's *Antichità di Pozzuoli*,

---

[1] Trapp (1984); see also Trapp (1986) and Hendrix, Chapter 14 in this volume.

published in Naples in 1768.[2] Other researchers and draughtsmen
associated with the new scholarly investigations of southern Italy
were also drawn to the site. For example, the architect Robert Adam
visited the tomb on his Grand Tour, writing from Naples on 8 April
1755 that its antiquity 'induced me to make several sketches of it'.[3]
Adam visited the site with his teacher in Rome, Charles Louis Clérisseau,
who himself issued an engraving of the spot in 1766.[4]

The tomb's fame made it an appropriate accompaniment to
a learned tribute to scholarship: Antoine Cardon's etching after
Giuseppe Bracci's original drawing of the tomb was dedicated to
the recently deceased Comte de Caylus and published in 1765 as a
plate in William Hamilton and Pierre François Hugues d'Hancarville's
*Etruscan, Greek and Roman Antiquities* (Figure 15.1).[5] At bottom

**Figure 15.1.** Antoine Alexandre Joseph Cardon after Giuseppe Bracci, 'View
of Virgil's tomb', Plate 4 of Pierre François Hugues d'Hancarville (ed.)
*Etruscan, Greek and Roman Antiquities from the Cabinet of the Honourable
William Hamilton* (Naples, 1766). Etching, 156 × 268 mm.

[2] Paoli (1768), alternative title page *Avanzi Delle Antichità Esistenti a Pozzuoli
Cuma e Baja*, Naples 1768, pl. x.

[3] National Archives of Scotland, Edinburgh, Clerk of Penicuik Collection, GD18/4769.

[4] The plate was reissued in 1823. Two drawings (pen, pencil, grey and brown
washes) by Clérisseau and Robert Adam, *c.*1755, are in the collection of the Soane
Musueum: Adam vol. 57/16 and 21.

[5] Hamilton and d'Hancarville (1766-7).

right, Virgil's supposed auto-epitaph is inscribed on a shelf of rock.[6]
The text below the plate's dedication quotes lines from Virgil's fifth
*Eclogue* and is designed to prompt thoughts on the legacy of Comte de
Caylus: *Daphnim ad astra feremus: amavit nos quoque Daphnis* ('I will
extol Daphnis to the stars: for me, too, Daphnis loved'). The combin-
ation in the plate of Virgil's verse and the image of his tomb extends the
fifth *Eclogue*'s focus on the tomb erected for Daphnis, the mythical
creator of pastoral poetry, to a meditation on Virgil's own grave
monument.[7] It shows the tomb, with Castello St Elmo in the back-
ground, and numbers and identifies both sites, an aid to viewers that
would soon become unnecessary as the spot became something of a
standard item in every tourist's itinerary.

Some artists chose to turn the view round, as for example Hubert
Robert's presentation, derived from his trip to Naples in 1760 and widely
known from an etching of 1771.[8] Irrespective of these variants in view-
points, most eighteenth-century depictions adopt the formula seen in
Cardon's and Clérisseau's engravings, and the majority of artists chose a
presentation that focused on the tomb to the exclusion of its wider
surroundings. What the visual record thus suggests is that there quickly
developed an optimal presentation of the site, with the tomb's entrance
clearly shown and the worn steps beside it suggesting a descent into a
liminal space where the intimate experience of the structure in its
immediate setting is paramount, removing it from the broader landscape
containing it. The dislocation of the tomb from its quotidian location is
designed to encourage reverence for Virgil and meditation on his legacy.

## 'VIRGIL'S TOMB': JOSEPH WRIGHT OF DERBY

Among English artists, Joseph Wright of Derby was the painter who
devised the most impressive tribute to the tomb. During Wright's
two-year Italian sojourn, in the years 1773 to 1775, he was based

---

[6] The text is quoted and translated at p. 1.

[7] Cf. *Eclogue* 5.42–4: *et tumulum facite, et tumulo superaddite carmen: / 'Daphnis
ego in silvis, hic usque ad sidera notus, / formosi pecoris custos, formosior ipse'* ('And
build a tomb, and on the tomb add this verse: "I was Daphnis amid the woods, known
from here to the stars; my flock was beautiful, but I, their shepherd, more so"').

[8] Adélaïde Allou after Hubert Robert, *Vue du tombeau de Virgile*, etching, from
Fragonard and Robert (1771). Six plates.

principally in Rome but his Italian travels included a visit to Naples, which took place from early October to mid November 1774. Virgil's tomb clearly struck him as a site whose imaginative potential had been somewhat under-exploited. After his arrival back in England, and his failure to establish himself as a portrait painter in Bath, Wright's return to Derby saw him turn increasingly to subject and landscape paintings as a source of revenue, among them canvases inspired by his Italian experiences. Virgil's tomb was one of these subjects: Wright's account book shows that he painted six pictures of it.[9] Wright's contribution to the stock of images of Virgil's tomb is so well known that it is easy to forget how innovative his response was, both in terms of the medium he chose and in his creative approach. Before him, when rendered visually, the site had been treated principally as an antiquarian feature and thus the preserve of topography, most typically recorded on paper, as a drawing or an engraving. Wright's treatment used oil paint, which in the circumstances of the late eighteenth century was considered a more serious medium. Arguably, he was the first artist to lift the tomb from the prosaic to the ideal, to accord it an imaginative response and to draw out its significance in visual terms.

Wright's first version was exhibited at the Royal Academy in 1779, carrying the long title *Virgil's Tomb, with the Figure of Silius Italicus, who bought an estate enriched with this very Tomb. He was frequent in his Visits to the Monument of his Master.*[10] The painting now in the collection of the Metropolitan Museum of Art, New York, is assumed to be the picture shown at the Royal Academy because it is signed at bottom right (Figure 15.2). It probably corresponds with the picture listed in Wright's account book as 'Virgil's Tomb £63'.[11] A review of the Royal Academy exhibition in the *St. James's Chronicle* includes an appraisal of the picture and indicates that Wright had succeeded in enhancing the associations of the spot to encourage the spectator to reflect on fame, mortality, and the value of letters: 'This is a Scene admirably painted, and calculated to warm the Imagination of a Poet.'[12] Wright's second version of this subject, now in the collection of the Yale Center for British Art, New Haven, is a replica, and it is assumed that

---

[9] National Portrait Gallery, London; MS 111.    [10] No. 359.
[11] National Portrait Gallery, London; MS 111.
[12] *St. James's Chronicle or, the British Evening Post*, Arts & Entertainment page, 29 April 1779 to 1 May 1779; Issue 2829.

**Figure 15.2.** Joseph Wright of Derby, *Virgil's Tomb by Moonlight, with Silius Italicus Declaiming,* 1779. Oil on canvas, 101.6 × 127 cm. Metropolitan Museum of Art, New York. 2013.155.

Metropolitan Museum of Art, New York. Public domain (CC0).

this picture was the one exhibited in 1784 at the Society for Promoting the Arts, Liverpool.

Silius Italicus' epic, *Punica,* was regularly cited in the eighteenth century as part of the common stock of classical literature,[13] and viewers with a good education—including the reviewer for the *St. James's Chronicle* who had no difficulty picking up the reference— may well have remembered Martial's epigrams or Pliny's account of Silius' cultivation of Virgil's tomb.[14] A new (seventh) edition of

---

[13] Bassett (1953).

[14] The reviewer for the *Chronicle* merely noted that 'there are some trifling Faults in the Figure of Silius Italicus, and the Poems of his Master are awkwardly held in his Hand', but had no trouble with the classical allusion: *St. James's Chronicle or, the British Evening Post,* Arts & Entertainment page, 29 April 1779 to 1 May 1779; Issue 2829. For Silius at Virgil's tomb in ancient sources, including Pliny and Martial *Ep.* 11.48 and 49, see Peirano Garrison's discussion at pp. 269–74 of this volume. For the popularity of Martial in the eighteenth century, see Sullivan (1991).

William Melmoth's popular English translations of Pliny's letters, first published in London in 1746, had appeared in 1777, two years before Wright exhibited his picture.[15] Melmoth's rendering of Pliny's letter to Caninius Rufus (3.7), which records Silius' veneration of Virgil, helps explain Wright's inclusion of him in his presentation of Virgil's tomb:

> He carried his taste for objects of *virtù* so far as to incur reprehension for greedy buying. He had several villas in the same district, and the last purchase was always the chief favourite, to the neglect of the rest. They were all furnished with large collections of books, statues and portraits, which he more than enjoyed, he even adored; above all the portrait of VIRGIL, whose birthday he celebrated with more solemnity than his own, especially at Naples, where he used to approach his tomb with as much reverence as if it had been a temple. In this tranquillity he lived to the seventy-sixth year of his age . . .[16]

Melmoth's was not the only version of Pliny's letters in circulation; John Boyle's rather more elegant translations were published in London and Dublin in 1751 and went through three editions by 1752.[17] For interested readers, therefore, the name of Silius Italicus and his cultivation of Virgil's memory—staged at the site of the poet's tomb—were well-understood references.

The reviewer of the Royal Academy exhibition in 1779 was right to describe the painting as 'calculated to warm the Imagination of a Poet'. Wright uses strong contrasts of light and darkness to remove the subject from a merely topographical understanding and exaggerate its otherworldliness. These abrupt transitions from light to shade had already been developed successfully by Wright in earlier paintings, such as his *An Experiment on a Bird in the Air Pump* (1768; National Gallery, London) and *An Academy by Lamplight* (1769; Yale Center for British Art, New Haven), but their use here is clearly designed to emphasize the numinous. As has long been recognized, the *mise en scène* that Wright devised for this presentation borrowed much of its emotional charge from a treatment already applied to a highly theatrical moment. David Garrick's staging of *Romeo and Juliet* in the 1750s had interpolated a scene in which Romeo discovers

---

[15] Melmoth (1777). For the publication of the first edition, see Tierney (1988), 106–8.
[16] Melmoth (1931), 209–11. For discussion, see also Peirano Garrison in this volume, pp. 269–74, who quotes and translates part of this text.
[17] Boyle (1751), 193–4.

Juliet in the Capulet tomb, the moon breaking through the clouds outside and lamplight within.[18] When he was a pupil of Thomas Hudson in London, Wright may conceivably have attended a performance of Garrick's *Romeo and Juliet*, which may very possibly have used an illuminated backdrop to depict the moonlight. If not that, we know in any case that Wright was familiar with the print made of Benjamin Wilson's painting of this scene, first published in 1751 and reissued in 1765.[19] Wright had included the moon, seen through a window, in *An Experiment on a Bird in the Air Pump* but he started using the device of a double light source as a major element contrasting natural and artificial illumination shortly afterwards with his *Philosopher by Lamplight* (*A Hermit Studying Anatomy*) of *c.*1769 (Derby Museum and Art Gallery). In Wright's treatment, the control of light is not merely a demonstration of artistic creativity and technical prowess in chiaroscuro but carries a symbolic charge contrasting natural illumination with human enlightenment. When using two light sources for Virgil's tomb, the contrast of the lantern's warm light with the cool silvery light of the moonbeams is meant to remind us of life and mortality. The ritual adopted by Silius Italicus, the light and warmth spread inside the tomb by the torch he carries, may temporarily restore Virgil's memory but it cannot restore his living presence.

Two other paintings of the tomb by Wright are in public collections. Neither includes the figure of Silius Italicus. The version in Derby is dated 1782 and the one in Belfast is dated 1785. A fifth version is in a private collection. The sixth was given by Wright to his friend the poet William Hayley but has not been identified. The Belfast painting is the only version that shows the tomb in daylight.[20] The differences between the five extant versions of the subject are worth noting: two paintings with Silius Italicus and three without; four night scenes and one in daylight. At one level, this variety merely points to the workings of the art market and the painter's need to avoid stale repetition and vary his stock: Wright thus refreshes his treatment of the tomb in different iterations for different audiences and/or patrons. We might also consider further how the presence of

---

[18] Bertelsen (1978), 311, 320.

[19] Wright certainly knew this print; he referred to it in a letter dated 23 December 1786, to William Hayley, concerning his painting *Romeo and Juliet: the Tomb Scene*, exhibited in 1790 (Derby Museum and Art Gallery). See Egerton (1990), 123–4.

[20] Nicholson (1968) 1, 83–4 & 258, no. 287; 2, 147; see also Nicholson (1988), 745–58.

Silius Italicus in the 1779 and 1784 versions elevates the subject from a topographical record of the tomb to the realm of history painting. The Roman author offers an authentic point of historical reference while at the same time acting as a surrogate for the eighteenth-century viewer's response to Virgil's legacy. Yet the fact that Wright felt free to discard this figure in other paintings of the tomb is significant. He may have estimated that the tomb's fame was sufficiently strong not to require an intermediary figure to act out the reverential response Wright's contemporaries had for Virgil.

## J. M. W. TURNER AND VIRGIL

J. M. W. Turner was born in the year in which Wright returned from Italy to England and it is traditional to think of the younger generation as ushering in a new set of priorities for painting. Nevertheless, in Turner's case especially, a good deal of the eighteenth-century academic legacy remained significant, not just in terms of the subject matter of many of his major paintings but also in terms of his understanding of the purpose of the arts within civil society. His investigation of Virgil's tomb resulted in no painting of it, despite exploring the site reasonably thoroughly in pencil sketches on his first visit to Italy in 1819. Yet by looking carefully at his wider engagement with Virgil we can come to some understanding of his reactions to the tomb.

By the time Turner got to Italy, Virgil had already proved to be a major source of inspiration to him. His reliance on the *Aeneid* as a source of subjects for pictures was part of his campaign to raise the dignity of landscape painting, whose detractors deprecated its practitioners for their unimaginative copying of observable nature and their inability to broach the ideal. Turner's response to this prejudice was to use his art to demonstrate forcibly that landscape painting could encompass a very wide spectrum of subjects, including historical painting, which was still considered to be the most exalted academic genre. A significant number of his oil paintings take their subjects from classical history and mythology, and among them the works prompted by Virgil are second only to those inspired by Ovid.

Around 1804–7 Turner drew up lists of possible subjects for pictures in several sketchbooks in which topics from the *Aeneid* are listed along with associated sketches of their compositions.[21] 'Aeneas and Evander', 'Pallas and Aeneas', and 'Aeneas parting from Evander' were listed among them but these subjects were not developed into paintings. The two stories that Turner did work on were those of Aeneas and the Sibyl, and Dido and Aeneas. The first of these resulted in *Aeneas and the Sibyl, Lake Avernus* (*c.* 1798; Tate), which he duplicated a decade and a half later, reworked in his current manner as *Aeneas and the Cumaean Sibyl, Lake Avernus* (1814–15; Yale Center for British Art, New Haven). The story of Dido and Aeneas prompted two pictures in the 1810s: *Dido and Aeneas; the Morning of the Chase*, exhibited at the Royal Academy in 1814 (Tate) and *Dido Building Carthage; or, the Rise of the Carthaginian Empire*, shown there the following year (National Gallery, London). He returned to Virgil's epic on three further occasions with pictures exhibited at the Royal Academy: *Dido Directing the Equipment of the Fleet; or, the Morning of the Carthaginian Empire* was shown in 1828 (Tate), *The Golden Bough* in 1834 (Tate), and in 1850, the year before he died, the last four pictures Turner exhibited there were all on the theme of Dido and Aeneas: *Aeneas Relating his Story to Dido*, *Mercury Sent to Admonish Aeneas*, *The Visit to the Tomb*, and *The Departure of the Fleet* (all Tate).[22]

The books in Turner's library demonstrate that he was as well read in the classics, at least in English translations, as many of those who viewed his pictures. He owned Pope's version of Homer's *Iliad* (in the 1773 edition), Edmund Bohun's translation of Livy (1686), Thomas North's edition of Plutarch's *Lives* (in a 1657 printing of the 1579 original), and Oliver Goldsmith's *The Roman History: From the Foundation of the City of Rome, to the Destruction of the Western Empire* (in a 1786 printing of the 1769 original). The posthumous inventory produced in November 1854 of Turner's house and studio also lists among his books *Virgilii opera folio*.[23] Although this publication is not among those still retained by Turner's family, it was

---

[21] See *Studies for Pictures, Isleworth* (*c.*1804–6); *Hesperides* (*c.*1804–6); and *Wey, Guildford* (*c.*1807) sketchbooks, London: Tate.

[22] *Aeneas Relating his Story to Dido* is no longer extant and is presumed to have been destroyed.

[23] For a list of Turner's library, see Wilton (2006), 247–8.

conceivably an edition based on John Ogilby's translation as adapted
in a folio text (1658), which was published with engravings by
Wenceslaus Hollar and others. But apart from its plates, this book
cannot have been of much use to the artist, who could not read Latin.
As F. S. Trimmer, the son of his would-be tutor, attested: 'Turner,
when beginning his great classical subjects from the *Aeneid*, regretted
his ignorance of Latin; my father undertook to teach him for instruc-
tion in painting in return. My father, who was accustomed to teach-
ing, has told me Turner sadly floundered in the verbs, and never
made any progress—in fact, he could not spare the time.'[24] In add-
ition to this Latin text, it is clear that Turner also owned one or more
English editions of Virgil. John Dryden's translation was used for the
epigraph that accompanied the painting *Dido and Aeneas; the Morn-
ing of the Chase* when it was exhibited at the Royal Academy in 1814.
Christopher Pitt's translation of the *Aeneid* in Joseph Warton's bilin-
gual edition of Virgil's works (1753) gave Turner the title for *The
Golden Bough*, shown in 1834. The same book may have been the one
Turner consulted when he added a line in Latin from the *Eclogues* to
his *Perspective Sketchbook* (1809; Tate).[25]

## TURNER AND VIRGIL'S TOMB

As shown in the record of subjects inspired by the *Aeneid*, there is no
question that Virgil mattered a great deal to Turner from early in his
career. It is therefore not at all surprising that he made a special
pilgrimage to sketch the poet's tomb when he visited Naples in 1819.
Indeed, when he later set about ordering his sketchbooks, Turner
included Virgil's tomb as a point of reference for the inscription he
added to one of them, the *Naples, Paestum and Rome* sketchbook,
writing in black ink on its cover, 'Vesuvius. Napoli. Virgils Tomb /
1 Journey to Salerno. Paestum / returning from Naples to Rome.'[26]

---

[24] Thornbury (1877), 123–4.

[25] *Non omnia possumus omnes / Virg Ec 8 ver 63* ('We cannot all do everything',
*Eclogues*, 8.63); inside front cover of Turner Bequest CVIII, Tate. Cf. Christopher Pitt,
Joseph Warton et al. *The Works of Virgil in Latin and English*, London: J. Dodsley
(1753); third edition (1778), vol. 1, p. 160.

[26] Turner Bequest CLXXXVI. Another original inscription by Turner on one of
this sketchbook's covers has been largely effaced: '12. Vesuvius. Napoli. V. Tomb. 1 R$^t$

In his *Italian Guide Book* sketchbook Turner provided himself with a
summary of passages from J. C. Eustace's *Tour through Italy* (1813),
including Eustace's account of the tomb.[27] Eustace compared the
neglect of Virgil's tomb with the recent destruction of Alexander
Pope's house and garden in Twickenham, and his reflections are
worth quoting at length. He begins by noting how the laurel trad-
itionally associated with the tomb no longer grows there, its place
taken by myrtle, ivy, and ilex.[28] From this botanical observation of
fact overcoming fancy, he moves on to remind his readers that even in
classical times, as Martial records, the tomb had been neglected. This,
in turn, leads Eustace to consider the fate of reputations and to
caution against any astonishment that Virgil's tomb could have fallen
into neglect so quickly:

> Our surprise, however, may cease when we recollect, that in the present
> most polished and enlightened century, in less than sixty years after
> Pope's death, at a time when his works were in the hands of every child,
> and had been translated into every language, his house was levelled with
> the ground, his grotto defaced, the trees planted by his own hand rooted
> up, and his whole retreat, the seat of genius and of the British muse,
> ravaged and stripped of the very ornaments which endeared them to the
> public, because they were the creation of the poet's fancy, and still
> seemed to bear the impression of his mind. Houses and gardens, grottos
> and sepulchres, are, it is true, the most perishable of monuments, and
> the Hero and the Poet must finally rest their hopes of fame on their
> virtues, and on their talents, the sole memorial *aere perennius*, superior
> to time and barbarism. Yet the longer even such frail monuments as the
> former are preserved the better; the attention paid to their conservation
> is a tribute to genius, and a proof of the influence of the arts, and of the
> prevalence of information, honourable to the country itself.[29]

The assault on Pope's estate at Twickenham took place in 1807 when
the new owner, Baroness Howe of Langar, demolished it to rid herself

---

to Salerno. Paestum, and Return from Naples to Rome.' Ironically, however, this
sketchbook contains no record of the tomb, unless the pillar-shaped structure in the
bottom right-hand corner of CLXXXVI 52 is identified as such.

[27] Turner Bequest CLXXII 13.

[28] For the ancient interest in the vegetation surrounding the tombs of poets, see
Montiglio's discussion in this volume, pp. 226–33.

[29] Eustace (1815), volume 2, 375f; *aere perennius*, 'more durable than bronze', is a
quotation from Horace, *Odes* 3.30.1: see further pp. 10–11 in this volume. Eustace's
work, originally published in 1813 as *A tour through Italy*, changed title in the revised
second edition of 1814 to *A classical tour through Italy*.

of the nuisance of a constant stream of visitors to Pope's garden and grotto. Turner had bought land in Twickenham himself in 1807 and was appalled by Lady Howe's action. In his *River* sketchbook (*c.*1807; Tate), he set out his view of the demolition as a national humiliation:

> O lost to honor and the sence of shame
> Can Britain so forget Pope's well earnd fame
> To desolation doom the poet's fane
> The pride of T[wickenham's] bower and silver Thames...[30]

He wrote further verses on that same episode in 1808, calling Pope 'the British Maro', a routine reference to the quality of his compatriot's classicizing verse, to be sure, but also an appellation that would facilitate the later comparison between the disgraceful lack of respect shown by those who should have venerated the material remains associated with both Virgil's and Pope's achievements:

> Dear Sister Isis tis thy Thames that calls
> See desolation hovers o'er those walls
> The scattered timbers on my margin lays
> Where glimmering Evening's ray yet lingering plays
> There British Maro sung by science long endear'd
> And to an admiring Country once rever'd
> Now to destruction doom'd thy peacefull grott
> Popes willow bending to the earth forgot...[31]

In the same year Turner also exhibited at his own gallery *Pope's Villa at Twickenham, During its Dilapidation* (private collection, USA), showing the house as it was being demolished.

Turner's attitude to the legacy of Alexander Pope indicates his belief that great creative achievement should ensure a place in national memory. In 1809, the year after he had exhibited *Pope's Villa*, Turner showed *Thomson's Aeolian Harp* in his own gallery, too (Manchester City Galleries). In the catalogue he produced for the occasion the painting was accompanied with what are arguably Turner's most successful lines of verse, themselves inspired by Thomson's poetry. The picture shows dancing figures, representing the Seasons, in front of a pedestal bearing Thomson's name and topped with a lyre. Turner's verses anticipate the sentiments he would later find

---

[30]  Turner Bequest XCVI, f. 71v.
[31]  'On the demolition of Pope-House at Twickenham', *Verse Book*, p. 11. For a full transcription, see Wilton and Turner (1990), 150.

in Eustace's remarks on Virgil's tomb. Eustace, we may recall, talked of how important it was to preserve such monuments as 'a tribute to genius, and a proof of the influence of the arts'. Yet he also acknowledged that because monuments perish, virtue and talent are 'the sole memorial . . . superior to time and barbarism'.[32] Turner, likewise, in the lines he supplied for *Thomson's Aeolian Harp* regrets the destruction of Pope's house at Twickenham, but locates Pope's and Thomson's memory in the landscape of the Thames itself, their achievement impervious to changes in taste and more sordid reckonings of the worth of a landscape:[33]

> On Thomson's tomb the dewy drops distil,
> Sad tears of pity shed for Pope's lost fane,
> To worth and verse adheres the memory still,
> Scorning to wear ensnaring fashion's chain.[34]

These lines must surely have been inspired by the review John Landseer published on *Pope's Villa* in 1808 and his remarks there on the fragility of reputation: 'At such a time the mind willingly enthralled by a certain feeling of melancholy pleasure, is instinctively led to compare the permanency of Nature herself with the fluctuations of fashion and the vicissitudes of taste . . . and not even the taste, the genius, and the reputation of Pope could retard the operations of Time, the irksomeness of satiety, and the consequent desire of change!'[35] Turner's two pictures honouring Pope and Thomson and the poetry he composed about them are manifestly of the same mind; they celebrate the permanence of creative genius whose memory transcends the coarser values of a subsequent age.

Turner's care in seeking out Virgil's tomb in 1819 was thus more than a tourist's idle curiosity: it was a dutiful homage by someone who set a very high value on poetry and felt that society as a whole should share the same respect for creative genius. It gave him the opportunity to see with his own eyes how posterity had neglected the presumed last resting place of one of his most important literary inspirations. The drawings he made in his *Pompeii, Amalfi, &c.* sketchbook show

---

[32] Eustace (1815), 375.
[33] On metaphors of nature, landscape, and vegetation as a means of thinking about poetic legacies, see also Montiglio in this volume, pp. 226–33.
[34] Wilton and Turner (1990), 134.
[35] *Review of Publications of Art*, June 1808, 155–9.

**Figure 15.3.** J. M. W. Turner 'Four Sketches of Virgil's Tomb on the Posillipo Hill; also Part of a View of Naples and Vesuvius' from *Pompeii, Amalfi, &c.*, Sketchbook CLXXXV 68 [D15865], 1819. Graphite on paper, 113 × 189 mm. © Tate.

him to have worked assiduously over the site.[36] As the guidebooks recommended, he took advantage of the views it offered over Naples, as for example the sketch on Folio 69 verso now identified as 'Naples and Vesuvius Seen from Virgil's Tomb' which looks east towards the headland of Castel dell'Ovo with Vesuvius seen rising behind it. On the opposite page in the sketchbook (Folio 70 recto) Turner made four sketches of Virgil's Tomb (Figure 15.3).

The top of the monument is recorded in the top right-hand portion of the page, with the steps from the tomb rising to the left. The tomb's interior is shown at bottom right. Next to it on the left is a view from the top looking down the steps towards the tomb. The Latin inscription, recorded at bottom left, was engraved in the sixteenth century on a marble tablet opposite the tomb, reading 'QUI CINERES TVMVLI HAEC VESTIGIA / CONDITVR OLIM / ILLE HOC QVI CECINIT PASCVA RVRA DVCES CAN REG MDLIIII'. At the bottom of the

---

[36] Turner Bequest *Pompeii, Amalfi, &c., Sketchbook* CLXXXV 68 a, 68, 69. These drawings can be consulted online at <http://www.tate.org.uk/art/artworks/turner-naples-and-vesuvius-seen-from-virgils-tomb-d15866> *et seq.* Two further sketches of the landscape around the tomb are contained in Turner's *Naples; Rome C. Studies* sketchbook (Turner Bequest CLXXXVII 14 and 55), also from 1819.

page on the right this inscription has been translated somewhat inaccurately, in handwriting unlike Turner's, as 'This [*sic*] are the remains of a Tomb which / contained the cinders of him who sang the / pastorals of the Country.'[37] On the next sheet (Folio 71 recto) Turner made another view looking out towards the panorama of the Bay of Naples, showing the city and Vesuvius. The inscription he transcribed here is another tribute to Virgil, this time a much more recent one:

> Près du chantre divin, dont la lyre immortelle
> Répéta des pasteurs les doux et tendres vœux,
> Sur ce banc consacré par l'amitié fidèle,
> Amis, reposez-vous et resserrez vos nœuds.
> 17 Ag. MDCCCXII

> Near the divine bard, whose immortal lyre
> Sounded the sweet and tender vows of shepherds,
> On this bench consecrated by faithful friendship,
> Friends, rest and renew your bonds.
> 17 August 1812

The verse was inscribed on a marble bench placed in the vicinity by admirers of Virgil. The lines had been composed by a French naval officer, Armand Louis Charles Rose de Lostanges, who rose to the rank of Vice-Admiral in the navy of the King of Naples from 1806 to 1817, occupying himself in his leisure time with archaeology and making a collection of antiquities.[38]

Although no picture was derived from these sketches—not, in itself, an unusual result given the number of places he visited on this tour—Turner's record of the site is instructive. Wright of Derby's radical presentation, removing the tomb from its everyday presentation to tourists, was not a method suitable for Turner's exploration of Italy, whose immediate concerns were principally exploratory and topographical. The fact that he chose not to produce a watercolour of the site may indicate that he felt its subject was already too hackneyed. What is immediately striking about the drawings he made of the

---

[37] For this sixteenth-century inscription (more accurately punctuated), and others like it, see Trapp (1984), 12 with Hendrix in this volume, pp. 292. Turner added further notes to help him remember details: 'Vines' centre left-hand edge, 'W | M[?yrtle] Vines' and 'over the Grotto toward the Elmo or Tomb'.

[38] Valentin (1826), 49–50 and Julvécourt (1832), letter xliv, dated Naples 16 November 1830, 146–7. Turner also includes further words which to date have not been identified: 'W Blackford / F R [?Misstez] / Gabriel Ally [?ses Auteurs]'.

tomb is how much attention has been paid to the inscriptions: the
textual paraphernalia which were part of the experience of the site
in 1819. Turner was no linguist, but here and elsewhere in Italy (for
example, in his record of the Via dei Sepolcri, Pompeii, which is also
included in this sketchbook) he copied carved texts.[39] Such data
could, of course, be utilized later were a fully realized image to be
produced, especially when drawing attention to details that helped
to deepen the historical register of the scene. This habit of making
a full record explains why he went to such pains to note down the
texts physically present in the vicinity of Virgil's tomb. These inscrip-
tions, however, were historically supplementary; they did not so
much anchor the tomb in its classical context as offer glosses on its
reception by subsequent generations of devotees. They were, to that
extent, an epigraphic equivalent to the discursive frame of reference
he had already explored through his preparatory reading of guide-
books such as Eustace's *Tour through Italy*. To the nineteenth-
century tourist, Virgil's material tomb was mediated by texts, whose
physical presence at the site as paratexts to the tomb itself helped to
codify visitors' reactions.

## TURNER AND OVID

Turner's failure to produce a finished work on the theme of Virgil's
tomb should not be taken to mean that his interest in classical poetry
would never be the subject of a fully realized picture. In fact, one of
his most significant paintings took the place of the poet in society as
its central theme.

*Ancient Italy—Ovid banished from Rome*, now in a private collec-
tion, was exhibited at the Royal Academy in 1838. It was paired with a
companion work *Modern Italy—the Pifferari* (Glasgow Museums).
The latter picture includes a small group of strolling musicians or
'pifferari', playing their traditional bagpipes and pifferi (oboe-like
instruments) who travelled to Rome from the Abruzzi during Advent
and played to the Madonna at roadside shrines. Contemporary travel
writers, such as Eustace, saw this as a continuation of a pagan tradition

---

[39] Turner Bequest, *Pompeii, Amalfi, &c., Sketchbook* CLXXXV 5 a.

**Figure 15.4.** James T. Willmore after J. M. W. Turner *Ancient Italy—Ovid Banished from Rome*, c.1842. Etching and engraving, engraver's proof, 527 × 711 mm. Yale Center for British Art, Paul Mellon Collection. B1977.14.8048.

Photo: Yale Center for British Art, Paul Mellon Collection. Public domain.

connected with Ovid, who encouraged the worship of the gods with music. The welcome given to their art in modern Rome is thus contrasted by Turner with Ovid's banishment under Augustus. The figure of the poet may be the man escorted by two soldiers in a group of figures at the left, and the possessions strewn at the water's edge in the foreground speak of a violent expulsion. The strongbox jemmied open looks rather like a codex, as though poetry itself has been assaulted.

Ovid was Turner's favourite classical author, so it is all but certain that he knew the canonical story that Ovid had probably died at Tomis and was buried there.[40] Yet here, in a detail that might at first pass unnoticed, Turner includes at bottom left a sarcophagus clearly inscribed 'Ovidius Naso.' This detail is most easily discerned in the engraving issued originally in 1842 (Figure 15.4). The form of the sarcophagus, with its pitched roof, is of the Attic type, and its humble appearance is contrasted very forcibly with the silhouette of the Mausoleum of Hadrian in the background, doing duty here for the Mausoleum of Augustus. Irrespective of its anachronistic inclusion, the point Turner is making very deliberately is the contrast between the modest sarcophagus of the exiled poet and the colossal monuments of the state that had expelled him. It speaks to a recurrent strain in Turner's paintings and in his writings concerning the place of the arts in modern life, the standard they upheld and the value they conferred upon society. Whether Virgil had been buried in Naples or Ovid in Tomis was immaterial—nor were their tombs, if discoverable, of ultimate significance. What kept the poets in memory, whether classical or modern, was the quality of their work and the lessons it imparted. This was a credo that all artists, Turner among them, needed to maintain if they were to practise their métier with integrity and ensure the survival of the creative arts in a material age.

---

[40] For other versions of Ovid's tombs, see Goldschmidt's discussion in Chapter 5 of this volume.

# Bibliography

Acosta-Hughes, B. (2002) *Polyeidea: The Iambi of Callimachus and the Archaic Iambic Tradition, Hellenistic Culture and Society* 35, Berkeley and Los Angeles CA.

Acosta-Hughes, B. (2007a) 'The Inscribed Voice: Lyric in Epigram', in Bing and Bruss (2007), 445–57.

Acosta-Hughes, B. (2007b) '"*Leukai phthengomenai selides*". Sulla fortuna di Saffo nella poesia alessandrina', *Philologia Antiqua* 1.

Acosta-Hughes, B. (2010) *Arion's Lyre: Archaic Lyric into Hellenistic Poetry*, Princeton NJ.

Acosta-Hughes, B. and Barbantani, S. (2007) 'Inscribing Lyric', in Bing and Bruss (2007), 429–58.

Addesso, C. A. (2005) 'Un "sepolcro di candidissimi marmi, & intagli eccellentissimi". Sannazzaro nelle "guide" di Napoli', *Studi rinascimentali*, 3, 171–200.

Agosti, G. (2005) 'L'etopea nella poesia greca tardoantica', in E. Amato and J. Schamp, eds, *ΗΘΟΠΟΙΙΑ. La représentation de caractères à l'époque impériale et tardive*, Salerne, 34–60.

Alcock, S. (1991) 'Tomb Cult and the Post-Classical Polis', *AJA* 95, 447–67.

Alcock, S. (1993a) *Graecia Capta: The Landscapes of Roman Greece*, Cambridge.

Alcock, S. (1993b) 'Landscape of Memory and the Authority of Pausanias', in J. Bingen, ed., *Pausanias historien, Entretiens de la Fondation Hardt* 41, Vandoeuvres-Geneva, 241–76.

Alexopoulou, A. A. and Karamanou, I. (2014) 'The Papyrus from the "Musician's Tomb" in Daphne: *ΜΠ* 7449, 8517-8523', *Greek and Roman Musical Studies* 2, 23–49.

Altmann, W. (1905) *Die Römischen Grabaltare der Kaiserzeit*, Berlin.

Antonaccio, C. M. (1994) 'Contesting the Past: Hero Cult, Tomb Cult, and Epic in Early Greece', *AJA* 98.3, 389–410.

Antonaccio, C. M. (1995) *An Archaeology of Ancestors: Tomb Cult and Hero Cult in Early Greece*, Lanham.

Asper, M. (2013) 'Minding the Gap: Archaeology and False Closure', in Grewing, Acosta-Hughes, and Kirchenko (2013), 63–82.

Assmann, A. (1999) *Erinnerungsräume. Formen und Wandlungen des kulturellen Gedächtnisses*, Munich.

Assmann, A. (2011) *Cultural Memory and Western Civilization: Arts of Memory*, Cambridge.

Assmann, A. and Assmann, J. (1989) 'Schrift, Tradition, Kultur', in P. Goetsch, W. Raible, and H.-R. Roemer, series eds, and W. Raible, vol. ed., *Scriptoralia* 6. *Zwischen Festtag und Alltag*, Tübingen, 25–49.

Assmann, J. (1992) *Das kulturelle Gedächtnis. Schrift, Erinnerung und politische Identität in den frühen Hochkulturen*, Munich.

Assmann, J. (1998) 'Kollectives, Gedächtnis und kulturelle Identität', in J. Assmann and T. Hölzchen (eds), *Kultur und Gedächtnis*, Frankfurt am Main, 9–19.

Assmann, J. (2011) *Cultural Memory and Early Civilization: Writing, Remembrance and Political Imagination*, Cambridge.

Austin, C. and Bastianini, G., eds (2002) *Posidippi Pellaei quae supersunt omnia*, Milan.

Babel, R. and Paravicini, W., eds (2005) *Grand Tour. Adeliges Reisen und Europäische Kultur vom 14. bis zum 18. Jahrhundert*, Ostfildern.

Badian, E. (1972) 'Ennius and his Friends', in O. Skutsch, ed., *Ennius, Entretiens de la Fondation Hardt* 17, Vandoeuvres-Geneva, 151–99.

Bakola, E. (2008) 'The Drunk, the Reformer and the Teacher: Agonistic Poetics and the Construction of Persona in the Comic Poets of the Fifth Century', *CCJ* 54, 1–29.

Bakola, E. (2010) *Cratinus and the Art of Comedy*, Oxford.

Bakola, E. (2013) 'Crime and Punishment: Cratinus, Aeschylus' *Oresteia*, and the Metaphysics and the Politics of Wealth', in E. Bakola, L. Prauscello, and M. Telò, eds, *Greek Comedy and the Discourse of Genres*, Cambridge, 226–55.

Bakola, E. (2014) 'Interiority, the "Deep Earth", and the Spatial Symbolism of Darius' Apparition in the Persians of Aeschylus', *CCJ* 60, 1–36.

Bakola, E. (2016) 'Textile Symbolism and the "Wealth of the Earth": Creation, Production and Destruction in the "Tapestry Scene" of Aeschylus' *Oresteia* (*Ag.* 905–78)', in M. Harlow, M.-L. Nosch, and G. Fanfani, eds, *Spinning Fates and the Song of the Loom: The Use of Textiles, Clothing and Cloth Production as Metaphor, Symbol and Narrative*, Oxford, 115–36.

Barbantani, S. (1993) 'I poeti lirici del canone alessandrino nell' epigramma-tistica', *Aevum(ant)* 6, 5–97.

Barbantani, S. (2010) *Three Burials (Ibycus, Stesichorus, Simonides): Facts and Fiction about Lyric Poets in Magnia Graecia in the Epigrams of the Greek Anthology*, Alessandria.

Barber, K. (2007) 'Improvisation and the Art of Making Things Stick', in E. Hallam and T. Ingold, eds, *Creativity and Cultural Improvisation, Association of Social Anthropologists Monographs* 44, Oxford and New York, 25–41.

Barchiesi, A. (1979) 'Palinuro e Caieta. Due "epigrammi" virgiliani (*Aen.* V 870 sg.; VII 1–4)', *Maia* 31, 3–11.

Barham, N. (2015) 'Ornament and Art Theory in Ancient Rome: An Alternative Classical Paradigm for the Visual Arts', PhD Diss., University of Chicago.

Barthes, R. (1967) 'The Death of the Author', R. Howard, trans., *Aspen* 5–6.

Barthes, R. (1974) *S/Z*, R. Miller, trans., London.

Barthes, R. (1975) *The Pleasure of the Text*, R. Miller, trans., New York.

Bassett, E. L. (1953) 'Silius Italicus in England', *CPh* 48.3, 155–68.

Bassino, P. (2017) 'On Constructive Conflict and Disruptive Peace: The *Certamen Homeri et Hesiodi*', in P. Bassino, L.-G. Canevaro, and B. Graziosi, eds, *Conflict and Consensus in Early Hexameter Poetry*, Cambridge, 190–207.

Basta Donizelli, G. (2003) 'Eschilo a Gela', in R. Panvini and F. Giudice, eds, *Ta Attika, Veder Greco a Gela*, Rome, 95–8.

Bathoe, W. (1758) *A Catalogue of the Collection of Pictures, & c. Belonging to King James the Second*, London.

Bauman, R. and Briggs, C. L. (1990) 'Poetics and Performance as Critical Perspectives on Language and Social Life', *Annual Review of Anthropology* 19, 59–88.

Baumbach, M., Petrovic, A., and Petrovic, I., eds (2010) *Archaic and Classical Greek Epigram*, Cambridge.

Beard, M. (2012) 'The "Pushy Parent" Syndrome in Ancient Rome', *BBC News Magazine*, 16 April, <http://www.bbc.com/news/magazine-17701080>.

Beckby, H., ed. (1965–8) *Anthologia Graeca*, 4 vols, Munich, 2nd edn.

Bell, M. (1981) *The Terracottas*, Princeton.

Bell, J. and Willette, T., eds (2002) *Art History in the Age of Bellori*, Cambridge.

Bellori, G. P. (1680) *Le pitture antiche del sepolcro de' Nasonii nella Via Flaminia*, Rome.

Beloch, K. J. (1879) *Campanien. Topographie, Geschichte und Leben der Umgebung Neapels im Alterthum*, Berlin.

Benario, H. (1959) 'Cocceius and Cumae', *CB* 35, 40.

Bérard, C. (1974) *Anodoi. Essai sur l'imagerie des passages chthoniens*, Rome.

Bérard, C. (1982) 'Récupérer la mort du prince: héroïsation et formation de la cité', in G. Gnoli and J.-P. Vernant, eds, *La mort, les morts dans le sociétés anciennes*, Cambridge and Paris, 89–105.

Berghoff, H. et al., eds (2002) *The Making of Modern Tourism: The Cultural History of the British Experience, 1600–2000*, Basingstoke.

Bergk, T. (1853) *Poetae Lyrici Graeci*, Leipzig, 2nd edn.

Bernabé, A., ed. (2004–7) *Poetae epici Graeci, testimonia et fragmenta*, part II, 3 vols, Munich.

Berndt-Ersöz, S. (2008) 'The Chronology and Historical Context of Midas', *Historia* 57, 1–37.

Berns, J. J. (1988) 'Peregrinatio academica und Kavalierstour. Bildungsreisen junger Deutschen in der Fruehen Neuzeit', in C. Wiedemann, ed., *Rom-Paris-London. Erfahrung und Selbsterfahrung deutscher Schriftsteller und Künstler in den fremden Metropolen*, Stuttgart, 155–81.

Bernsdorff, H. (1997) 'Q. Sulpicius Maximus, Apollonios von Rhodos und Ovid', *ZPE* 118, 105–12.

Bertelsen, L. (1978) 'David Garrick and English Painting', *Eighteenth Century Studies* 11, 311–20.

Beschi, L. (1967/68) 'Il monumento di Telemachos, fondatore dell'*Asklepieion* Ateniese', *Annuario della Scuola Archeologica di Atene e delle Missioni Italiane in Oriente* 45/46, 381–436.

Betegh, G. (2004) *The Derveni Papyrus: Cosmology, Theology and Interpretation*, Cambridge.

Bettenworth, A. (2007) 'The Mutual Influence of Inscribed and Literary Epigram', in Bing and Bruss (2007), 69–94.

Bettini, M. (1976) 'L'epitaffio di Virgilio, Silio Italico, e un modo di intendere la letteratura', *DArch* 9, 439–48.

Biles, Z. P. (2002) 'Intertextual Biography in the Rivalry of Cratinus and Aristophanes', *AJPh* 123, 169–204.

Bing, P. (1988a) *The Well-Read Muse: Present and Past in Callimachus and the Hellenistic Poets*, Hypomnemata 90.

Bing, P. (1988b) 'Theocritus' Epigrams on the Statues of Ancient Poets', *A&A* 34, 117–23.

Bing, P. (1993) 'The *Bios*-Tradition and Poets' Lives in Hellenistic Poetry', in R. Rosen and J. Farrell, eds, *Nomodeiktes: Greek Studies in Honor of Martin Oswald*, Ann Arbor MI, 619–31.

Bing, P. (1995) '*Ergänzungsspiel* in the Epigrams of Callimachus', *A&A* 41, 115–31.

Bing, P. (2002) 'The Un-Read Muse? Insribed Epigram and Its Readers in Antiquity', in Harder, Regtuit, and Wakker (2002), 39–66.

Bing, P. (2005) 'The Politics and Poetics of Geography in the Milan Posidippus, Section One: On Stones (AB 1–20)', in K. Gutzwiller, ed., *The New Posidippus: A Hellenistic Poetry Book*, Oxford, 119–40.

Bing, P. (2009) *The Scroll and the Marble: Studies in Reading and Reception in Hellenistic Poetry*, Ann Arbor MI.

Bing, P. (2014) 'Inscribed Epigrams in and out of Sequence', in Harder, Regtuit, and Wakker (2014), 1–24.

Bing, P. and Bruss, J. P., eds (2007) *Brill's Companion to Hellenistic Epigram*, Leiden.

Bischoff, B. (1952) 'Eine mittelalterliche Ovid-Legende', *Historisches Jahrbuch* 71, 268–73.

Bleisch, P. (1999) 'The Empty Tomb at Rhoeteum: Deiphobus and the Problem of the Past in *Aeneid* 6.494–547', *ClAnt* 18, 187–226.

Bloch, A. (1970) '*Arma virumque* als heroisches Leitmotiv', *MH* 27, 206–11.

Bloomer, K. (2000) *The Nature of Ornament: Rhythm and Metamorphosis in Architecture*, New York and London.

Boedeker, D. (1993) 'Hero Cult and Politics in Herodotus: The Bones of Orestes', in C. Dougherty and L. Kurke, eds, *Cultural Poetics and Archaic Greece: Cult, Performance, Politics*, Cambridge, 164–77.

Bolmarcich, S. (2002) 'Hellenistic Sepulchral Epigrams on Homer', in Harder, Regtuit, and Wakker (2002), 67–83.

Borg, B. E. (2013) *Crisis and Ambition: Tombs and Burial Customs in Third-Century CE Rome*, Oxford.

Boschung, D. (1987) *Antike Grabaltäre aus den Nekropolen Roms*, Bern.

Bowie, A. M. (1993) *Aristophanes: Myth, Ritual and Comedy*, Cambridge.

Bowra, C. M. (1952) 'Orpheus and Eurydice', *CQ* 11, 113–26.

Boyer, M. (2005) *Histoire générale du tourisme du XVIe au XXIe siècle*, Paris.

Boyle, J. (1751) *The Letters of Pliny the Younger, With observations on each letter; and an essay on Pliny's life*, printed by George Faulkner, Dublin.

Braudy, L. (1986) *The Frenzy of Renown: Fame and its History*, Oxford.

Bravi, L. (2006) *Gli epigrammi di Simonide e le vie della tradizione*, Rome.

Breitenbach, A. (2009) *Kommentar zu den Pseudo-Seneca-Epigrammen der Anthologia Vossiana*, Hildesheim.

Brelich, A. (1958) *Gli eroi greci. Un problema storico-religioso*, Rome.

Bremmer, J. (1991) 'From Guru to Gay', in P. Bourgeaud, ed., *Orphisme et Orphée. En l'honneur de Jean Rudhardt*, Geneva, 13–30.

Bremmer, J. (2006) 'The Rise of the Hero Cult and the New Simonides', *ZPE* 158, 15–26.

Briggs, C. L. and Bauman, R. (1992) 'Genre, Intertextuality, and Social Power', *Journal of Linguistic Anthropology* 2.2, 131–72.

Brink, C. O. (1971) *Horace on Poetry*, vol. 2, Cambridge.

Briscoe, J. (2008) *A Commentary on Livy: Books 38–40*, Oxford.

Bruss, J. S. (2004) 'Lessons from Ceos: Written and Spoken Word in Callimachus', in Harder, Regtuit, and Wakker, eds, *Callimachus II*, Leuven, 49–69.

Bruss, J. S. (2005) *Hidden Presences: Monuments, Gravesites, and Corpses in Greek Funerary Epigram*, Hellenistica Groningana 10, Leuven, Paris, and Dudley MA.

Burck, E. (1984) *Historische und epische Tradition bei Silius Italicus*, Zetemata, Munich.

Burges Watson, S. (2013a) 'Muses of Lesbos or (Aeschylean) Muses of Pieria? Orpheus' Head on a Fifth-century Hydria', *GRBS* 53.3, 441–60.

Burges Watson, S. (2013b) 'Orpheus: A Guide to Selected Sources', *Living Poets*, Durham <https://livingpoets.dur.ac.uk/w/Orpheus:_A_Guide_to_Selected_Sources>.

Burges Watson, S. (2015) '*Mousikê* and Mysteries: A Nietzschean Reading of Aeschylus' *Bassarides*', *CQ* 65, 455–75.

Burke, S. (1992) *The Death and Return of the Author*, Edinburgh.

Burkert, W. (1985) *Greek Religion: Archaic and Classical*, Cambridge MA.

Burnett, A. P. (1983) *Three Archaic Poets: Archilochus, Alcaeus, Sappho*, London.

Burris, S., Fish, J., and Obbink, D. (2014) 'New Fragments of Book 1 of Sappho', *ZPE* 189, 1–28.

Burzachechi, M. (1962) 'Oggetti parlanti nelle epigrafi greche', *Epigraphica* 24, 3–54.

Butler, S. (2011) *The Matter of the Page: Essays in Search of Ancient and Medieval Authors*, Madison CT.

Cachey, T. J. (2002) *Petrarch's Guide to the Holy Land: Itinerary to the Sepulchre of Our Lord Jesus Christ*, Notre Dame.

Cairns, F. (1996) 'Asclepiades AP 5.85 = Gow-Page 2 again', *PLLS* 9, 323–6.

Calame, C. (1997) 'Figures of Sexuality and Initiatory Transition in the Serveni Theogony and its Commentary', in A. Laks and G. Most, eds, *Studies on the Derveni Papyrus*, Oxford.

Caldelli, Maria Letizia (1993) *L'Agon Capitolinus. Storia e protagonisti dall'istituzione domizianea al IV secolo*, Rome.

Camden, W. (1600) *Reges, Reginae, Nobiles et alii in Ecclesia Collegiata B. Petri Westmonasterii sepulti, usque ad annum reparatae salutis 1600*, London.

Camden, W. (1627) *Tomus Alter Annalium Rerum Anglicarum, et Hibernicarum, regnante Elizabetha*, London.

Cameron, A. (1968) 'The *Garlands* of Meleager and Philip', *GRBS* 9, 323–49.

Cameron, A. (1980) 'The Garland of Philip', *GRBS* 21, 43–62.

Cameron, A. (1993) *The Greek Anthology: From Meleager to Planudes*, Oxford.

Campbell, D. A. (1967) *Greek Lyric Poetry: A Selection of Early Greek Lyric, Elegiac and Iambic Poetry*, London.

Campbell, L. (2008) 'Garden Tombs in Roman Italy', *Arctos* 42, 31–43.

Campbell, V. (2008) 'Stopping to Smell the Roses: Garden Tombs in Roman Italy', *Arctos* 42, 31–43.

Capasso, M. (1983) *Il sepolcro di Virgilio*, Naples.

Carabell, P. (1995) 'Finito and Non-Finito in Titian's Last Paintings', *RES: Anthropology and Aesthetics* 28, 78–93.

Carabell, P. (2014) 'Figura Serpentinata: Becoming over Being in Michelangelo's Unfinished Works', *Artibus et Historiae* 69, 79–96.

Carlson, R. D. (2015) 'The Honey Bee and Apian Imagery in Classical Literature', PhD Diss., University of Washington.

Carrella, A. (2000) *La chiesa di Santa Maria del Parto a Mergellina*, Naples.

Caruso, G. (1999) 'Sepulcrum: Q. Sulpicius Maximus', in E. M. Steinby, ed., *Lexicon Topographicum Urbis Romae*, IV, *P-S*, Rome, 300 and 499 fig. 153.

Casali, S. (2006) 'The Poet at War: Ennius on the Field in Silius's *Punica*', *Arethusa* 39, 569–93.

Caviglia, F. (1990) 'Titiro', *Enciclopedia Virgiliana*, V*, Rome, 196–201.

Champlin, E. (2003) *Nero*, Cambridge MA and London.

Christian, T. (2015) *Gebildete Steine. Zur Rezeption literarischer Techniken in den Versinschriften seit dem Hellenismus*, Göttingen.

Chytraeus, N. (1594) *Variorum in Europa itinerum Deliciae seu ex variis manuscriptis selectiora tantum inscriptionum maxime recentum monumenta*, Herborn.

Ciofi, L. (1871) *Inscriptiones Latina et Graeca cum carmine Graeco extemporali Quinti Sulpicii Maximi in eius monumento nuper reperto ad portam Salariam, adjecta interpretatione Latina cum notis per Aloisium C.*, Rome, 2nd edn.

Ciofi, L. (1872) *Lectio inscriptionum in sepulchro Q. Sulpicii Maximi ad portam Salariam, iterum vindicata per Aloisium C.*, Rome.

Claassen, J.-M. (2008) *Ovid Revisited: The Poet in Exile*, London.

Clark, R. J. (1991) 'Vergil's Poetic Treatment of Cumaean Geography', *Vergilius* 37, 60–8.

Clark, W. (2006) *Academic Charisma and the Origins of the Research University*, Chicago IL.

Clay, D. (2004) *Archilochos Heros: The Cult of Poets in the Greek Polis*, Cambridge MA.

Clay, J. S. (2003) *Hesiod's Cosmos*, Cambridge.

Coarelli, F. (1972) 'Il Sepolcro degli Scipioni', *Dialoghi di Archaeologia* 6, 36–105.

Cocchia, E. (1889) *La Tomba di Virgilio. Contributo alla topografia dell'antica città di Napoli*, Turin.

Coldstream, J. N. (1976) 'Hero-Cults in the Age of Homer', *JHS* 96, 8–17.

Cole, T. (1969) 'The Saturnian Verse', *YCS* 21, 3–73.

Coleman, K. M. (1988) *Silvae IV*, Oxford.

Coleman, K. M. (2015) 'Hybrid identity in Flavian Rome: the case of Quintus Sulpicius Maximus', *Historical Research* 3, 186–88, 192.

Connolly, A. (1998) 'Was Sophocles Heroised as Dexion?', *JHS* 118, 1–21.

Conte, G. B. (2007) 'Aristaeus, Orpheus, and the *Georgics*: Once Again', in J. S. Harrison, ed., *The Poetry of Pathos: Studies in Virgilian Epic*, Oxford, 123–49.

Corrêa, P. de C. (2008) 'The Muses Buy a Cow', in Katsonopoulou, Petropoulos, and Katsarou (2008), 191–202.

Cosgrove, D. E. (2001) *Apollo's Eye*, Baltimore MD.

Cougny, E. (1890) *Epigrammatum Anthologia Palatina cum Planudeis et appendice nova epigrammatum veterum ex libris et marmoribus ductorum* [ . . . ], *III, instr. E. C.*, Paris.

Courtney, E. (1993) *The Fragmentary Latin Poets*, Oxford.

Croon, J. H. (1952) 'The Palici: An Autochthonous Cult in Ancient Sicily', *Mnemosyne* 5, 116–29.

Csapo, E. (2013) 'Comedy and the *Pompe*: Dionysian Genre-crossing', in E. Bakola, L. Prauscello, and M. Telò, eds, *Greek Comedy and the Discourse of Genres,* Cambridge, 40–80.

Csapo, E., and Wilson, P. (2015) 'Drama Outside Athens in the Fifth and Fourth Centuries BC', *Trends in Classics* 7, 316–95.

Culasso Gastaldi, E. (1979) 'Eschilo e l'Occidente', in L. Burelli et al., eds, *I tragici greci e l'Occidente*, Bologna, 19–89.

Currie, B. (2005) *Pindar and the Cult of Heroes*, Oxford.

Dahlmann, H. (1962) *Studien zu Varro 'De Poetis'*, Mainz.

Da Morano, N. G. (1871) *Le ricreazioni letterarie sui colli di Paussillipo e Mergellina, ossia una visita alle tombe di Virgilio di Sannazaro e di Leopardi. Libro di lettura amena*, Napoli.

Daraki, M. (1985) *Dionysos*, Paris.

Daraki, M. (1999) *Dionysos et la déesse Terre*, Paris.

D'Arms, J. H. (1970) *Romans on the Bay of Naples: A Social and Cultural Study of the Villas and their Owners from 150 B.C. to A.D. 400*, Cambridge MA.

Dart, J. (1723) *Westmonasterium, Or The History and Antiquities of the Abbey Church of St. Peter's Westminster*, vol. 1, London.

Davidson, J. (2003) 'Carcinus and the Temple: A Problem in the Athenian Theater', *CPh* 98, 109–22.

Davies, M. (2004) 'Simonides and the "grateful dead"', *Prometheus* 30, 275–81.

Day, J. (2010) *Archaic Greek Epigram and Dedication: Representation and Reperformance*, Cambridge.

Day, J. (2007) 'Inscribed Epigram in Pre-Hellenistic Literary Sources', in Bing and Bruss (2007), 29–48.

de Armas, F. A. (2002) 'Cervantes and the Virgilian Wheel: The Portrayal of a Literary Career', in P. Cheney and F. A. de Armas, eds, *European Literary Careers: The Author from Antiquity to the Renaissance*, Toronto, 268–86.

Degrassi, A., ed. (1965) *Inscriptiones Latinae liberae rei publicae. Imagines*, Berlin.

De Jong, I., and Sullivan, J. P., eds (1994) *Modern Critical Theory and Classical Literature*, Leiden.

Del Corso, L. (2010) 'Scritture epigrafiche e scritture su papiro in età ellenistico-romana. Spunti per un confronto', in A. Bravo García and I. Pérez Martín, eds, *The Legacy of Bernard de Montfaucon: Three Hundred Years of Studies on Greek Handwriting*, Turnhout, 3–16, 661–8.

Della Corte, F. (1984) 'Creteo', *Enciclopedia virgiliana*, I [A-DA], Rome, 930.

Deramaix, M. and Laschke, B. (1992) '"Maroni musa proximus et tumulo". L'église et le tombeau de Jacques Sannazar', *Revue de l'art* 95, 25–39.

Desport, M. (1952) 'L'incantation virgilienne. Essai sur les mythes du poète enchanteur et leur influence dans l'oeuvre de Virgile', PhD Diss., Bordeaux.

Dessau, H., ed. (1892: I), (1902: II/1), (1906: II/2), (1916: III) *Inscriptiones Latinae selectae*, Berolini.

Detienne, M. (1986) 'Dionysos et ses parousies. Un dieu épidémique', in C. Bérard and C. Bron, eds, *L'Association dionysiaque dans les sociétés anciennes, Collection de l' école francaise de Rome* 89, Rome, 53–83.

Didi-Huberman, G. (1999) 'Wax Flesh, Viscous Circles', in M. Von Düring, G. Didi-Huberman, and M. Poggesi, eds, *Encyclopaedia Anatomica: A Complete Collection of Anatomical Waxes.* Cologne, 64–74.

Dilthey, C. (1869) 'Sarcofaghi di Medea', *Annali dell'Instituto di Corrispondenza Archeologica* 41, 5–69.

Di Marco, M. (1993) 'Dioniso ed Orfeo nelle *Bassaridi* di Eschilo', in A. Masaracchia, ed., *Orfeo e l'orfismo*, Rome, 101–53.

Dimmick, J. (2002) 'Ovid in the Middle Ages', in P. R. Hardie, ed., *The Cambridge Companion to Ovid*, Cambridge, 264–87.

Dinter, M. (2005) 'Epic and Epigram: Minor Heroes in Virgil's *Aeneid*', *CQ* 55.1, 153–69.

Dinter, M. (2013) 'Epitaphic Gestures in Statius and Silius Italicus', in A. Augustakis, ed., *Ritual and Religion in Flavian Epic*, Oxford, 267–83.

Divenuto, F. (2009) '"Deos nemorum invocat in extruenda domo". Iacopo Sannazaro e la sua casa a Mergellina', in P. Sabbatino, ed., *Jacopo Sannazaro. la cultura napoletana nell'Europa del Rinascimento*, Florence, 237–60.

Döpp, S. (1996) 'Das Stegreifgedicht des Q. Sulpicius Maximus', *ZPE* 114, 99–114.

Dolansky, F. (2011) 'Honouring the Family Dead on the Parentalia: Ceremony, Spectacle and Memory', *Phoenix* 65, 125–57.

D'Ovidio, S. (2014) 'The Crypta Neapolitana: Perception of a Roman Tunnel throughout History', in L. Kouneni, ed., *The Legacy of Antiquity: New Perspectives in the Reception of the Classical World*, Newcastle upon Tyne, 8–27.

Dover, K. J. (1989) *Greek Homosexuality*, Cambridge MA, 2nd edn.

Dover, K. J., ed. (1993) *Aristophanes Frogs*, Oxford.

Duffett, M. (2013) *Understanding Fandom: An Introduction to the Study of Media Fan Culture*, London.

Dyer, R. (2000) *Suda* entry: σ441 Adler Σιμωνίδης. *Suda Online*, <http://www.stoa.org/sol/> (consulted 2/4/15).

Eagle, R. (1956) 'The Search for Spenser's Grave', *Notes & Queries* 201, 282–3.

Edmonds, J. M. (1931) 'Simmias XI, 6, Epitaph on Sophocles', *PCPhS* 7, 148–50.

Edmonds, R. G. III (2013) *Redefining Ancient Orphism: A Study in Greek Religion*, Cambridge.

Edmunds, L. (1981) 'The Cults and Legends of Oedipus', *HSPh* 85, 221–38.

Egerton, J. (1990) *Wright of Derby*, London.

Ekroth, G. (1999) 'Pausanias and the Sacrificial Rituals of Greek Hero-Cults', in R. Hägg, ed., *Ancient Greek Hero Cult: Proceedings of the Fifth International Seminar on Ancient Greek Cult*, Stockholm, 145–58.

Ekroth, G. (2002) *The Sacrificial Rituals of Greek Hero-cults in the Archaic to the Early Hellenistic Periods*, Liège.

Ekroth, G. (2007) 'Heroes and Hero-Cults', in D. Ogden, ed., *A Companion to Greek Religion*, Malden MA, 100–14.

Elsner, J. (1995) *Art and the Roman Viewer: The Transformation of Art from the Pagan World to Christianity*, Cambridge.

Engels, D. and Nicolaye, C., eds (2008) *Ille operum custos. Kulturgeschichtliche Beiträge zur antiken Bienensymbolik und ihrer Rezeption*, Spudasmata118, Hildesheim, Zurich, and New York.

Erll, A. (2011) *Memory in Culture*, S. B. Young, trans., Basingstoke and New York.

Erskine, A. (2002) 'Life after Death: Alexandria and the Body of Alexander', *G&R* 49, 163–79.

Eustace, J. C. (1815) *A Classical Tour through Italy*, 4 vols, London, 3rd edn.

Fantham, E. (2006) '*Dic si quid potes de Sexto Annali*: The Literary Legacy of Ennius's Pyrrhic War', *Arethusa* 39.3, 549–68.

Fantuzzi, M. (2007) 'Epigram and the Theatre', in Bing and Bruss (2007), 477–96.

Fantuzzi, M. (2008) 'La doppia gloria di Menas (e di Filostrato)', in A. M. Morelli, ed., *Epigramma longum. da Marziale alla tarda antichità*, Cassino, 603–22.

Fantuzzi, M. (2010) 'Typologies of Variation on a Theme in Archaic and Classical Metrical Inscriptions', in Baumbach, Petrovic, and Petrovic (2010), 289–310.

Fantuzzi, M. and Hunter, R. (2004) *Tradition and Innovation in Hellenistic Poetry*, Cambridge.

Faraone, C. (2004) 'Orpheus' Final Performance: Necromancy and a Singing Head on Lesbos', *SIFC* 97, 5–27.

Farley, P. and Symmons Roberts, M. (2017) *Deaths of the Poets*, London.

Farnell, L. R. (1921) *Greek Hero Cults and Ideas of Immortality*, Oxford.

Farrell, J. (1999) 'The Ovidian *corpus*: Poetic Body and Poetic Text', in Hardie, Barchiesi, and Hinds (1993), 127–41.

Fayant, M.-C. (2014) *Hymnes Orphiques*, Paris.

Fearn, D. (2013) '*Kleos* vs. Stone? Lyric Poetry and Contexts for Memorialization', in Liddel and Low (2013), 231–53.

Feeney, D. (1982) 'A Commentary on Silius Italicus Book 1', DPhil. Diss., University of Oxford.

Felici, L. (2009) 'Theodor Zwinger's *Methodus Apodemica*: An Observatory of the City as Political Space in the Late Sixteenth Century', *Cromohs* 14, 1–18.

Felton, D. (2007) 'The Dead', in D. Ogden, ed., *A Companion to Greek Religion*, Malden MA and Oxford, 86–99.

Fendt, T. (1574) *Monumenta sepulchrorum cum epigraphis ingenio et doctrina excellentium virorum aliorumque tam prisci quam nostri seculi memorabilium hominum*, Vratislava [Breslau].

Feraudi-Gruénais, F. (2001) *Ubi diutius nobis habitandum est. Die Innendekoration der kaiserzeitlichen Gräber Roms, Palilia* 9, Wiesbaden.

Fernández Delgado, J. A. and Ureña Bracero, J. (1991) *Un testimonio de la educación literaria griega en época romana: IG XIV 2012 = Kaibel, EG 618*, Badajoz.

Ferrari, F. (2014) 'Saffo e i suoi fratelli e altri brani del primo libro', *ZPE* 192, 1–19.

Ferrari, G. (2004) 'The *"anodos"* of the Bride', in D. Yatromanolakis and P. Roilos, eds, *Greek Ritual Poetics*, Cambridge MA, 245–60.

Festugière, A.-J. (1973) 'Tragédie et tombes sacrées', *RHR* 184, 3–24.

Flower, H. (1996) *Ancestor Masks and Aristocratic Power in Roman Culture*, Oxford.

Foley, H. P. (1992) '*Anodos* Dramas: Euripides' *Alcestis* and *Helen*', in R. Hexter and D. Selden, eds, *Innovations of Antiquity*, New York, 133–60.

Fontannaz, D. (2008) 'L'ENTRE-DEUX-MONDES: Orphée et Eurydice sur une hydrie proto-Italiote du sanctuaire de la source à Saturo', *Antike Kunst* 51, 41–72.

Ford, A. (2002) *The Origins of Criticism: Literary Culture and Poetic Theory in Classical Greece*, Princeton NJ.

Fortuna, S. (1993) 'Sofocle, Sositeo, il dramma satiresco (Dioscoride, *AP* VII 37 e 707)', *Aevum(ant)* 6, 237–49.

Fowler, D. P. (1989) 'First Thoughts on Closure: Problems and Prospects', *Materiale e Discussione* 22, 75–122, reprinted in Fowler (2000), 239–83.

Fowler, D. P. (1994) 'Postmodernism, Romantic Irony and Classical Closure', in De Jong and Sullivan (1994), 231–56, reprinted in Fowler (2000), 5–34.

Fowler, D. P. (1997) 'Second Thoughts on Closure', in Roberts, Dunn, and Fowler (1997), 3–22, reprinted in Fowler (2000), 284–308.

Fowler, D. P. (2000) *Roman Constructions: Readings in Postmodern Latin*, Oxford.

Fraenkel, E. (1954) 'VRBEM QVAM STATVO VESTRA EST', *Glotta* 33, 157–9.

Fränkel, H. (1975) *Early Greek Poetry and Philosophy*, M. Hadas and J. Willis, trans., Oxford.

Fragonard, J.-H. and Robert, H. (1771) *Différentes vues dessinées d'après nature dans les environs de Rome et de Naples*, printed by Pierre François Basan, Paris.

Frank, T. (1930) *Life and Literature in the Roman Republic*, Berkeley.

Fratantuono, L. (2012) *Madness Triumphant: A Reading of Lucan's* Pharsalia, Lanham MD.

Frederiksen, M. (1984) *Campania*, London.

Freeman, P. (1998) 'The Saturnian Verse and Early Latin Poetics', *JIES* 26, 61–90.

Frings, I. (1998) '*Mantua me genuit*. Vergils Grabepigramm auf Stein und Pergament', *ZPE* 123, 89–100.

Fuscano, I. B. (1531) *Stanze sopra le bellezze di Napoli*, Rome.

Fuscano, I. B. (2007) *Stanze sopra le bellezze di Napoli*, C. A. Adesso, ed., Naples.

Gabathuler, M. (1937) *Hellenistische Epigramme auf Dichter*, Diss. Basel, Leipzig.

Gadamer, H.-G. (1975) *Truth and Method*, G. Barden and J. Cumming, trans., New York.

Gaifman, M. (2013) 'Timelessness, Fluidity, and Apollo's Libation', *RES: Anthropology & Aesthetics* 63/64, Wet/Dry, 39–76.

Galán Vioque, G. (2001) *Dioscórides, Epigramas. Introducción, edición critica, traducción y comentario filológico*, Huelva.

Ganiban, R. (2010) 'Virgil's Dido and the Heroism of Hannibal', in A. Augoustakis, ed., *Brill's Companion to Silius Italicus*, Leiden and Boston, 73–98.

Gantz, T. (1993) *Early Greek Myth: A Guide to Literary and Artistic Sources*, Baltimore MD.

Garulli, V. (2007) 'Callimaco e Simonide. Ancora sul fr.64 Pf.', *Eikasmos* 18, 251–63.

Garulli, V. (2012) *Byblos lainee. Epigrafia, letteratura, epitafio*, Bologna.

Garulli, V. (2014) 'Stones as Books: The Layout of Hellenistic Inscribed Poems', in Harder, Regtuit, and Wakker (2014), 125–69.

Genette, G. (1983) *Narrative Discourse: An Essay in Method*, Jane E. Lewin, trans., Ithaca NY.

Genette, G. (1997) *Paratexts: Thresholds of Interpretation*, Cambridge.

Gercke, W. (1968) *Untersuchungen zum Römischen Kinderporträt*, Hamburg.

Gerritsen, W. (2003) 'Hoefnagel en Ortelius zwervend door Europa', *Omslag. Bulletin van de universiteitsbibliotheek Leiden en het Scaligerinstituut* 2, 5–8.

Ghisalberti, F. (1946) 'Mediaeval Biographies of Ovid', *JWI* 9, 10–59.

Godman, P. (1995) 'Ovid's Sex-Life: Classical Forgery and Medieval Poetry', *Poetica* 27, 101–12.

Goldberg, S. (1995) *Epic in Republican Rome*, Oxford.

Goldhill, S. (1994) 'The Naïve and Knowing Eye: Ecphrasis and the Culture of Viewing in the Hellenistic World', in S. Goldhill and R. Osborne, eds, *Art and Text in Ancient Greek Culture*, Cambridge, 197–223.

Goldschmidt, N. (2013) *Shaggy Crowns: Ennius' Annales and Virgil's Aeneid*, Oxford.

Goldschmidt, N. (forthcoming) *Afterlives of the Roman Poets: Biofiction and the Reception of Latin Poetry*, Cambridge.

Gordon, A. E. (1958) *Album of Dated Latin Inscriptions: Rome and the Neighborhood, Augustus to Nerva*, in collaboration with J. S. Gordon, Berkeley and Los Angeles CA.

Gow, A. S. F. and Page, D. L., eds (1965) *The Greek Anthology: Hellenistic Epigrams*, 2 vols, Cambridge.

Gow, A. S. F. and Page, D. L., eds (1968) *The Greek Anthology: The Garland of Philip and Some Contemporary Epigrams*, 2 vols, Cambridge.

Graf, F. (1974) *Eleusis und die orphische Dichtung Athens in vorhellenistischer Zeit*, Berlin.

Graf, F. (1980) 'Milch, Honig und Wein. Zum verständnis der Libation im griechischen Ritual', in *Perennitas. Studi in onore di Angelo Brelich promossi dalla Cattedra di Religioni del mondo classicso dell' Università degli Studi di Roma*, Rome, 209–21.

Graf, F. (1987) 'Orpheus: A Poet among Men', in J. Bremmer, ed., *Interpretations of Greek Mythology*, London, 80–106.

Graf, F. (2003) 'Hero Cult', in H. Cancik, H. Schneider, and M. Landfester, eds, *Brill's New Pauly*, vol. 2, Leiden.

Graf, F. and Johnston, S. I. (2007) *Ritual Texts for the Afterlife*, London.

Grant, M., trans. (1971) *Cicero: On the Good Life*, London.

Graziosi, B. (2002) *Inventing Homer: The Early Reception of Epic*, Cambridge.

Green, J. R. (1990) 'Carcinus and the Temple: A Lesson in the Staging of Tragedy', *GRBS* 31, 281–5.

Grewing, F. F., Acosta-Hughes, B., and Kirichenko, A., eds (2013) *The Door Ajar: False Closure in Greek and Roman Literature and Art,* Heidelberg.

Griffin, J. (1979) 'Virgil, the Fourth *Georgic* and Rome', *G&R* 26, 61–80.

Griffin, J. (1980) *Homer on Life and Death*, Oxford.

Griffith, M. (1978) 'Aeschylus, Sicily, and Prometheus', in R. Dawe, J. Diggle, and P. E. Easterling, eds, *Dionysiaca: Nine Studies in Greek Poetry by Former Pupils, Presented to Denys Page on his Seventieth Birthday*, Cambridge, 105–39.

Griffith, M. (2013) *Aristophanes' Frogs*, Oxford.

Gruen, E. (1992) *Culture and National Identity in Republican Rome*, Ithaca NY.

Guardì, T. (1990) 'L'attività teatrale nella Siracusa di Gerone I', *Dioniso* 51, 25–47.

Guentner, W. A. (1993) 'British Aesthetic Discourse, 1780–1830: The Sketch, the Non Finito, and the Imagination', *Art Journal* 52.2, 40–7.

Gurd, S. A. (2007) 'Meaning and Material Presence: Four Epigrams on Timomachus' Unfinished Medea', *TAPA* 137.2, 305–31.

Guthrie, W. (1952) *Orpheus and Greek Religion: A Study of the Orphic Movement*, London.

Gutzwiller, K. (1997a) 'Genre Development and Gendered Voices in Erinna and Nossis', in Y. Prins and M. Shreiber, eds, *Dwelling in Possibility: Women Poets and Critics on Poetry*, Ithaca NY, 202–22.

Gutzwiller, K. (1997b) 'The Poetics of Editing in Meleager's *Garland*', *TAPA* 127, 169–200.

Gutzwiller, K. (1998) *Poetic Garlands: Hellenistic Epigrams in Context*, Hellenistic Culture and Society 28, Berkeley CA.

Gutzwiller, K. (2002) 'Art's Echo: The Tradition of Hellenistic Ecphrastic Epigram', in Harder, Regtuit, and Wakker (2002), 85–112.

Gutzwiller, K. (2010a) 'Literary Criticism', in J. J. Clauss and M. Cuypers, eds, *A Companion to Hellenistic Literature*, Malden NJ.

Gutzwiller, K. (2010b) 'Heroic Epitaphs of the Classical Age: The Aristotelian *Peplos* and Beyond', in Baumbach, Petrovic, and Petrovic (2010), 219–49.

Gutzwiller, K. (2014) 'Anacreon, Hellenistic Epigram and the Anacreontic Poet', in M. Baumbach and N. Dümmler, eds, *Imitate Anacreon! Mimesis, Poiesis and the Poetic Inspiration in the Carmina Anacreontea*, Berlin, 47–66.

Haarløv, B. (1977) *The Half-Open Door: A Common Symbolic Motif within Roman Sepulchral Sculpture*, Odense.

Habash, M. (1995) 'Two Complementary Festivals in Aristophanes' *Acharnians*', *AJPh* 116, 559–77.

Habicht, C. (1998) *Pausanias' Guide to Ancient Greece*, Sather Classical Lectures 50, Berkeley and Los Angeles CA.

Habinek, T. (1990) 'Sacrifice, Society, and Vergil's Ox-born Bees', in M. Griffith and D. J. Mastronarde, eds, *Cabinet of the Muses*, Berkeley and Los Angeles CA, 209–23.

Hackworth Petersen, L. (2006) *The Freedman in Roman Art and Art History*, Cambridge.

Hadfield, A. (2012) *Edmund Spenser: A Life*, Oxford.

Hägg, R. and Alroth, B., eds (2005) *Greek Sacrificial Ritual, Olympian and Chthonian, Proceedings of the Sixth International Seminar on Ancient Greek Cult*, Stockholm.

Hall, E. (2006) 'Casting the Role of Trygaios in Aristophanes' *Peace*', in E. Hall, *The Theatrical Cast of Athens: Interactions between Modern Greek Drama and Society*, Oxford, 321–52.

Hamilakis, Y. (2007) *The Nation and its Ruins*, Oxford.

Hamilton, W. and D'Hancarville, P. F. H. (1766–7) *Collection of Etruscan, Greek, and Roman Antiquities from the Cabinet of the Hon. W. Hamilton his Brittanick Majesty's Envoy Extraordinary at the Court of Naples; Antiquités Etrusques, Grecques, et Romaines Tirées du Cabinet de M. Hamilton. . . .* Naples [but 1766–76].

Hanink, J. (2008) 'Literary Politics and the Euripidean *Vita*', *CCJ* 54, 115–35.

Hanink, J. (2010) 'The Classical Tragedians, from Athenian Idols to Wandering Poets', in I. Gildenhard and M. Revermann, eds, *Beyond the Fifth Century: Interactions with Greek Tragedy from the Fourth Century BCE to the Middle Ages,* Berlin, 39–68.

Hanink, J. (2014) *Lycurgan Athens and the Making of Classical Tragedy,* Cambridge.

Hanink, J. and Uhlig, A. S. (2016) '"My poetry did not die with me": Aeschylus and his Afterlife in the Classical Period', in S. Constantinidis and B. Heiden, eds, *The Reception of Aeschylus' Plays through Shifting Models and Frontiers,* Leiden, 51–79.

Hansen, P. A., ed. (1983) *Carmina epigraphica Graeca saeculorum VIII–V a. Chr.N.,* Berlin.

Hantelmann, D. von (2014) 'The Experiential Turn', in E. Carpenter, ed., *On Performability, Living Collections Catalogue* 1.2, Walker Art Center, <http://walkerart.org/collections/publications/performativity/experiential-turn>.

Harder, M. A. (1998) '"Generic Games" in Callimachus' *Aetia*', in M. A. Harder, R. F. Regtuit, and G. C. Wakker, eds, *Genre in Hellenistic Poetry,* Groningen, 95–113.

Harder, M. A. (2012) *Callimachus*: Aetia, Oxford.

Harder, M. A., Regtuit, R. F., and Wakker, G. C., eds (2002) *Hellenistic Epigrams, Hellenistica Groningana* 6, Leuven.

Harder, M. A., Regtuit, R. F., and Wakker, G. C., eds (2014) *Hellenistic Poetry in Context, Hellenistica Groningana* 20, Leuven.

Hardie, P. R. (1986) *Virgil's Aeneid: Cosmos and Imperium,* Oxford.

Hardie, P. R. (1993) *The Epic Successors of Virgil: A Study in the Dynamics of a Tradition,* Cambridge.

Hardie, P. R. (2002) *Ovid's Poetics of Illusion,* Cambridge.

Hardie, P. R. (2012) *Rumour and Renown: Representations of 'Fama' in Western Literature,* Cambridge.

Hardie, P., Barchiesi, A., and Hinds, S., eds (1999) *Ovidian Transformations: Essays on Ovid's Metamorphoses and its Reception, PCPhS Suppl.* 23, Cambridge.

Hardie, P. R. and Moore, H., eds (2010) *Classical Literary Careers and their Reception,* Cambridge.

Harding, P. (1994) *Androtion and the Atthis,* Oxford.

Harissis, H. V. (2009) 'Aristaeus, Eurydice and the Ox-Born Bee: An Ancient Educational Beekeeping Myth', in H. V. Harissis and A. V. Harissis, eds, *Apiculture in the Prehistoric Aegean. Minoan and Mycenaean Symbols Revisited, BAR International Series 1958,* Oxford.

Harrison, J. E. (1908) *Prolegomena to the Study of Greek Religion,* Cambridge, 2nd edn.

Hartung, J. A., ed. and trans. (1857) *Die griechische Lyriker,* vol. 6, Leipzig.

Heath, J. (1994) 'The Failure of Orpheus', *TAPA* 124, 163–96.

Heizmann, J. (2016) '*Der Tod des Vergil*', in M. Kessler and P. M. Lützeler, eds, *Hermann Broch Handbuch*, Berlin, 167–97.

Helbig, W. (1966) *Führer durch die öffentlichen Sammlungen klassischer Altertümer in Rom*, II. *Die städtischen Sammlungen Kapitolinische Museen und Museo Barracco* [ . . . ], Tübingen, 4th edn.

Hellekson, K. and Busse, K., eds (2014) *The Fan Fiction Studies Reader*, Iowa City.

Henderson, J., ed. and trans. (2002) *Aristophanes*, vol. IV (*Frogs, Assemblywomen, Wealth*), Cambridge MA and London.

Hendon, J. A. (2000) 'Having and Holding: Storage, Memory, Knowledge, and Social Relations', *American Anthropologist* 102.1, 42–53.

Hendrickson, T. (2013) 'Poetry and Biography in the Athenaion Politeia: The Case of Solon', *CJ* 109, 1–19.

Hendrix, H. (2013) 'Topographies of Poetry: Mapping Early Modern Naples', in M. Calaresu and H. Hills, eds, *New Approaches to Naples c.1500–c.1800: The Power of Place*, Farnham, 81–101.

Hendrix, H. (2014) 'Plagio e commercio nelle guide tardocinquecentesche dedicate a Napoli e Pozzuoli', *Incontri. Rivista europea di studi italiani* 29, 41–53.

Hendrix, H. (2015) 'City Branding and the Antique: Naples in Early Modern City Guides', in J. Hughes and C. Buongiovanni, eds, *Remembering Partenope: The Reception of Classical Naples from Antiquity to the Present*, Oxford, 217–41.

Hendrix, H. (2018) 'Epigraphy and Blurring Senses of the Past in Early Modern Travelling Men of Letters', in K. Ottenheym and K. Enenkel, eds, *The Quest for an Appropriate Past*, Leiden and Boston (in press).

Henrichs, A. (1991) 'Namenlosigkeit und Euphemismus. Zur Ambivalenz der chthonischen Mächte im attischen Drama', in H. Hofmann and A. Harder, eds, *Fragmenta dramatica. Beiträge zur Interpretation der griechischen Tragikerfragmente und ihrer Wirkungsgeschichte*, Göttingen, 161–201.

Henrichs, A. (1993) 'The Tomb of Aias and the Prospect of Hero Cult in Sophokles', *ClAnt* 12, 165–80.

Henry, O. and Kelp, U., eds (2016) *Tumulus as Sema: Space, Politics, Culture and Religion in the First Millenium BC*, 2 vols, Berlin.

Henzen, G. (1871) 'Sepolcri antichi rinvenuti alla porta Salaria', *Bullettino dell'Instituto di Corrispondenza Archeologica* 5 (May), 98–115.

Herington, C. J. (1967) 'Aeschylus in Sicily', *JHS* 87, 74–85.

Heslin, P. J. (2018) *Propertius, Greek Myth, and Virgil: Rivalry, Allegory, and Polemic*, Oxford.

Heubeck, A. and Hoekstra, A. (1989) *A Commentary on Homer's Odyssey*, vol. 2, Oxford.

Heurgon, J. (1932) 'Orphée et Eurydice avant Virgile', *Mélanges d'archéologie et d'histoire* 49, 6–60.

Hexter, R. (1999) 'Ovid's Body', in J. Porter, ed., *Constructions of the Classical Body*, Michigan, 327–54.

Hexter, R. (2011) 'Shades of Ovid: Pseudo- (and para-) Ovidiana in the Middle Ages', in J. G. Clark, F. Coulson, and K. McKinley, eds, *Ovid in the Middle Ages*, Cambridge, 285–309.

Heyworth, G. (2009) *Desiring Bodies: Ovidian Romance and the Cult of Form*, Notre Dame.

Highet, G. (1957) *Poets in a Landscape*, London.

Hinds, S. (1987) *The Metamorphosis of Persephone: Ovid and the Self-conscious Muse*, Cambridge.

Hinds, S. (1998) *Allusion and Intertext: Dynamics of Appropriation in Roman Poetry*, Cambridge.

Hinz, V. (1998) *Der Kult von Demeter und Kore auf Sizilien und in der Magna Graecia*, Wiesbaden.

Hirsch, E. (1966) 'Zum Kranz des Philippos', *Wissenschaftliche Zeitschrift der Universität Halle* 16, 401–17.

Hodder, I. (2012) *Entangled: An Archaeology of the Relationships between Humans and Things*, Malden.

Hölscher, T. (2009) 'Architectural Sculpture: Messages? Programs? Towards Rehabilitating the Notion of "Decoration"', in P. Schultz and R. Von den Hoff, eds, *Structure, Image, Ornament: Architectural Sculpture in the Greek World, Proceedings of an International Conference Held at the American School of Classical Studies, 27–28 November 2004*, Oxford and Oakville, 54–67.

Höschele, R. (2006) *Verrückt nach Frauen. Der Epigrammatiker Rufin*, Tübingen.

Höschele, R. (2007) 'The Traveling Reader: Journeys through Ancient Epigram Books', *TAPA* 137, 333–69.

Höschele, R. (2010) *Die blütenlesende Muse: Poetik und Textualität antiker Epigrammsammlungen, Classica Monacensia, Münchener Studien zur Klassischen Philologie* 37, Tübingen.

Höschele, R. (2013) '"If I am from Syria—So What?": Meleager's Cosmo-poetics', in S. Ager and R. Faber, eds, *Belonging and Isolation in the Hellenistic World*, Toronto, 19–32.

Höschele, R. (2014) 'Honestus' Heliconian Flowers: Epigrammatic Offerings to the Muses at Thespiai', in Harder, Regtuit, and Wakker (2014), 171–94.

Höschele, R. (2017) '"Harvesting from a New Page": Philip of Thessalonike's Editorial Untertaking', *Aitia* 7.1 <http://journals.penedition.org/aitia/1727>.

Höschele, R. (forthcoming) 'A Garland of Freshly Grown Flowers: The Poetics of Editing in Philip's *Stephanos*', in C. Carey, M. Kanellou, and I. Petrovic, eds, *Reading Greek Epigram from the Hellenistic to the Early Byzantine Era*, Oxford.

Horsfall, N. M. (1993) 'Empty Shelves on the Palatine', *G&R* 40.1, 58–67.

Horsfall, N. M. (1995) *A Companion to the Study of Virgil*, Mnemosyne Suppl. 151, Leiden.

Horsfall, N. M. (2000) *Virgil Aeneid 7: A Commentary*, Leiden.

Horsfall, N. M. (2008–9) 'Dictys's Ephemeris and the Parody of Scholarship', *ICS*, 33–4, 41–63.

Horsfall, N. M. (2013) *Virgil, Aeneid 6: A Commentary*, Berlin.

Hosking, G. A. and Schöpflin, G., eds (1997) *Myths of Polish Nationhood*, New York.

Hughes, C. J. (2008) 'Buried in the Churchyard: A Good Story, at Least', *New York Times*, 12th December.

Hulls, J.-M. (2011) 'Re-Casting the Master: Further Faces of Virgil in Imperial Rome', *PVS* 27, 155–83.

Hunter, R. (1996) *Theocritus and the Archaeology of Greek Poetry*, Cambridge.

Hunter, R. (2009) *Critical Moments in Classical Literature: Studies in the Ancient View of Literature and its Uses,* Cambridge.

Hutton, W. (2005) *Describing Greece: Landscape and Literature in the Periegesis of Pausanias*, Cambridge.

Ingleheart, J. (2012) 'Ovid's *scripta puella*: Perilla as Poetic and Political Fiction in *Tristia* 3.7', *CQ* 62.1, 227–41.

Inglis, F. (2010) *A Short History of Celebrity*, Princeton NJ.

Inglis, F. (2015) 'City Branding and the Antique: Naples in Early Modern City Guides', in J. Hughes and C. Buongiovanni, eds, *Remembering Parthenope: The Reception of Classical Naples from Antiquity to the Present*, Oxford, 217–41.

Isager, S. and Pedersen, P., eds (2004) *The Salmakis Inscription and Hellenistic Halikarnassos*, Odense.

Iser, W. (1978) *The Act of Reading: A Theory of Aesthetic Response*, Baltimore MD.

Jaeger, M. (1997) *Livy's Written Rome*, Ann Arbor MI.

Jaeger, M. (2002) 'Cicero and Archimedes' Tomb', *JRS* 92, 49–61.

James, E. O. (1961) *Seasonal Feasts and Festivals*, London.

Jansen, L., ed. (2014) *The Roman Paratext: Frame, Texts, Readers*, Cambridge.

Jardine, L. (1995) *Erasmus Man of Letters: The Construction of Charisma in Print*, Princeton NJ.

Jashemski, F. W. (1970–1) 'Tomb Gardens at Pompeii', *CJ* 66, 2, 97–115.

Jauss, H. R. (1982) *Toward an Aesthetic of Reception*, T. Bahti, trans.; introduction by P. de Man, Minneapolis MN.

Jenkins, H. (1992) *Textual Poachers: Television Fans and Participatory Culture*, New York.

Jenkyns, R. (1998) *Virgil's Experience: Nature and History; Times, Names, and Places*, Oxford.

Johannowsky, W. (1952) 'Contributi alla topografia della Campania antica', *Rendiconti della Accademia di Archeologia, Lettere e Belle Arti 27*, Naples, 84–146.

Johnston, S. I. (1999) *Restless Dead: Encounters between the Living and the Dead in Ancient Greece*, Berkeley CA.

Jones, C. P. (2010) *New Heroes in Antiquity From Achilles to Antinoos*, Cambridge MA.

Jones, N. F. (2004) *Rural Athens under the Democracy*, Philadelphia.

Jones, N. F. (2015) 'Androtion of Athens (324)', in I. Worthington, ed., *Brill's New Jacoby* <http://referenceworks.brillonline.com.ezphost.dur.ac.uk/browse/brill-s-new-jacoby>.

Joyce, H. E. (2002) 'From Darkness to Light: Annibale Carracci, Bellori, and Ancient Painting', in Bell and Willette (2002), 170–88.

Julvécourt, P. de (1832) *Mes souvenirs de bonheur, ou, Neuf mois en Italie*, Paris.

Kaibel, G. (1878) *Epigrammata Graeca ex lapidibus conlecta*, Berolini.

Kania, R. (2016) *Virgil's Eclogues and the Art of Fiction: A Study of the Poetic Imagination*, Cambridge.

Katsonopoulou, D., Petropoulos, I., and Katsarou, S., eds (2008) *Archilochus and his Age, Proceedings of the Second International Conference on the Archaeology of Paros and the Cyclades, Paroikia, Paros, 7–9 October 2005*, Paros 2, Athens.

Kay, N. M. (1985) *Martial Book XI: A Commentary*, London.

Kearns, E. (1989) *The Heroes of Attica, BICS Supplement 57*, London.

Kermode, F. (2000) *The Sense of an Ending: Studies in the Theory of Fiction*, Oxford, 2nd edn.

Kimmel-Clauzet, F. (2013) *Morts, tombeaux et cultes des poètes grecs. Étude de la survie des grands poètes des époques archaïque et classique en Grèce ancienne*, Bordeaux.

Kirstein, R. (2002) 'Companion Pieces in the Hellenistic Epigram (Call. 21 and 35 Pf; Theoc. 7 and 15 Gow; Mart. 2.91 and 2.92; Ammianos *AP* 11.230 and 11.231)', in Harder, Regtuit, and Wakker (2002), 113–35.

Kivilo, M. (2010) *Early Greek Poets' Lives: The Shaping of the Tradition*, Leiden and Boston.

Kleiner, D. E. E. (1987) *Roman Imperial Funerary Altars with Portraits*, Rome.

Klooster, J. (2011) *Poetry as Window and Mirror: Positioning the Poet in Hellenistic Poetry*, Leiden.

Klopsch, P., ed. (1967) *Pseudo-Ovidius, De vetula. Untersuchungen und Text*, Leiden.

Knauer, O. (1935) 'Die Epigramme des Asklepiades von Samos. Text und Kommentar', Diss. Tübingen (reprinted in S. L. Tarán, ed. (1987) *The Greek Anthology*, New York, vol. 2).

Kontoleon, N. M. (1952) 'Νέαι Ἐπιγραφαὶ περὶ Ἀρχιλόχου ἐκ Πάρου', *ArchEph*, 32–95.

Kontoleon, N. M. (1956) 'Archiloque d'apres la nouvelle inscription de Paros', *L'Hellénisme contemporain* 10, 397–406.

Kossatz-Deissmann, A. (1978) *Dramen des Aischylos auf westgriechischen Vasen*, Mainz.

Kouremenos, T., Parássoglou, G., and Tsantsanoglou, K., eds (2006) *The Derveni Papyrus: Edited with Introduction and Commentary*, Florence.

Kowalzig, B. (2007) 'The Aetiology of Empire? Hero-Cult and Athenian Tragedy', in J. Davidson, F. Muecke, and P. Wilson, eds, *Greek Drama III: Essays in Honour of Keven Lee, BICS Supplement* 87, London, 79–98.

Kowalzig, B. (2008) 'Nothing to Do with Demeter, Something to Do with Sicily! Theatre and Society in the Greek West', in O. Revermann and P. Wilson, eds, *Performance, Iconography, Reception: Studies in Honour of Oliver Taplin*, Oxford, 128–57.

Kramer, R. (2008) *Unfinished Music*, Oxford.

Kraus, C. S. (1994) '"No Second Troy": Topoi and Refoundation in Livy, Book V', *TAPA* 124, 267–89.

Krieken, R. van (2011) *Celebrity Society*, London.

Kubíková, B., ed. (2010) *Monumenta Sepulcrorum*, E. Mellander, trans., Prague.

Kwapisz, J. (2013) *The Greek Figure Poems. Hellenistica Groningana* 19, Leuven, Paris, and Walpole.

Kyriakidēs, S. (1998) *Narrative Structure and Poetics in the Aeneid: The Frame of Book 6*, Bari.

Lada-Richards, I. (1999) *Initiating Dionysus: Ritual and Theatre in Aristophanes' Frogs*, Oxford.

Lafaye, G. (1883) 'De poetarum et oratorum certaminibus apud veteres', PhD Diss., Paris.

Laird, A. (1999) *Powers of Expression, Expressions of Power*, Oxford.

Laird, A. (2001a) 'Paradox and Transcendence: The Prologue as the End', in A. Kahane and A. Laird, eds, *A Companion to the Prologue of Apuleius' Metamorphoses*, Oxford, 267–81.

Laird, A. (2001b) 'The Poetics and Afterlife of Virgil's Descent to the Underworld: Servius, Dante, Fulgentius and the *Culex*', *PVS* 24, 49–80.

Laird, A. (2009) 'Virgil: Reception and the Myth of Biography', *Cento Pagine* 3, 1–9.

Laird, A. (2016) 'Recognising Virgil', in J. Hanink and R. Fletcher, eds, *Creative Lives*, Cambridge, 75–99.

Laird, A. (2017) 'Fashioning the Poet: Biography, pseudepigraphy and textual criticism', in P. R. Hardie and A. Powell, eds, *Ancient Lives of Virgil*, Swansea, 29–49.

Laqueur, T. (2015) *The Work of the Dead: A Cultural History of Mortal Remains*, Princeton NJ.

Lardinois, A. (2014) 'Sappho en haar broers. Een nieuw lied van Sappho', *Lampas* 47, 179–201.

Larson, J. (1995) *Greek Heroine Cults*, Madison WI.

Laschke, B. (2002) 'Arma et litterae. Tugendkonzeptionen an neapolitanische Dichtergrabmaelern', in J. Pöschke, B. Kusch, and T. Weigel, eds, *Praemium virtutis. Grabmonumente und Begrabniszeremoniell im Zeichen des Humanismus*, Münster, 61–82.

Lattimore, R. (1962) *Themes in Greek and Latin Epitaphs*, Urbana IL.

Lausberg (1982) *Das Einzeldistichon. Studien zum antiken Epigramm*, Munich.

Leach, E. W. (2001) 'G. P. Bellori and the *Sepolcro dei Nasonii*: Writing a "Poet's" Tomb', in A. Barbet, ed., *La peinture funéraire antique IV siècle av. J.-C.–IVe siècle apr. J.-C.*, Paris, 69–77.

Lee, H. (1996) *Virginia Woolf*, London.

Lee, H. (2005) *Body Parts: Essays in Life Writing*, London.

Lee, M. O. (1996) *Virgil as Orpheus*, New York.

Lefkowitz, M. R. (1978) 'The Poet as Hero: Fifth-Century Autobiography and Subsequent Biographical Fiction', *CQ* 28, 459–69.

Lefkowitz, M. R. (2012) *The Lives of the Greek Poets*, Baltimore MD, 2nd edn (1st edn, London, 1981).

Lehmann, P. (1927) *Pseudo-antike Literatur des Mittelalters*, Leipzig.

Leibetseder, M. (2004) *Die Kavalierstour. Adlige Erziehungsreisen im 17. und 18. Jahrhundert*, Cologne, Weimar, and Vienna.

Lenzinger, F. (1965) *Zur griechischen Anthologie*, Zurich.

Leonard, M. (2009) 'Reception Studies', in G. R. Boys-Stones, B. Graziosi, and P. Vasiunia, eds, *The Oxford Handbook of Hellenic Studies*, Oxford, 835–45.

Levaniouk, O. (2008) 'Lament and Hymenaios in Erinna's Distaff', in A. Suter, ed., *Lament: Studies in the Ancient Mediterranean and Beyond*, Oxford, 200–32.

Liddel, P. and Low, P., eds (2013) *Inscriptions and Their Uses in Greek and Latin Literature*, Oxford.

Lidov, J. B. (2002) 'Sappho, Herodotus, and the *Hetaira*', *CPh* 97, 203–37.

Linforth, I. (1941) *The Arts of Orpheus*, London.

Lipking, L. (1981) *The Life of the Poet: Beginning and Ending Poetic Careers*, Chicago IL.

Lissarrague, F. (1994) 'Orphée mis à mort', *Musica e storia* 2, 269–307.

Livrea, E. (2006) 'La tomba di Simonide da Callimacho a S. Saba', *ZPE* 156, 53–7.

Lolos, G. (2000) 'Σαλαμινιακές έρευνες, 1998–2000. Μέρος Α΄. Το Ιερό του Διονύσου υπό το σπήλαιο του Ευριπίδη', *Dodone* 29, 113–65.

Lolos, G. (2003) 'Το Σπήλαιο του Ευριπίδη στη Σαλαμίνα: Η Προϊστορία του χώρου', in E. Konsolaki-Giannopoulou, ed., *Πρακτικά του Α΄ Διεθνούς Συνεδρίου Ιστορίας και Αρχαιολογίας του Αργοσαρωνικού, Πόρος, 26–29 Ιουνίου 1998*, Athens, 85–101.

Lolos, G. (2013) 'Νεώτερα πορίσματα από την εξέλιξη της πανεπιστημιακής ανασκαφής Σαλαμίνος', in M. Donka-Toli and S. Oikonomou, eds, *ΑΡΧΑΙΟΛΟΓΙΚΕΣ ΣΥΜΒΟΛΕΣ*, vol. *A*, Athens, 81–91.

Lossau, M. (1987) 'Palinuro', *Enciclopedia Virgiliana*, III [IO-PA], Rome, 936–8.

Lowrie, M. (2013) 'Foundation and Closure', in Grewing, Acosta-Hughes, and Kirichenko (2013), 83–102.

Luce, T. (1977) *Livy: The Composition of his History*, Princeton NJ.

Luck, G. (1954) 'Die Dichterinnen der griechischen Anthologie', *MH* 11, 170–87.

Lugli, G. (1938) *I monumenti antichi di Roma e suburbio, III. A traverso le regioni*, Rome.

Luz, C. (2010) *Technopaignia. Formspiele in der griechischen Dichtung*, Mnemosyne Suppl. 324, Leiden.

Lygouri-Tolia, E. (2014) 'Two Burials of 430 B.C. in Daphne, Athens: Their Topography, and the Profession of the So-Called "Poet" in Tomb 2', *Greek and Roman Musical Studies* 2, 3–22.

Lyne, R. O. A. M. (1987) *Further Voices in Vergil's Aeneid*, Oxford.

Mac Góráin, F. (forthcoming) 'Untitled/Arma virumque', *CPh*.

Machor, J. L. and Goldstein, P., eds (2001) *Reception Study: From Literary Theory to Cultural Studies*, New York and London.

MacLachlan, B. (2012) 'The Grave's a Fine and Funny Place: Chthonic Rituals and Comic Theater in the Greek West', in K. Bosher, ed., *Theater Outside Athens: Drama in Greek Sicily and South Italy*, Cambridge, 343–64.

MacPhail, J. (2005) Review of Clay (2005), *BMCR* 2005.09.32.

Mączak, A. (1998) *De ontdekking van het reizen*, Utrecht.

Männlein-Robert, I. (2007a) *Stimme, Schrift und Bild. Zum Verhältnis der Künste in der hellenistischen Dichtung*, Bibliothek der klassischen Alter-tumswissenschaften 119, Heidelberg.

Männlein-Robert, I. (2007b) 'Epigrams on Art: Voice and Voicelessness in Hellenistic Epigram', in Bing and Bruss (2007), 251–74.

Männlein-Robert, I. (2007c) 'Hellenistische Selbstepitaphien. Zwischen Auto-biographie und Poetik', in M. Erler and S. Schorn, eds, *Die griechische Biographie in hellenistischer Zeit*, Berlin, 363–83.

Malamud, M. (1995) 'Happy Birthday, Dead Lucan: (P)Raising the Dead in Silvae 2.7', *Ramus* 24, 1–30.

Malkin, I. (1998) *The Returns of Odysseus*, Berkeley CA.

Minchin, E. (2012) 'Commemoration and Pilgrimage in the Ancient World: Troy and the Stratigraphy of Cultural Memory', *G&R* 59, 76–89.

Mangoldt, B. von (2013) *Griechische Heroenkultstätten in klassischer und hellenistischer Zeit. Untersuchungen zu ihrer äusseren Gestaltung, Ausstat-tung und Funktion*, Tübingen.

Manieri, A. (2014) 'Sulpicio Massimo e un concorso di poesia greca a Roma. Riflessioni su alcune questioni agonistiche', *QUCC* 108, 145–68.

Marchesi, I. (2008) *The Art of Pliny's Letters: A Poetics of Allusion in the Private Correspondance*, Cambridge.

Marcon, L. (2012) *Un giallo a Napoli. La seconda morte di Giacomo Leopardi*, Naples.

Marconi, C. (2004) '*Kosmos*: The Imagery of the Greek Temple', *Res: Anthropology and Aesthetics* 45, 211–24.

Marincola, J. (1997) *Authority and Tradition in Ancient Historiography*, Cambridge.

Markson, D. (2016) *This is Not a Novel and Other Novels*, Berkeley CA.

Markwald, G. (1986) *Die Homerischen Epigramme. Sprachliche und inhaltliche Untersuchungen*, Königstein.

Marrou, H.-I. (1964) Μουσικὸς ἀνήρ. *Étude sur les scènes de la vie intellectuelle figurant sur les monuments funéraires romains*, Rome, 2nd edn.

Marshall, P. D. (1997) *Celebrity and Power: Fame in Contemporary Culture*, Minneapolis MN.

Marshall, P. D. (2006) *The Celebrity Culture Reader*, New York.

Martelli, F. (2013) *Ovid's Revisions: The Editor as Author*, Cambridge.

Martindale, C. (1993) *Redeeming the Text: Latin Poetry and the Hermeneutics of Reception*, Cambridge.

Martindale, C. (2013) 'Reception—a New Humanism? Receptivity, Pedagogy, and the Transhistorical', *Classical Receptions Journal* 5.2, 169–83.

Martins de Jesus, C. A., ed. (2015) *Pseudo-Aristotle, Epitaphs for the Heroes = Pepli Epitaphia (Appendix Planudea): Introduction, Text, and Commentary*, Berlin.

Marx, W. (2012) *Le tombeau d'Oedipe. Pour une tragédie sans tragique*, Paris.

Mason, Z. (2010) *The Lost Books of the Odyssey*, New York.

Massimilla, G. (2006) 'Il sepolcro di Simonides (Callimaco, fr.64 Pf.)', in A. Martina and A-T Cozzoli, eds, *Callimachea I. Atti della prima giornata di studi su Callimaco*, Rome, 33–52.

Mastronarde, D. J., ed. (2002) *Euripides: Medea*, Cambridge.

Matthews, S., ed. (2004) *Poetical Remains: Poets' Graves, Bodies, and Books in the Nineteenth Century*, Oxford.

Mayer, E. (2012) *The Ancient Middle Classes: Urban Life and Aesthetics in the Roman Empire, 100BCE–250 CE*, Cambridge MA.

Mazzella, S. (1591) *Sito, ed antichità della città di Pozzuolo e del suo amenissimo distretto*, Naples.

McCrum, M. and Woodhead, A. G., eds (1966) *Select Documents of the Principates of the Flavian Emperors Including the Year of Revolution A.D. 68–96*, Cambridge.

McKay, A. G. (1971) *Vergil's Italy*, Somerset.

Melmoth, W. (1777) *The letters of Pliny the consul: with occasional remarks*, printed by George Faulkner, London.

Melmoth, W. (1931) *Pliny, Letters*, revised by W. M. L. Hutchinson, London.

Mendelsohn, D. (1992) 'συγκεραυνόω: Dithyrambic Language and Dionysiac Cult', *CJ* 87, 105–24.

Méndez Dosuna, J. (2008) 'The Literary Progeny of Sappho's Fawns: Simias' Egg (*AP* 15.27.13-20) and Theocritus 30.18', *Mnemosyne* 61, 192–206.

Mercado, A. (2012) *Italic Verse: A Study of the Poetic Remains of Old Latin, Faliscan, and Sabellic*, Innsbruck.

Merrills, A. H. (2005) *History and Geography in Late Antiquity*, Cambridge.

Messineo, G. (2000) *La Tomba dei Nasonii*, Rome.

Meuli, K. (1921) *Odyssee und Argonautika*, Berlin.

Meyer, D. (2007) 'The Act of Reading and the Act of Writing in Hellenistic Epigram', in Bing and Bruss (2007), 187–210.

Michalski, S. (1977) 'Seyfreida Rybischa i Tobiasza Fendta "Monumenta Sepulcrorum cum Epigraphis", in J. Bialostocki, ed., *O ikonografii swieckiej doby humanizmu. Tematy—symbole—problemy*, Warsaw, 77–158.

Michaud, C. (2006) *Johann Heinrich Schönfeld. Un peintre Allemand du XVIIe Siécle en Italie*, Munich.

Miles, G. (1995) *Livy: Reconstructing Early Rome*, Ithaca NY and London.

Mindt, N. (2013) *Martials 'epigrammatischer Kanon'*, Munich.

Mines, John Flavel (1890) 'Who Was Charlotte Temple?', *Leslie's Popular Monthly*, November, 600–6.

Mitchell-Boyask, R. (2008) *Plague and the Athenian Imagination: Drama, History, and the Cult of Asclepius*, Cambridge.

Mitescu, A. (1972) 'Ovid's Presence in Romanian Culture', *Romanian Review* 26, 54–7.

Mlinko, A. (2017) 'In Coleridge's Bed', *London Review of Books* 39.8, 20.4.2017, 39–40.

Mole, T. (2009) *Romanticism and Celebrity Culture*, Cambridge.

Mommsen, T. (1864–79) *Römische Forschungen*, Berlin.

Montiglio, S. (2000) *Silence in the Land of Logos*, Princeton NJ.

Morand, A.-F. (2001) *Études sur les Hymnes Orphiques*, Leiden.

More, T. (1989) *Utopia*, G. George, M. Logan, and R. M. Adams, eds, Cambridge.

Moretti, L. (1979) *Inscriptiones Graecae urbis Romae*, vol. 3, Rome.

Morgan, K. (1993) 'Pindar the Professional and the Rhetoric of the *komos*', *CPh* 88, 1–15.

Morrison, A. (2013) 'Speaking from the Tomb? The Disappearing Epitaph of Simonides in Callimachus, *Aetia* fr.64 Pf.', in Liddel and Low (2013), 289–301.

Mouritsen, H. (2011) *The Freedman in the Roman World*, Cambridge.

Müller, L. (1595) *Septentrionalische Historien, oder Warhaffte Beschreibung der fürnembsten Polnischen, Lifflandischen, Moscowiterischen, Schwedischen und andern Geschichten*, Hamburg.

Muir, J. V. (2001) *Alciamas: The Works and Fragments*, London.

Murray, J. and Rowland, J. M. (2007) 'Gendered Voices in Hellenistic Epigram', in Bing and Bruss (2007), 211–32.

Musti, D. (1984) 'L'itinerario di Pausania. Dal viaggio alla storia', *QUCC* 17, 7–18.

Mustilli, D. (1939) *Il Museo Mussolini*, Rome.

Myers, K. S. (2005) 'Garden Ownership and Configurations of Leisure in Statius and Pliny the Younger', *Arethusa* 38, 103–29.

Mynors, R. A. B. (1990) *Virgil: Georgics*, Oxford.

Nagy, G. (1979) *The Best of the Achaeans: Concepts of the Hero in Archaic Greek Poetry*, Baltimore MD.

Nagy, G. (1983) '*Sēma* and *nóēsis*: Some illustrations', *Arethusa* 16, 35–55.

Nagy, G. (1989) 'Early Greek Views of Poets and Poetry', in G. A. Kennedy, ed., *The Cambridge History of Literary Criticism, I, Classical Criticism*, Cambridge, 1–77.

Nagy, G. (1990a) *Pindar's Homer: The Lyric Possession of an Epic Past*, Baltimore.

Nagy, G. (1990b) *Greek Mythology and Poetics*, Ithaca NY.

Nagy, G. (2008) 'Convergences between God and Hero in the Mnesiepes Inscription', in Katsonopoulou, Petropoulos, and Katsarou (2008), 259–65.

Nagy, G. (2012) 'Signs of Hero Cult in Homeric Poetry', in F. Montanari, A. Rengakos, and C. Tsagalis, eds, *Homeric Contexts: Neoanalysis and the Interpretation of Oral Poetry*. Berlin and Boston MA, 27–71.

Nagy, G. (2013) *The Ancient Greek Hero in 24 Hours*, Cambridge MA.

Neer, R. (2010) *The Emergence of the Classical Style in Greek Sculpture*, Chicago IL.

Neger, M. (2012) *Martials Dichtergedichte. Das Epigramm als Medium der poetischen Selbstreflexion*, Tübingen.

Nelson, J. R. (1903) 'The boy poet Sulpicius: a tragedy of Roman education', *The School Review* 11, 384–95.

Neri, C. (1996) *Studi sulle testimonianze di Erinna*, Bologna.

Neri, C. (2003) *Erinna. Testimonianze e frammenti*, Bologna.

Nervegna, S. (2014) 'Performing Classics: The Tragic Canon in the Fourth Century and Beyond', in E. Csapo, H. R. Goette, J. R. Green, and P. Wilson, eds, *Greek Theatre in the Fourth Century B.C.*, Berlin, 157–87.

Nicholson, B. (1968) *Joseph Wright of Derby: Painter of Light*, London.

Nicholson, B. (1988) 'Wright of Derby, Addenda and Corrigenda', *Burlington Magazine* 130, October 1988.

Niola, M. (2013) 'Aiutateci alla maturità'. Studenti in pellegrinaggio sulle tombe dei grandi poeti. Napoli, l'ultimo rito prima dell'esame, in coda da Virgilio e Leopardi', *La Repubblica*, 10 June, 1, 23.

Nisbet, R. and Rudd, N. (2004) *A Commentary on Horace, Odes Book III*, Oxford.

Nocita, M. (2000) 'L'ara di Sulpicio Massimo. Nuove osservazioni in occasione del restauro', *BCAR* 101, 81–100.

Nocita, M. (2012) 'A Via in Context: Via Salaria in Rome', *Spolia: Journal of Medieval Studies* <http://www.spolia.it/online/it/argomenti/archeologia/materiale_antico/2012/salaria.htm>.

Noirot-Maguire, C. (2012) 'The Politics of *Translatio*: Du Bellay and the Death of Palinurus', in P. J. Usher and I. Fernach, eds, *Virgilian Identities in the French Renaissance*, Woodbridge, 189–212.

Nooteboom, C. and Sassen, S. (2009) *Tumbas. Tombes de poètes et de penseurs*, Barcelona.

Nora, P., ed. (1984–92) *Les Lieux de mémoire*, 7 vols, Paris.

Nora, P. (1989) 'Between Memory and History: Les lieux de mémoire', *Representations* 26, 7–24.

Nora, P. (1996) 'From lieux de mémoire to Realms of Memory', in P. Nora and L. D. Kritzman, eds, *Realms of Memory: Rethinking the French Past, Vol. 1: Conflicts and Divisions*, New York, xv–xxiv.

Obbink, D. (2011) 'Vanishing Conjecture: The Recovery of Lost Books from Aristotle to Eco', in D. Obbink, R. B. Rutherford, and P. Parsons, eds, *Culture in Pieces: Essays on Ancient Texts in Honour of Peter Parsons*, Oxford.

Obbink, D. (2014) 'Two New Poems by Sappho', *ZPE* 189, 32–49.

O'Higgins, D. (1990) 'Sappho's Splintered Tongue: Silence in Sappho 31 and Catullus 51', *AJPh* 111, 156–67.

Olson, S. D. (1998) *Aristophanes Peace*, Oxford.

Ornaghi, M. (2009) *La lira, la vacca e le donne insolenti. Contesti di recezione e promozione della figura e della poesia di Archiloco dall' arcaismo all' ellenismo*, Alessandria.

O'Sullivan, N. (2008) 'The Authenticity of [Alcidamas] *Odysseus*: Two New Linguistic Considerations', *CQ* 58, 638–47.

O'Sullivan, P. (2003) 'Victory Statue, Victory Song: Pindar's agonistic poetics and its legacy', in D. J. Phillips and D. Pritchard, eds, *Sport and Festival in the Ancient Greek World*, Swansea, 75–100.

Oswald, A. (2011) *Memorial*, London.

Otto, W. F. (1965) *Dionysus: Myth and Cult*, R. B. Palmer, trans., Bloomington IN.

Pache, C. O. (2004) *Baby and Child Heroes in Ancient Greece*, Urbana.

Page, D. (1955) *Sappho & Alcaeus*, Oxford.

Page, D., ed. (1962) *Poetae Melici Graeci*, Oxford.

Page, D., ed. (1975) *Epigrammata Graeca*, Oxford.

Pane, G. and Valerio, V. (1987) *La città di Napoli tra vedutismo e cartografia. Piante e vedute dal XV al XIX secolo*, Naples.

Pansa, G. (1924) *Ovidio nel medioevo e nella tradizione popolare*, Sulmona.

Paoli, P. (1768) *Antichità di Pozzuoli,* Naples.

Paratore, E. (1977) 'Virgilio e Cuma', in *I Campi Flegrei nell'archeologia e nella storia: Atti dei Convegni Lincei 33, Roma, 4–7 Maggio 1976,* 9–39, Rome.

Parke, H. W. (1958) 'The Newly Discovered Delphic Responses from Paros', *CQ* 8, 90–4.

Parke, H. W. (1977) *Festivals of the Athenians,* London.

Parker, J. H. (1877) *The Archaeology of Rome, Vol. IX: Tombs in and near Rome,* Oxford and London.

Parker, R. (1995) 'Early Orphism', in A. Powell, ed., *The Greek World,* London, 483–510.

Parker, R. (2005) *Polytheism and Society at Athens,* Oxford.

Parker, R. (2011) *On Greek Religion,* Ithaca NY and London.

Parry, A. (1963) 'The Two Voices of Virgil's *Aeneid*', *Arion* 2.4, 66–80.

Parsons, J. (1999) 'A New Approach to the Saturnian Verse and its Relation to Latin Prosody', *TAPA* 129, 117–37.

Paton, W. R. (1917) *The Greek Anthology, Book 9, Loeb Classical Library* 84, Cambridge MA.

Payne, M. (2007) *Theocritus and the Invention of Fiction,* Cambridge.

Pearsall, D. (1995) 'Chaucer's Tomb: The Politics of Reburial', *Medium Aevum* 64, 51–72.

Pée, H. (1971) *Johann Heinrich Schönfeld. Die Gemälde,* Berlin.

Peek, W., ed. (1955) *Griechische Versinschriften I. Grab-Epigramme,* Berlin.

Peek, W., ed. (1960) *Greichische Grabgedichte,* Berlin.

Peirano, I. (2014) '"Sealing" the Book: the *Sphragis* as Paratext', in Jansen (2014), 224–42.

Pelliccia, H. (forthcoming) Review of *The Greek Anthology, Books 1–5,* W. R. Paton, trans., revised by M. A. Tueller, *Loeb Classical Library* 67, Cambridge MA, in *the New York Review of Books.*

Pelliccia, H. (2009) 'Simonides, Pindar and Bacchylides', in F. Budelmann, ed., *The Cambridge Companion to Greek Lyric,* Cambridge, 240–62.

Pelling, C. B. R. (2002) *Plutarch and History: Eighteen Studies,* Swansea.

Penny Small, J. (1997) *Wax Tablets of the Mind: Cognitive Studies of Memory and Literacy in Classical Antiquity,* London and New York.

Peradotto, J. J. (1964) 'Some Patterns of Nature Imagery in the *Oresteia*', *AJPh* 85, 378–93.

Perkell, C. G. (1989) *The Poet's Truth: A Study of the Poet in Virgil's Georgics,* Berkeley and Los Angeles CA.

Petrain, D. (2013) 'Visual Supplementation and Metonymy in the Roman Public Library', in J. König, K. Oikonomopoulou, and G. Woolf, eds, *Ancient Libraries,* Cambridge, 332–46.

Petrovic, A. (2005) 'Kunstvole Stimme der Steiner, sprich! Zur Intermedialität der griechischen epideiktischen Epigramme', *A&A* 51, 30–42.

Petrovic, A. (2007) *Kommentar zu den simonideischen Versinschriften*, Leiden.

Philbrick, N. (2006) *Mayflower: A Story of Courage, Community, and War*, New York.

Pickard-Cambridge, A. (1968) *The Dramatic Festivals of Athens*, Oxford.

Platner, S. B. and Ashby, T. (1929) *A Topographical Dictionary of Ancient Rome*, Oxford.

Platt, V. J. (2011) *Facing the Gods: Epiphany and Representation in Graeco-Roman Art, Literature and Religion*. Cambridge.

Platt, V. J. (2012) 'Framing the Dead on Roman Sarcophagi', *RES* 61/62: 213–27.

Platt, V. J. (2018) 'Orphaned Objects: The Phenomenology of the Incomplete in Pliny's *Natural History*', *Art History* 41.1.

Platt, V. J. (forthcoming) 'Beeswax: The Natural History of an Archetypal Medium', in A. Anguissola and A. Grüner, eds, *The Nature of Art: Pliny the Elder on Materials*, Turnhout.

Poccetti, P. (2002) 'Il filo dell'onomastica e la trama della rappresentazione letteraria della Campania in Virgilio', *Il Nome nel testo* 6, 171–200.

Pöhlmann, E. (2013) 'Excavation, Dating and Content of Two Tombs in Daphne, Odos Olgas 53, Athens', *Greek and Roman Musical Studies* 1, 7–23.

Pöhlmann, E. and West, M. L. (2012) 'The Oldest Greek Papyrus and Writing Tablets: Fifth-century Documents from the "Tomb of the Musician" in Attica', *ZPE* 180, 1–16.

Poli-Palladini, L. (2001) 'Some reflections on Aeschylus' *Aetnae(ae)*', *Rheinisches Museum* 144, 287–325.

Poli-Palladini, L. (2013) *Aeschylus at Gela: An Integrated Approach*, Alexandria.

Poltera, O., ed. (2008) *Simonides Lyricus. Testimonia und Fragmente*, Basel.

Porter, J. I. (2001) 'Ideals and Ruins: Pausanias, Longinus, and the Second Sophistic', in S. Alcock, J. Cherry, and J. Elsner, eds, *Pausanias: Travel and Memory in Roman Greece*, Oxford, 63–92.

Potter, D. (2010) 'Sulpicius Maximus: Child Prodigy', *Classics Convivium* 22 (Spring).

Potts, J. (2009) *A History of Charisma*, Basingstoke.

Prendergast, T. A. (2015) *Poetical Dust: Poets' Corner and the Making of Britain*, Pennsylvania PA.

Pretzler, M. (2007) *Pausanias: Travel Writing in Ancient Greece*, London.

Prinzen, H. (1998) *Ennius im Urteil der Antike*, Stuttgart.

Prioux, É. (2007) *Regards alexandrins. Histoire et théorie des arts dans l'épigramme hellénistique*, Hellenistica Groningnana 12, Leuven.

Psaroudakēs, S. (2013) 'The Daphnē Aulos', *Greek and Roman Musical Studies* 1, 93–121.

Pugliese Carratelli, G. (1974) 'Un sepolcro di Hipponion e un nuovo testo orfico', *PP* 29, 108–26.

Purcell, N. (1987) 'Tomb and Suburb', in H. von Hesberg and P. Zanke, eds, *Römische Gräberstrassen. Selbstdarstellung, Status, Standard, Kolloquium in München vom 28. bis 30. Oktober 1985*, Munich, 25–41.

Rädke, G. (1981) *Viae Publicae Romanae*, G. Sigismondi, trans., Bologna.

Raleigh Nelson, J. (1903) 'The Boy Poet Sulpicius: A Tragedy of Roman Education', *The School Review* 11, 384–95.

Ramsby, T. R. (2007) *Textual Permanence: Roman Elegists and the Epigraphic Tradition*, London.

Rawles, R. (2013) 'Aristophanes' Simonides: Lyric Models for Praise and Blame', in E. Bakola, L. Prauscello, and M. Telò, eds, *Greek Comedy and the Discourse of Genres*, Cambridge, 175–201.

Rawles, R. (2018) *Simonides the Poet: Intertextuality and Reception*, Cambridge.

Rawson, B. (1999) 'Education: The Romans and Us', *Antichthon* 33, 81–98.

Redfield, J. (1991) 'The Politics of Immortality', in P. Borgeaud, ed., *Orphisme et Orphée. En l'honneur de Jean Rudhardt*, Geneva, 103–17.

Reece, S. (1994) 'The Cretan Odyssey: A Lie Truer than Truth', *AJPh* 115, 157–73.

Reggiani, A. M. (1990) *Vita e costumi dei Romani antichi X. Educazione e scuola*, Rome.

Reid, J. D. (1993) *The Oxford Guide to Classical Mythology in the Arts, 1300–1990s*, Oxford.

Reitzenstein, R. (1893) *Epigramm und Skolion. Ein Beitrag zur Geschichte der alexandrinischen Dichtung*, Gießen.

Ricoeur, P. (2004) *Memory, History, Forgetting*, K. Blamey and D. Pellauer, trans, Chicago.

Ridder-Symoens, H. de (1983) 'Peregrinatio academica doorheen Europa (13e–18e eeuw) in vogelvlucht', *Batavia academica* 1, 3–11.

Ridgeway, W. (1910) *The Origin of Tragedy with Special Reference to the Greek Tragedians*, Cambridge.

Ripoll, F. (2000) 'Silius Italicus and Cicero', *LEC* 68, 147–73.

Robathan, D. M., ed. (1968) *The Pseudo-Ovidian De Vetula:Text, Introduction, and Notes*, Amsterdam.

Roberts, D., Dunn, F., and Fowler, D. P., eds (1997) *Classical Closure: Reading the End in Greek and Latin Literature*, Princeton NJ.

Rohde, E. (1921) *Psyche. Seelenkult und Unsterblichkeitsglaube der Griechen*, Tübingen, 7th and 8th edns.

Rohde, E. (1925) *Psyche: The Cult of Souls and Belief in Immortality Among the Greeks*, W. B. Hills, trans., London.

Roochnik, D. (2009) 'The Political Drama of Plato's *Republic*', in S. Salkever, ed., *The Cambridge Companion to Ancient Greek Political Thought*, Cambridge, 156–77.

Rosati, G. (1996) 'Sabinus, the Heroides and the Poet-Nightingale. Some Observations on the Authenticity of the Epistula Sapphus', *CQ* 46, 207–16.

Rosen, R. (2007) 'The Hellenistic Epigrams on Archilochus and Hipponax', in Bing and Bruss (2007), 459–76.

Rosenmeyer, P. A. (1992) *The Poetics of Imitation: Anacreon and the Anacreontic Tradition*, Cambridge.

Rosenmeyer, P. A. (1997) 'Her Master's Voice: Sappho's Dialogue with Homer', in S. Hinds and D. P. Fowler, eds, *Memory, Allusion, Intertextuality = MD* 39, 123–49.

Rosenmeyer, P. A. (2006) 'Sappho's Iambics', *Letras Clássicas* 10, 11–36.

Rosenmeyer, T. G. (1982) *The Art of Aeschylus*, Berkeley CA.

Ross, D. (1969) *Style and Tradition in Catullus*, Cambridge MA.

Rossi, L. (2001) *The Epigrams Ascribed to Theocritus: A Method of Approach*, Leuven and Paris.

Rostagni, A., ed. (1961) *Virgilio Minora*, Rome.

Rothstein, E. (1976) 'Ideal Presence and the "Non Finito" in Eighteenth-Century Aesthetics', *Eighteenth-Century Studies* 9.3, 307–32.

Rotstein, A. (2010) *The Idea of Iambos*, Oxford.

Rotstein, A. (2014) 'The Parian Marble and the Mnesiepes Inscription', *ZPE* 190, 3–9.

Rotstein, A. (2015) *Literary History in the Parian Marble, Hellenic Studies* 68, Cambridge MA.

Rowson, S. H. (1905) *Charlotte Temple: A Tale of Truth, With an historical and biographical introduction, bibliography, etc. by Francis W. Halsey*, 2 vols, New York.

Rubiés, J.-P. (1996) 'Instructions for Travellers: Teaching the Eye to See', *History and Anthropology*, 9, 139–90.

Rudd, N. (1989) *Horace: Epistles II and Epistle to the Pisones (Ars Poetica)*, Cambridge.

Ruiz Pérez, A. (1995) 'Oráculo y profecía en el mito griego. las Familias de Tántalo y Cadmo', PhD Diss., University of Valladolid.

Sansone, D. (1985) 'Orpheus and Eurydice in the Fifth Century', *CM* 36, 53–64.

Santamaria, M. A. (2012) 'Orfeo y el orfismo: actualización bibliográfica (2004–2012)', *Ilu Revista de Ciencias de las Religiones* 17, 211–52.

Sarnelli, P. (1685) *Guida de' forestieri curiosi di vedere e d'intendere le cose più notabili della Regal Città di Napoli e del suo amenissimo distretto*, Naples.

Sauppe, H. (1871) review of Visconti (1871), *GGA*, 1036–40.

Sbordone, F. (1984) 'Averno', in F. Della Corte, ed., *Enciclopedia Virgiliana* I, 430–2.

Scaffai, M. (2004) 'Il console Marcello e Archimede nei Punica di Silio Italico', *Paideia* 59, 483–509.

Scharffenberger, E. W. (2007) '*Deinon Eribremetas*: The Sound and Sense of Aeschylus in Aristophanes' *Frogs*', *CW* 100, 229–49.

Schein, S. L. (1984) *The Mortal Hero: An Introduction to Homer's Iliad*, Berkeley CA.

Schiesaro, A. (2001) 'Virgil in Bloomsbury', *PVS* 24, 31–47.

Schliemann, H. (1878) *Mycenae: A Narrative of Researches and Discoveries at Mycenae and Tiryns*, New York.

Schmidt, M. (1967) 'Dionysien', *Antike Kunst* 10, 70–81.

Scott, W. C. (1966) 'Wind Imagery in the *Oresteia*', *TAPA* 97, 459–71.

Scullion, S. (1994) 'Olympian and Chthonian', *ClAnt* 13, 75–119.

Seaford, R. (1994) *Reciprocity and Ritual: Homer and Tragedy in the Developing City-state*, Oxford.

Seaford, R. (2005) 'Mystic Light in Aeschylus' *Bassarai*', *CQ* 55, 602–6.

Segal, C. (1982) *Dionysiac Poetics and Euripides' Bacchae*, Princeton NJ.

Segal, C. (1989) *Orpheus: the Myth of the Poet*, Baltimore MD.

Sens, A. (2003) 'Asclepiades, Erinna, and the Poetics of Labor', in P. Thibodeau and H. Haskell, eds, *Being There Together: Essays in Honor of Michael C. J. Putnam on the Occasion of his Seventieth Birthday*, Afton, 78–87.

Sens, A. (2007) 'One Thing Leads (Back) to Another: Allusion and the Invention of Tradition in Hellenistic Epigrams', in Bing and Bruss (2007), 373–90.

Sens, A. (2011) *Asclepiades of Samos: Epigrams and Fragments*, Oxford.

Sfameni Gasparro, G. (2000) '"Anodos" e "kathodos". Movimento nello spazio e ritorno al tempo mitico', in D. Pezzoli-Olgiati and F. Stol, eds, *Cartografia religiosa. Organizzazione, codificazione e simbologia dello spazio nei sistemi religiosi*, Bern, Berlin, et al., 83–106.

Sfyroeras, P. (2008) '*Πόθος Εὐριπίδου*: Reading *Andromeda* in Aristophanes' *Frogs*', *AJPh* 129, 299–317.

Shapiro, A. (1998) 'Autochthony and the Visual Arts in Fifth-century Athens', in D. Boedeker and K. Rauflaub, eds, *Democracy, Empire and the Arts in Fifth Century Athens*, Cambridge MA, 127–51.

Sherwin-White, A. N. (1969) *Fifty Letters of Pliny*, Oxford. 2nd edn.

Shoji, S., Nanjo, M. and Dahlgren, R. (1994) *Volcanic Ash Soils: Genesis, Properties and Utilization*, Amsterdam.

Sider, D. (2007) '*Sylloge Simonidea*', in Bing and Bruss (2007), 113–30.

Silverstein, M. and Urban, G., eds (1996) *Natural Histories of Discourse*, Chicago IL.

Simon, E. (1989) 'Hermeneutisches zur Anodos von Göttinnen', in H.-U. Ulrich Cain, H. Gabelmann, and D. Salzmann, eds, *Beiträge zur Ikonographie und Hermeneutik. Festschrift für Nikolaus Himmelmann*, Mainz, 197–203.

Simon, E. (2005) 'Libation', in *Thesaurus Cultus et Rituum Antiquorum* [*ThesCRA*], Los Angeles CA, 236–53.

Skiadas, A. (1965) *Homer im griechischen Epigramm*, Athens.

Skutsch, O., ed. (1985) *The Annals of Q. Ennius*, Oxford.

Smith, H. and Wilson, L., eds (2011) *Renaissance Paratexts*, Cambridge.

Snodgrass, A. M. (1982) 'Les origines du culte des heros dans la Grece antique', in G. Gnoli and J.-P. Vernant, eds, *La mort, les morts dans le sociétés anciennes*, Cambridge and Paris, 107–19.

Solmsen, F. (1949) *Hesiod and Aeschylus*, Ithaca NY.

Sommerstein, A. H., ed. and trans. (2008) *Aeschylus*, 2 vols, Cambridge MA.

Sommerstein, A. H. (2010) *Aeschylean Tragedy*, London, 2nd edn.

Sourvinou-Inwood, C. (1987) 'Myth as History: The Previous Owners of the Delphic Oracle', in J. Bremmer, ed., *Interpretations of Greek Mythology*, London, 215–41.

Sourvinou-Inwood, C. (1995) *'Reading' Greek Death to the End of the Classical Period*, Oxford.

Squire, M. J. (2010) 'Making Myron's Cow Moo? Ecphrastic Epigram and the Poetics of Simulation', *AJPh* 131, 589–634.

Stagl, J. (1983) *Apodemiken. Eine räsonnierte Bibliographie der reisetheoretischen Literatur des 16., 17. und 18. Jahrhunderts*, Paderborn.

Stagl, J. (1995) *A History of Curiosity: The Theory of Travel, 1550–1800*, Chur.

Stallings, A. E. (2006) *Hapax*, Chicago IL.

Stannek, A. (2001) *Telemachs Brüder. Die höfische Bildungsreise des 17. Jahrhunderts*, Frankfurt and New York.

Stehle, E. (1997) *Performance and Gender in Ancient Greece: Nondramatic Poetry in its Setting*, Princeton NJ.

Stehle, E. (2001) '"The Good Daughter: Mothers" Tutelage in Erinna's Distaff and Fourth-Century Epitaphs', in A. Lardinois and L. McClure, eds, *Making Silence Speak: Women's Voices in Greek Literature and Society*, Princeton NJ, 179–200.

Steiner, D. (1993) 'Pindar's "Oggetti Parlanti"', *HSPh* 95, 159–80.

Stewart, A. (1993) *Faces of Power: Alexander's Image and Hellenistic Politics, Hellenistic Culture and Society*, Berkeley CA and Oxford.

Suerbaum, W. (1968) *Untersuchungen zur Selbstdarstellung älterer römischer Dichter. Livius Andronicus, Naevius, Ennius, Spudasmata* 19, Hildesheim.

Sullivan, J. P. (1991) *Martial: The Unexpected Classic*, Cambridge.

Sung-Yul Park, J. and Bucholtz, M. (2009) 'Public Transcripts: Entextualization and Linguistic Representation in Institutional Contexts', *Text & Talk* 29.5, 485–502.

Sutton, D. F. (1975) 'The Staging of *anodos* Scenes', *RSC* 23, 347–55.

Svenbro, J. (1993) *Phrasikleia: An Anthropology of Reading in Ancient Greece*, J. Lloyd, trans., Ithaca NY.

Taplin, O. (1978) *Greek Tragedy in Action*, London.

Taplin, O. (2007) *Pots and Plays: Interactions between Tragedy and Greek Vase-painting of the Fourth Century B.C.*, Los Angeles CA.

Taplin, O. (2013) 'Epiphany of a Serious Dionysus in a Comedy?', in S. D. Olson, ed., *Ancient Comedy and Reception: Essays in Honor of Jeffrey Henderson*, Berlin and Boston MA, 62–8.

Tarkow, T. A. (1982) 'Achilles and the Ghost of Aeschylus in Aristophanes' *Frogs*', *Traditio* 38, 1–16.

Taylor, D. (2003) *The Archive and the Repertoire: Performing Cultural Memory*, Chapel Hill NC.

Tervoort, A. (2005) *The Iter Italicum and the Northern Netherlands: Dutch Students at Italian Universities and Their Role in the Netherlands' Society (1426–1575)*, Leiden.

Terzēs, Ch. (2013) 'The Daphnē Harp', *Greek and Roman Musical Studies* 1, 123–49.

Thalmann, W. G. (1978) *Dramatic Art in Aeschylus's Seven against Thebes*, New Haven CT and London.

Thomas, B. (2003) 'Finding Ovid through Raphael in the Schools of the Tombs', *Art on the Line* 1.2, 1–11.

Thomas, R. F., ed. (1988) *Virgil Georgics*, 2 vols, Cambridge.

Thomas, R. F. (1999) *Reading Virgil and His Texts: Studies in Intertextuality*, Ann Arbor MI.

Thomas, R. F. (2014), 'The Two Voices Theory', in R. F. Thomas and J. M. Ziolkowski, eds, *The Virgil Encyclopaedia*, Oxford, 1310f.

Thornbury, W. (1877) *The Life of J. M. W. Turner*, London.

Tierney, J. E., ed. (1988) *The Correspondence of Robert Dodsley, 1733–1764*, Cambridge.

Todisco, L. (2002) *Teatro e spettacolo in Magna Grecia e in Sicilia. Testi, immagini, architettura*, Milan.

Touchette, L.-A. (1990) 'A New Interpretation of the Orpheus Relief', *Archäologischer Anzeiger* 1, 77–90.

Touring Club Italiano (2005) *Guida Touring Club Italiano Napoli e dintorni*, Rome.

Toynbee, J. M. C. (1971) *Death and Burial in the Roman World*, Baltimore MD.

Trapp, J. B. (1973) 'Ovid's Tomb: The Growth of a Legend from Eusebius to Laurence Sterne, Chateaubriand and George Richmond', *JWI* 36, 35–76.

Trapp, J. B. (1984) 'The Grave of Vergil', *JWI* 47, 1–31.

Trapp, J. B. (1986) 'Virgil and the Monuments', *PVS* 18, 1–17.

Trapp, J. B. (1990) 'Archimedes's Tomb and the Artists: A Postscript', *JWI* 53, 286–8.

Trapp, J. B. (2006) 'Petrarchan Places: An Essay in the Iconography of Commemoration', *JWI* 69, 1–50.

Trepesch, C., Müller, S., and Sedelmeier, W., eds (2010) *Maler von Welt. Johann Heinrich Schönfeld im Bestand der Kunstsammlungen und Museen Augsburg*, Munich.

350 *Bibliography*

Troia, A. M. (2016) 'The Epitaph for Bion: Agonism and Fictional Biography as Literary Criticism in Late Bucolic', PhD Diss., Brown University, Providence.

Trümpy, C. (2010) 'Observations on the Dedicatory and Sepulchral Epigrams and Their Early History', in Baumbach, Petrovic, and Petrovic, eds (2010), 167–80.

Tsagalis, C. (2008) *Inscribing Sorrow: Fourth-Century Attic Funerary Epigrams*, Berlin.

Tueller, M. A. (1991) *Mortals and Immortals: Collected Essays*, F. Zeitlin, ed., Princeton NJ.

Tueller, M. A. (2008) *Look Who's Talking: Innovations in Voice and Identity in Hellenistic Poetry*, Leuven.

Tueller, M. A. (2010) 'The Passer-by in Archaic and Classical Epigram', in Baumbach, Petrovic, and Petrovic (2010), 42–60.

Usher, P. J. (2013) *Epic Arts in Renaissance France*, Oxford.

Valentin, L. (1826) *Voyage en Italie fait en l'année 1820*, Paris.

Van Sickle, J. (1987) 'The *Elogia* of the Cornelii Scipiones and the Origin of Epigram at Rome', *AJPh* 108.1, 41–55.

Vérilhac, A.-M. (1978: I), (1982: II) Παῖδες ἄωροι. *Poésie funéraire*, Athens.

Vermeule, E. (1979) *Aspects of Death in Early Greek Art and Poetry*, Berkeley and Los Angeles CA.

Vernant, J.-P. (1990) *Figures, Idoles, Masques*, Paris.

Vessey, D. (1974) 'Pliny, Martial and Silius Italicus', *Hermes* 102, 109–16.

Vestrheim, G. (2010) 'Voice in Sepulchral Epigrams: Some Remarks on the Use of First and Second Person in Sepulchral Epigrams, and a Comparison with Lyric Poetry', in Baumbach, Petrovic, and Petrovic (2010), 61–78.

Visconti, C. L. (1871) *Il sepolcro del fanciullo Quinto Sulpicio Massimo nel terzo agone Capitolino coronato fra i poeti greci recentemente scoperto nella struttura della Porta Salaria, [...] con dichiarazione del monumento ed interpretazione dei versi greci*, Rome.

Visscher, F. de (1963) *Le droit des tombeaux romains*, Milan.

Visser, M. (1982) 'Worship your Enemy: Aspects of the Cult of Heroes in Ancient Greece', *Harvard Theological Review* 75, 403–28.

Voss, H. (1964) *Johann Heinrich Schönfeld. Ein schwäbischer Maler des 17. Jahrhunderts*, Biberach an der Riß.

Wace, A. J. B. and Stubbings, F. H. (1962) *A Companion to Homer*, London.

Walbank (1967) *A Historical Commentary on Polybius I–II*, Oxford.

Walker, A. (1997) 'Oedipal Narratives and the Exilic Ovid', *Ramus* 26, 194–204.

Wallace-Hadrill, A. (2008) *Rome's Cultural Revolution*, Cambridge.

Walsh, P. (1961) *Livy, His Historical Aims and Methods*, Cambridge.

Walter, O. (1953) 'Das Priestertum des Sophocles', Γέρας Ἀντωνίου Κεραμοπούλου, 469–79.

Weick, K. (2009) 'Reflexionen zur malerischen Aneigung von Antike. Schönfelds Schatzgräberdarstellungen', in Zeller, Waike, and Kaulbach (2009), 114–31.

Weisshäupl, R. (1889) *Die Grabgedichte der griechischen Anthologie*, Vienna.

Weisshäupl, R. (1896) 'Zu den Quellen der Anthologia Palatina', *Serta Harteliana*, Vienna, 184–8.

Wellenbach, M. (2016) 'Herodotus' Tragic Choruses', *Trends in Classics* 8, 17–32.

Wenzel, S. (2011) 'Ovid from the Pulpit', in J. G. Clark, F. Coulson, and K. McKinley, eds, *Ovid in the Middle Ages*, Cambridge, 160–76.

West, M. L., ed. (1966) *Hesiod: Theogony*, Oxford.

West, M. L. (1977) 'Erinna', *ZPE* 25, 95–119.

West, M. L. (1983) *The Orphic Poems*, Oxford.

West, M. L. (1990) 'The Lycurgus Trilogy', in M. L. West, ed., *Studies in Aeschylus*, Stuttgart, 26–50.

West, M. L. (2005) '*Odyssey* and *Argonautica*', *CQ* 55, 39–64.

West, M. L. (2013) 'The Writing Tablets and Papyrus from the Tomb II in Daphni', *Greek and Roman Musical Studies* 1, 73–92.

West, M. L. (2014) 'Nine Poems of Sappho', *ZPE* 191, 1–12.

White, P. (1998) 'Latin Poets and the *Certamen Capitolinum*', in P. Knox and C. Foss, eds, *Style and Tradition: Studies in Honor of Wendell Clausen*, Stuttgart, 84–95.

Whitmarsh, T. (2009) 'Performing Heroics: Language, Landscape and Identity in Philostratus' *Heroicus*', in E. Bowie and J. Elsner, eds, *Philostratus*, Cambridge, 205–29.

Whittaker, H. (1991) 'Pausanias and his use of inscriptions', *SO* 66, 171–86.

Wifstrand, A. (1926) *Studien zur griechischen Anthologie*, Lund Univ. Arsskrift 23.3, Lund.

Wilamowitz-Moellendorff, U. von (1913) *Sappho und Simonides: Untersuchungen über griechische Lyriker*, Berlin.

Wilamowitz-Moellendorff, U. von (1914) *Aeschyli Tragoediae*, Berlin.

Wilamowitz-Moellendorff, U. von (1924) *Hellenistische Dichtung in der Zeit des Kallimachos*, 2 vols, Berlin.

Wilamowitz-Moellendorff, U. von (1932) *Der Glaube der Hellenen II*, Basel.

Wilde, O. (1891) 'The Decay of Lying: An Observation', in O. Wilde, *Intentions*, London, 1–55.

Wilkins, E. H. (1955) *Studies in the Life and Works of Petrarch*, Cambridge MA.

Wilson, M. (2004) 'Ovidian Silius', *Arethusa* 37, 225–49.

Wilson, P. (2007) 'Sicilian Choruses', in P. Wilson, ed., *The Greek Theatre and Festivals: Documentary Studies*, Oxford, 351–77.

Wilson, P. (2015) 'The Festival of Dionysos in Ikarion: A New Study of IG I3 254', *Hesperia*, 84, 97–147.

Wilson, P. (forthcoming a) 'Eleusis', in E. Csapo and P. J. Wilson, eds, *Historical Documents for the Greek Theatre to 300 BC*, 2 vols, Cambridge.

Wilson, P. (forthcoming b) 'Thorikos', in E. Csapo and P. J. Wilson, eds, *Historical Documents for the Greek Theatre to 300 BC*, 2 vols, Cambridge.

Wilson, P. (forthcoming c) 'Ikarion', in E. Csapo and P. J. Wilson, eds, *Historical Documents for the Greek Theatre to 300 BC*, 2 vols, Cambridge.

Wilton, A. (2006) *Turner in his Time*, London.

Wilton, A. and Turner, R. M. (1990) *Painting and Poetry: Turner's 'Verse Book' and his Work of 1804–1812*, London.

Woodman, A. J. (1974) '*Exegi monumentum*: Horace, *Odes* 3.30', in A. J. Woodman and D. West, eds, *Quality and Pleasure in Latin Poetry*, Cambridge, 115–28.

Wölfflin, E. (1892) 'Die Dichter der Scipionenelogien', *Sitz. Bayer. Akad.*, Munich, 188–219.

Wright, T., ed. (1842) *A Selection of Latin Stories from Manuscripts of the Thirteenth and Fourteenth Centuries: A Contribution to the History of Fiction During the Middle Ages*, London.

Yatromanolakis, D. (2007) *Sappho in the Making: The Early Reception*, Washington DC.

Zanker, P. and Ewald, B. C. (2008) *Vivere con i miti. L'iconografia dei sarcofagi romani*, G. Adornato, ed., F. Cuniberto, trans., Turin.

Zeller, U., Waike, M., and Kaulbach, H.-M., eds (2009) *Johann Heinrich Schönfeld. Welt der Götter, Heiligen und Heldenmythen*, Cologne.

Zetzel, J. (2007) 'The Influence of Cicero on Ennius', in W. Fitzgerald and E. Gowers, eds, *Ennius Perennis: The Annals and Beyond*, *CCJ Supplement* 31, Cambridge, 1–16.

Zevi, F. (1970) 'Considerazioni sull'elogio di Scipione Barbato', *Studi Miscellanei* 15, 63–74.

# Index